# Gendering the Renaissance

## *Text and Context in Early Modern Italy*

Edited by
Meredith K. Ray and Lynn Lara Westwater

University of Delaware
University of Delaware Press
*Newark*

Library of Congress Cataloging-in-Publication Data

Names: Ray, Meredith K., 1969– editor. | Westwater, Lynn Lara, editor.
Title: Gendering the renaissance : text and context in early modern Italy / edited by Meredith K. Ray and Lynn Lara Westwater.
Description: Newark : University of Delaware Press, 2023. | Series: The early modern exchange | Includes bibliographical references and index.
Identifiers: LCCN 2022037672 | ISBN 9781644533048 (paperback) | ISBN 9781644533055 (hardback) | ISBN 9781644533062 (epub) | ISBN 9781644533079 (pdf)
Subjects: LCSH: Women—Italy—History—Renaissance, 1450–1600. | Sex role—Italy—History. | Social structure—Italy—History.
Classification: LCC HQ1149.I8 G464 2023 | DDC 305.420945—dc23/eng/20221207
LC record available at https://lccn.loc.gov/2022037672

A British Cataloging-in-Publication record for this book is available from the British Library.



∞ The paper used in this publication meets the requirements of the American National Standard for Information Sciences—Permanence of Paper for Printed Library Materials, ANSI Z39.48-1992.

udpress.udel.edu

Distributed worldwide by Rutgers University Press

# GENDERING THE RENAISSANCE

## The Early Modern Exchange



SELECTED TITLES

*The Waxing of the Middle Ages: Revisiting Late Medieval France,* edited by Tracy Adams and Charles-Louis Morand-Métivier

*Storytelling in Sixteenth-Century France: Negotiating Shifting Forms,* edited by Emily E. Thompson

*England's Asian Renaissance,* edited by Su Fang Ng and Carmen Nocentelli

*Performative Polemic: Anti-Absolutist Pamphlets and Their Readers in Late Seventeenth-Century France,* Kathrina Ann LaPorta

*Innovation in the Italian Counter-Reformation,* edited by Shannon McHugh and Anna Wainwright

*Milton among Spaniards,* Angelica Duran

*The Dark Thread: From Tragical Histories to Gothic Tales,* edited by John D. Lyons

*Women Warriors in Early Modern Spain: A Tribute to Bárbara Mujica,* edited by Susan L. Fischer and Frederick A. de Armas

*Per Elissa, con stima e affetto*

# Contents

# Acknowledgments

This volume is a tribute to Elissa Weaver and her enormous influence on the study of Italian literature in the United States and Italy. It collects essays from those colleagues, students, and friends who have been most impacted by her rigorous intellectual approach and her boundless scholarly generosity. Versions of these essays were presented in Professor Weaver's honor at the 2019 Renaissance Society of America (RSA) conference. With their range, depth, and subtlety, the presentations gave an exciting overview of the state of the field, and we knew immediately that they should appear in print. It has been our great honor and pleasure to gather these contributions into a book—Professor Weaver's most beloved object—as a sign of gratitude for all that she has done for each of us and for our notions of what Italian literature is and how it should and can be studied.

We are grateful to the volume's contributors for all the work they have put into making this volume a reality. We would also like to thank Julia Oestreich of the University of Delaware Press for shepherding the project into print; Gary Ferguson, coeditor of the Early Modern Exchange Series at the University of Delaware Press, for his support of the project; and the two anonymous readers for their invaluable feedback. We are grateful to Giuseppe Bruno-Chonin, for translating an essay and helping with the bibliography, and to Luciana Vernola, for her assistance with copyediting and proofreading. Our thanks also go, as always, to our families for their love and support.

INTRODUCTION

# Beyond the Wall

## Gender as Nexus in Renaissance Italy

MEREDITH K. RAY AND LYNN LARA WESTWATER

In her seminal work on the theater of Renaissance nuns, Elissa B. Weaver reveals the porous and constantly shifting boundaries between the social, literary, and religious worlds of the early-modern convent—an inherently gendered space in a Renaissance context in which sex and gender were inextricably linked—and "il mondo," the world just outside it. Noting the multidirectional influence of these spaces upon one another, Weaver draws upon archival documents to underscore how the very existence of convent walls inspired efforts to overcome them, revealing the clear visibility of the convent's "invisible" inhabitants. In one early essay, for instance, she relates a 1629 account in which the cloistered nuns of San Michele in Prato gathered at the windows during Carnival, showing themselves off in costumes assumed for the plays they performed in, while the *parlatorio*—the semiprivate, highly permeable receiving space inside the convent—was filled with visitors, "constant dancing . . . and other similar entertainments."[1] As Weaver wrote then, "the outside world was as curious as the nuns to see beyond the wall," and the wall itself had only limited efficacy in separating them.[2]

The essays in this volume stem from a series of conference panels organized in 2019 for the Renaissance Society of America to recognize and celebrate the impact of Weaver's scholarly legacy. As Weaver's work has always made clear, only by deliberately reinserting women into the literary and historical picture can we begin to obtain a more accurate account of the early modern. By gendering the Renaissance—that is, by reintroducing women as key actors in a field long dominated by scholarly focus on male authors and experience—we make gender not only a useful, but an essential, category of historical analysis, or to paraphrase Joan Scott: a signifier not only of sex but also of power differentials.[3] The convent walls on which Weaver has focused serve, metaphorically, as invitations to meditate on the role of gender in early-modern Italy. They urge the decloistering of normative spaces thought to be defined and certain: the physical and social spaces of convent, court, or home, and the literary spaces of established genres, from religious plays to Renaissance treatises and epic poetry. They also remind us to ask what might obscure our view of texts and archives and to interrogate absence as well as presence in the historical record.

In the same way that Weaver approached the convent walls of Renaissance Prato to investigate the dynamic interactions between spaces and among text, spectacle, and communities, her scholarship has interrogated the disciplinary divisions that have traditionally characterized much scholarship on early modern literature. By means of insightful textual criticism and archival historiography, Weaver has carved out a rich interdisciplinary space that weaves together literature, history, religion and gender, much as these strands were intertwined in the early-modern world. Weaver's open approach allows text and context to speak for themselves, without imposing preconceived schema upon them, understanding that to tease them out and study them separately would be to ignore and decontextualize the source material. Embracing interdisciplinary and collaborative perspectives, Weaver's methodology illuminates multivalent historical and literary sources and the social and cultural networks that produced them.

When Weaver began her academic career, Italian literary studies were still dominated by a rigid view of the canon, where only a handful of masterpieces by men were considered worthy of attention and the fields of women's studies or gender studies did not yet exist. Even in her early work on well-known male writers, she applied the lens of gender and sexuality, opening a path that still provides wonderfully rich study, as essays in this volume demonstrate. But her hallmark contribution has been to uncover women's writing that was languishing in archives or rare book collections—ignored by other scholars—and to bring it into the mainstream, analyzing the nuances of gender that shape and animate it. Founded on the intrinsic pairing of archival research and literary analysis and fueled by a determination to recenter women's writing, Weaver's school of literary study does not consider text without context, or context without text. As Daria Perocco has noted, Weaverian scholarship shows "the confidence of allowing the texts to speak in the historical, social, and literary context that generated them."[4] Weaver intuited and then proved that women's writing matters and has demonstrated time and again that the artificial erasure of women from literary history created a partial and inaccurate story about the development of culture. Numerous critics have described her transformative effect on the field of early-modern studies: for Beatrice Collina, Weaver has "radically changed the paradigms of early modern studies,"[5] while Maria Teresa Guerra Medici credits her with helping scholars to understand "the influence of women on the development of culture and language."[6]

From the nuanced examination of nuns' performance in Prato cited above, Weaver went on to pioneer the study of early-modern convent theater: her path-breaking studies include her 1990 edition of Beatrice del Sera's convent play *Amor di virtù: Commedia in cinque atti* (1548) and her 2002 monograph *Convent Theatre in Early Modern Italy: Spiritual Fun and Learning for Women*.[7] Evident in all her work is an attention to the transitory and flexible boundaries of literal and literary spaces and the imaginative application of the traditional tools of literary and historical analysis to rediscover the presence of women in early-modern Italy and to reorient perspectives on canonical and newly recovered texts and the contexts out of which they emerged. Weaver's scholarship has brought gender to the fore by highlighting its primacy in sometimes unexpected places, from the epic poetry of Boiardo, the satire of Berni, and the novellas of Boccaccio to convent theater (which often included nuns' reworkings of canonical texts) and the feminist polemics of the Venetian nun Arcangela Tarabotti.[8]

The essays in this collection build upon Weaver's critical methodology. They are intended to showcase the numerous and fruitful ways in which scholars can expand her coalescent approach that creates bridges between Italian and Anglophone scholarly traditions and that is informed by a political and social sensibility that insists on foregrounding those figures and experiences that have historically remained marginal. Collina notes that Weaver's scholarship has been driven by an urgent question: "Why did women remain invisible as literary, historical and social subjects while their presence and participation in those fields is a matter of historical fact?"[9] Weaver's answer to this question reveals as much about the modern academy as it does about early-modern society: she has shown us again and again that women were not in fact invisible in the Renaissance world. They were central drivers in literature, culture, and society, even if subsequent literary and historical studies erased or forgot this presence. Sparked by Weaver's con/textual approach and inspired by her rigorous techniques of textual recovery and close reading, the essays in this volume suggest new ways to interrogate gendered discourses of genre, identities, and sanctity. Organized into groupings around these three themes, they offer a complex picture of gender in early-modern Italian literature and culture through overlapping lenses that bring into focus myriad other issues, from race and religion to schooling and storytelling. Read in dialogue with one another, these essays provide a multifaceted view of currents in the study of gender in early-modern Italy.

More broadly, this collection is an example of the kind of study that can be done when a barrier becomes an invitation to its crossing, showing the ways in which scholars can, and should, violate disciplinary, temporal, and institutional walls. Here again, gender provides the fissure, the ladder, and the key. At the same time, Weaver's approach, and that of this volume, can also be described with the figure of the path. Weaver's scholarship has been pathbreaking, leading to such essential and now generally accepted concepts as the porousness of the convent wall. And as with any path worth following, her work has opened new routes to others, as the essays in this collection so vividly demonstrate. Using careful archival and philological work, and attending to absence as well as presence, Weaver has unmasked the historiographical distortions that erase women, providing a model for how to reveal and reverse other erasures, how to break down barriers that obscure, separate, or deny the fluidity of race, sexuality, identity, spirituality, and genre. This collection, therefore, points to a rich landscape of future possibilities for exploring text and context within early-modern studies.

The volume opens with Part One: "Gendering Genre." The three essays in this section challenge conventional ideas of genre by investigating a diverse set of literary texts through the lens of gender. The essays shed new light on the early-modern genres of *sacra rappresentazione* (the religious play in verse), dialogue, novella, fairy tale, and epic poem by showing women's agency within various textual spaces even as they grapple with the constrictions and consequences of patriarchal norms: violence against women, control of women's bodies and discourses, and the co-opting of women for social, political, or religious agendas. From within established generic conventions, women writers and female voices test those bounds to question and reshape standing literary parameters, demonstrating the power of genre as a vehicle for alternative and marginalized perspectives as well as for hegemonic political goals. The first and third essays in this section pair the exploration of gender with the discussion of race and colonialism, too long ignored by many scholars under the improbable premise that Italy's anomalous position in early-modern Europe as a failed colonial power meant that issues of race and colonialism did not appear in its literature. These essays apply Weaver's exacting literary techniques of textual recovery and rereading to demonstrate the numerous ways in which early-modern Italian writers insistently revisited questions of race and colonialism (with frequent slippage between race and religion), while at the same time failing to recognize the inescapable relevance of these matters to a peninsula that was itself a pawn of colonial powers: "più stiava che li Ebrei," as Machiavelli famously wrote, "sanza capo, sanza ordine, battuta, spogliata, lacera, corsa" ("more slave than the Jews . . . without a leader, without order, beaten, despoiled, lacerated, overrun . . .").[10] The second contribution instead foregrounds the interplay of genre and the discourse of early-modern feminist thought, showing how the novella and the fairy tale could be inverted, subverted, and exploited to tell other, often-invisible stories about marginalization, imagined communities, and possible remedies for injustice.

First in this section is Anna Wainwright's study of the widow motif in a religious play by the fifteenth-century writer Antonia Tanini Pulci (1452/4–1501)—fittingly, an author restored to literary history through the seminal work of Weaver.[11] In "Widows, Lament, and Ottoman Anxieties in Renaissance Florence," Wainwright examines how cultural preoccupations about gender, race, and religion are entwined in Pulci's *The Destruction of Saul and the Lament of David*. Weaver's work on Pulci revealed how the writer engaged with themes of gender, religion, and power to advance a body of work that was at once orthodox and implicitly destabilizing to established literary and social norms. Wainwright's analysis expands that lens to interrogate how Pulci—a widow and a tertiary—employs the *sacra rappresentazione*, a genre considered appropriate to women writers, to articulate an oblique commentary on gender roles that also touched on racialized religious anxieties about the perceived Ottoman threat after the siege of Otranto in 1480. As Wainwright's essay deftly highlights, Pulci's play subverts conventional tropes broadly employed in canonical texts by Dante, Petrarch, and Boccaccio of the widow as a danger to civic stability. Instead, Pulci introduces Saul's queen (virtually absent from the Old Testament story) as her protagonist and heroine, activating "racialized fears of a common enemy" to portray "Saul's widow as a representative of collective [civic] mourning." Playing on contemporary anxieties about Ottoman power, it is not the Hebrews who attack the widow in Pulci's play but the Philistine soldiers (relabeled by Pulci as "Turks") who violently assault her, resulting in her martyrdom and the consequent glorification of Christianity over Islam. As Wainwright demonstrates, Pulci uses the *sacra rappresentazione* as a medium through which to reframe the power of the widow, while simultaneously making a political commentary that projects religious disquiet about the Jews onto racialized fears about the Ottoman Muslims as a perceived threat to Italian Christian women and society.

Suzanne Magnanini's essay, "Unhappily Ever After: Moderata Fonte's Fairy Tale," delves into another gendered genre, investigating the fairy tale from a feminist perspective. Magnanini examines the production of *novelle* by Fonte, the versatile sixteenth-century Venetian writer who is best known for her dialogue *Il merito delle donne* (*The Worth of Women*), published posthumously in 1600. Magnanini looks at the three *novelle* told within the frame of *Il merito* and focuses in particular on the dynamics of storytelling and reception within the diverse group of seven women who gather in a walled Venetian garden to discuss men's merits and defects. Magnanini develops the concept of "concensureship," or a reading that fuses consensus and censure (in particular of antiwoman bias), to describe the reactions of the women, whom Magnanini terms "savvy feminist literary critics."

Magnanini considers in particular at the tale of Lioncorno and Biancarisa, narrated by the character Corinna. Corinna tells the sorrowful story of these star-crossed lovers, whose happiness is forever thwarted when Climene, Phaeton's mother, turns the new groom into a unicorn in misdirected vengeance for Apollo's faithlessness. Magnanini characterizes this account as an "anti-tale," that is, a story that takes certain elements of the fairy tale genre and subverts them. Drawing on a broad range of Italian fairy tales, Magnanini shows in particular how Fonte's tale, which implicitly critiques the gender bias inherent to conventional fairy tales, is exceptional in its treatment of Climene, who—far from a traditional, one-dimensional female villain—is given a sympathetic backstory that justifies her destructive actions. The tale also challenges the "radical hopefulness" of the fairy tale genre, which is predicated on the knowledge that justice will be done. Corinna's tale is instead one of hopelessness, since the original villain (Apollo, whose betrayal of Climene set the plot into motion) remains unpunished and Climene is left as both victim and perpetrator of wrongdoing. Returning to the concept of "consensureship," Magnanini argues that the group of women censures, but does not censor, the tale of Lioncorno and Biancarisa, allowing the telling of the tale, even with a negative female character, in part because the fantastic tale is far from the virtuous reality of the women themselves, in part because it is instructive to women about the dangers they face, and in part because it was a man who was ultimately to blame for the negative outcome. Magnanini therefore reads the fantastic tale as ultimately realistic, acknowledging that, just as men have created the systems that subjugate women, so too must they be involved in overhauling them.

The final essay in this section, Nathalie Hester's "Amerigo Vespucci and African Amazons: Reinventing Italian Exploration in Baroque Epic Poetry," explores the role of race, gender, and colonial ambition in this genre par excellence of the Italian tradition. Hester focuses in particular on the role of the Amazon in these epic tales, an intriguing and elusive figure that drew inspiration from a variety of sources, including the Amazonian-inspired warrior women in the preceding Italian epic tradition; the reports in European chronicles of the Americas that described Amazon-like territories in the "New" World; and the pervasive appearance of the figure in a wide variety of other genres, including treatises on illustrious women, operas, and public spectacles. The Amazon became a means for discussing a number of issues, including women's relationship to political and social power and to warfare and violence, as well as a way to express anxiety about European encounters with "global otherness." In typical Italian epic narratives about the Americas, the Amazon women are defeated, converted, and domesticated, signaling "the providential imposition of the patriarchal, Catholic religious and social order." In contrast, Hester offers the unusual example of the 1650 *L'America* by the Florentine Girolamo Bartolomei Smeducci, which sets a significant portion of the story in or near Africa and offers a distinctive treatment of armed women.

In Bartolomei's celebratory narrative of Florentine exploration, which centered on ultimately futile colonial hopes, the warrior Lampedona, rather than being a target for conversion, is a generous host who helps the hero Vespucci and his crew to leave Africa and continue their journey to the Americas. Lampedona's figure allows Bartolomei to present Florentine colonial ambitions as peaceful and humane, in contrast to Portuguese and Spanish violence, within a genre that also, in its use of the Tuscan vernacular and Dantean and Petrarchan literary references, celebrates Florentine cultural achievement. But Bartolomei also departs in important ways from the tradition: while he describes

Lampedona—who is Black, in contrast to the white Ethiopian warrior Clorinda of Tasso's *Gerusalemme liberata*—in Petrarchan terms, he foregrounds Lampedona's morality and agency, rather than male desire. Hester reads Lampedona as an ultimately ambiguous figure who expresses her own desires, is not converted, and reports on the brutality of colonialism; nonetheless she is situated in a narrative that desires, however unrealistically, Florentine colonial expansion. She becomes an emblem of Italian colonial ambitions that remained a mere fictional projection, while also representing the troubled history of the early-modern European colonization of Africa.

If Part One considers the literary possibilities of working within, against, and beyond established genre conventions, the essays in Part Two, "Gendering Identities," take a sociocultural turn to explore alternative paths to autonomy, education, and self-realization for early-modern women, on and beyond the established paths of marriage and convent. Charting women's agency within gendered physical and social spaces, the essays draw on the archive and a careful revisiting of primary texts to show the complexity and richness of the lives of early-modern women across social strata, lives that were constructed around religious identity, societal expectations, gender norms, and personal ambition. At root, the essays in this section explore the interpenetrations between religious and lay life in early-modern Italy, examining movement in both directions: on the one hand, through women using religious identity as a launching pad for active participation in the secular world, and on the other, through lay women who yearned for certain aspects of religious life. The essays show, in short, that women inside and outside the convent led highly mobile and fluid lives that resist easy categorization.

In her essay on Suor Eleonora d'Este (1515–1575), daughter of Lucrezia Borgia, Gabriella Zarri explores the ways in which the Renaissance convent intersected with issues of gender and power for early-modern elite women, functioning not as a closed world but as an alternative and porous space that allowed for the pursuit of intellectual and artistic goals as well as continued engagement with the secular world. Zarri's pioneering work as a historian of gender and religion has long illuminated the importance of convents in the establishment and reproduction of networks of female power. Her rigorous contextualization of archival documents has shed invaluable light on the creative and spiritual aspects of monastic life for early-modern women (which found its dark side in the practice of forced monachization, which is discussed in an essay in Part Three of this volume).

Here, in her essay "The Princess Nun: The Familiar Letters of Suor Eleonora d'Este (1515–1575), Daughter of Lucrezia Borgia," Zarri again employs the archive to bring to light the experience of Leonora Barbara (Suor Eleonora), who entered the convent of Corpus Domini in Ferrara—the "family convent," as Zarri writes—at only five years of age, after the death of her mother. Despite her youth and the challenges she surely faced in this transition, Eleonora was able to find the foundation for a varied and extensive education that included music and medicine (she was also proficient in Latin and Greek), eventually serving as the convent apothecary and earning the attention of the noted physician Antonio Musa Brasavola, who dedicated a work on medical simples to her in 1536. Notably, Zarri also documents that Eleonora was active in the *parlatorio*, having received an unusual dispensation that allowed her to meet freely (and even secretly) with secular figures, and maintained an active interest and engagement with the political affairs of her family, perhaps offering counsel to her brother Ercole II, as he navigated the rocky spiritual currents of his marriage to Renée of France. Zarri's multifaceted examination of Eleonora's life is deepened by her examination of the princess nun's familiar correspondence, which shows her to have been active in providing advice and introductions (often to help her convent sisters) and in intervening on behalf of those in need (including, in at least two cases, women facing domestic violence). Zarri's essay shows that convent walls could indeed become permeable conduits for religious, political, and cultural exchange—especially for elite women of Eleonora's rank. Read in conjunction with the final essay of this volume, which examines the experience of the convent from another perspective, Zarri's study reinforces the notion that walls invite their own breaching.

The next essay in this section, by Emanuela Zanotti Carney, returns us to a figure central to Weaver's work, considered from a different angle than in the first essay in this volume by Wainwright: the prolific Antonia Tanini Pulci. Weaver's study of Pulci established her as a significant figure in the literary and religious history of Renaissance Florence, whose writings provided strong models of female spirituality and appealed to an engaged audience of women, while Wainwright's essay examines the motif of the widow in one of her plays. In "A Christian Romance for Married Women: Marriage, Female Spirituality, and the Pursuit of Saintliness in Antonia Pulci's *Rappresentazione di Santa Guglielma*," Carney builds on our understanding of Pulci's oeuvre to interrogate how this play, walking a careful line between seeming conformity to Florentine ideologies of marriage and an implicit challenge to the submissive role accorded women by the Church, the state, and the family, presented women with the possibility of an inherently radical alternative: the pursuit of a chaste spiritual vocation within marriage. Carney shows how Pulci—herself an *ammantellata*, or tertiary—used the legend of Santa Guglielma to explore this path, by which women could obtain spiritual authority within marriage, redefining and sanctifying wedlock as a chaste union in order to create an autonomous space of female power.

As Carney points out, there is multivalent meaning behind Pulci's choosing as heroine the historical Guglielma, who was hailed as an emblem of women's salvation and then posthumously deemed a heretic. Guglielma pursues spiritual authority, transcending the confines of marriage and a husband's prerogative by submitting obediently to Christ and, especially, to the Virgin Mary (whose cult would develop and grow over the next centuries, as discussed in the volume's last essay). Her story also resituates female chastity within women's own purview. Pulci's *Santa Guglielma* was enormously popular with early-modern audiences, published over thirty times by the mid-seventeenth century. Carney's close examination of this text and its history offers an important key to reading female authority, sexuality, and spirituality in the early Renaissance.

The final essay in this second grouping, Jennifer Haraguchi's study of public education for women in early-modern Lazio, has reverberations into the early eighteenth century and beyond. In "Maestre Pie Venerini e Filippini: Instituting Public Education for Women in Seventeenth- and Eighteenth-Century Lazio," Haruguchi brings to the fore the understudied history of women's organized education in Italy, examining the interdependence of female-led schools with the motives and aims of the Church, whose hierarchy supported their development with the goal not only of providing girls from poor families with a better future but also of imparting to them Christian morals and gender ideologies. Again building on the work of Zarri for the earlier Renaissance period, Haraguchi argues that the *terzo stato*, or "third status" (socially acceptable alternatives to convent or traditional marriage that included lay communities of women such as the Maestre Pie), was by no means anomalous in the early-modern period and warrants deeper investigation into its forms and impact.

Haraguchi's study traces the development of lay educational institutions as an alternative to the cloistered environments of the convent (especially for families who could not afford the convents' spiritual dowries). These lay institutions gave women instruction not only in Christian morals and ideals but also in literacy (in part to prepare them to read spiritual books) and taught them the tangible skills they needed for professional careers. As Haraguchi points out, though the schools established by the Maestre Pie in many respects supported, and were as a result supported by, Church leaders, their very existence functioned to destabilize social and religious norms and hierarchies of gender and class (notably, the teachers trained there were required to remain *zitelle*, that is, unmarried, without responsibilities to the home). Haraguchi argues for the importance of accounting for networks, and in this case, collaborative relationships between men and women, in contextualizing the development of institutions that promoted both a female apostolate and professional careers for women as itinerant teachers and in a variety of other fields.

Part Three of this collection, titled "Gendering Sanctity," brings together essays that explore the possibilities and limits for early-modern women who lived in, and tried to move beyond, tightly defined and socially prescribed roles in the convent and the court, on the stage and the page. Exploring the multifaceted identities of such varied personas as duchess, performer, and nun, the essays address the extensive, onerous, and often contradictory gendered norms that subtended the notion of how women, both secular and religious, were expected to occupy their positions. How and when could they stray from a strictly defined and closely controlled role without inviting censure? The essays show a remarkably consistent solution: that women could achieve social sanction for an ambition that led them beyond accepted gender bounds by associating themselves—and all women—with female saints, most importantly with the Virgin Mary.

Michael Sherberg's essay, "The State of Grace in the *Libro Del Cortegiano*," investigates transcendence and female power in Baldassare Castiglione's sixteenth-century masterpiece about "depicting in words a perfect courtier." Sherberg terms the work "a quintessential work of escapist fiction," as the court at Urbino both evades the reality of the imminent death of the duke (who, languishing in illness, is absent from all of the story's events) and also plans for a more hopeful future under the idealized leader described through conversation. Underscoring the importance of the duchess and the "exalting power" with which she is vested to authorize the court's proceedings, Sherberg's essay centers women and female authority in the text. He revises a common critical reading of the work that sees women as largely invisible within the text and transcended by a male power that is both political and intellectual.

Sherberg offers another view of transcendence, a central concept to his essay at which he arrives by means of the *Cortegiano*'s central concept of *grazia*, grace. The word provides Sherberg a key to interpreting issues of power, gender, and spirituality in the work. *Grazia* is at once an enigmatic aesthetic quality, shared by men and women alike, and political currency, the means by which rulers reward loyalty and service. *Grazia* is also a central term in both Neo-Platonic and Christian thought, which Castiglione goes to lengths to weave together, creating a notion of it that is both aesthetic (from the former) and political (from the latter). Sherberg points out that the New Testament, which refers to Mary as *gratia plena* ("full of grace"), situates grace in the female body, making a discussion of gender inherent in the term. The *Cortegiano*'s speakers go to some lengths to insist that grace, for men, does not imply preening effeminacy, which would in fact compromise the more material grace—that is, largesse—that a courtier must seek from the prince; a manly grace instead secures princely favor. This is not the only gender-inflected discussion of grace within the *Cortegiano*. In the text's famous exchange over women's roles and worth, its nod to the contemporary *querelle des femmes*, Giuliano de' Medici, women's defender, points to the many untold tales of religious women who follow the example of the Virgin Mary. These cloistered women have direct transcendence, direct access to grace, as opposed to the courtiers, who have to seek its diminished material form from their lord. The ineluctable association of grace with the feminine creates a fundamental tension at court, Sherberg demonstrates, intensifying a gender crisis that has already been set into motion by the manifest example of female power at its center. Read in connection with Magnanini's essay on Moderata Fonte's imagined, all-female alternative to the space of the court, Sherberg's essay suggests that the court itself could be the locus of female power, even as tensions around women's authority—in both works—play out both mimetically and diegetically.

Courtney Quaintance approaches similar questions of gender, authority, and religion, while moving into the seventeenth century and to a different center of power: the papal city of Rome. In her essay, "Singing Women, Saint Cecilia, and Self-Fashioning in Seventeenth-Century Rome," Quaintance brings an interdisciplinary lens and rich archival discoveries to the examination of the prolific seventeenth-century writer, singer, and musician Margherita Costa (c. 1600–post-1657). Quaintance begins her exploration with an engraved portrait of the *virtuosa* that features the many musical instruments that were the tools of the singer's trade. The portrait recalls Raphael's *The Ecstasy of Saint Cecilia*, which similarly features a display of worldly musical instruments, even as Saint Cecilia herself gazes upward toward choirs of angels. While Quaintance does not argue that the images are directly related, she uses them as a jumping-off point to uncover the factors that shaped singing women's careers in a time of shifting norms. These shifts were driven by two important and disparate factors that took root in the seventeenth century: on the one hand, the emergence of opera, and on the other, the religious reform that followed from the Council of Trent, which focused attention not only on the potential dangers of the arts but also on their spiritual potential. In this context, the figure of the musical Saint Cecilia assumed a special importance, especially given the intensification of the saint's cult in Rome in the seventeenth century after the 1599 discovery of her miraculously incorrupt body in the Basilica of Santa Cecilia in Trastevere—a body that, contemporary observers marveled, physically signaled its virginity.

But even as this saintly female musician attracted followers, Rome proved to be an unfriendly space for others: elsewhere in Italy, women were achieving new levels of fame, and compensation, on the opera stage, while women singers in Rome, where women's presence on stage was actively discouraged, were instead forced to perform in private settings. Female performance elicited intense anxiety about the power of women's bodies and women's voices and consequent judgments about women's honor being compromised through public spectacle. Quaintance argues that one tool Costa used to fend off such negative associations was her 1644 sacred poem on Saint Cecilia's life, *Cecilia martire,* dedicated to Pope Urban VIII's nephew Francesco Barberini. The work was the only devotional one that she published and the only one printed in Rome, her bid to court Barberini's patronage as well as legitimacy by associating herself (but never so closely as to be offensive) with the musical saint who was dear to Roman hearts. Though Costa's attempt to use this work to curry long-term favor in Rome foundered, she nevertheless continued to use her *Cecilia martire* to seek Barberini's patronage. By examining Costa's complex effort to authorize and fund her work as a musician by associating herself with Saint Cecilia, Quaintance's essay provides a case study, in exquisite detail, of how female sanctity could be strategically deployed to authorize women's worldly activities.

In the final essay of Part Three, "'Polemics That Might Seem Spiteful in Heaven': Female Spiritual Authority in Arcangela Tarabotti's *Paradiso Monacale,*" Meredith K. Ray and Lynn Lara Westwater continue the exploration of female sanctity and the construction of female identity and power in Counter-Reformation Italy by examining the depiction of female saints in the works of the Venetian nun and polemicist Arcangela Tarabotti (1604–1652). In a context far removed from that of sixteenth-century Eleonora d'Este, presented in

Zarri's essay, Tarabotti was forced against her will to become a nun and dedicated her life to protesting the practice of forced monachization and other injustices against women. Ray and Westwater demonstrate that Tarabotti's hallmark advocacy for women and her tendency to thwart prevailing cultural trends are both manifest in her unconventional approach to female saints. The writer capitalizes upon the example of these inviolate women, whose sanctity and power had been authorized by the Church, to demonstrate the key role women played in the history of the Church and to decry men's abuses against women in religious and secular contexts. Ray and Westwater identify two religious figures who have particular resonance for Tarabotti: Saint Catherine of Siena and the Virgin Mary. Saint Catherine, mentioned frequently if fleetingly throughout Tarabotti's oeuvre, is a powerful implicit presence in the Venetian nun's writing, Ray and Westwater argue, her life story resonating strongly with Tarabotti.

While Catherine often serves as subtext or inspiration in Tarabotti's writing, the Virgin Mary instead occupies the explicit place of honor in many of her works, most important in her signature devotional work, her 1643 *Paradiso monacale* (*Convent Paradise*). Tarabotti's emphasis on the Virgin was connected to a surge in Marian devotion in the early-modern period, and certain elements of Mary's story that Tarabotti emphasizes—for example, the Virgin's role as coredemptrix with her son and mediatrix—were consonant with broader tendencies within Counter-Reformation Catholicism, in which devotion to the Virgin became an important rallying point to counter the Protestant threat. Much traditional worship of Mary emphasized her humility and obedience, and even as Mary became a tool in the fight against Protestantism, she was often depicted unthreateningly, though many women writers sought to highlight her spiritual authority. Tarabotti instead imagines an actively forceful Mary, even naming her, rather than Peter, as the first pope. To contextualize Tarabotti's use of Catherine and Mary in seventeenth-century Venice, Ray and Westwater also consider the example of the other prominent woman writer in mid-century Venice, Lucrezia Marinella (1571–1653), who wrote several hagiographic works, including two dedicated to Catherine of Siena and the Virgin Mary, whose publication preceded Tarabotti's *Paradiso*. Ray and Westwater explore the varying strategies in these works, seeing Tarabotti's depiction as "perhaps the apex of such expression by women writers in the Counter Reformation." Even in Tarabotti's depiction of convent "paradise," where she seeks to accept female submission to a religious vocation, she highlights avenues to female activism and resistance by making female sanctity and female power self-reinforcing. An unwilling nun for whom the pen is both weapon and salvation, Tarabotti seeks in the authoritative women of the Church an alternative state, in which a religious life does not mean sacrificing power beyond convent walls.

We have deliberately chosen to close this volume with an essay devoted to Arcangela Tarabotti, a figure whom, like Antonia Pulci, Weaver was instrumental in bringing to the attention of scholars. In the dynamic atmosphere of Counter-Reformation Venice, Tarabotti, benefiting from the city's relatively open publishing climate, enjoyed a certain degree of intellectual freedom even as she lived in tight physical constraint. Her life and her work are a study in the thwarting of fixed boundaries, and her thought, in its remarkable prescience, pointed a path to a future of possibilities that was as vivid in her imagination as it was antithetical to her own imprisoned circumstances. Perhaps we can see, as a way station along this path to the freer future she imagined, two well-known eighteenth-century Venetian paintings by Francesco Guardi. This pendant pair—like the work of Elissa Weaver—evokes the crossing of boundaries and the penetration of spaces, the spectacle and the little-noticed but essential detail, the intermixing of sacred and secular. We would like to conclude our introductory reflections with a brief consideration of these paintings as emblems of the sort of scholarly approach this volume embodies and hopes to transmit for new lines of inquiry.

The more famous of these paired images depicts the lively atmosphere of a Venetian convent, San Zaccaria, a scene often pointed to for its vivid visualization of the porousness between religious and secular worlds. The nuns in the *Parlatorio delle monache di San Zaccaria* (1750) sit on one side of three open, grilled windows, the interlocking quadrants large enough to permit clear views, the exchange of letters or small objects, and even the touch of a hand through the bars. On the other side, their visitors—men, women, and children—engage with them, and with each other, enthusiastically. Some are seated, some are standing, their gazes drawing us through the open and hidden spaces of the convent.

As scholars have pointed out, there is a distinctly theatrical aspect to the ambience (and indeed, San Zaccaria was known for its theatrical activities): the grilled, partially curtained windows are suggestive of a delineated stage; the nuns or visitors become the performers or the audience, depending on the viewer's perspective. The theatrical element is reinforced, quite literally, by the animated puppet show to one side, eagerly observed by two small boys, while,

Figure I.1. *Il Parlatorio delle monache di San Zaccaria*. Francesco Guardi (1750). Wikimedia Commons, https://commons.wikimedia.org/wiki/File:Ca%27_Rezzonico_-_Il_Parlatorio_delle_monache_di_San_Zaccaria_-_Francesco_Guardi.jpg.

on the other side, a beggar appears to seek alms. Notable in the painting is the intermingling of gender and social, as well as secular and spiritual, status. If the grilled windows evoke exchange and circulation (as well as division and segregation), the open door to the viewer's far right, through which the blue sky over the cloister can be glimpsed, presents yet another permeable, not-quite-knowable space that hints at unseen connections and exchanges. Though the Venetian religious and political authorities went to great lengths to assure the impenetrability of the city's convents through measures such as limiting visits and correspondences, walling up exterior windows, and restricting access to the convent by locking and monitoring doors, the repeated prohibitions that litter the archives reflect the futility of this campaign rather than its success.

The pendant pair to Guardi's *Parlatorio* is his *Il Ridotto di palazzo Dandolo a San Moisé* (1746), which depicts a gathering of men and women in the sitting room of a Venetian palazzo, where they have convened, in a Carnival-like atmosphere, to visit and gamble. The viewer is immediately struck by the similarities in composition between the two paintings, which, as part of a pictorial genre juxtaposing convent parlors and *ridotti,* were intended to provoke comparison and contemplation between these spaces.[12] As Christine Scippa Bhasin notes, the physical pairing of these images "testifies to the complementary space that secular sitting room and cloister parlor occupied in the Venetian mindset."[13] The grille that separates the nuns from their visitors in Guardi's *Parlatorio* is, as Bhasin and other scholars have pointed out, suggestive at once of both separation and exchange, evoking the "paradox of restriction and possibility," in the words of Alison Findlay.[14]

Guardi's companion *ridotto* image is similarly evocative, rewarding close examination of what is present as well as what is absent, what is fixed and what is fluid. Here, too, the environment is marked by elements of performance and spectacle, with masked figures—a mix of men and women, the latter primarily courtesans and actresses—moving through the foreground. Their clothing and postures suggest a range in status and role, an open social circulation, and even the possibility of sexual availability amid Carnival's customary, temporary subversion of social and gender mores. (Indeed, the scale of gambling in Venice, focus of the *ridotto,* increased throughout the early-modern period as Carnival—that period of boundary crossings with which this essay opened—became more important).[15] As Marc Neveu notes, masks were typical, even expected, at such gatherings, a theatrical practice that allowed a degree of anonymity and that "dramatically" enhanced the "potential to socialize with those individuals

Figure I.2. *Il Ridotto di palazzo Dandolo a San Moisè*. Francesco Guardi (1746). Wikimedia Commons, https://commons.wikimedia.org/wiki/File:Ca%27_Rezzonico_-_Il_Ridotto_di_palazzo_Dandolo_a_San_Moise_-_Francesco_Guardi.jpg.

with whom one might not normally interact."[16] A closer study of this image further underscores this theatrical and potentially disruptive element, revealing in the foreground a pair of figures whose costume evokes the stock commedia dell'arte figures of Columbine and Harlequin. A basket on her arm, Columbine banters with a cloaked gentleman, while her diminutive companion extends a playful hand to a dog. Wielding his traditional wooden spatula or "slapstick," the figure wears the distinctive black mask common to the character. Meant to evoke his comic function, the mask also introduces the specter of race (its presence, distortions, and erasures) into the image, though it has gone largely unremarked. Harlequin, as Robert Hornback has noted—a "malleable" figure who combines elements of racial difference with social satire—developed from longstanding, even ancient, blackface traditions, eventually becoming a "key figure in the transmission of comic blackface and its cultural meanings across the Old World into the New."[17]

Race, together with gender, sexuality, and social status, is thus present in Guardi's painting as an element of the underlying dynamics of exchange and permeability at work in the image, while, as in the *Parlatorio*, the open doorways in the background—and mirrors hanging still beyond—suggest people, encounters, and exchanges taking place just beyond the viewer's scope.[18] Partially obscured, and situated at unusual angles, these semiprivate, ambiguous zones invite the viewer to consider the relationship between protagonists and spaces, to ponder the function and limitations of doors, windows, walls, and other architectural and metaphorical delineations between categories. This volume shows the provocative and generative scholarship that results from applying this perspective to interrogate Renaissance texts and contexts—from seeking out, through the lens of gender, the obscured or absent spaces around genre, identity and sanctity, and from drawing out the permeable, flexible, and transmutative connections between the archive and the text, and between the worldly and the religious, in order to scale the walls to the past.

Notes

1. Elissa B. Weaver, "Convent Comedy and the World: The Farces of Suor Annalena Odaldi (1572–1638)," *Annali d'italianistica* 7, Women's Voices in Italian Literature (1989): 191.

2. Weaver, "Convent Comedy," 191.

3. Joan W. Scott, "Gender: A Useful Category of Historical Analysis," *American Historical Review* 91, no. 5 (1986): 1053–1075. Always at play as well are the dynamics of gender as performance, theorized by Judith Butler; see, for example, her *Gender Trouble: Feminism and the Subversion of Identity* (New York: Routledge, 1990).

4. Daria Perocco, "Thought Pieces for Elissa Weaver," *Modern Philology* 106, no. 4 (May 2009): 713.

5. Beatrice Collina, "Thought Pieces for Elissa Weaver," 705.

6. Maria Teresa Guerra Medici, "Thought Pieces for Elissa Weaver," 707.

7. Beatrice del Sera, *Amor di virtù: Commedia in cinque atti (1548)*, ed. Elissa Weaver (Ravenna: Longhi Editore, 1990); Elissa B. Weaver, *Convent Theatre in Early Modern Italy: Spiritual Fun and Learning for Women* (Cambridge: Cambridge University Press, 2002).

8. In addition to the studies mentioned above, Weaver's books include such critical editions as Francesco Buoninsegni and Arcangela Tarabotti, *Satira ed Antisatira*, ed. and with an introduction by Elissa Weaver (Rome: Salerno Editrice, 1998); Arcangela Tarabotti, *Antisatire: In Defense of Women, against Francesco Buoninsegni*, ed. and trans. and with an introduction by Elissa B. Weaver (Toronto: Iter Press and the Arizona Center for Medieval and Renaissance Studies, 2020); Antonia Pulci, *Saints' Lives and Bible Stories for the Stage*, ed. Elissa B. Weaver, trans. James Wyatt Cook, with introduction by Elissa B. Weaver (Toronto: Iter Press/Centre for Reformation and Renaissance Studies, 2010); several edited volumes, including *The Decameron First Day in Perspective*, ed. and with introduction and bibliography by Elissa B. Weaver (Toronto: University of Toronto Press, 2004); *Arcangela Tarabotti: A Literary Nun in Baroque Venice*, ed. and with an introduction by Elissa B. Weaver (Ravenna: Longo Editore, 2006); and *Scenes from Italian Convent Life: An Anthology of Theatrical Texts and Contexts*, ed. Elissa B. Weaver (Ravenna: Longo Editore, 2010). Since she began publishing in 1975, Weaver has also authored more than four dozen articles and book chapters, in English or Italian.

9. Collina, "Thought Pieces for Elissa Weaver," 705.

10. Niccolò Machiavelli, *Il Principe e altre opere politiche*, ed. Stefano Andretta, introduction by Delio Cantimori, 14th edition (Milan: Garzanti, 1994), 94 (cf. *Machiavelli: Political, Historical and Literary Writings*, eds. Mark Jurdjevic and Meredith K. Ray, trans. Meredith K. Ray [Philadelphia: University of Pennsylvania Press, 2019, 79]).

11. See Pulci, *Saints' Lives*.

12. This term stems from the verb *ridurre*, or *to enclose*, and came to be equated in later seventeenth- and early eighteenth-century Venice with gaming salons.

13. Christine Scippa Bhasin, "Prostitutes, Nuns, Actresses: Breaking the Convent Wall in Seventeenth-Century Venice," *Theatre Journal* 66, no. 1 (2014): 30.

14. Alison Findlay, *Playing Spaces in Early Women's Drama* (Cambridge: Cambridge University Press, 2006), 1; cited in Bhasin, "Prostitutes, Nuns, Actresses," 30.

15. Jonathan Walker, "Gambling and Venetian Noblemen c.1500–1700," *Past & Present* 162, no. 1 (1999): 57.

16. Marc Neveu, "The Space of the Mask: From Stage to Ridotto," in *Architectural Space in Eighteenth-Century Europe: Constructing Identities and Interiors*, eds. Denise Amy Baxter and Meredith Martin (London: Routledge, 2010), 152.

17. Robert Hornback, "Harlequin as Theatergram: Transmitting the Timeworn Black Mask, Ancient to Antebellum," in *Racism and Early Blackface Comic Traditions, From the Old World to the New*, ed. Robert Hornback (New York: Palgrave Macmillan, 2018), 35.

18. Indeed, early *ridotti* often had "secret doors for entry and exit" (Neveu, "The Space of the Mask," 150).

PART I

# Gendering Genre

CHAPTER ONE

# Widows, Lament, and Ottoman Anxieties in Renaissance Florence

ANNA WAINWRIGHT

Widows played a central yet sometimes controversial role in how the medieval and Renaissance Italian city was conceptualized, especially in times of political crisis. The figure of the widow often served as a powerful symbol of a city's mourning, but it could also speak to its resilience and the possibility of healing from collective trauma. From the fifteenth century onward, the public voices of widows—prophetic, saintly, sometimes rife with anger or indignation—were amplified through texts by women writers, offering a new perspective on the social and political function the widow served.[1] In this essay, I consider how the widow's voice could be used to symbolize collective suffering in the face of political violence—and also to complicate it. I take as my case study the little-discussed *sacra rappresentazione*, or sacred play, by Antonia Tanini Pulci (1452/54–1501), *La rappresentazione della distruzione di Saul e del pianto di Davit* (*The Destruction of Saul and the Lament of David*), in which we see Saul's widow tortured and killed by Philistine soldiers.[2] After her gruesome onstage death, the widowed queen is flown away by angels, her killers left behind in a deep sleep. Through this one unusual and striking scene, Saul's widow becomes a key protagonist in a story from which she is excluded in the Old Testament.

Tanini Pulci's play is one of the first instances of an Italian widowed writer writing about a widowed character, following her fellow Florentine Lucrezia Tornabuoni's sacred narrative of the Hebrew widow Judith and Christine de

Pizan's panoply of widowed figures in *The Book of the City of the Ladies*.[3] Unlike these more well-known examples, this play offers us something unique: a widow whose story is almost entirely the author's own invention. Tanini Pulci presents a unique portrait of a widow's suffering, and the threatening power of a widow's voice, through the medium of a religious play. Moreover, the author destabilizes common scholarly understandings of how widows functioned in civic society. As I elaborate below, the widow's voice was often used in Italian literature as a metaphorical representation of the city itself, yet the voices of widowed citizens themselves were frequently constrained or even silenced. By adding the woes of Saul's widow to the story of Saul and David, Tanini Pulci asks her audience to confront this longstanding societal anxiety over widows' emotional expression, while she flips it on its head. During her onstage murder, criticism of the widow's voice comes not from the mouths of Hebrews—stand-ins for Tanini Pulci's contemporary Florentines—but from the Philistine soldiers who capture and kill her. Even more striking, Tanini Pulci labels the soldiers as "Turks," exploiting contemporary Florentine fears around the powerful Ottoman Empire's violent incursions onto Italian soil, most notably the invasion and capture of Otranto a decade earlier in 1480–81.[4] Common Florentine fears of the widow's voice are thus displaced onto the shoulders of the Muslim enemy, as the Hebrew widow is transformed into a Christian martyr. The audience is expected to empathize with her wailed lament as she dies; at the same time, they are asked to bear witness to the violence perpetrated by her Philistine assassins through a contemporary lens. Tanini Pulci thereby reinforces the broader cultural project racializing Ottoman Muslims as a "barbarian" threat to Italian Christian women—and by extension, to the Italian city itself.

Tanini Pulci operated within a broader circle of writers who incorporated contemporary Florentine social and political anxieties into their work. Late-Quattrocento Florence was an especially fruitful and influential period for writers of the Medici family and its court, from Lucrezia Tornabuoni (1427–1482) and her sacred narratives, to her son Lorenzo de' Medici (1449–1492) and his poems and *sacra rappresentazione*, to Angelo Poliziano (1454–1494) and his *Stanze*. These writers worked to build up the nascent dynasty's brand with religious and humanist themes speaking to the desired relationship between Florence and its "first family," as well as Medici aspirations in international politics. To highlight one instance with particular relevance to the subject at hand, Andrea Moudarres has recently tied the epic-chivalric poem *Il Morgante maggiore* by Tanini Pulci's brother-in-law Luigi Pulci (1434–1484) to the Pazzi conspiracy of 1478, demonstrating how the epic poet weaves "the internal rivalries that may eventually consume [a city's] political body" into his text.[5] Luigi Pulci's sprawling poem, composed in the 1470s and 1480s, also engages actively with the renewed obsession with the Crusades following the Fall of Constantinople to the Ottomans in 1453.[6] Like her more famous relative, Tanini Pulci tapped into the tumult of the Florentine political world, but she focused her lens on the external menace of the Ottoman Empire rather than on the disastrous domestic divisions revealed by the Pazzi conspiracy.

In the following pages, I explore how Tanini Pulci offered her own contribution to the broader political conversation on the Ottomans, as she destabilized long-standing characterizations of the widowed voice in Florence, highlighting the ingrained value of widows to the city. Through the genre of the sacred play—a safe and decorous medium for a woman writer who was both widow and tertiary—Tanini Pulci stealthily joined the broader clamor across the peninsula for a new united crusade to combat what was viewed almost universally as the existential threat in Constantinople. This was a conversation conducted overwhelmingly through male voices, and it played out in genres dominated by male authors: epic, oration, and history.[7] And yet as scholars have demonstrated in recent years, women's voices were also audible, from the humanist Isotta Nogarola (1418–1466) in Quattrocento Venice to the lyric poets Veronica Gambara (1485–1550) and Isabella Cervoni (1575–c. 1600) in the sixteenth century.[8] Here, I ask: how does Antonia Tanini Pulci's play engage with this wider political discussion? How might her own identity as a widowed writer be important for our understanding of the development of the widow character in her play? How does the representation of this character diverge from the representation of widows in canonical Florentine literature, from Dante to Savonarola? And finally, how does the author reinforce the value of the widow's voice through her use of the racialized trope of the threatening Turk? I begin with a brief portrait of Tanini Pulci herself, and then expand my focus, tracing the significance of the widow's voice as a political instrument in late medieval and early Renaissance Florentine culture. I then turn to the text of the Saul play and its female protagonist to suggest that Tanini Pulci adopts the contemporary and well-developed antipathy toward the "Turk" in order to challenge existing tropes about widows in her own society.

## Antonia Tanini Pulci and the Florentine Idea of Widowhood

Scholars have done much in recent years to bring Antonia Tanini Pulci's innovative work and biography to our attention. This is especially true in the case of Elissa Weaver, whose "groundbreaking" scholarship, as Nerida Newbigin has rightly classified it, has transformed the playwright from the "mere" female relative of the more famous Luca and Luigi Pulci to an important and compelling author worthy of study.[9] We now have two critical editions of her plays in the *Other Voice in Early Modern Europe Series,* as well as important archival scholarship that tells us a great deal about her life and fortunes in fifteenth-century Florence, from her childhood to her marriage into the Pulci family to her years as a tertiary following her husband's death.[10] She was born sometime between 1452 and 1454 to a Tuscan merchant father, Francesco di Antonio di Giannotto Tanini, and a Roman mother, Jacopa di Torello di Lorenzo Torelli. She would have been a young teenager when her father died in 1467, leaving her mother a widow with seven children.[11] Jacopa corresponded with fellow Roman Clarice Orsini, who married Lorenzo de' Medici in 1469; Weaver suggests that the influential Orsini may have had a hand in Antonia's marriage to Bernardo Pulci, of the noble but impoverished literary family, in 1470 or 1471.[12] By 1488, widowed and childless, she returned to live at her mother's house. She died in 1501.

Like many of her contemporaries, after her husband's death Tanini Pulci became an *ammantellata,* or Third Order tertiary, ultimately founding her own order, Santa Maria della Misericordia.[13] As documented by her friend and biographer Fra' Dolciati, she spent much of her time in solitude (he makes an interesting and touching comparison between her and the Hebrew widow Judith, who loomed so large in the Quattrocento Florentine imagination).[14] Mother and daughter were part of the city's substantial population of widows, which included prominent women like Lucrezia Tornabuoni and the prolific letter writer Alessandra Strozzi (1408–1471), as well as the many widow residents of the Orbatello.[15] As David Herlihy and Christiane Klapisch-Zuber demonstrated with their landmark study of the famous 1427 *catasto* (or tax census), widows in that year made up an extraordinary 25 percent of the population in the city of Florence; the percentage was 13.6 percent in other Tuscan cities. Eighteen percent of women over 40 were widowed; 45 percent of women over 50 were. Widowers, on the other hand, were far fewer in number: according to the *catasto,* they accounted for less than 5 percent of the Florentine population in 1427.[16] This discrepancy was in part due to the substantial age gap between men and women that typified Florentine marriages (Antonia, in our example here, was fourteen years younger than her husband).[17] Furthermore, property-owning men of all ages across Quattrocento Italy routinely remarried after the deaths of their wives. Women generally remarried only if they were still comparatively young when their husbands died. By the time a woman was thirty-seven—the age Tanini Pulci was when her husband Bernardo died—it was unlikely that she would remarry.

Widows also played a prominent, even outsized, role in the cultural imagination of medieval and Renaissance Florence, and they served an important allegorical function in the very idea of the Italian city. More scholarly attention has been paid to the common casting of Rome as a widow bereft in the years of the Avignon Papacy, which drew on the model of the widowed city of Jerusalem in Lamentations, but city-as-widow was a prominent trope in Tre- and Quattrocento Florence as well.[18] Lamentations, whose authorship is traditionally attributed to the prophet Jeremiah, opens with a description of Jerusalem as "widowed" of her people following the historical destruction of Jerusalem by the Babylonian general Nebuchadnezzar in 587 BCE: "How doth the city sit solitary that was full of people! how is the mistress of the Gentiles become as a widow: the princes of provinces made tributary . . . The ways of Sion mourn, because there are none that come to the solemn feast: all her gates are broken down: her priests sigh: her virgins are in affliction, and she is oppressed with bitterness."[19] Widowed Jerusalem is given voice and cries out, bewailing her status as a sorrowful, aggrieved victim: "Oh all ye that pass by the way, attend, and see if there be any sorrow like to my sorrow . . . From above he hath sent fire into my bones, and hath chastised me: he hath spread a net for my feet, he hath turned me back: he hath made me desolate, wasted with sorrow all the day long."[20] Across the five books of Lamentations, the widowed city of Jerusalem is continuously depicted, in her own words and those of others, as the female victim of war, sexually assaulted, her virgins captured—a blunt reminder not only of war's toll on cities but also of the profound violation of a city's women.[21]

Lamentations has long served as an affective template, a model for how to grieve loss. The widowed city mourning her lost population in Lamentations is read in the Christian tradition as an allegory for the Christian people mourning the death of Christ, with Christ in the position of bridegroom and the Christian people that of the grieving, widowed Jerusalem: the faithful will be reunited with their savior through his return to earth; the widow will be reunited with her beloved husband through her own death. In the Italian literary tradition, we see one important appropriation of the Lamentations model in Dante's angry Epistle XI to the Italian cardinals in conclave at Carpentras after the death of Clement V. For Dante, Rome is now the widowed city, the cardinals corrupt priests like those in Jerusalem in the days before the destruction of the temple.[22] Dante returns to this theme in his angry apostrophe in *Purgatorio* VI, in which Italy is a female body degraded—"non donna di province, ma bordello!" ("not a ruler of provinces, but a whore!")—and Rome, a widow abandoned by the pope, cries out in anguish:

Vieni a veder la tua Roma che piagne
vedova e sola, e dì e notte chiama:
"Cesare mio, perché non m'accompagne?"

Come and see your Rome,
which weeps widowed and alone, and day and night calls out:
"My Caesar, why do you not keep me company?"[23]

Dante first employed the trope of the widowed city much earlier, in a different and more personal context, and in that instance it was Florence who was cast as aggrieved widow. Halfway through his *Vita nuova*, he quotes the opening lines of Lamentations in the Vulgate before describing his native city as "quasi vedova" because of his beloved Beatrice's death. "Poi che fue partita da queso secolo, rimase tutta la sopradetta cittade quasi vedova dispogliata da ogni dignitade . . ." ("Because she had departed from this world, the entire abovenamed city was like a widow despoiled of all majesty . . .") (*Vita nuova*, 30:1).[24] "Widowing" the city of his birth, he places Florence in a collective of mourning, widowed cities alongside Jerusalem and Rome. Unlike the political widowings of Rome and Jerusalem, however—traumas inflicted on the entire population of those cities—Dante widows Florence because of the death of a single, beloved citizen, a private event Dante grants an astonishingly public import.[25]

Florence-as-widow was a foundation upon which Tre- and Quattrocento Florentine literary texts built a pantheon of widowed characters, and visual art too gave widows prominence in the city. Widowed saints—including Anne, Felicity, Birgitta of Sweden, Monica, and Anna of Phanuel—were common in fourteenth- and fifteenth-century Florentine art, serving as models of virtuous widowhood as well as examples of female piety more generally.[26] Dante highlighted the crucial diplomatic role widows play for their husbands in his *Purga-*

*torio*, where we learn of numerous women who devote their lives to praying their departed husbands up the mountain of Purgatory and into Heaven. The contrasting trope of the "merry widow"—a woman who neglects her sacred duty to memorialize her dead husband through somber behavior and dutiful prayer and instead engages in reckless sexual behavior—was codified by Boccaccio through several *novelle* in his *Decameron*.[27] This widow type reached its apex with his *Il Corbaccio* (1365), in which a lover laments his heartbreak over a widow who has left him for another lover and who is comforted (and fed misogynist vitriol) by the shade of her dead husband.[28] (The shade is most indignant that he is stuck in Purgatory because his widow has neglected her duties while she gallivants on earth.) The vital importance of widows as powerful intercessors, not only for their husbands but for society at large, was reflected in societal organizations as well as in literature. In a prominent Florentine example, the Orbatello home for widows was founded in the early 1370s by the merchant Niccolò Jacopo degli Alberti (1327–1377), who was hopeful that the widowed residents would work together to pray him into Heaven.[29]

Despite the high value placed on the rhetorical power of a widow's prayers, however, the potential civic consequences of a widow's grief were concurrently the focus of great anxiety, in Florence and elsewhere. This is perhaps illustrated most famously in Petrarch's "How a Ruler Ought to Govern His State," when the poet beseeches the lord of Padua, Francesco I da Carrara (1325–1393), to move any ostentatiously mourning, weeping women indoors, in order to prevent such "loud and indecent wailing so that someone who did not know what was happening could easily think that here was a madman on the loose or that the city was under enemy attack."[30] The two threats to the city for which the weeping women's wails might be mistaken—either a citizen gone mad or an attack by the enemy—is a reminder that grieving women were viewed as potential agents of chaos, a danger to civic order. While Petrarch speaks in this example not of Florence but of Padua, his letter nevertheless remains an important source for understanding how the humanist project, which so dominated civic life in Quattrocento Florence, worked to constrain female voices.[31] Sharon Strocchia has demonstrated how Florentine leaders employed an assortment of methods of control in order to rein in widows and their public performances of grief, from barring women from public funerals to broader ideological shifts in what kinds of emotion were deemed socially acceptable at all.[32] In addition to increasingly stringent ideas around emotional expression, sumptuary statutes revealed a persistent mistrust of widows and the suspicion that their public performance of grief might not be real. This often played out in the very clothes signaling a woman's identity as a widow: in 1459, when Tanini Pulci was a young child, Florentine lawmakers complained that the city's widows were dressed too fashionably and in too sexually suggestive a manner. There were also concerns that beneath their widow's weeds, some women might be wearing provocative clothing to entice potential lovers.[33]

Some Florentine widows, of course, were praised by their humanist compatriots: in 1450, the Italian bookseller Vespasiano da Bisticci singled out the young Alessandra Bardi as the ideal widow because of her modest habit.[34] Vespasiano is a helpful hinge for thinking about the ways in which Florentine intellectuals balanced the question of "real" widows and their role in civic life on the one hand, and the metaphorical widowed city of Lamentations on the other. Thirty years after his praise of Bardi, Vespasiano's *Lamento d'Italia per la presa d'Otranto fatta dai Turchi nel 1480*, published in Florence in 1480, borrows heavily from Jeremiah and Lamentations. He begins his lament with the opening lines from Jeremiah 9: "Who will give water to my head, and a fountain of tears to my eyes? And I will weep day and night for the slain of the daughter of my people."[35] He also cites directly from Lamentations, in which the prophet takes on the voice of the widowed Jerusalem—"oh all ye that pass by the way, attend, and see if there be any sorrow like to my sorrow"—remarking that one can easily apply this traditional lament to the *misera Italia*.[36] Vespasiano's depiction of postincursion Italy as a ravaged widow is a natural progression from earlier explorations of Italian cities "widowed" by political or religious strife, as well as the repeated use of the same imagery in laments mourning the loss of Constantinople after 1453.[37] Vespasiano blames Florence, along with the rest of Italy, for what he views as their culpability in the catastrophe unfolding at Otranto: they have been blind to the Turkish menace and have been punished as a result. His logic chimes with that of Lamentations, in which the destruction of the temple at Jerusalem is presented as punishment of the Hebrews themselves. Italy as a defiled widow was a prevalent image in the 1480s and 1490s in the refrains of pro-Crusade preachers who centered the sexual violations of Italian women at the hands of the Ottomans at Otranto.[38]

## Tanini Pulci's Idea of a True Widow

Widowhood as both metaphorical concept and lived reality was on people's minds, then, in Antonia Tanini Pulci's world, as she came of age as a woman and as a writer and was then widowed. Her contemporary, the notorious friar and firebrand Girolamo Savonarola (1452–1498), was himself somewhat preoccupied with the important role widows played in the Christian community, and many of his closest women followers were themselves widowed.[39] His 1491 *Libro della vita viduale* (*The Book on the Life of the Widow*), written in the early years of his tenure in Florence, was one of the earliest, and most popular, Renaissance conduct manuals for widows and was printed several times in the first half of the sixteenth century.[40] His ideal widow is a conventional Christian "vera vedova" in the mold of Saint Paul's "vere vidua"—a widow who gives up all earthly pleasures and community to devote herself to God. As Konrad Eisenbichler has argued, the aim of Savonarola's treatise was clearly to control the substantial Florentine widowed population.[41] And yet it is worth highlighting a few particular ways in which the preacher's instructions to widows dovetailed with the earlier strategies of the Florentine humanists he so despised. Taking as his main example the devout and simple widow Anna of Phanuel from Luke 2:36–38—who recognizes Jesus as the savior of Israel when she sees him at the temple—Savonarola cautions widows throughout his treatise against speaking too often, too loudly, or, if possible, to men at all.[42] "Grave widows," he observes, "remain alone and keep themselves from any type of conversation, knowing that Jesus is not found except in solitude."[43] Savonarola insists that the only "true" widows are not only chaste and obedient but also silent, unassuming, and know their place; his ideal widow is far removed from the many fierce Florentine widows of literature and history who made their presence felt in the city.

Tanini Pulci most likely thought up her widowed character during the very same years Savonarola was composing his treatise, and she had an important role model in one of those fierce women: the "first lady" of Florence, Lucrezia Tornabuoni (1427–1482). Tanini Pulci was surely aware of Tornabuoni's sacred narratives, most of which were written in the 1470s.[44] The widow of Piero de' Medici (1416–1469) turned loose a compelling version of the Old Testament Judith in which the modest and virtuous Hebrew widow is compelled to leave her life of solitude to rescue the hapless Israelites from the Babylonians. With Tornabuoni, we see a Florentine widowed writer adapting a famous widowed character in a pointed way. Given the Medici matriarch's political position, it does not seem accidental that she chooses to portray a widowed woman who is celebrated as the savior of her people. As Jane Tylus has noted, Tanini Pulci's brother-in-law Luigi also mentions Judith in his *Morgante*, arguing that her violence against the Babylonian general Holofernes should be considered both justified and lawful because she was fighting on behalf of the Hebrew people.[45] Judith Bryce has argued that we should consider Lucrezia Tornabuoni and Antonia Tanini Pulci together, and indeed, Judith and the version of Saul's widow in Tanini Pulci's play present similar examples of widows' virtues that would have appealed to the Florentine imagination, especially through their acts of resistance to an external, "barbarian" enemy.

While Tornabuoni's sacred narratives circulated only in manuscript, Tanini Pulci published actively and was one of the first women writers in Italy to be published.[46] Her work first appeared in print with the publication of three plays in an anthology alongside plays written by her husband, perhaps as early as 1483.[47] The Saul play, however, is a unique case. It only turns up in a later print edition with no author name attached, and Weaver has convincingly identified it as Tanini Pulci's Saul play described by Dolciati in his posthumous biography of the author.[48] That the play is not known to exist in an earlier version also makes it likely that Tanini Pulci authored the play after she was widowed in 1488. Like Tornabuoni's Judith narrative, Tanini Pulci's Saul play presents the heroic story of an Old Testament widow's encounter with a foreign and threatening superpower. In an important difference, Tanini Pulci's representation of the widow is not a retelling of an established narrative, but instead an audacious addition: she inserts a character and a narrative arc that are not present in the original. The Bible does not tell us anything about Saul's wife other than her name—Ahinoam—but Tanini Pulci builds her out and makes her central to the story.[49]

The play is organized around King Saul's battle against the Philistines, his defeat, and his subsequent suicide, the account of which occurs in the First Book of Samuel during the epic struggle of the Israelites against the Philistines. As I mention above, Tanini Pulci identifies the Philistines in stage directions throughout the play as both "Filistei" and, several times, as "turchi"; the Philistines are very clearly meant to be read as stand-ins for contemporary Florence's own menacing enemy superpower, the Ottomans. Tanini Pulci signals her play's departure from the original story of Saul in the opening lines, when an angel tells the audience that they will be witness to the travails of *three* protagonists, rather than two.

> L'ANGELO *in prima dice*:
> Popolo, attento sta con divozione,
> e vedrai oggi di Davit il pianto,

il qual fe' per Saul orazione.
Prima gedrite le battaglie intanto,
e di Saul la suo distruzïone,
e de' figliuoli ancore vedrete alquanto;
e vo' della reina anche tu senti
come fu morta, però state attenti.

*First an* ANGEL *speaks:*
O people, with devotion close attend,
And David's lamentation you will see—
That David who once prayed for Saul. First bend
Your gaze on battles, though, and you will see
King Saul's destruction. You'll observe the end
As well, that Saul's sons suffered. Finally
I want to tell you too about the queen—
How she was slain, so closely watch the scene.[50]

Positioning the queen's story as the final piece in this exposition is significant, as is the wording. By way of angelic proxy, Tanini Pulci is instructing her audience to listen closely to the queen's story, and *especially* how she was killed and made martyr. "State attenti," she says. ("Watch carefully.") It is a rather bold rhetorical move on Tanini Pulci's part. She here implies that the queen was given short shrift in the biblical tale—where was she, after all, when Saul was killed? What happened to *her?*— and also trumpets her own authorial prowess by expanding the traditional biblical narrative to include the moving story of a woman neglected by the Old Testament. Throughout the play, we are witness to the important, sometimes tricky, political role played by women in times of war: of note, Saul hands over power to his wife before he leaves to fight the Philistines, asking her to rule in his stead should something happen to him, and she readily obeys.[51] In the main action of the play, Saul and his sons fight against the Philistines in an uneven match; his sons are killed off, one by one. Saul, defeated and grief-stricken, chooses to fall on his own sword rather than face death at the hands of his enemies. In his dramatic final speech before his suicide, he woefully describes his love for each of his sons—but makes no mention of his queen.[52] Tanini Pulci, however, has not forgotten about her, and at this crucial moment in the play's action, the author departs from the traditional story and provides her audience with an entirely new and innovative scene.

Philistine soldiers, who believe Saul is still alive and thus a present danger, capture the queen at her palace and bring her back to their own king. She insists defiantly that she does not know where her husband is and that she has not seen him since he left. The exchange between the soldiers and the queen is interrupted by the "primo turco" Carfase, who complains that the queen is, like all other women, a terribly annoying chatterbox.

> CARFASE, *Primo Turco, dice:*
> Non sa' tu che le donne son di pruova
> e sempre le si fan pregare assai?
> Ora una scusa ed or un'altra truova:
> gli è 'l più bel dondol ch'i' vedessi mai
> e sempre le bugie ella rinuova.
> Oh, s'a mie modo di questo farai,
> dara'li mort' e non cercar più nulla!
> Non vedi tu com'ella ti trastulla?

> *CARFASE, the First Turk, says:*
> Don't you know how trying women are?
> They always make you ask repeatedly;
> One pretext first, another then she brings;
> At changing things she surely takes the prize,
> But always she renews her pack of lies.
> Indeed, if you will do what I advise,
> You'll kill her now and let this quiz be through.
> Do you not see the game she plays with you?[53]

The Philistine king agrees that the Hebrew queen is indeed tiresome. With brutally precise instructions, he orders his men to take her away, to tie her to a tree by her hair, and to "thrash her," before leaving her remains to be picked over by birds.[54] On their way to her execution site, she begs the soldiers to allow her to pray for news of her husband and the Jewish people. Her captors, described here as "e turchi, cioè e filistei" ("the Turks, that is, the Philistines"), fall asleep. An angel appears, and reveals to the queen that Saul is dead, bestows on her the martyr's palm, and disappears. Once he has gone, her captors wake up; unaware of what has just transpired, "primo turco," Carfase asks if she is ready to die. Now aware of her husband's death and her own new status as widow, she affirms that she is. In few words, she humbly asks God to grant her grace, while her captors grouse incongruously yet again about her "loquacity"; they carry out their king's command and tie her by her hair to a tree. She cries out in pain and distress, again asking God to take pity on her. The violence and brutality of her execution is hinted at when she exclaims, "Oimè, quest'albor tira così forte!" ("This tree pulls with such force!")[55]

After her death, the Philistine-Turks fall spontaneously asleep yet again, and angels reappear. Rescuing her corpse from the gruesome fate the Philistine king had desired, they carry her body away to Limbo. The soldiers wake up; alarmed and confused to find her missing, they resolve not to report her disappearance to the king. In the very next scene, we see the triumphant Philistine king reuniting happily with his wife, a bitter reminder for the play's audience that Saul and *his* queen will never enjoy a similar reunion.

Tanini Pulci's addition of the queen figure to her sacred play is extraordinary, both in the fact of it and in the prominent and original role the widow is granted: she is made central to the story and to the political action of the play. This is dramatically different from her negligible role in the Old Testament. Tanini Pulci reminds her audience repeatedly of the queen's importance and also of how shabbily she is treated by all the men in the piece—the omission of her name from her husband's speech before he dies, the Philistine-Turk soldiers' verbal abuse and murderous violence. Weaver has pointed out that the scene of the queen's torture is the most dramatic, and dynamic, of the whole play, and would have been the most exciting for actors to perform and for an audience to witness.[56] It seems likely that the Hebrew queen's death scene would have also been the most memorable. It is therefore particularly important that in these scenes we see Tanini Pulci engage explicitly with contemporary Italian fears about Ottoman violence against Italian women, through continuous reminders to the audience that the queen's captors are not only Philistines, but Turks as well.

## Philistine Soldiers and the Racialized "Turk" in Quattrocento Literature and Thought

Scholars have recently begun to identify the ways in which the Philistines were racialized as Turks in early modern representations—proxies, like the Babylonians, for foreign enemies of European Christians, who were themselves so often cast as the persecuted ancient Israelites in visual art and literature.[57] While more investigation is needed on just how widespread the Italian practice was of using Philistines in particular as stand-ins for the Ottomans and other Muslims, work on humanist perceptions of the Ottoman Empire has expanded our understanding of the broad program of racialization of Ottomans in Renaissance Italy after 1453, as well as how that racialized view affected the broader perception of Muslims and the fervor for new crusades to "liberate" Jerusalem once again. Nancy Bisaha has shown that Turks were perceived not just as a religious threat to Catholicism but as an "uncultivated race" with no business occupying the cultural capital of Constantinople.[58] Humanists, including Coluccio Salutati, Lauro Quirini, and Francesco Filelfo, identified Ottomans not only as "infidels," a threat because of their religion, but also as "barbarians"—innately different and possessing an "inborn ferocity." Shortly after the 1453 takeover of Constantinople by Mehmed II, Quirini described the Turks as a "gens barbara, gens inculta, nullis certis moribus, nullis legibus" ("a barbarous race, an uncivilized race, living without set customs or laws"); Filelfo went even further, describing them as "completely unrestrained and savage beasts."[59] That these "uncivilized barbarians" were in charge of the cultural and political center of Constantinople was viewed not just as a religious threat to the supremacy of Catholicism but also as a threat to the supremacy of European intellectualism: humanists feared a backslide at the height of humanism, ground lost in the conquest of texts and objects as well as of land. Moreover, there was a continued conflation of "Turk"—with its dual connotations of "barbarian" and "infidel"—and all Muslims, which reinforced the "streamlined" lexicon used to describe Muslims in the Christian crusading mind since the Middle Ages.[60] In this same period, the emerging notion of "European"—an identity imagined in express contrast with the Ottomans—was put forth by Enea Silvio Piccolomini (1404–1464; Pope Pius II, 1458–1464), creating a new sense of Europeans as a "collective" or cultural group who existed against the new Philistines in Constantinople.[61] Humanists began to weaponize the classical texts they studied and extolled, reading them as anticipating the Ottoman menace and seeing the Fall of Constantinople as foretold through misfortunes suffered by the Romans.[62] It was not only humanists who found ways to insert anti-Ottoman racism into their texts: as Eisenbichler notes in a particularly relevant example for our purposes here, in *The Book on the Life of the Widow,* Savonarola changes the enemies of the righteous from "Gentiles" to "infidels" when quoting Saint Paul.[63]

Tanini Pulci's *La rappresentazione della distruzione di Saul e del pianto di Davit* is a reminder that the racialized narrative of the threatening Turk was not limited to humanist orations and treatises on classical texts but was pervasive across the cultural landscape, present even in sacred plays written by women and aimed at predominantly female audiences. Working in parallel to the humanist circles imposing revisionist political prophecy on classical texts, Tanini Pulci takes the well-worn, racialized foil of the barbarous, uncultivated "Turk" and slides him into the Old Testament story she adapts for the stage. Her text suggests that works aimed at women were stretched to accommodate new fears of and prejudices against the Muslim superpower.

Tanini Pulci's exploitation of familiar anxieties over Ottoman violence against Italian women seems to have a clear aim: to destabilize the deeply ingrained cultural mistrust of widows and their voices, especially when they speak too much or cry too loudly. Consider the queen's captors who, in the scene of her torture and death, complain repeatedly about her excessive wailing as she is tortured, tied to a tree, and threatened with death. Carfase asks her impatiently "Ha' tu tanto grachiato, berghinella?" ("Have you chattered on enough, you hag?")[64] The Tuscan word "berghinella" boasts rich misogynistic overtones, and is translated by John Florio in 1611's *Queen Anna's World of Words* as "a prattling whore."[65] The word also carries significant class implications: defined by La Crusca as "femmina plebea di bassa condizione, e talora di non buona fama" ("A common female of low estate, and on occasion of ill repute"), "berghinella" is a terrific insult to lob at the wife of the Hebrew king, a woman who has been made ruler in his stead. This disrespect is compounded by the "third Turk" or Philistine soldier, who urges his fellows on to kill her quickly: "Or caviànne le man ché gli è sera; la grachierebbe insin a primavera." ("Let's cut off her hands now, for it is already evening; she could keep jabbering on until spring!")[66] The clear formula laid out by the third Turk—hurt her now so that she will stop talking—is not so different from the rationale behind Florentine controls of female grief, which left unchecked might wreak havoc on the broader community of a city. The complaints repeated by the three Turks over how much the queen speaks are especially noteworthy when we consider that she is a character who has no "lines" at all in the Old Testament and to whom Tanini Pulci has quite literally given voice. The queen's dying lament invites the audience to bear witness to her suffering; with her "vedi ch'i stento" ("look how I'm suffering"), the public is reminded of the widowed city of Lamentations and the line lifted by Vespasiano in his 1480 *Lamento*: "O all ye that pass by the way, attend, and see if there be any sorrow like to my sorrow."[67] Speaking in the imperative, the queen is calling on the Christian, Florentine audience to bear witness to her torment at the hands of her captors. Her lament—described by the Philistine-Turks, alternately, as inconsequential chatter and dangerous distraction—invites the audience to grieve her violation and death, an echo of the author's own initial command: "state attenti." The martyred Hebrew queen, defiled by Philistines, becomes a symbol for widowed Italy herself, the Christian collective both wounded and existentially threatened by Turkish incursions.

## Conclusion

Tanini Pulci does all this in a genre suitable for a widowed tertiary in late-Quattrocento Florence. She is not, however, writing outside of history. While *sacre rappresentazioni* are less traditionally "political" than the humanist, masculine-coded texts produced in the same years, they can offer us important evidence about just how widespread certain cultural beliefs were and who participated in their promulgation.[68] Indeed, it is worth thinking, in conclusion, about how Tanini Pulci's play might offer paths forward for exploring how both gender and race were weaponized in Renaissance Italy, including those paths by women writers. With her uncovering of and definitive attribution of the play, Elissa Weaver has gifted scholars with fresh evidence not just of "new" work by an early-modern woman writer but of the complicated, sometimes complicit, role of those women. Unlike Judith, unlike the widowed city of Jerusalem, Saul's queen is not a fleshed-out character before Tanini Pulci has her way with her. It is the Florentine woman playwright who provides her with a way to speak, to lament her own death and that of her husband, to pray for the fate of the Israelites, and to stand on a stage. She bestows upon the widowed queen an honorable martyrdom. And as she uplifts Saul's widow, a new representative of collective, communal mourning, Tanini Pulci also contributes to the ever-escalating racialization of Muslims in Renaissance Italy.

Notes

1. This essay is part of my larger project on widows and the political community, *Widow City: Gender, Emotion and Politics in Renaissance Italy.* I have discussed Antonia Tanini Pulci's play before, in Anna Wainwright, "Teaching Widowed Women, Community, and Devotion in Quattrocento Florence with Lucrezia Tornabuoni and Antonia Tanini Pulci," *Religions* 9 (3), no. 76 (2018): 1–13. My heartfelt thanks go to Elissa Weaver for suggesting long ago that I consider the case of Saul's widow and for her invaluable mentorship and encouragement over the last two decades. I am also indebted to the editors of this volume, Meredith Ray and Lynn Westwater, for generously including me in the 2019 RSA panel in Elissa Weaver's honor, at which I first presented this research on Antonia Tanini Pulci,

and to Melissa Swain, Shannon McHugh, and Jessica Goethals for their thoughtful comments on this piece.

2. I use the critical edition and translation of the play in Antonia Pulci, *Saints' Lives and Bible Stories for the Stage*, ed. Elissa B. Weaver, trans. James Wyatt Cook, with introduction by Elissa B. Weaver (Toronto: Iter Press/Centre for Reformation and Renaissance Studies, 2010). Translations by Wyatt unless otherwise noted. I have chosen here and elsewhere to refer to her as "Antonia Tanini Pulci." In a 2003 essay, Elissa Weaver points out that "Antonia Pulci," which is the most common name in scholarship, is anachronistic, a symptom of a broader mischaracterization of the author ("Antonia Tanini Pulci (1452–1501), Playwright and Wife of Bernardo Pulci (1438–1488)," in *Essays in Honor of Margo Cottino-Jones*, eds. Laura White, Andrea Fedi, and Kristin Phillips [Florence: Edizioni Cadmo, 2003], 23–37). "Most scholars who have written about her, or simply mentioned her, have claimed that little is known of her life," Weaver argues. "This was true, but only because no one investigated, or, if they had, they sought to find her among members of a family to which she did not belong" (23). As Weaver has demonstrated through her significant archival discoveries about the author, Tanini Pulci's identity as a member of the wealthy Tanini family is as important for understanding her biography as is her connection by marriage to the literary Pulci family.

3. While Christine de Pizan made her career in France, she bears considering in the context of Italian widowed writers, especially for her important representations of heroic widows. See Cynthia Brown, "The Reconstruction of an Author in Print: Christine de Pizan in the 15th and 16th Centuries," in *Christine de Pizan and the Categories of Difference*, ed. Marilynn Desmond (Minneapolis: University of Minnesota Press, 1998), 215–235. Judith Bryce has pointed out the likely connections between Tornabuoni and Tanini Pulci in "Adjusting the Canon for Later Fifteenth-Century Florence: The Case of Antonia Pulci," in *The Renaissance Theatre: Texts, Performance, Design* (New York: Routledge, 1999), 133–145.

4. Weaver notes this important anachronism in her 2010 editor's introduction to *Saints' Lives* (57) and analysis of the Saul play.

5. Andrea Moudarres, *The Enemy in Italian Renaissance Epic: Images of Hostility from Dante to Tasso* (Newark: University of Delaware Press, 2019). The Pazzi Conspiracy was a high-profile but unsuccessful plot to seize control of Florence from the Medici family, organized by Francesco de' Pazzi, Francesco Salviati, and Girolamo Riario, and sanctioned by Pope Sixtus IV. It was carried out in public by numerous members of influential Florentine families; Giuliano de' Medici was killed, Lorenzo de' Medici wounded. Dozens were executed as punishment, and the Pazzi family was exiled from Florence.

6. On Luigi Pulci's thorny relationship with Lorenzo de' Medici, see Constance Jordan, *Pulci's* Morgante: *Poetry and History in Fifteenth-Century Florence* (Washington, DC: The Folger Shakespeare Library, 1986), 28–38.

7. Nancy Bisaha has addressed the humanist discourses on the Ottoman Empire post-1453 in *Creating East and West: Renaissance Humanists and the Ottoman Turks* (Philadelphia: University of Pennsylvania Press, 2004). Virginia Cox points out that Pulci's choice of *sacra rappresentazione* "conforms . . . to traditional circumscriptions of women's proper sphere." Virginia Cox, *Women's Writing in Italy, 1400–1650* (Baltimore: Johns Hopkins University Press, 2008).

8. See Isotta Nogarola, *Complete Writings: Letterbook, Dialogue on Adam and Eve, and Orations*, ed. Margaret L. King and Diana Robin (Chicago: The University of Chicago Press, 2003), 179–86, and Anna Wainwright, "A Simple Virgin Speaks: Authorial Identity and Persuasion in Isabella Cervoni's Oration to Pope Clement VIII," *The Italianist* 37, no. 1: 1–19. DOI: 10.1080/02614340.2016.1258877.

9. See Nerida Newbigin, *Making a Play for God: The* Sacre Rappresentazioni *of Renaissance Florence* (Toronto: University of Toronto Press, 2021), 442.

10. The two *Other Voice in Early Modern Europe* volumes are Antonia Pulci, *Florentine Drama for Convent and Festival: Seven Sacred Plays*, trans. James Wyatt Cook, ed. James Wyatt Cook and Barbara Collier Cook (Chicago: The University of Chicago Press, 1996); and Antonia Pulci, *Saints' Lives*. Weaver's critical introduction to *Saints' Lives* contains a rich biography and contextual analysis of her works. Newbigin's comprehensive 2021 study of Florentine sacred plays analyzes several of Tanini Pulci's works and also firmly ensconces her as an important contributor to the genre (*Making a Play for God*). See also Judith Bryce, "Adjusting the Canon," and Nerida Newbigin, "Antonia Pulci and the First Anthology of *Sacre rappresentazioni* (1483?)," *La Bibliofilia* 118, no. 3 (2016): 337–361.

11. On the details of her father's life and business in Florence and nearby Scarperia, see Weaver, "Editor's Introduction," in Pulci, *Saints' Lives*, especially 6–12.

12. On Tanini family connections to the Medici family, see also Bryce, "Adjusting the Canon."

13. On tertiaries in Florence, see Anna Benvenuti Papi, "Mendicant Friars and Female Pinzochere in Tuscany: From Social Marginality to Models of Sanctity," in *Women and Religion in Medieval and Renaissance Italy*, ed. Daniel Borstein and Roberto Rusconi (Chicago: The University of Chicago Press, 1996), 85–106.

14. On Judith in Quattrocento Florence, see Elena Ciletti, "Patriarchal Ideology in the Renaissance Iconography of Judith," in *Refiguring Woman: Perspectives on Gender and the Italian Renaissance*, eds. Marilyn Migiel and Juliana Schiesari (Ithaca, NY: Cornell University Press, 1991), and Lucrezia Tornabuoni, *Sacred Narratives*, ed. and trans. Jane Tylus (Chicago: The University of Chicago Press, 2001).

15. On the Orbatello, see Richard Trexler, "A Widow's Asylum of the Renaissance: the Orbatello of Florence," in *The Women of Renaissance Florence. Power and Dependence in Renaissance Florence*, 3 vols. (Binghamton, NY: Medieval and Renaissance Texts and Studies, 1993), 2:75.

16. David Herlihy and Christiane Kapsch-Zuber, *Tuscans and Their Families: A Study of the Florentine Catasto of 1427* (New Haven, CT: Yale University Press, 1985), 216–217. For Klapisch-Zuber's important discussion of the troubled fate of Florentine widows, especially those with children, see Christiane Klapisch-Zuber, "The 'Cruel Mother': Maternity, Widowhood, and Dowry in Florence in the Fourteenth and Fifteenth Centuries," in *Women, Family, and Ritual in Renaissance Italy* (Chicago: The University of Chicago Press, 1985), 117–131.

17. Herlihy and Klapisch-Zuber, *Tuscans and Their Families*, 207–211.

18. For the discourse of the widowed city in fourteenth-century Rome, see especially Cristelle Baskins, "Trecento Rome: The Poetics and Politics of Widowhood," in *Widowhood and Visual Culture in Early Modern Europe*, ed. Allison Levy (London: Routledge,

2003), 197–209, and Unn Falkeid, *The Avignon Papacy Contested: An Intellectual History from Dante to Catherine of Siena* (Cambridge, MA: Harvard University Press, 2017), especially 95–120.

19. Lamentations 1:1, 1:4.

20. Lamentations 1:12–13.

21. Gerry Milligan troubles the conventional narrative of women as victims of war in early-modern Italian literature in his *Moral Combat: Women, Gender and War in Italian Renaissance Literature* (Toronto: University of Toronto Press, 2018).

22. On Lamentations in Dante, see Ronald J. Martinez, "Dante between Hope and Despair: The Tradition of Lamentations in the *Divine Comedy*," *Logos: A Journal of Catholic Thought and Culture* 5, no. 3 (2002): 45–76.

23. From *Purgatorio*, VI.112–114: "Come and see your Rome, which weeps widowed and alone, and day and night calls out: 'My Caesar, why do you not keep me company?'" Dante Alighieri, *Purgatorio*, ed. and trans. Robert M. Durling and Ronald J. Martinez (New York: Oxford University Press, 2003).

24. See especially Ronald L. Martinez, "Mourning Beatrice: The Rhetoric of Threnody in the *Vita nuova*," *MLN* 113, no. 1 (1998): 1–29. On Dante's "widowed words" and Petrarch's subsequent imitation of them, see Nancy J. Vickers, "Widowed Words: Dante, Petrarch, and the Metaphors of Mourning," in *Discourses of Authority in Medieval and Renaissance Literature*, ed. Kevin Brownlee and Walter Stephens (Hanover, NH: University Press of New England, 1989), 97–108. Dante Alighieri, *Vita Nova*, trans. Andrew Frisardi (Evanston, IL: Northwestern University Press, 2012).

25. On this see especially Olivia Holmes, *Dante's Two Beloveds: Ethics and Erotics in the* Divine Comedy (New Haven, CT: Yale University Press, 2008), 140.

26. Catherine Lawless, "Widowhood was the time of her greatest perfection: Ideals of Widowhood and Sanctity in Florentine Art," in *Widowhood and Visual Culture in Early Modern Europe*, ed. Allison Levy (London: Routledge, 2003), 19–38.

27. For a particularly astute reading of his most famous widow *novella*, VIII.7, and precursor to the *Corbaccio*, see Teodolinda Barolini, "The Scholar and the Widow: Corrupt Appetite and Moral Failure in Society's Intellectual Elite (VIII.7)," in *The Decameron Eighth Day in Perspective* (Toronto: University of Toronto Press, 2020), 148–189.

28. Katherine Clark Walter points to the broader influence of the *Corbaccio* across Europe on the idea of the "merry widow," perhaps most famously in the figure of Chaucer's Wife of Bath (*The Profession of Widowhood: Widows, Pastoral Care, and Medieval Models of Holiness* [Washington, DC: Catholic University Press, 2018], 337.)

29. Trexler, "A Widow's Asylum of the Renaissance," 66.

30. Francesco Petrarch, "How a Ruler Ought to Govern His State," in *The Earthly Republic: Italian Humanists on Government and Society*, trans. Benjamin G. Kohl, eds. Benjamin G. Kohl and Ronald J. Witt (Philadelphia: University of Pennsylvania Press, 1978), 78.

31. Baskins also references this famous letter of Petrarch's, which has become emblematic of humanist anxieties around women's mourning in public. Baskins, "Trecento Rome." Kindle location 6215.

32. Sharon Strocchia, *Death and Ritual in Renaissance Florence* (Baltimore: The Johns Hopkins University Press, 1992), especially 10–15.

33. Strocchia, *Death and Ritual*, 174.

34. Strocchia, *Death and Ritual*, 173–174. Weaver points out that Vespasiano's bookshop was down the street from Antonia Tanini Pulci's childhood home, in the introduction to Pulci, *Saints' Lives*, 57. For further examples of the Quattrocento Florentine debate on widows, see Konrad Eisenbichler, "At Marriage End: Girolamo Savonarola and the Question of Widows in Late Fifteenth-Century Florence," in *The Medieval Marriage Scene: Prudence, Passion, Policy*, eds. Sherry Roush and Cristelle L. Baskins (Tempe: ACMRS, 2005), 23–35.

35. Vespasiano da Bisticci, "Lamento d'Italia per la presa d'Otranto fatta dai Turchi nel 1480," Archivio Storico Italiano 4, no. 1 (1843): 452.

36. Jeremiah 1:12. "Ben si può adducere questa lamentazione e dolorosa voce alla misera Italia." Vespasiano, "Lamento d'Italia," 462.

37. Perhaps most famous is Guillaume Dufay's *Lamentatio sanctae matris ecclesiae Constantinopolitanae*, which he mentioned in a letter to Piero and Giovanni de' Medici in 1454. Hans Kühner, "Ein Unbekannter Brief Von Guillaume Dufay." *Acta Musicologica* 11, no. 3 (1939): 114–115.

38. See Bisaha, *Creating East and West*, 141.

39. See Girolamo Savonarola, *A Guide to Righteous Living and Other Works*, ed. and trans. Konrad Eisenbichler (Toronto: University of Toronto Press, 2003), 8 n 9. On Savonarola's influence on women and reform in the decades following his death, see Tamar Herzig, *Savonarola's Women: Visions and Reform in Renaissance Italy* (Chicago: The University of Chicago Press, 2008). On Savonarola's engagement with the Charlemagne Prophecy, an important tool for pro-Crusade actors, see Bisaha, *Creating East and West*, 40–41.

40. For the full translated text by Eisenbichler, see Savonarola, "Book of the Life of the Widow," in *A Guide to Righteous Living*, 191–226. On Italian Renaissance conduct manuals for widows, including Savonarola's, see Helena Sanson, "Conduct for the *Real* Widow: Giulio Cesare Cabei's *Ornamenti della gentildonna vedova* (1574)" in *Conduct Literature for and about Women in Italy 1470–1900: Prescribing and Describing Life*, eds. Helena Sanson and Francesco Lucioli (Paris: Classiques Garnier, 2016), 41–61.

41. Eisenbichler, "At Marriage End," 31.

42. On the broader significance of Anna of Phanuel in Florence, see Lawless, "Widowhood as the time of her greatest Perfection."

43. Savonarola, "Book of the Life of the Widow," 211.

44. See especially Bryce, "Adjusting the Canon."

45. Jane Tylus, introduction to "The Story of Judith, Hebrew Widow," in Tornabuoni de' Medici, *Sacred Narratives*, 119.

46. See Weaver, "Editor's Introduction," in Pulci, *Saints' Lives*, 2.

47. On the dating of the anthology by Miscomini, see Weaver, "Editor's Introduction," 2 n 1. On the popularity of Tanini Pulci's plays, see Cox, Women's Writing in Italy, Appendix A.

48. For an explanation of this attribution, see Weaver, "Editor's Introduction," in Pulci, *Saints' Lives*, 54. She comments that the play "seems to represent a coming together of many elements we have found earlier in Antonia Pulci's theater." Newbigin affirms the persuasiveness of Weaver's attribution in *Making a Play for God*, 481–482.

49. "And the name of Saul's wife was Ahinoam, the daughter of Ahimaaz." 1 Samuel 14.50.

50. Pulci, *Saints' Lives*, 364–365.

51. Pulci, *Saints' Lives*, 386–87. This mirrors corulership patterns in the courts of Quattrocento Italy, in which noblewomen often became de facto princes after the deaths of their husbands. See especially Melissa Swain, "Spousal Sovereignty: The Ruling Couple and Its Representations in Quattrocento Italy" (PhD diss., New York University, 2016).

52. Pulci, *Saints' Lives*, 396–397.

53. Pulci, *Saints' Lives*, 424–427.

54. "EL RE *dice:* Or oltre presto, senza più indugiare, /Dapoi che voi volete, son contento. /Andatela a un albore attacare/Per le suo chiome, ognun con ardimento!/E vo' con verghe l'abbiate a frustrare, /Poi agli uccelli la lasciate al vento!" ("*The KING says:* Now, speedily, with no more dithering, /Since that is what you wish, I am content. /Go all of you and take her to a tree and by her hair/ With stout determination hang her there!/ And I want you to thrash her there with rods,/ Then leave her twisting in the wind for birds.") Pulci, *Saints' Lives*, 426–427.

55. Pulci, *Saints' Lives*, 430–431.

56. Pulci, *Saints' Lives*, 59.

57. Colby Gordon pointed to this racialization in the English early-modern context in his December 2020 talk for the University of Toronto Early Modern Critical Race Studies Working Group, "Trans Mayhem in *Samson Agonistes*."

58. Bisaha, *Creating East and West*, 2004, 77–78. If, as Ian Smith states, "Renaissance transitive logic specifically equates the ancient barbarian type with the early modern African" in the English imaginary, the "transitive logic" of humanist Italy generally equated the barbarian with the Turk. See Ian Smith, *Race and Rhetoric in the Renaissance: Barbarian Errors* (New York: Palgrave Macmillan, 2010), 5.

59. Margaret Meserve, *Empires of Islam in Renaissance Historical Thought* (Cambridge, MA: Harvard University Press, 2008), 227.

60. Bisaha, *Creating East and West*, 2004, 88. On the "streamlining" of Muslim identity in the European Middle Ages, seen Geraldine Heng, *The Invention of Race in the European Middle Ages* (Cambridge: Cambridge University Press, 2018), 110.

61. Bisaha, *Creating East and West*, 88.

62. Bisaha, *Creating East and West*, 44.

63. See Savonarola, *A Guide to Righteous Living*, 200 n 6.

64. Pulci, *Saints' Lives*, 428–429.

65. Florio defines the related verb *berghinellare* as "to gad abrode a gossiping, as a prattling, love-pot woman." Italian definition from Accademia della Crusca, *Compendio del Vocabolario degli Accademici della Crusca formato sulla edizione quarta del medesimo*, vol. 1 (Florence: Appresso Domenico Maria Manni, 1739), 240.

66. Original Italian in Pulci, *Saints' Lives*, 430. Translation my own.

67. See note 38 above.

68. On the history of scholarly contempt for the genre, see Newbigin, *Making a Play for God*, especially 40–41.

CHAPTER TWO

# Unhappily Ever After

## Moderata Fonte's Fairy Tale

SUZANNE MAGNANINI

The feminist recovery of texts written by early-modern Italian women begun in the 1980s has radically altered our understanding of the sixteenth-century literary landscape and women's place in it. This recuperation set the stage for revision. If, in the 1960s, Carlo Dionisotti could convincingly assert that it was only during the mid-sixteenth century that female authors "fanno gruppo" ("are a group") rather than an exception and that they penned primarily lyric poetry and letters, then such assertions were no longer tenable a few decades later.[1] In her 1983 study of Moderata Fonte and Lucrezia Marinella, Adriana Chemello identified a "rigogliosa produzione di scrittura femminile che abbraccia più generazioni" ("thriving production of female writing that spans multiple generations").[2] Print and digital projects born in the 1990s served as the foundations on which to construct new literary histories that more accurately assessed the role of women writers in the shaping of early-modern Italian literary culture. To name just two such endeavors, The Other Voice in Early Modern Europe series has published over 145 volumes to date, forty of which include texts by Italian women writers, and the University of Chicago Library's Italian Women Writers digital database makes available biographies and texts of fifty-two women writing between 1450 and 1700.[3] Research on these female authors has shown that such writers came from many different ranks and stations: they were cloistered nuns and courtesans; virgins, wives, mothers, and widows; actresses and political actors; and, on occasion, members of literary academies.

Indeed, in *Women's Writing in Italy, 1400–1650* (2008), Virginia Cox argues that not only were there many women writing and publishing throughout this period but also that they adopted a wide array of literary genres, many more than scholars had previously imagined, including those, such as tragedy, that had long been considered the exclusive purview of men.[4]

While Dionisotti viewed the reforms of the Council of Trent as limiting women's participation in literary life, Cox, surveying a literary landscape now densely populated with recuperated texts, saw things quite differently. Writing about the years 1580–1620, Cox notes that the efforts to reform literature paradoxically created a more open and welcoming environment for women writers:

> An unintended consequence of this comprehensive "reform" of vernacular literature was to open up a greater space for women within Italian literary culture and to allow for their more comprehensive integration within that culture. Genres such as the comedy, romance, and *novella,* as they had been practiced in the early Cinquecento, were problematic for "decent" women in their frank celebration of extramarital sexual pleasure. While there is much evidence of women ignoring the carping of moralists and enjoying this literature as readers, it is difficult to imagine a respectable woman writer in this period, at least in an Italian context, putting her name publicly with impunity to a work of such "lascivious" nature. Such problems did not arise with the reborn literature of the post-Tridentine period, which was far more easily morally consonant with a female authorial persona.[5]

While there is no extant female-authored collection of Italian tales akin to Marguerite de Navarre's *Heptameron* (1558) or Maria de Zayas's seventeenth-century collections of exemplary tales, a few Italian women, such as Giulia Bigolina (c. 1518–c. 1569) and Moderata Fonte (1555–1592), were indeed *novellieri,* or authors of tales.[6]

Although we do not primarily think of Fonte as a *novelliere,* I will argue in this essay that we should add *novelle* (tales), more specifically fairy tales, to the extensive list of literary genres in which she excelled.[7] Although, in Fonte's lifetime, fairy tales had long been associated with female narrators, only men had published fairy tales, either in Boccaccian tale collections or embedded in prose romances. To consider Fonte a *novelliere* revives the opinions of nineteenth-century scholars who catalogued her tales in their annotated bibliographies and republished them in volumes separate from the dialogue in which they originally appeared, *Il merito delle donne* (1600), which was completed before her death in 1592 and published posthumously by her family. She is, for example, included in Giambattista Passano's bibliography *I novellieri italiani in prosa* (1864).[8] There, Passano lists Fonte as the author of two novellas and references their (re)publication, first in the Bolognese journal *L'eccitamento* in 1858 and then in a separate volume in 1859, both edited by Anicio Bonucci.[9] These two tales in prose both come from the Second Day of Fonte's *Il merito delle donne*. The first is the tragic tale of Lioncorno and Biancarisa, and the second is the comic-realistic tale of the ironmonger hoping to prepare his son for university exams by having him practice speaking before pots and pans. There is also a third tale in verse at the very end of the dialogue that recounts how the goddess Juno blunted Love's arrows, leading to the end of the honest and sincere love men once felt for women. In designating this poem as a "novella in verso," or a tale in verse, I am again using a category employed by nineteenth-century literary scholars.[10]

In the pages that follow, I first demonstrate that the female interlocutors in Fonte's dialogue prove to be skilled storytellers, whom Fonte depicts as savvy feminist literary critics. The women recognize the political stakes of storytelling and operate a form of what I call "concensureship," or a critique arising from consensus and censure, which, without ever silencing the tellers or their tales, denounces the potentially antiwoman conventions of the fairy tale genre. Through a formalist reading, I argue that we should consider the narrator Corinna's story of Lioncorno and Biancarisa as an anti-tale that implicitly interrogates the same gender bias of fairy tales that her companions in the dialogue openly condemn. I suggest that this anti-tale also functions as an "esempio," or cautionary tale, that warns of the risks and limitations of open revolution against the patriarchy. No such critique arises later in the dialogue when Corinna recites her "stanze," the mythological tale in verse about Love (Amore in Italian, often translated as Cupid in English) and Juno. By this point, the group seems to have come to accept that fantastic folklore, whether myth or fairy tale, is the proper space for portraying the vices of women.

## Storytelling in the Garden: Fairy Tales, Fables, and Realistic Novellas

Fonte's dialogue *Il merito delle donne* begins with five female friends of varying ages and marital statuses gathered at the home of a sixth friend, a widow named

Leonora who has inherited a lovely Venetian palazzo from her aunt and who has sworn never to remarry. Soon, a seventh friend, the young bride Elena just returned from her honeymoon, arrives. The group includes the older widow Adriana and her unmarried daughter Virginia; Lucrezia, who has been married for many years; the young married woman Cornelia; and the poet Corinna, who is called a *dimessa*, a term that indicates that she is a single, noncloistered woman who will not marry.[11]

As in many Renaissance dialogues, the text begins with the friends casting about for a diversion to structure their conversation under the leadership of the eldest woman of the group, Adriana, whom the others have elected "queen." They will eventually hold a debate, with three women defending the merits of men (there are few) and three decrying men's defects (there are many), while their queen Adriana referees the proceedings. The teams are far from equal: the defenders of men include those women who are the least experienced with them, the virgin Virginia and the newlywed Elena, as well as the more seasoned wife Lucrezia, whose name suggests the violence men perpetrate on women. Assigned the task of defending men's injurious behavior towards women, all three women are depicted in terms of their relation to a husband: Virginia is "figliuola da marito" ("daughter of marriageable age"); Elena is "di fresco maritata" ("a young bride"); and Lucrezia has been "maritata da assai tempo" ("married for a long time").[12] Not surprisingly, this group will advance the status quo. Denouncing the defects of men and upholding the worth of women are the more articulate and educated members of the group: Leonora, Corinna, and Cornelia. The group decrying men are all described in terms of their youth and will provide a new viewpoint on relations between the sexes.[13]

Before settling on the plan to debate the merits of men, the group considers telling tales as if they were an all-female Boccaccian *brigata*, or group of friends, that had left Santa Maria Novella before Panfilo, Filostrato, and Dioneo arrived and were recruited to accompany the women to the countryside.[14] In their own *locus amoenus*, the walled garden of Leonora's villa, where they are protected from the prying eyes and controlling ways of men, the newlywed Elena suggests, "averemo più piacere se noi novellamo, o ragionamo di qualche materia . . ." ("it would be more fun for us to tell each other stories or have a discussion on some subject that interests us . . ").[15] Indeed, Katherine McKenna has argued convincingly that "Fonte's dialogue, as well as her pro-woman treatment of women's voices and the social female collective, represent a feminist adaptation of Boccaccio."[16] Although ultimately the women decide against storytelling as a pastime, at various points in the dialogue Fonte nonetheless represents these female friends as knowledgeable consumers and skilled creators of all sorts of tales, this even though women had long been discouraged from reading the *Decameron*, and other collections of tales, because of their lascivious content. For example, in his influential treatise, *On the Education of Christian Women* (1524), Juan Luis Vives says that laws and magistrates should concern themselves "with those pernicious books like those popular in Spain," by which he means chivalric romances. He also denounces the *Decameron* and Poggio Bracciolini's *Facetiae*, collections of tales which he claims "were written by idle, unoccupied, ignorant men, the slaves of vice and filth."[17] Vives anticipates the censorial impulses and actions of the Council of Trent and the Church's successive *Indexes of Prohibited Books* that would ban or require the expurgation of anticlerical and lascivious materials for all readers, not just women. On occasion, concrete actions were taken to bar women from accessing these texts, a clear sign they were not heeding such proscriptions.[18] As Cox notes, such "carping" never really did stop women from reading tales, and by Fonte's day women would have had access to expurgated editions of the *Decameron* which had been approved by the Church.[19]

Throughout the discussion of the vices of men, the women will display their knowledge of multiple subgenres in the varied Italian tale tradition. Like the courtly male interlocutors who dominate the conversation in Baldassare Castiglione's dialogue *Il libro del cortegiano* (1528), Fonte's women cite the proverbial wisdom of Aesop's fables and reference specific tales from Boccaccio's *Decameron*.[20] Aesop's fables enter the dialogue at three different moments, and their presence ranges from a brief, passing reference to a more thorough recounting. While speaking about the hollowness of the praise male writers heap on women, Cornelia recounts in detail Aesop's fable of the fox who flatters the crow by claiming it has a lovely voice so that when the bird sings it will drop a piece of cheese that it has been holding in its mouth.[21] When Elena asks why women are more kind, innocent, and trusting than men, Corinna attributes women's nature to their humoral complexion (cold and phlegmatic), but urges women to use their intellect to counter these natural dispositions so as not to be deceived by men.[22] Women should, Corinna tells her companions, be like the sensible lamb in Aesop's fable, who is not tricked by the wolf at the gate that is imitating its mother the ewe's voice, and she references the fable with just a few words.[23] Cornelia, decrying men's blindness to women's worth, declares that men "fanno come fé il gallo, che trovando la gioia nel fango la disprezzò, poiché non era cosa per lui e seguì una vil carogna, come cibo suo proprio" ("act like that cockerel who found a jewel in the dirt and ignored it because he didn't know how what to do with it and instead rooted around after some disgusting piece of filth, recognizing his natural diet").[24] The women thus use the proverbial wisdom of Aesop's fables as both cautionary tales and analogies for illustrating human vice, just as they were used by male authors such as Giovanni Maria Veridizotti. In Verdizotti's illustrated *Cento favole morali* (1570), in fact, conclusions and morals related to two of the fables cited above, the fox and the crow and the cockerel and the jewel, engage key concepts in the dialogue: *merito*, or merit, and the perils of ignorance and deception.[25] The women, however, deploy these generalized morals in a new, specific context aimed at critiquing abusive male power and cautioning women against falling into the hands of deceitful male lovers.

Clearly these women also know the realistic novellas of Giovanni Boccaccio's fourteenth-century *Decameron* quite well, because when they reference his tales to prove a point during their conversations, they need only mention the first name of the protagonist of the tale or a key element from the plot. Boccaccio famously dedicated his *Decameron* to women in love, claiming that by reading the one hundred tales such women would derive "parimento diletto delle sollazzevoli cose in quelle mostrate e utile consiglio potranno pigliare, in quanto potrannno cognoscere quello che sia da fuggire e che sia similmente da seguitare" ("not only pleasure from the entertaining material they contain, but useful advice as well, for the stories will teach them how to recognize what they should avoid, and likewise, what they should pursue").[26] Rather than advice for women in love, Fonte's ladies instead find in Boccaccio's text an authority to cite in order to prove their points regarding human behavior and the natural history of birds and stones. For example, as Corinna argues, "se l'uomo contiene in sé qualche buon costume, lo ha dalla donna con cui pratica" ("if a man has virtues, he has picked them up from the woman he lives with"),[27] she furnishes as proof of women's civilizing effect on men Boccaccio's tale of Cimone (V.1), a brutish young man inspired to become an educated gentleman after falling in love with Efigenia. She concludes her argument on the civilizing powers of women by stating, "come avvenne (per essempio) a Cimone e molti altri" ("Just look at the examples of Cimone and many others").[28] When on the second day of their conversation, the ladies are discussing the edibility of various species of raptors, Lucrezia, speaking of falcons, notes that "il Bocacio [*sic*] ci afferma, che fu mangiato e fu anco delicatissimo al gusto" ("Boccaccio tells us about a falcon being eaten and tasting delicious"),[29] a clear reference to the tale of the impoverished but noble Federigo degli Alberighi (V.9) who, after spending his fortune to court Monna Giovanna, cooks his prized bird in order to provide a suitable meal for her.

When the seven women are discussing the properties of various stones and Lucretia wonders aloud whether the heliotrope can truly render one invisible, Corinna orders: "Lasciamo le favole" ("Let's not get sidetracked by those old yarns").[30] Although Corinna does not explicitly reference Boccaccio's *Decameron* at this moment in the conversation, her quick dismissal of the alleged powers of the heliotrope as nonsense recalls one of Boccaccio's four tales of the foolish, and often haughty, Florentine painter Calandrino, who is repeatedly *beffato*, or tricked, by his friends. In the first of the four Calandrino tales in the *Decameron* (VIII.3), his fellow painters Bruno and Buffalmacco, along with their clever accomplice Maso del Saggio, trick Calandrino into believing that an ordinary stone that he has found along the banks of the Mugnone river is a heliotrope that makes him invisible. If we take Corinna's reference to the *favola* here to mean the tall tale that Maso del Saggio recounts in the Church of San Giovanni to dupe Calandrino into believing in the powers of the heliotrope and other stones, then we have a double reference: broadly to Boccaccio's tale (VIII.3) and more specifically to the legend of Bengodi or Cuccagna, a fantastic land of plenty that Maso describes, where there is a mountain made of cheese and rivers of Vernaccia wine free for the taking and where magical stones are found.[31]

Stories of lands of plenty like Bengodi or Cuccagna circulated not only in Boccaccio's tale but also in cheaply printed chapbooks primarily written in verse (octaves) and often adorned with woodblock illustrations.[32] From the beginning of printing through the nineteenth century, all sorts of stories circulated in this format: chivalric adventures of knights and ladies, saints' legends, mythological stories, ghost stories, tragic and triumphal love stories, verse retellings of Boccaccio's "novelle," and fairy tales.[33] The women in Fonte's dialogue seem to know certain tales from this popular tradition as well as they know the tales of Boccaccio's *Decameron*, because they can metonymically reference a chapbook with the mere mention of a character and magical motif, as occurs when Corinna states that they will turn to discuss false and deceitful lovers. During this exchange, Queen Adriana suggests that Corinna will need either Love's wings or the wax wings of Daedalus to escape the wrath of dishonest men who would surely turn on Corinna if they were to hear her address this vast and difficult subject. Lucrezia adds, "Più presto . . . lei sarà di mestiero il mantello di Leombruno per girsene coperta e invisibile" ("Or rather . . . she will need Leombruno's magic cloak so that she will escape hidden and invisible").[34] This is a reference to the hero of a fairy tale in verse, *Historia di Lionbruno*, attributed to Cirino d'Ancona, but printed anonymously. The text circulated widely in various editions printed between the 1480s and early 1600s.[35] Sold to the devil by his impoverished fisherman father, Leombruno or Lionbruno is saved from the demon's clutches by a woman named Aquilina, who, in the shape of an eagle, carries him off to her castle. Fairy-like Aquilina magically completes the four-hundred-day journey in just one night and becomes a beautiful woman once again, when they arrive at her home. Her agency in this tale in determining her own romantic fate must have appealed to Corinna and her friends. After receiving a proper education in arms and letters, Lionbruno marries Aquilina, but he loses her and the wealth she provided when he fails to abide by her interdiction not to boast of her. During his search for Aquilina, he happens upon a group of feuding robbers and cleverly steals from them a cloak of invisibility and seven-league boots. With this magical attire, he discovers Aquilina's whereabouts from the wind, and the couple is happily reunited. Interestingly, this fairy tale in octaves was sometimes circulated with a *capitolo* by the humanist and Petrarchan poet Panfilo Sasso (1455–1527), in which a woman denounces a faithless lover. The poem, "d'una che si lamenta del suo Amante" ("about a woman who complains about her lover"), includes the following tercets berating the male lover's deceptive words:

Quante volte m'hai detto o vis'adorno
Mai non ti lascierò fin che sei vivo
& fin che volg'il ciel la ruota intorno
Hor se mutato, & cerchi d'esser privo,
del mio servir, & far dolente strazio
di me che per te sola al mondo vivo.
O poca fede, o cor di freddo diaccio
Son queste le promesse, o bella cosa,
una donna stratiar legata al laccio.

How many times have you said to me, "O adorned visage,
I will never leave you, as long as you live
And the heavens turn the wheel."
Now you have changed and seek to shed
My service and painfully massacre

Me who lives in this world only for you.
O faithless one! O cold heart of ice!
These are your promises, a fine thing,
A woman tortured, bound by a snare.[36]

Thus, in these editions that contain Sasso's *capitolo,* the story of Lionbruno and his cloak of invisibility is linked to the lament of a woman spurned by a man whose words cannot be trusted, precisely the subject of the women's discussion at the moment in Fonte's text in which Leombruno is mentioned. Through these citations and references in the dialogue, the women gathered in Leonora's garden reveal an expansive, shared knowledge of tales, from animal fables to realistic Boccaccian novellas to fairy tale chapbooks.

## Unhappily Ever After: Fonte's Fairy Tale

The second day of Fonte's dialogue stands in marked contrast to the first day's sharp focus on discussing the vices of men. After the women have gathered once again at Leonora's home, they begin their conversation with a sustained consideration of the nature of friendship. The dialogue then expands into a rambling, encyclopedic discussion that covers numerous topics, including medicine, poetry, oratory, geology, biology, and the law. Rather than a complete break from the first day's discourse, scholars of Fonte's work have viewed the second day as a logical continuation of a discussion of the ways in which men oppress women that aims to provide women with a model for gaining access to an education that was typically denied them, while simultaneously providing a new model for female education.[37] It is during the course of this varied and edifying discussion that Fonte's characters recount two prose tales, one a fairy tale and one a comic-realistic novella, as well as a mythological narrative in verse.[38]

Thanks to the insistence of one character, Leonora, the conversation on the second day never strays completely from the critique of men and their mistreatment of women. When her companions meander too far from what Leonora sees as the group's proper topic of conversation, she steers the group back to their discussion of men's wrongdoings. In this way, the conversation on the second day unfolds, with one topic leading to another, like links in a chain.[39] For example, when Leonora observes that although she speaks ill of men, she claims that she does so openly, while men cover their poison with honeyed words. After Leonora mentions poison, the conversation shifts to a discussion of antidotes, including the ancient Greek cure-all theriac and a remedy made from a unicorn's horn. This observation inspires Corinna to recount for her friends the *favola* of Biancarisa and Lioncorno (Italian for unicorn).

Corinna's fairy tale begins not with a description of the young lovers Lioncorno and Biancarisa but with the tragic backstory of the female villain, Climene, whose son Fetonte (Phaeton) was struck dead by his father Apollo and whose daughters were changed into poplar trees. As Climene wanders the earth in misery, another one of Apollo's male offspring, King Alciteo, happily reigns over his city of Felicia in India. The fame of Alciteo's virtue has spread throughout Asia and the "più eccellenti cavallieri" ("finest knights") are flocking to his court; among them is Lioncorno of Phrygia.[40] These two virtuous young men immediately strike up a loving friendship, which also serves to link this tale to the extended discussion of friendship at the beginning of the second day. Only after Lioncorno and Alciteo's brotherly bond has been described in detail do we learn that Alciteo has a "bellissima sorella da marito, detta Biancarisa, la qual di raro ad occhio umano si lasciava mirare" ("a very beautiful sister of marriageable age, called Biancarisa, who only very rarely exposed herself to human gaze").[41] Biancarisa is a sort of princess in the tower, but unlike Sleeping Beauty, she is fully awake, and unlike Rapunzel, her decision to remain far from prying eyes is her own. One day, while the two young men are horsing around, their ball flies into Biancarisa's window, and Lioncorno follows it. He and Biancarisa lock eyes, and the two fall in love. Once each is assured of the other's affection, they marry clandestinely, thus creating a perfectly chaste love story that would, at least in regard to the lack of lascivious material, satisfy Counter-Reformation censors. At the same time, Corinna upends our expectations for a fairy tale wedding: the princess enters into matrimony on the basis of reciprocal affection of her own accord, not as a passive prize awarded to the hero. And the union takes place toward the beginning of the couple's adventures, not as the closing act of the tale.

We then learn that Apollo is so pleased with his son Alciteo that he has forgotten about the pain Fetonte's death caused him. At this point, Climene arrives in the kingdom and witnesses this other son of Apollo flourishing. Overcome by *cordoglio, invidia,* and *gelosia* (grief, envy, and jealousy), Climene concocts a poison using knowledge she acquired from Apollo, a detail that again anchors this fantastic tale to the women's discussion of poison and antidotes. She bribes an unscrupulous servant to deliver the poisoned cup to unsuspecting Alciteo. As Lioncorno is on his way to consummate his clandestine marriage to Biancarisa, he overhears this plot. In that moment, "prevalse la ragion l'appetito" ("his reason overcame his appetite"), and Lioncorno decides to delay his own sexual gratification in order to save his beloved friend by knocking the cup of poison to the ground.[42] After the unfaithful servant has confessed under torture, Climene, fearing for her own life, flees to a wood, where she prays to Venus. Climene's centrality in the tale is underscored by the fact that she is the only character to speak in direct discourse, and Corinna supplies her with a speech in which she denounces Apollo's betrayal and callous behavior and then makes common cause with Venus against the Sun God. Climene's lament, however, seems misdirected, as she targets Lioncorno, who ruined her plans for revenge. Venus, hesitating only a moment because of her love for her faithful servant Lioncorno, quickly resolves to aid Climene and to avenge her own mistreatment by Apollo. The goddess sprinkles magic dust over Lioncorno, which turns him into a unicorn as he is about to consummate his marriage. Alciteo weeps bitterly at the loss of his beloved friend, as does Lioncorno's bride Biancarisa, and she swears never to remarry. No mention is made of the fate of Climene.

The response to Corinna's tale is mixed. On the one hand, her friends acknowledge that it is an entertaining, sentimental story, but the unflattering depiction of the behavior of female characters does not sit well with Leonora. Some of the women have tears in their eyes at the conclusion of the tale, but Leonora reacts by stating, "Questa è ben una bella novella, ma par che sia più in favor de gli uomini che delle donne" ("Well, that's a very fine tale, but it seems to put men in a rather better light than women").[43] The narrator Corinna dismisses the antiwoman charge by underscoring the fact that she has told a fantastic *favola* rather than a verisimilar novella: "Fate conto . . . d'aver udito una favola" ("Ah, but you have to remember . . . that what you've just heard was a fairy tale").[44] Lucrezia then moves to change the subject back to natural history, but not before noting that *favole* are one of the only literary genres in which one can speak ill of women: "Sì sì . . . però diteci pur così di qualche altro animale, né restate, benché dite mal delle donne, che in ogni modo il ben de gli uomini, come 'l mal delle donne non si può dire se non in favola." ("Oh, I know . . . Go on, tell us about some other animals. And don't worry if it means speaking ill of women: we all know that it's only in fairy tales that it's possible to speak ill of women").[45] In this period, the highly polysemous word *favola* (plural: *favole*), referred to fairy tales, fables, pastoral tales of shepherds and nymphs, and mythological stories like those in Ovid's *Metamorphoses*. Lucrezia's joke hinges on understanding that *favola* refers to the sort of fantastic fictions that make no claim to realism, but it may also be read as a critique of the depiction of women in such fictions.

In her English translation of Fonte's dialogue, Virginia Cox renders *favola* as "fairy tale" in this exchange. Initially, it might be difficult for us modern readers to classify as a fairy tale this tragic story featuring metamorphosis, gods, and goddesses, which perhaps seems closer to Ovid's *Metamorphoses* than to the sixteenth-century literary fairy tales of Giovan Francesco Straparola and Lorenzo Selva.[46] But we must remember that in Fonte's day, one of the most widely circulating fairy tales was the story of Cupid and Psyche found in Apuleius's Latin novel, *The Metamorphosis or The Golden Ass*. The Latin novel, a source for a number of Boccaccio's tales in the *Decameron*, circulated widely throughout Europe in print during the sixteenth century.[47] Italian translations by both Matteo Maria Boiardo and Agnolo Firenzuola were reprinted throughout the sixteenth century, and visual representations of the story of Cupid and Psyche abounded in engravings, paintings, and frescoes. Recounted by an older woman to a young woman who has been kidnapped by robbers on her wedding day, the story focuses on a favorite topic of Fonte's interlocutors: envy. Psyche is a persecuted maiden who suffers because of the jealousy of other women: the goddess Venus who envies her beauty and her sisters who are jealous of the riches her mysterious lover (Cupid) has bestowed upon her. Despite the many trials Psyche endures at the hands of these jealous women, the tale ends happily, with Cupid and Psyche married before the gods, Psyche deified and giving birth to their daughter Pleasure, and Venus even dancing at their wedding. As I will show below, Fonte tells her own story of Cupid, or Love, in the narrative poem in octaves that appears toward the end of the second day of *Il merito delle donne*. Although both in Apuleius's novel and Fonte's tale, it is female jealousy and envy that drives the plots forward, Fonte's fairy tale of Lioncorno and Biancarisa provides no such happy ending. For this reason, too, Fonte's story might not initially seem to be a fairy tale.

## Fairy Tales and Anti-Tales

As Catriona McAra and David Calvin argue in the introduction to their edited volume *Anti-tales: The Uses of Disenchantment* (2011), an anti-tale "takes some aspects of the fairy tale genre, and its equivalent genres, and reimagines, subverts, inverts, deconstructs, or satirizes elements of them to present an alternate narrative interpretation, outcome or morality."[48] For McAra and Calvin, anti-tales are a type of "subversive re-assemblage" of fairy tale plot elements. I will use this concept to examine how Fonte's anti-tale implicitly critiques the gender bias of traditional fairy tales, while simultaneously functioning as a cautionary tale regarding open female rebellion against patriarchal oppression. While the term "anti-tales" might first conjure in our minds postmodern retellings of tales of the sort examined in McAra's and Calvin's volume, they remind us that concept of anti-tale is not a contemporary one.[49] Indeed, they note that in his chapter on fairy tales in his seminal *Simple Forms* (1930), André Jolles recognizes that anti-tales have long existed alongside fairy tales as their inverse. Jolles observes that fairy tales often "give us a sense of injustice and a feeling that this injustice must be corrected."[50] Such is the case, he argues, in "Puss-in-Boots," in which a youngest son receives a seemingly useless inheritance, while his brothers receive profitable property and goods.

Jolles sees fairy tales as expressing a naïve morality, as opposed to philosophical ethics that answers the question, "What should I do?" For Jolles, fairy tales express an "ethical judgment concerned not with *actions*, but with *events*" by answering the question "How should events happen in the world?"[51] Indeed, he finds this expectation of justice as central to the fairy tale form: "This expectation of how things should really happen in the world seems to be normative for the form 'fairy tale': it is the mental disposition of the fairy tale."[52] From this demand for justice in an unjust world springs both the fairy tale and its opposite, the anti-tale: "We might expect that this doubly directed activity of the mental disposition would also produce two forms, that besides the form in which the way of the world is ordered so that it answers completely to the demands of naïve morality we would find a form in which the naively immoral world, the tragic world is condensed: in short, there must be an anti-*Märchen*, an anti-fairy tale."[53] Fonte's tale is just such an anti-fairy tale, a story in which unresolved injustices abound and no one receives a happy ending.

Furthermore, in her anti-tale, Fonte selects and reassembles narrative structures and motifs of the traditional fairy tale to highlight the experience and actions of the older female villain rather than those of Lioncorno and Princess Biancarisa, who initially might seem to be more typical fairy tale protagonists. In his seminal study *Morphology of the Folktale* (1928), the Russian formalist Vladimir Propp argues that all fairy tales share one structure. Propp identifies thirty-one possible functions (which we can think of as the actions of the characters) that are typical of fairy tales. According to Propp, you do not need to have all thirty-one functions to have a fairy tale, but the functions that do appear must follow a fixed order. Who carries out an action is not as important as what happens, the action itself, and the order in which actions unfold.[54] In a typical fairy tale, we would expect to find heroes or heroines who absent themselves from home because of an act of villainy or a lack that propels the plot and a donor who provides magic that leads to the liquidation of that villainy or lack. For Propp, fairy tales often conclude with the punishment of the villain, an act that restores justice, followed by rewards and/or weddings for the heroes or the heroines.[55]

Fonte challenges our expectations by collapsing the heroine and the villain into one figure. If we analyze Corinna's story from the point of view of the characters that we would expect to be the hero or the heroine, Lioncorno or Biancarisa, the story hardly seems a fairy tale. Lioncorno does leave home, but not because of any villainy or lack, and the villainy eventually perpetrated on him, his metamorphosis, is never undone. Biancarisa marries a handsome prince who later turns into a beast, but, unlike most European animal-bridegroom tales, the tale ends in a kind of tragic suspension. Never having consummated her marriage, she is neither truly wife nor truly widow. Instead, the character whose narrative trajectory most resembles the fairy tale structure outlined by Propp is Climene. Corinna's tale begins with the villainy she endures: the murder/death of her son Fetonte and the arboreal transformation of her daughters (they become poplar trees). Climene initially attempts to redress this wrong with the poison she sends to Alciteo, but ultimately, she must revert to magic. She receives the magic from a donor, Venus, a sort of evil fairy godmother, who then carries out the revenge for Climene, but this does not neatly undo the original villainy. Climene does not get her son back, and the vengeance and punishment intended for Apollo never directly touches him. Instead, Venus's magic destroys the Kingdom of Felicia: Alciteo loses his best friend, and his sister Biancarisa is, in effect, widowed, as she will never enjoy the company of her human husband. In Corinna's reconfiguration of the traditional fairy tale structure, the character who usually occupies the role of villain, the older female who thwarts the marriage plans of the young couple, becomes the protagonist of the tale.

By providing Climene with a sympathetic backstory, Corinna rebels against a genre that more often than not depicted older women as one-dimensional villains. Examples of such wicked stepmother figures abound, and for vivid examples we need look no further than another Venetian text featuring female narrators that was popular in Fonte's day, Giovan Francesco Straparola's two volume collection of tales, *Le piacevoli notti* (2 vols: 1550, 1553). In one of Straparola's dragon-slayer tales (Night 10, Tale 3), a mother joins with her daughters to poison her dragon-slayer son, because the women are envious of his marriage to a princess and the wealth it has brought him. In another, Night 4, Tale 3, a baker's daughter manages to marry a prince by promising to bear him three marvelous offspring with stars on their brows. When she delivers on the promise by birthing a set of prodigious triplets, her jealous sisters and mother-in-law convince the midwife to remove the infants and replace them with three mongrel pups. The princess will be jailed in a fetid room beneath the kitchen in the castle for this "crime." Similarly, fairy tale chapbooks in verse, such as Francesco Corna da Soncino's *Historia di Santa Oliva* and the anonymous *Historia di Regina Stella e Mattabruna,* featured envious female villains who viciously persecute their daughters-in-law and (temporarily) destroy their marriages through false accusations of monstrous births. In short, although many fairy tales from this period depict strong female protagonists who exercised a considerable amount of agency,[56] stories of women behaving badly towards other women were equally plentiful.[57]

Unlike the evil women in the aforementioned fairy tales, who are motivated purely by envy, greed, or lust, Climene possesses a sympathetic motive for her destructive actions: the death of her son, the arboreal metamorphoses of her daughters, and her abandonment and betrayal at the hands of an unfaithful lover. Corinna also depicts her female villain as capable of collaboration with other women to fight their own mistreatment. Venus and Climene's alliance might appear to be based more on their mutual hatred for Apollo than on the sort of true friendship binding the tale's narrator to her listeners in the dialogue, but they are united in opposition to the systematic mistreatment of women by the patriarchal power Apollo. And their angry actions are not aimed at directly harming another female. Biancarisa's marital disappointment is collateral damage, not the primary target of their rage. Perhaps most surprising in this anti-tale is the narrator's unwillingness to punish the female malefactors. At the end of Straparola's fairy tales and the chapbooks mentioned above, the female villains are always executed, usually by being burned alive. But Corinna refrains from enacting such punishment; in fact, we simply do not know what becomes of Climene and Venus, as the narrative shifts focus to the victim of their actions: Lioncorno. Thus, in Corinna's tragic anti-tale, Fonte rewrites two key misogynist motifs of the fairy tale: the patriarchal marriage and the wicked stepmother or mother-in-law. Her subversive reassemblage of fairy tale tropes implicitly critiques the forms of oppression embedded in the dominant narrative structures of the genre by its negation of the possibility of a resolution for the villainies committed. As long as Apollo persists in misbehaving, there will be no happy ending for anyone. In this way, the tale echoes a central theme in the dialogue: if men persist in mistreating women, there can be no harmony in the world.

Fonte's anti-tale, however, does much more than subvert generic conventions. As McAra and Calvin note, anti-tales are not simply inversions of the narratives they deform: "Often the anti-tale may be thought of more in line with what David Hopkins has recently termed 'dark poetics,' a tale with malevolent undercurrents which lurk just beneath the surface."[58] As Jolles and contemporary scholars of the fairy tale have noted, traditional fairy tales are a genre of radical hopefulness full of the certain knowledge that justice will be done in an unjust world.[59] Good people will ultimately be rewarded, and the wicked will be brought to swift, violent, often vengeful justice, as Propp's final set of functions indicate: the villain is punished (XXX), and the hero is married and ascends the throne (XXXI).[60] Corinna's tale is, instead, a story of hopelessness. The true villain, the unfaithful lover and forgetful father Apollo, is never brought to justice; the villainy he perpetrates persists. Climene occupies an impossible position as heroine and villain, one that negates all possibility of a happy ending, because, unable to undo the villainy she endured, she now replicates and displaces this villainy onto others. Her narrative is circular rather than linear, looping through acts of villainy rather than charging ahead to a resolution, a liquidation of the villainy and a punishment of the villain. Thus, what lurks below Fonte's anti-tale is a chilling "esempio," or cautionary tale, that helps to explain what can seem to contemporary readers to be the anticlimactic ending to the dialogue.

## Conclusion

When in the final pages of the dialogue Virginia declares that the other women's discussion of the vices of men has convinced her not to marry, her mother Adriana responds, "Non dire così figliuola mia . . . che egli è forza che io ti mariti" ("Don't say that, daughter dear! . . . Because I have no choice but to find a husband for you").[61] So two days of rousing, rebellious conversation, and insightful analysis of gender inequality end not with revolution but with the acceptance of patriarchal marriage and a return to the status quo. Perhaps, in part, this is because the story of Climene reveals the possibility of catastrophic outcomes when the oppressed adopt the strategies of their oppressors, when women combat the patriarchy by acting like men.

While Adriana seeks to reassure her daughter that she will seek a decent man for her husband, Leonora declares that if Virginia should find such a man, then she should marry him. If she fails, however, which Leonora feels is the most likely outcome of such a search, Virginia should "guardarsene più che dal fuoco" ("shun marriage like the plague").[62] In the same breath, Leonora reinforces her doubts on finding a worthy husband who will love her sincerely, by recalling a poem that Corinna has written and by asking her to recite it. Although Corinna initially demurs, stating that the thirty-six-octave poem is "tropo [*sic*] la materia lunghetta" ("longish"), Adriana pulls rank and commands her to recite her verse.[63]

Corinna's *stanze*, or narrative in verse, tells of a Golden Age of Love, during which Love's sharp arrows pierce only hearts that love honestly. The love he sparks in human hearts is so pure and strong that kings and princes disregard the social class of their beloveds; the lack of a dowry never prevents a union; love inspires poetry and literature; and men are never unfaithful. In such a world, humans turn to worshiping Love and ignore the temples of Juno, who becomes jealous. Uniting with Superbia (Pride) and Avarizia (Avarice), two other immortals who are spurned thanks to the pure desire Love engenders in humans, Juno sees that Love's arrows are blunted. The result is the imperfect love and male treachery that now operates in the women's world. Unlike Apuleius's story of Cupid and Psyche, which concludes happily with Psyche's marriage and the birth of her daughter, Corinna's narrative poem of Love (Cupid) and Juno, like her tale of Biancarisa and Lioncorno, finishes unhappily with the establishment of an imperfect, debased form of love now reigning in the world.

After this tale is told, no one censures the depiction of Juno as an envious woman who plots with accomplices to ruin love for everyone, mortals and gods alike. As in the tale of Lioncorno and Biancarisa, female envy is safely contained within the bounds of fantastic fictions, and none of Corinna's listeners feels the need to comment upon this negative portrayal of women. Instead, the women are struck by the aesthetic aspects of the poem, its beauty and inventiveness. It is as if there was no need to repeat what they had agreed upon after hearing the fairy tale of Lioncorno and Biancarisa: it is only in *favole* that women can be spoken of badly.

Reformed literature, as Cox asserts, allowed women to participate more fully in literary life by "cleaning up" lascivious genres, so, paradoxically, censorship empowered their voices. The women in Fonte's dialogue are well aware that they can speak so freely precisely and only because they find themselves in a protected, all-female space. The enclosed *locus amoenus* of their friend's garden protects them from the men who would censure and censor their conversation, and the women treasure and celebrate this freedom. Yet, in that same garden, they practice their own form of censorship, "concensureship." After Corinna tells the anti-tale of Lioncorno and Biancarisa, rather than simply condemning the negative depiction of women, banning such tales outright, the group seems to reach a consensus to censure, but not to censor fantastic stories that depict some female characters negatively. In fact, Corinna's mythological tale of Cupid and Juno, which also features a jealous female who irreparably harms lovers, although indirectly by blunting Love's arrows, meets with no such criticism. While the tale of Lioncorno and Biancarisa is censured, such tales may be recounted, in part because the fantastic fairy tale and mythic spaces they create stand in stark contrast to the reality of their tellers, where all seven women are virtuous, mutually supportive, even when they disagree, and free of envy. Of course, the women are under no pretense that all women behave so virtuously beyond the walls of the garden, but they do recognize the importance of such cautionary tales in instructing women how to live virtuously, of tales that warn of the perils of female envy that pit women against women, just as *invidia* is the cause for men abusing women.

In her reading of *Il merito delle donne*, Adriana Chemello observes that throughout the dialogue, male *invidia* is consistently contrasted with female *merito* but that Corinna's fairy tale momentarily reverses the binary. Climene's *invidia* stands in stark contrast to Lioncorno's *merito* and Biancarisa's virtue; her self-serving alliance with Venus appears the inverse of Lioncorno's selfless love for his friend Alciteo. Spurred on by envy, the emotion so closely associated with men in this dialogue, Climene exacts her revenge. Both her agency and her *invidia* masculinize her and lead to the destruction of the harmonious, homosocial, and heterosexual bonds that kept the Kingdom of Felicia happy. Corinna's companions understand the moral of her story quite well; there will be no happy endings until Apollo changes his ways. So perhaps women failing to rebel at the end of the dialogue is not a failure of courage but an acknowledgment that any significant societal change will demand a change in men, their attitudes, their behavior, and the structures, narrative and social, that they have built to control women.

Notes

1. Carlo Dionisotti, "La letteratura italiana nell'età del concilio di Trento," in *Geografia e storia della letteratura italiana* (Turin: Giulio Einaudi Editore, 1967), 191–192.

2. Adriana Chemello, "La donna, il modello, e l'immaginario: Moderata Fonte e Lucrezia Marinella," in *Nel cerchio della luna: figure di donne in alcuni testi del XVI*, ed. Marina Zancan (Venice: Marsilio, 1983), 97. All translations are my own unless otherwise indicated.

3. For a complete list of volumes in the series *The Other Voice in Early Modern Europe*, see http://www.othervoiceineme.com. For the University of Chicago Library's Italian Women Writers Project, see https://www.lib.uchicago.edu/efts/IWW/. Elissa Weaver, whose research on early-modern Italian women has inspired and informed this essay, made significant contributions to both projects. She is the general editor, along with Catherine M. Mardikes, of the Italian Women Writers Project, and she translated, edited, and contributed to a number of volumes for The Other Voice series, including Antonia Pulci, *Saints' Lives and Bible Stories for the Stage: A Bi-lingual Edition*, ed. Elissa B. Weaver, trans. James Wyatt (Toronto: Iter Press/Centre for Reformation and Renaissance Studies, 2010), and Arcangela Tarabotti, *Antisatire: In Defense of Women, Against Francesco Buoninsegni*, ed. and trans. Elissa B. Weaver (Toronto: Iter Press/Tempe: ACMRS, 2020).

4. For example, we now list as authors of pastoral dramas not just the famed actress Isabella Andreini, whose *La Mirtilla* was published in 1588, but also Barbara Torelli Benedetti (*Partenia*, c. 1586) and Maddalena Campiglia (*Flori*, 1588). The list of women writers of epic poems includes not only Tullia D'Aragona, mentioned by Dionisotti, but also Moderata Fonte, Lucrezia Marinella, and Margherita Sarrocchi.

5. Virginia Cox, *Women's Writing in Italy 1400–1650* (Baltimore: The Johns Hopkins University Press, 2008), 136.

6. Only one tale circumscribed by a framing narration of Bigolina's has survived, but archival documents suggest that she had written a collection of tales. See Valeria Finucci's introduction in Guilia Bigolina, *Urania: A Romance*, ed. and trans. Valeria Finucci (Chicago: The University of Chicago Press, 2005); Christopher Nissen's introduction in Giulia Bigolina, *Urania: The Story of a Young Woman's Love, & The Novella of Giulia Camposanpiero and Thesibaldo Vitaliani*, ed. and trans. Christopher Nissen (Tempe: Arizona Center for Medieval and Renaissance Studies, 2004); and Virginia Cox, *Women's Writing in Italy*, 113.

7. Modesta Pozzo (1555–1592) published in a wide variety of genres under the pseudonym Moderata Fonte. Her oeuvre includes the chivalric epic poem *I tredici canti di Floridoro* (1581), the banquet play *Le feste* (1581), and religious verse in octaves *La passione di Christo* (1582) and *La resurrettione di Gesù Christo nostro Signore* (1592), as well as occasional verse. Her dialogue discussed here, *Il merito delle donne*, was published by her uncle and her children as a response to Giuseppe Passi's misogynist *I donneschi difetti* (1599). On this controversy, see Stephen Kolsky, "Moderata Fonte, Lucrezia Marinella, Giuseppe Passi: An Early Seventeenth-Century Feminist Controversy," *Modern Language Review* 96, no. 4 (October 2001): 973–989. On the dialogue as a space for the verse and prose that Fonte wrote during her marriage, see Beatrice Collina, "Moderata Fonte e *Il Merito delle donne*," *Annali d'italianistica* 7 (1989): 142–165. On Fonte's dedication of *Floridoro* to Francesco de' Medici and Bianca Capello, see Eleanora Carinci, "Una lettera autografa inedita di Moderata Fonte (al granduca di Toscana Francesco I)," *Critica del Testo* 5, no. 3 (2002):

1–11. For a modern edition and translation of *Le feste*, see Courtney Quaintance, "*Le feste*: Written by Moderata Fonte," in *Scenes from Italian Convent Life: An Anthology of Convent Theatrical Texts and Contexts*, ed. Elissa B. Weaver (Ravenna, Italy: Longo Editore, 2009), 193–231. The only monograph dedicated exclusively to Fonte is Paola Malpezzi-Price, *Moderata Fonte: Women and Life in Sixteenth-Century Venice* (Madison, NJ: Fairleigh Dickinson University Press, 2003). Biographies by Virginia Cox can be found in the Italian Women Writers Project and in "Moderata Fonte and *The Worth of Women*," in Moderata Fonte, *The Worth of Women: Wherein Is Clearly Revealed Their Nobility and Their Superiority to Men*, ed. and trans. Virginia Cox, The Other Voice in Early Modern Europe. (Chicago: The University of Chicago Press, 1997), 2–6. For an annotated bibliography of Fonte's work and critical studies, see Suzanne Magnanini, "Moderata Fonte," *Oxford Bibliographies: Renaissance and Reformation* (Oxford: Oxford University Press, 2019), https://www-oxfordbibliographies-com.colorado.idm.oclc.org/view/document/obo-9780195399301/obo-9780195399301-0416.xml; doi:10.1093/obo/9780195399301-0416.

8. Giambattista Passano, *I novellieri italiani in prosa* (Milan: Libreria Antica e Moderna di G. Schiepatti, 1864), 323–324.

9. Passano, *I novellieri italiani in prosa*, 324.

10. Giovanni Passano, *I novellieri in verso indicati e descritti da Giambattista Passano* (Bologna: Gaetano Romagnoli, 1868).

11. On the figure of the *dimessa* in the works of authors from the Veneto region, see Adriana Chemello, "Letteratura di condotta e vita delle donne nelle opera di Moderata Fonte e Lucrezia Marinella," in *Conduct Literature for and about Women in Italy, 1470–1900: Prescribing and Describing Life*, eds. Helena Sanson and Francesco Lucioli (Paris: Classiques Garnier, 2016), 137–58.

12. Chemello, "La donna, il modello, e l'immaginario," 113.

13. Chemello, "La donna, il modello, e l'immaginario," 113.

14. Fonte, *The Worth of Women*, 45 n 5.

15. Moderata Fonte, *Il merito delle donne*, ed. Adriana Chemello (Venice: Eidos, 1988), 23. English translations from Fonte, *The Worth of Women*, 56.

16. Katherine McKenna, "Women in the Garden: The *Decameron* Reimagined in Moderata Fonte's *Il merito delle donne*," *Early Modern Women: An Interdisciplinary Journal* 13, no. 2 (Spring 2019), 65.

17. Juan Luis Vives, *The Education of a Christian Woman*, ed. and trans. Charles Fantazzi (Chicago: The University of Chicago Press, 2000), 74–75.

18. In Lucca in 1585, the *Ordine per monache* banned nuns from reading romances, novellas, and anything containing sensual or explicit words, while in Verona in 1667, the bishop ordered that all nuns' cells be searched for "all books of chivalry, novellas, or poetry hidden in armoires or under their beds" (Valeria Finucci, "Moderata Fonte and the Genre of Women's Chivalric Romances," in *Floridoro, A Chivalric Romance* by Moderata Fonte, trans. Julia Kisacky [Chicago: The University of Chicago Press, 2006], 18–19).

19. Three expurgated editions were published in the late sixteenth century, first by the Medici-elected committee of Deputati in Florence led by Vincenzo Borghini (1573), then by the Florentine philologist Lionardo Salviati (1582), and finally by the blind poet Luigi

Groto (1588) in Venice. Since the women all cite from tales that were not heavily censored, it is difficult to determine whether we are to understand them as having read an expurgated edition of the *Decameron*.

20. McKenna notes that in *Joining the Conversation: Dialogues by Renaissance Women* (Ann Arbor: University of Michigan Press, 2005) Janet Levarie Smarr recognized Boccaccio's *Decameron* and Castiglione's *The Book of the Courtier* as the two key intertexts for Fonte's dialogue. See McKenna, "Women in the Garden," 65.

21. Fonte, *Il merito delle donne*, 43; Fonte, *The Worth of Women*, 79.

22. Fonte, *Il merito delle donne*, 46; Fonte, *The Worth of Women*, 83.

23. ". . . dandoli quell'udienza e quella fede che diè la savia pecorella all'ingordo lupo quando, fingendo egli la voce della madre di lei, l'essortava ad aprirli la porta" (Fonte, *Il Merito delle donne*, 47). "In fact, we should pay about as much attention to them and give them about as much credence as the sensible little lamb gave to the wolf when it was imitating its mother's voice and begging to open the gate" (Fonte, *The Worth of Women*, 83).

24. Fonte, *Il merito delle donne*, 70; Fonte, *The Worth of Women*, 115.

25. See, for example, Verdizotti's conclusion to the fable of the fox and the crow, which emphasizes both "merito" and "inganno": "Colui, che in tua presenzia assai ti loda,/ A tua simplicitade inganno ordisce;/E di giudicio assai manca e fallisce/Chi suol fede prestare à finta loda." ("He who praises you greatly to your face/Plots to deceive your simplicity;/And lacking in judgment and at fault/ is he who tends to lend credence to false praise.") The moral of this tale is: "La lode senza mer[i]to è fraude espressa." ("Praise without merit is fraud spoken.") (Giovanni Maria Verdizotti, *Cento favole morali dei più illustri antichi et moderni autori Greci e Latini* (Venice: Francesco Ziletti, 1586), 185–86. Verdizotti (1525–1600) was an artist and Titian's secretary; his own engravings adorn this volume, which was first printed in 1570.

26. Giovanni Boccaccio, *Opere. Decameron. Elegia di Madonna Fiammetta. Ninfe fiesolane*, ed. Cesare Segre, notes by Maria Consigli Segre (Milan: Mursia, 1966), 9; Giovanni Boccaccio, *Decameron*, ed. and trans. Wayne Rebhorn (New York: W. W. Norton, 2013), 3.

27. Fonte, *Il merito delle donne*, 25; Fonte, *The Worth of Women*, 58.

28. Fonte, *Il merito delle donne*, 26; Fonte, *The Worth of Women*, 59.

29. Fonte, *Il merito delle donne*, 87; Fonte, *The Worth of Women*, 138.

30. Fonte, *Il merito delle donne*, 128; Fonte, *The Worth of Women*, 185.

31. Of course, by not referencing Boccaccio's tale directly, Corinna spares her listeners from recalling the ending of Calandrino's adventures, where mistakenly thinking his wife Tessa has undone the magic of the stone, Calandrino savagely beats her.

32. For example the chapbook *Capitolo di Cuccagna dove se intendono le maravigliose cose che sono in quel paese, dove chi piu dorme piu guadagna, & a chi parla di lavorare li sono rotte le braccia* (s.d., s.p). The colophon indicates that the text was "Composta per M. Mariano de Patrica improvisatore, alias Tocadiglia."

33. For an overview of the sorts of tales and texts that circulated in this format, see Arnoldo Segarizzi's bibliography of the holdings in the Marciana Library: Arnoldo Segarizzi, *Bibliografia delle stampe popolari italiane: Stampe Popolari delle Biblioteca Marciana* (Bergamo: Istituto D'Arti Grafiche, 1913). For a discussion of fairy tales in this format,

see Luisa Rubini, "Fiabe in ottava rima: Il cantare fiabesco a stampa (1475–1530)," in *Il cantare italiano fra folklore e letteratura*, eds. Michelangelo Piccone and Luisa Rubini Messerli (Florence: Olschki, 2007), 414–440.

34. Fonte, *Il merito delle donne*, 38; Fonte, *The Worth of Women*, 73.

35. The attribution comes from Giuseppe Molini, *Operette bibliografiche* (Florence: Cellini, 1858), 495. For a descriptions of extant editions, see Giambattista Passano, *I novellieri in verso indicati e descritti da Giambattista Passano* (Bologna: Gaetano Romagnoli, 1868), 68–69, who lists editions printed in Venice, Florence, and Bologna, as well as Segarizzi, who describes an edition from 1550 printed in Siena and a seventeenth-century edition printed in Bologna and Pistoia (Segarizzi, *Bibliografia delle stampe popolari italiane*, 159, 76). For an English translation and facsimile of what is believed to be the *editio princeps* (Venice 1476), see *The Story of Lionbruno*, ed. and trans. Beatrice Corrigan (Toronto: Toronto Public Library, 1976).

36. *Historia di Liombruno il quale fu lasciato dal padre per povertà in preda del diavolo, & scampando fu portato da una donna in forma d'Aquila in una Città, & facendo egli dipoi varij viaggi rubò a certi malandrini un Mantello, & un paio di Stivali con li quali andò invisibile, & vinse il vento. Con un capitolo di Panfilo Sasso Nuovamente Ristampato* (Florence: Giovanni Baleni, 1583), c. 6v. The *capitolo* also appears in the 1550 edition printed in Siena.

37. Virginia Cox describes the second day of the dialogue "as a symbolic first step toward the task of empowering women by equipping them with the kind of practical and theoretical knowledge from which they had been excluded" (Cox, "Moderata Fonte and *The Worth of Women*," 10). Sarah Ross views this part of the dialogue as depicting a sort of salon that serves to educate women outside of the convent (Sarah Gwyneth Ross, *The Birth of Feminism: Woman as Intellect in Renaissance Italy and England* [Cambridge, MA: Harvard University Press, 2009], 193–234. Meredith Ray sees in this wide-ranging conversation that covers many scientific fields a sort of weapon with which women can defend themselves, because the knowledge imparted teaches women how to care for themselves, to liberate themselves from men, and to participate capably in scientific discussions (Meredith K. Ray, *Daughters of Alchemy: Women and Scientific Culture in Early Modern Italy* (Cambridge, MA: Harvard University Press, 2015), 73–110. I have interpreted the second day as a performance of the *selva* genre (Suzanne Magnanini, "Una selva luminosa: The Second Day of Moderata Fonte's *Il merito delle donne*," *Modern Philology* 101, no. 2 [2003]: 278–296), and Chemello has called it a "piccola 'enciclopedia' del sapere" ("little 'encyclopedia' of knowledge") ("La donna, il modello, e l'immaginario," 137).

38. A full discussion of the comic-realistic novella Leonora recounts of the ironmonger is beyond the scope of this essay (for the tale see Fonte, *Il merito delle donne*, 135–136; Fonte, *The Worth of Women*, 193–194). The ironmonger has his son practice speaking before pots and pans in order to prepare for his university exams, but the young man fails to perform when he speaks in front of his human examiners. Leonora inserts this tale into the conversation by asking whether Adriana is suggesting that she is like the ironmonger's son, after Adriana notes that she has successfully defended women in front of their all-female group, "But I'm not sure how much success you'd have persuading the men!" The tale does show, however, that Corinna is not the only woman versed in the tale tradition

and that storytelling is used to inject humor and delight, as the women all laugh at Leonora's joke.

39. Chemello, "La donna, il modello, e l'immaginario," 136–137.

40. Fonte, *Il merito delle donne,* 107; Fonte, *The Worth of Women,* 162.

41. Fonte, *Il merito delle donne,* 107; Fonte, *The Worth of Women,* 162.

42. Fonte, *Il merito delle donne,* 109; Fonte, *The Worth of Women,* 163.

43. Fonte, *Il merito delle donne,* 111; Fonte, *The Worth of Women,* 166.

44. Fonte, *Il merito delle donne,* 111; Fonte, *The Worth of Women,* 166.

45. Fonte, *Il merito delle donne,* 111; Fonte, *The Worth of Women,* 166.

46. Chemello, in fact, suggests that Fonte's description of the transformation of Lioncorno is inspired by a passage from Ovid's *Metamorphoses* describing Lycaon's lupine transformation. Chemello, "La donna, il modello, e l'immaginario," 125 n 59.

47. Ruth B. Bottigheimer, "Cupid and Psyche vs. Beauty and the Beast: The Milesian and the Modern," *Marvels and Tales* 3, no. 1 (1989): 9.

48. Catriona McAra and David Calvin, "Introduction," in *Anti-Tales: The Uses of Disenchantment,* eds. Catriona McAra and David Calvin (Cambridge, UK: Cambridge Scholars Publishing, 2011), 4.

49. McAra and Calvin, "Introduction," 4.

50. André Jolles, *Simple Forms* (1930), foreword by Fredric Jameson, trans. Peter J. Schwartz (New York: Verso, 2017), Kindle edition, loc. 3828 of 5364. All citations are from Jolles's chapter on the fairy tale in the Kindle edition.

51. Jolles, *Simple Forms,* Kindle edition, loc. 3842 of 5364.

52. Jolles, *Simple Forms,* Kindle edition, loc. 3839 of 5364.

53. Jolles, *Simple Forms,* Kindle edition, loc. 3861 of 5364.

54. Vladimir Propp, *Morphology of the Folktale,* trans. Laurence Scott, ed. Louis Wagner, introduction by Alan Dundes (Austin: University of Texas Press, 1996), 21–23.

55. Propp, *Morphology of the Folktale,* 25–65.

56. To provide three examples from Straparola's *The Pleasant Nights*: in Night 3 Tale 1, Luciana takes control of a magic tuna that grants her foolish husband's wishes and uses wishes to change her husband from an ugly oaf into a handsome gentleman, to create a castle and garden for them, and to return to her father's good graces. In Night 4, Tale 1, when she is deprived of a dowry, princess Costanza, who has been educated in both womanly arts and manly arms and letters, cross-dresses in order to leave her kingdom, captures a satyr, and win's a king's hand in marriage. In Night 3, Tale 4, Doralice sails out on the ocean and successfully schemes to save her husband from a Siren who has swallowed him.

57. On the topic of villainous mothers-in-law see Marina Warner's chapter "Wicked Stepmothers: The Sleeping Beauty," in *From the Beast to the Blonde* (New York: Farrar, Straus, and Giroux, 1994), 218–240.

58. McAra and Calvin, "Introduction," 5. They cite David Hopkins, *Childish Things* (Edinburgh: Fruitmarket Gallery, 2010), 72.

59. Marina Warner writes in *Once Upon a Time: A Short History of Fairy Tale* (Oxford: Oxford University Press, 2014), xviii: "Angela Carter called the spirit of the fairy tale 'heroic optimism,' a better phrase for the promise of a happy ending. Others identify it as

blind hope or wishful thinking, the life principle in action. It carries the tales of terrible dark deeds to their unlikely conclusion."

60. Propp, *Morphology of the Folktale*, 63.

61. Fonte, *Il merito delle donne*, 170; Fonte, *The Worth of Women*, 238.

62. Fonte, *Il merito delle donne*, 172; Fonte, *The Worth of Women*, 240.

63. Fonte, *Il merito delle donne*, 172; Fonte, *The Worth of Women*, 241.

CHAPTER THREE

# Amerigo Vespucci and African Amazons

## Reinventing Italian Exploration in Baroque Epic Poetry

NATHALIE HESTER

As the production of epic poetry continued to thrive in Italy through the late sixteenth and early seventeenth centuries, so emerged poetic attention to the voyages of Christopher Columbus, Amerigo Vespucci, and the exploration and conquest of the Americas. From 1581 to 1650, poets from a variety of courtly, professional, and regional contexts published, in Latin or the vernacular, initial cantos on or complete epic poems on the subject of the "New" World. Warrior women have significant roles in several of these poems, either as armed women from Europe or as Amazons who resist, for the most part unsuccessfully, European invaders.

That Amazons figure regularly and sometimes prominently in these texts is no surprise. Armed female characters were expected elements of the epic-chivalric tradition, and two of the most celebrated, armed female protagonists in the Italian tradition, Marfisa and Bradamante, were considered part of an Amazonian heritage.[1] In addition, as Eleonora Stoppino notes, "In the epic-chivalric tradition of the fifteenth-century, both in prose and in verse, the staging of some of the action in the legendary kingdom of the Amazons becomes a commonplace."[2] Furthermore, the European chronicles and reports about the Americas that informed poetic renditions of the "New" World often included references to territories inhabited by only women, which European readers would have associated with the Amazons of classical antiquity. In the first published account of Christopher Columbus's initial voyage, Columbus reports being told of Matitino, an island of women who disdain domestic chores and who wield bows, arrows, and copper spears.[3] The chronicler Peter Martyr of Anghiera gives a similar version of Columbus's claim.[4] Friar Gaspar de Carvajal, who accompanied Francisco de Orellano's expedition in the Amazon region in 1541, recounts that Orellano's men fended off an attack by tall, white Amazons who rule over neighboring Indigenous groups.[5] Such stories, although dismissed by some contemporary historians, provided enticing material for poetic renditions.

Amazons were also pervasive in a variety of literary genres and arts of the sixteenth and seventeenth centuries, for example in biographies of or treatises on illustrious women, the Venetian novel, theater, painting, and opera. In addition, Amazon characters figured in courtly events and official celebrations well into the seventeenth century. For example, during the festivities organized for Queen Christina of Sweden's official entry into Rome in December 1655, the procession in the courtyard of the Palazzo alle Quattre Fontane included twelve cavalrymen dressed as Amazons.[6] Certainly, Amazons represented appealing and intriguing mythical characters for readers and spectators, as did warrior women in general.

As scholars have observed, the extent and variety of representations of Amazons reflected continued preoccupations with and attention to gender roles and their connection to fictional and historical "virile" women. For example, Elissa Weaver writes that "the warrior heroine dramatizes at least admiration and fear of the power of women and of love."[7] Andrea Garavaglia, in his study of Amazons in Italian baroque opera, terms the preoccupations about the prominence of women "anxieties of gynocracy" concerning the reality of contemporary women in positions of social and political influence.[8] In epic poetry, women warriors were not just required variations of archetypes whose adventures readers delighted in following but also loci for discourses about, for example, genealogy and politics, women's relation to war and violence, and gender roles in general.[9] Furthermore, representations of Amazons specifically, symbols of exotic difference, were also deeply connected to anxieties about European encounters with global otherness. They evoked both a long history of tales of ethnographic variety and also pressing questions about contact with non-Christian peoples in the age of European exploration and colonial expansion.

In Italian epic poems about the Americas, which celebrate narratives of Christian evangelization, Amazons are generally portrayed as skilled warriors inimical to male invaders, and their near uniform defeat, conversion, and domestication signal the providential imposition of a patriarchal, Catholic religious, and social order.[10] An early example of a complete epic poem about the American conquest in the Italian vernacular, Giovanni Giorgini's *Mondo nuovo* (1596), focuses on Columbus and the conquest of Mexico. Columbus sends an Indigenous ally, the King of Borichen, to the island of Matitino to meet the Amazons.[11] The warrior women, subdued on shore by an offering of fine Italian wine and made aware that their Carib allies have been defeated, do not take up arms and instead swiftly convert and agree to marry Spanish men.[12] In this episode of reverse hospitality on a Caribbean beach, any threat of violence or harm on the part of the women is immediately cast aside. In the better-known heroic poem of Columbus's voyages, Tommaso Stigliani's *Mondo nuovo* (1617, 1628), Columbus arrives in the Americas with a vast army and engages in numerous battles, including one with the Amazons. They live in the city of Pimpa on an island in the middle of the Amazon River. They resist invaders violently, but after killing their queen, who has fallen in love with an Italian condottiere, they are defeated and agree to convert to Christianity.[13] Again, albeit in a more dramatic and graphic way, the Amazons cannot maintain their independence in a narrative of conquest and conversion.

In this corpus of poems, with the Amazons defeated and converted, Florentine academician Girolamo Bartolomei Smeducci's *L'America* (1650) offers a striking variation on representations of armed women in narratives of Italian navigators in the "New" World.[14] Unlike the poems that focus on Columbus or Amerigo Vespucci's transatlantic movement, *L'America* describes ahistorical travels in Northern Europe and also around the Cape of Good Hope, toward the Horn of Africa. Although the principal narrative thread is Vespucci's providential journey to Brazil, half of the forty cantos take place in Cape Verde or on the African continent and its surrounding seas, as storms and monstrous encounters separate the ships of Vespucci's expedition and, in Canto 8, send him to the southeastern coastlines of the African continent.[15] In contrast with earlier epic poems about the Americas, this one situates Amazons in Africa, as they were described in some classical sources.[16] Vespucci and his crew rely on assistance from Lampedona, the leader of the Amazon guards they encounter in the kingdom of Monomotapa.[17] Later, Lampedona plays a key role in ushering Vespucci and his crew safely to their ships and on to their voyage back around the African continent and to the Americas.

In this epic poem, Vespucci's global navigation—both the voyage itself and its recounting in the Tuscan literary vernacular—is a recognizably Florentine creation. The poem acclaims the travels of a measured and wise Vespucci, an ideal Medici subject who brings the example of Christian piety from Europe to Africa and the Americas. Bartolomei (1584–1662), a member of the Accademia della Crusca and the Accademia Fiorentina, dedicates his poem to Louis XIV and, in the initial canto, praises the French king's imperial forays in the Americas, a reflection of pro-French Medici politics of the time. *L'America* follows the model of the *Odyssey*, not the *Iliad*, and, as allowed by generic conventions, poetic invention eclipses historical accuracy.[18] Certainly the author's decision to write an Odyssean narrative required a meandering, lengthy navigation that accounts of Vespucci's historical voyages did not match. The poem recounts Vespucci's navigations to the Americas, Africa, then back to Brazil, where, in the last canto, Vespucci, Aeneas-like, founds the city of San Salvador de Bahia.[19] There, inhabitants joyfully convert to Catholicism, and Vespucci's nephew marries the Indigenous princess Tunimba. Vespucci is of course a Dantean figure himself, a pilgrim embarking on a daunting journey to another world. *L'America,* in keeping with narrative expectations of the time, comprises a dramatic array of storms, monsters, encounters, and adventures, and pays homage regularly to the Florentine past and Medici power and patronage. In Africa, calcio, an early form of soccer, is played and praised, and Vespucci encounters a telescope-wielding hermit who shows him the (Medici) moons of Jupiter. In several episodes Vespucci converses with members of other European expeditions, a convenient narrative strategy for including Columbus's and Vasco de Gama's navigations, among others. The poem also incorporates elements reminiscent of Dante's *Inferno,* for example when Vespucci speaks with damned souls in a volcano in the Americas. At the end of each canto, a section entitled "Allegoria" explains the Christian symbols featured and the meanings of the various episodes.

In this reinvention of Italian and Florentine global travel, the prominence of Africa, along with the significant role played by an African Amazon, invites further consideration. The geographical reach of the poem reflects not only the framing of Vespucci's travels within global Catholic evangelization but also the legacy of the Medici's ambition to establish colonies in both Africa and the Americas. Grand Duke Ferdinand I (1549–1609) had expanded commercial activities in the port of Livorno and, in 1608, sent an exploratory expedition to Brazil.[20] He hoped to bring, among other resources, sugarcane to Livorno to be refined. In addition, the grand duke attempted to purchase land in Sierra Leone, again with the intention of founding a colony and exploiting local resources, including human ones.[21] Although Spanish and Portuguese claims to Africa and the Americas rendered the Medici plans impossible, references to the Medici's global influence continued to appear in Tuscan literary and cultural production.[22] Even several decades after Ferdinand I's death, representations of Vespucci's navigations served as powerful cultural indicators of the Medici's international influence and potential role in European colonial expansion.

In Bartolomei's *L'America*, the Amazon Lampedona occupies a key position in the narrative of Vespucci's pluricontinental travels and Bartolomei's highly original recasting of Italian and Florentine exploration. By assisting Vespucci, she establishes a connective thread from Africa to the Americas, evoking the Medici desire to participate in imperial endeavors. She also represents a new kind of Amazon for narratives of navigation and conquest: not an antagonist to be converted but a benevolent supporter of Christian endeavors and a generous host to Tuscan outsiders.[23] In *L'America*, Amazons are not an impediment to travel and Christian conversion but helpful ushers to Tuscan travelers. As a warrior woman who falls in love with Vespucci's nephew, Vespuccio, she is an exotic "other" but also a highly legible protagonist as an armed woman who has forsaken love but finds herself struck by Cupid's arrow. Finally, she is the character who helps express a critique of Portuguese colonialism in Africa, echoing denunciations of Spanish violence in the Americas earlier in the poem and implying by contrast that Vespucci and his Florentine companions, representatives of Medici power, are the valid protagonists of global exploration and Christian evangelization.[24] She makes her final appearance as a vision at the end of the last canto, chiding Vespucci for doubting the success of his voyages and urging him to continue his mission in Brazil. Her presence at the end of the poem reinforces her significance as a novel figure that bridges classical antiquity and contemporary contexts.[25]

Lampedona is a composite figure whose origins incorporate both classical and contemporary sources. In canto 12, Vespucci and his crew reach southeastern Africa, and a Portuguese crewman explains that they will go to the land of the King Monomotapa, who trades in gold and ivory. Importantly, it is explained that his people do not worship idols and believe in one God, an indicator that conversion to Christianity may be possible.[26] In line with Diodorus Siculus's depiction of Libyan Amazons, Lampedona comes from a society where traditional gender roles are reversed and the warrior women do not live in isolation:[27]

Ma l'africane, che n'imbruna il sole
Scacciar no, ma ritennero i mariti,
Se marito può dirsi uom, cui mogliera
Com' a mancipio suo superba impera.
Scosse l'armi alla man, tolto il governo
Posero i maschi all'opere femminili,
Donar conocchia, che l'istate e 'verno
Spogli il marito, mentre lana fili.
Altri locaro a più dispregio e scherno
Della cucina a tutti offizi vili,
Sol gli onorar, mentre del proprio letto
Fer gli uomini consorti in tempo eletto.[28]

But the African Amazons, with skin burned by the sun,
did not turn away their husbands, but kept them,
if one can call "husband" a man whose wife
rules haughtily over him as her property.
Wielding their weapons, having taken power,
they put the men to work at women's tasks,
giving the distaff to the men to undo in the summer and winter,
while weaving wool.
Others they placed, with more disdain and contempt,
in the kitchen for all the wretched chores.
The Amazons honored them only at the chosen time,
by bringing them as consorts into their beds.

These verses repeat the classical trope of the sun causing the skin of Africans to darken, and the description of women disdaining traditional women's work is compatible with both Diodorus Siculus and early-modern texts that describe warrior women. Furthermore, the association between Lampedona and the Kingdom of Monomotapa recalls earlier texts that place Amazons in Africa. For example, Amazons from Monomotapa figure in discussions of powerful women in Giovanni Botero's *Relazioni universali* (1598) and in Tommaso Campanella's *Città del Sole* (1602), in which an overview of women rulers includes Bona Sforza, Isabella of Castille, and Amazons who live between Nubia and Monomotapa.[29] In *L'America*, the African Amazons are as militarily skilled and powerful as the Asian ones, and Lampedona, although named after one of the two founding Asian Amazon queens, comes from the Kingdom of Damot, in present-day Ethiopia.[30]

Both literary precedents and travel narratives appear to be sources for Lampedona's geographical origins. Several early-modern travel accounts describe Amazons or warrior women as originating from Damot, and not Monomotapa. For instance, Portuguese missionary Francisco Alvares describes a matriarchal society in Damot in the early sixteenth century, calling the women Amazons and specifying that they live with men.[31] The Portuguese Jesuit João dos Santos mentions Alvares as a source when describing Amazons in and around Damot as well. Dos Santos also claims that they live with men and, in emphasizing the reversal of traditional gender roles, deplores the husbands' femininity: "Their husbands are very cowardly and effeminate, either because of their nature or their custom, which began already many years ago, of doing the tasks that women were supposed to do."[32] Dos Santos refutes earlier accounts of Monomotapa, including that of Filippo Pigafetta, which claim Amazons live there.[33] Indeed, Pigafetta describes Monomotapan warrior women who follow the customs of the ancient Amazons and who fight the king's enemies.[34] The association of Lampedona with Damot and Monomotapa suggests that Bartolomei combined both classical and contemporary sources.

Lampedona, like Vespucci, is an outsider in Monomotapa. She has left Damot because her older sister has been chosen as the new queen. Lampedona, convinced that she possesses skills superior to those of her sister, cannot accept the decision and leaves the kingdom with one hundred companions.[35] Her woes echo the concerns about lineage and legitimacy in Moderata Fonte's *Floridoro* (1581), for instance, in which the warrior woman Risamante, separated from her family at a young age, seeks her rightful inheritance from her twin sister Biondaura, queen of Armenia, who refuses to share her kingdom.[36] Like Risamante, Lampedona must prove her valor and worth away from her homeland, and she is destined to reach posterity through stories of her generosity towards Vespucci and his crew.

Unlike American Amazons in earlier Italian poems, Lampedona remains outside the discourses of conversion, marriage, and domestication. The exchanges between Lampedona and the Europeans are courteous and replete with mutually laudatory pronouncements. Lampedona is characterized only in positive terms, as a warrior who avoids violence and conflict when possible. As is typical in descriptions of warrior women in the chivalric-epic tradition,

Lampedona embodies both the attributes of a skilled fighter and those of a beautiful woman. However, unlike Clorinda, the white Ethiopian warrior woman of Torquato Tasso's *Gerusalemme liberata,* who converts to Christianity upon her death at the hands of Tancredi, Lampedona is Black, and she does not mention conversion in her dialogues with Vespuccio.[37] She is first described in full armor, and, in Amazonian tradition, she has one burned breast.[38] She does not engage in battle but takes Vespucci and his travel companions on a dramatic elephant hunt. Her Black beauty is characterized in Petrarchan terms, which describe her flowing hair as she jumps on her elephant:

Ciò dettò la magnanima donzella,
Nova gloria d'Amazzoni rimonta
D'un leve salto all'elefante in sella,
E a destro corso lo rivolge pronta:
Su' vivi ebani suoi sparsa la bella
Sua negra chioma più che d'oro conta,
Ondeggia all'aure erranti, e 'n vari modi
Or si rivolge, or forma groppi, e nodi.

That said, the noble maiden,
the new glory of Amazons, with a quick jump
gets back in the saddle and quickly turns the elephant
in the right direction.
On her ebony shoulders flows her beautiful
black hair. It shines brighter than gold,
blows in the meandering breezes, and in multiple ways,
now twisting, now forming strands and knots.[39]

The lexicon borrows from the Petrarchan blazon ("sparsa," "chioma," "aure," "nodi"), but the depiction of Lampedona's exotic beauty, and in particular the brightness of her dark skin, recall the figurative language of Giambattista Marino's sonnet, usually identified by the title "la bella schiava" ("the beautiful slave").[40]

Marino's sonnet is worth quoting, as it develops an aesthetic of contrasts between, as well as conjunctions of, night and day, and dark and light:[41]

Nera sì, ma se' bella, o di natura
fra le belle d'Amor leggiadro mostro.

Fosca è l'alba appo te, perde e s'oscura
presso l'ebeno tuo l'avorio e l'ostro.
Or quando, or dove il mondo antico o il nostro
vide sì viva mai, sentì sì pura,
o luce uscir di tenebroso inchiostro,
o di spento carbon nascere arsura?
Servo di chi m'è serva, ecco ch'avolto
porto di bruno laccio il core intorno,
che per candida man non fia mai sciolto.
Là 've più ardi, o sol, sol per tuo scorno
un sole è nato, un sol che nel bel volto
porta la notte, ed ha negli occhi il giorno.

You are black, yes, but beautiful, o charming wonder
of nature among Love's beauties.
Dawn seems dark next to you.
Compared to your ebony skin, your ivory and your lips are lost and dim.
But how or where did the Ancient world and ours
see or feel such a vivid, pure light come out of murky ink,
or a burning thirst emerge from burnt coal?
A servant of she who serves me, here I
carry around my heart a dark snare,
which will never be released by a pale hand.
There where you burn the most, oh sun, only to scorn you
was another sun born, a sun who
carries night in her beautiful face,
and holds daylight in her eyes.[42]

Marino here plays on paradoxes, according to which dawn appears darker than night and darkness emits light. Bartolomei's poem echoes Marino's sonnet, in particular the image of ebony skin as a source of brightness and light. However, in a manner quite different from the construction of the desiring male gaze of lyric poetry, the narrator emphasizes the woman's courage and the contrasting forces of love and war that she embodies:

Ben porta la luna, mentre adduce
Ne' suoi begli occhi ella del sol la luce.
[ . . . ]
Bruna la fronte sì, bruna le chiome,

Ma 'l bruno non le fura il pregio adorno
Di grazia e di beltade, e nota come
Vaga si sposi in lei la notte al giorno:
Com' all'opra risponda il suo bel nome
Da' lampi risonante, mentre intorno
Raggi di beltà vibra, e di valore,
Guerriera in un Marte, e 'n un d'Amore.

She carries the moon [her shield]
and proffers the sun's light from her beautiful eyes.
[ . . . ]
Her forehead is dark, as is her hair,
but the darkness does not rob her of her excellence, adorned
with grace and beauty, and shows how
wonderfully night and day come together in her,
and how her appearance reflects her lovely name,
resonant with lightning flashes,
while rays of beauty reverberate around her, and also of courage;
a warrior woman for Mars, and also for Love.[43]

Here Bartolomei plays on her name Lampedona and *lampo,* lightning, to build upon the image of radiating light and brilliance, which links her beauty to her bravery and her status as a warrior. The accompanying lexicon—"risonante" and "vibra"—recalls the thunder that follows lightning and reinforces the depiction of Lampedona's power as an armed woman. Thus Lampedona is not portrayed as the passive object of desire, but, the verses suggest, she will be a dynamic participant in the adventures of the Tuscan crew.

Although the Amazon's primary function is that of assisting Vespucci with his travels, the text provides a novel depiction of the role of Amazons in narratives of global travel. Lampedona's agency is expressed, for example, through internal monologues, as she must admit her losing battle with Love, a sentiment she only confesses to Vespuccio when she helps the Tuscans escape the now-hostile king of Monomotapa. Several octaves of Canto 17 comprise Lampedona's musing about having fallen in love:

Dunque tai palmi e nobili trofei
Io gloria del mio sesso riportai,
Ond'io gli ceda altrui, che sia felice

Vincitor dell'altera vincitrice?
Un giovin pellegrin vinse guerriera,
Che nemici atterrò, deluse amanti,
Ed è possente a farla prigioniera
A' primi affronti appena offerto avanti,
Consentir deggio, che beltà straniera
Della vittoria del mio cor si vanti?

I, who brought back noble trophies and prizes
for the glory of my sex, must I concede
those to others, so that the man will be happy,
a victor over the lofty woman victor?
A young traveler won over a warrior woman
who defeated enemies and disappointed suitors,
and is powerful enough to make her a prisoner
from the very first encounter.
Must I concede that a foreign beauty
boast of victory over my heart?[44]

Here she rehearses the associations between love and war, both characterized by victory and defeat, and she also conveys pride in her martial accomplishments as a woman ("vincitrice," "guerriera"). These misgivings of a virgin warrior woman in love, while hardly new to this genre, add a certain appeal and depth to the character, who is not simply an unquestioning facilitator of European navigations but a protagonist with ambivalent sentiments about her desires and obligations.

The use of interior monologue for the character of Lampedona continues later on, when the king of Monomotapa, suspicious that his guests are yet another group of violent European invaders, orders Lampedona to kill the Europeans. She expresses her indignation, refusing to go against the law of hospitality and to take arms against those she is supposed to protect:

Io vibrar deggo l'armi
Omicida di quelli, a cui fedele
Dianzi promise protettrice farmi?
Io d'orrori ministra? Io l'infedele
Violatrice d'ospizio? Io quella, ch'armi
La man del fatal ferro, onde n'apporte
D'ospizio in vece a' pellegrini morte?

Must I take up arms
as a murderer of those to whom, faithfully,
I promised earlier to protect?
I, minister of horrors? I, the unfaithful
violator of hospitality? I, the one who, armed
with a fatal sword, does not bring
hospitality but rather death to these travelers?[45]

Again, the monologue conveys the moral considerations of a protagonist with a significant role in Vespucci's travels. Her loyalty to the Tuscans signals a tragic end for her and underscores the unquestionable legitimacy of the Tuscans' voyage and their American destiny. Within the narrative of the Tuscan journey, Lampedona's decision not to follow the king's orders earns her fame in the glorious memory of Vespucci's voyage. She wakes up Vespuccio and tells him to run for the harbor, purposely deceiving him by telling him that Vespucci, his uncle, is probably already at the port and ready to sail. The narrator praises Lampedona:

Esempio di valore e di pietate
Sarai nomata, e'l tuo preclaro nome,
Vivrà immortale con sublime vanto,
Se tal può darti vita un umil canto.

You will be renowned as an example of valor and piety,
and your illustrious name
will live immortally, with sublime praise,
if a humble song can give you life.[46]

The reference to immortality indicates that she will pay with her life for her disobedience to the king and that her reward will be to reach posterity, since fealty to Vespucci has made his journey possible. In the explanation of the allegory of the canto, Lampedona represents sacrifice and loyalty reminiscent of models from classical antiquity: "[R]isplende eroica virtù della donna amazzona, accorsa fra rischi estremi di vita a preservarne il toscano giovine, ponendo perciò a manifesto pericolo la salute propria, a farsi conservatrice dell'altrui . . . [e] come una novella Alceste si proferisce di morire, non per ravvivarne come quella l'estinto consorte, ma sì per mantenerne in vita lo straniero amante; dignissima perciò che le sia intessuta corona d'oliva fra lauri delle sue vittorie"[47] ("The heroic virtue of the Amazon woman shines. She rushed, running extreme risks to her life, to save that of the young Tuscan, putting in obvious danger her own safety, in order to save others . . . She, just as Alcestis, offers to die, not to revive her deceased consort, but instead to keep alive her foreign beloved; very worthy therefore of a crown of olive and laurel branches for her victories"). With this comparison to Alcestis's act of marital sacrifice, the allegorical explanation erases Lampedona's identity as a warrior woman. In choosing love and self-sacrifice over war, she eschews her martial life as an Amazon in order to support the cause of Tuscan global navigation.

Furthermore, Lampedona has a significant voice in expressing misgivings and fear of Portuguese colonialism, implying indirectly that Tuscan voyages are preferable. Indeed, references to Portuguese greed and cruelty are recurring elements of the narrative of Vespucci's navigations around Africa, although these criticisms are never voiced by the Tuscans. When the king of Monomotapa first hears of the arrival of European ships, he explains to Lampedona why they must be prepared to fight the invaders:

> Altre volte infettò nostre marine
> De' rei langari la malnata razza,
> Che da' fulmini suoi porta ruine;
> Mozzabingue lo sa, Quiloa, Mombazza.

> Other times our seas were sullied
> by the wicked race of the Portuguese kings,
> and brought ruin with its blasts.
> Mozambique knows this, and Quiloa, and Mombasa.[48]

His complaint underscores, by contrast, the peaceful and courteous Tuscan crew. When Vespucci and some of his men get to shore, they are surrounded by Amazons mounted on elephants, and Vespucci expresses clearly that he and the Tuscans travel out of curiosity and not to exploit resources or bring harm to other peoples. Theirs is a spiritual and exploratory journey:

> Da questo a noi natìo nido giocondo
> Movemmo a ricercar l'altrui confine,
> Vaghi toscani di vagar pel mondo
> A veder genti e terre pellegrine.

From our happy native nest
we left to seek out others' frontiers,
Tuscans eager to wander the world
and see the expanse of people and lands.[49]

In this rewriting of Vespucci's historical voyage, the pluricontinental traveler makes the case for Florentine exceptionalism, free of greed and thirst for conquest. Lampedona's response serves to corroborate Vespucci's claims and explicitly distinguishes his expedition from an Iberian one:

Ma come mostri al volto, e alle parole,
Tu non discendi no da' lidi ispani.
Uom non se' tu, che l'altrui frutti invole,
Noie recando a' prossimi e lontani.

But as your face and words show,
you do not come from Spanish shores.
You are not a man who covets the fruits of others,
bringing trouble to others near and far.[50]

Lampedona's words serve to legitimize the nonviolent aims of the Tuscans and to support their global endeavors. Through the African Amazon, the narrative confirms stories of Portuguese cruelty, while asserting Florentine respectability.[51] When Lampedona tells Vespuccio he must leave to escape the wrath of the king of Monomotapa, she refers to his fears of Portuguese colonialism:

L'imperator, che qua mantien l'impero,
Io non so come da rapporti indegni
Conceputo ha di voi sospetto fero,
Che qua giungeste a spiar terre, e regni:
Genti discese dal paese ibero
Soggette al re langario, ch'i suoi legni
Altre volte mandò fra questi mari
A far prede, conquiste, e strazi amari.

The emperor, who rules the empire here,
I don't know from which humiliating encounter,
has conceived a strong suspicion

that you came here to spy on lands and kingdoms:
people who came from Iberia,
subjects of the Portuguese king, who sent his ships
other times to these seas
to loot, conquer, and bring bitter torments.[52]

The repeated mentioning of the African leader's concerns about Portuguese incursions echoes the narrative threads of cantos 4 through 7, which illustrate the brutality of Spaniards in the New World at the time of Columbus's expeditions. "Dal paese ibero" alludes to the Iberian peninsula as a whole, implicitly connecting Portuguese to Spanish expansion.

Perhaps most indicative of Lampedona's central role in the story is her appearance in the final canto of the poem as an allegory of glory. Vespucci, after founding a city in Brazil, laments that converted peoples might not remain faithful Christians and that colonial settlements may not bear fruit. Lampedona comes to him at this crucial moment of doubt:

Ne' lamenti il pio tosco oltre seguiva,
Ma l'interruppe un improviso aspetto,
Vaga ninfa gli apparve immortal diva,
Ch'a lui cangiò l'affanno in bel diletto:
La scorta già fra l'etiopa riva
Adorna ravvisò d'abito eletto,
Vergine bella chiara più che 'l sole,
La gloria che del ciel beata prole.

The pious Tuscan continued with his laments,
but a sudden apparition interrupted him:
a graceful nymph appeared before him, immortal goddess,
who changed his worry into delight.
He recognized his guide from before, on the Ethiopian shores,
adorned in her given dress,
a beautiful virgin, more luminous than the sun,
the glory that comes from the Heavens.[53]

Here Lampedona has been transformed into a symbol of glory and goes on to reassure Vespucci that support from Europe is on the way. The description is again Petrarchan: "vergine bella" and the comparison to the sun recall the last poem of the *Rerum vulgarium fragmenta,* the prayer to the Virgin Mary. It is striking that, unlike Italian epic poems that depict divine intervention on the part of the Virgin Mary, angels, and saints, here an African Amazon, albeit in ethereal form, reassures the hero of the success of his Christian mission. Even though there are no physical descriptions or references to Lampedona's warrior attributes, the fragrance she leaves behind evokes her exotic origins:

> Ciò detto ella disparve, e l'aria intorno
> Sparsa tutta lasciò d'arabi odori,
> E novi fregi d'aurea luce al giorno
> Aggiunse da' suoi tremoli splendori.
>
> With that said, she disappeared, and left the surrounding air
> replete with Arabian fragrances,
> and to her resonant splendors
> added new beams of golden light.[54]

While the emphasis remains on light and air, the scent of Arabian perfumes ("arabi odori") links Christian and non-Christian worlds.[55] This last appearance of Lampedona, in the final canto, again connects Africa to America, and although Vespucci's destiny lies in Brazil, not in Damot, the link between the two continents once again underscores the global reach of Vespucci's journey and by extension Medici power.

In the end, Lampedona remains an ambiguous figure. On the one hand, she is a tamed Amazon, dedicated more to love than to war, and, in the context of European global expansion, she plays a role similar to that of the Indigenous woman go-between. On the other hand, she is accorded textual space to express her desires, and she maintains her autonomy with regard to domestication and religious conversion. Most significantly, she conveys to the Tuscans the suffering of Africans at the hands of the Portuguese, connecting Portuguese colonialism in Africa to the cruelties of the Spanish in the Americas that are recounted in other cantos of the poem. Nevertheless, these denunciations of Portuguese and Spanish greed serve to bolster a Florentine-Christian reinvention of Italian navigation, an expression of colonial desire that endures only in poetic expression. Lampedona is both part of a fictional projection of an alternative colonial Italian past and an emblem of the real, historical, early-modern European colonization of Africa.

Notes

1. As Jo Ann Cavallo writes of the representation of Marfisa (or Marphisia) in Matteo Maria Boiardo's *Orlando innamorato* (1495), "There are elements of Marphisia's character and story line that have led readers from the sixteenth century on to associate her with the Amazon queen Penthesilea and Virgil's warrior maiden Camilla" (Jo Ann Cavallo, *The World beyond Europe in the Romance Epics of Boiardo and Ariosto* [Toronto: University of Toronto Press, 2013], 73). Eleonora Stoppino points out that Marfisa is likely a transliteration of Marpesia. See Eleonora Stoppino, *Genealogies of Fiction: Women Warriors and the Dynastic Imagination in the* Orlando Furioso (New York: Fordham University Press, 2012), 83. Marfisa, a protagonist of *Orlando innamorato* and Ludovico Ariosto's *Orlando furioso* (1516, 1532), becomes queen of India and eventually converts to Christianity. Marpesia is also one of the Amazon queens described by Giovanni Boccaccio in *De claris mulieribus* (1361–1362). Bradamante, also an armed heroine of both Boiardo's and Ariosto's poems, marries and founds the Este dynasty of Ferrara.

2. Stoppino, *Genealogies of Fiction*, 66.

3. Christopher Columbus, "Lettera al Santángel," in *Scopritori e viaggiatori del Cinquecento*, vol. 1, ed. Ilaria Luzzana Caraci (Milan: Ricciardi editore, 1996), 37–38.

4. In Peter Martyr's account of Columbus's first voyage, the Spanish expedition sails by the island of Matityna, where only women live. Martyr repeats Columbus's assertion that the armed women are consorts of cannibals. See Peter Martyr of Anghiera, "Sommario dell'istoria dell'Indie occidentali," in Giovanni Battista Ramusio, *Navigazioni e viaggi*, vol. 5, ed. Marica Milanesi (Turin: Einaudi, 1985), 38.

5. Gaspar de Carvajal, *Descubrimiento del río de la Amazonas* (Bogotà: Prensas de la Biblioteca Nacional, 1942), accessed March 15, 2021, http://www.cervantesvirtual.com/obra-visor/descubrimiento-del-rio-de-las-amazonas—0/html/0039c0ae-82b2-11df-acc7-002185ce6064_7.html.

6. Andrea Garavaglia, *Il mito delle Amazzoni nell'opera barocca italiana* (Milan: LED Edizioni universitarie, 2015), 22–24.

7. Elissa Weaver, review of *The Fortunes of the Warrior Heroine in Italian Literature*, by Margaret Tomalin, *Renaissance Quarterly* 36, no. 3 (Autumn 1983): 459.

8. Garavaglia, *Il mito delle Amazzoni*, 13.

9. "The warrior woman is at the juncture of two debates, one about women, which comes out of a civic and courtly context, and the other about war, which comes out of a military context." (Frédérique Verrier, *Le miroir des Amazones. Amazones, viragos et guerrières dans la littérature italienne des XVe et XVIe siècles* [Paris: L'Harmattan, 2003], 213). All translations are mine unless noted otherwise. Eleonora Stoppino, for example, reads warrior women as inextricably connected to questions of dynastic legitimacy in the early-modern courts of Italy: "In the epic-chivalric tradition, the rule of the Amazons is clearly connected with fears of loss of control over reproduction and threats of illegitimacy" (*Genealogies of Fiction*, 71). Gerry Milligan explores women's militancy and the *virago* in the context of Renaissance constructions of gender and war. See Gerry Milligan, *Moral*

*Combat: Women, Gender, and War in Italian Renaissance Literature* (Toronto: University of Toronto Press, 2018).

10. Margaret Tomalin sees the role of warrior women as diminished and strictly circumscribed in epic poetry after the Catholic Reformation, noting a "return to a classical epic and an Amazon heroine who figured in a dramatic and appealing death scene" (Margaret Tomalin, *The Fortunes of the Warrior Heroine in Italian Literature* [Ravenna: Longo, 1982], 221).

11. In Lorenzo Gambara's *De navigatione Christophori Columbi* (1581), the earliest Latin epic poem about Columbus's voyages, armed women who live in caves are the consorts of a bellicose tribe of cannibals. They are mentioned by the Caribs, a rival tribe, as possible allies in the fight against the Spanish invaders.

12. The king of Borichen serves as ambassador to the Amazons and offers them libations: "Così dicendo di spumante vino/tracanna una gran coppa, o fosse Greco,/over Trebiano, o Moscatel più fino,/E invitò ciascuna a bever seco,/ Quai poscia, che gustar licor divino/'Liete certo dal ciel portasti teco/(Dicean) si dolce ben,' grand'accoglienze/Fur fatte a quel con molte riverenze." ("As he says this, he gulps from a large cup of sparkling wine, whether it was the finest Greco, or Trebbiano, or Moscatello, and invited each woman to drink with him, and they said happily, after tasting the divine liquor, 'Of course this most sweet thing you brought with you must come from the heavens!' And they gave him a grand welcome, with many expressions of respect"). Giovanni Giorgini, *Il mondo nuovo* (Iesi: Pietro Farri, 1596), 105, canto 17, octave 36.

13. Stigliani's Amazons receive vicious punishments at the hands of the Spanish. The torture and execution of the Amazons comprise a particularly violent and categorical rejection of female power and cultural otherness.

14. The poet's name is spelled either as Bartolomei or Bartolommei.

15. Historical documents provide evidence of two transatlantic voyages for which Amerigo Vespucci served as navigator: the first, 1499–1500, a Spanish-funded navigation led by Alonso de Ojeda and Juan de la Costa, and a second, 1501–1502, for the Portuguese, led by Gonçalo Coelho. Some historians support claims of a third voyage. Today, the travel accounts by Vespucci considered authentic are three manuscript letters sent to his patron, Lorenzo di Pierfrancesco de' Medici, which did not come to light until the nineteenth century. German cartographer Martin Waldseemüller's *Universalis Cosmographia* (1507) is the first known map to name the continent after Vespucci. The only surviving complete copy is held at the U.S. Library of Congress. See https://www.loc.gov/rr/geogmap/waldexh.html.

16. While the ancient Greeks generally situated the Amazons geographically on the banks of the Thermodon River, in Scythia, Diodorus Siculus writes of an ancient tribe of Amazons who lived in Lybia. See Garavaglia, *Il mito delle Amazzoni*, 148–149.

17. Monomotapa, or Mwene Matapa, also spelled Mwene Mutapa, was a kingdom located in what is now Zimbabwe and Mozambique. The Portuguese invaded the realm in the 1500s. "Mwene Matapa," accessed March 15, 2021, https://www.britannica.com/topic/Mwene-Matapa.

18. In the preface, Bartolomei praises the *Odyssey* as a preferable epic model for Vespucci's voyage and underscores the centrality of the journey rather than the battles of the *Iliad*. Indeed, Bartolomei's poem stands in stark contrast to the scenes of violent conquest in Stigliani's *Mondo nuovo*.

19. San Salvador de Bahia was founded by the Portuguese in 1549. For a consideration of *L'America* as an expression of global epic poetry, see Nathalie Hester, "Transnationalism and the Epic Tradition in Baroque Italian Travel Literature," in *Transnational Italian Studies*, eds. Charles Burdett and Loredana Polezzi (Liverpool: Liverpool University Press, 2020), 107–124.

20. For an overview of Medici interest in Brazil, see Brian Brege, "Renaissance Florentines in the Tropics: Brazil, The Grand Duchy of Tuscany, and the Limits of Empire," in *The New World in Early Modern Italy, 1492–1750*, eds. Elizabeth Horodowich and Lia Markey (Cambridge: Cambridge University Press, 2017), 206–222.

21. See P. E. H. Hair and Jonathan D. Davies, "Sierra Leone and the Grand Duke of Tuscany," *History in Africa* 20 (1993): 61–69.

22. For an excellent study of the Medici reception of the Americas, particularly in the visual arts, see Lia Markey, *Imagining the Americas in Medici Florence* (University Park: Pennsylvania University Press, 2016).

23. While the expedition is acknowledged as funded by the king of Portugal and includes Portuguese crew members, Vespucci is described as the leader and his companions primarily as Tuscans. The downplaying of the Portuguese presence is similar to earlier Florentine poems about Vespucci's travels, such as Raffaello Gualterotti's incomplete *L'America*, dedicated to Grand Duke Cosimo II of Tuscany (Florence: Giunti, 1611). Bartolomei's poem could also be read as Florentine displacing of Luís Vaz de Camões's *The Lusiads* (1572), the Portuguese national epic about Vasco da Gama's voyage around the African continent to India. In *L'America*, the impetus to recast Portuguese colonial endeavors as problematic points to the Medici competition with imperial powers and may also reflect Portugal's loss of influence after the Iberian Union of Spain and Portugal, beginning in 1580, when Philip II of Spain gained control of Portugal.

24. Amazons who fall in love with European warriors are not an unusual occurrence in epic poetry of the time. In Ascanio Grande's *Tancredi* (1632), for example, the Amazon Tigrina loves a Christian knight, Hidro, but perishes in a battle with a rival, Roberta.

25. Carla Aloé reads the absence of American Amazons in the poem as a sign of resignation regarding Italian participation in European expansion. See Carla Aloè, "The New World Mythology in New World Epic Poetry, 1492–1650" (PhD diss., University of Birmingham, 2015), 88–89. However, given the Medici interests in both Africa and America, Lampedona fits into the modern navigational-expansionistic logic of the poem. Lampedona, while an allusion to classical sources and to the past, conveys awareness of contemporary geopolitics and resembles the warrior women described in more contemporary travel accounts. Furthermore, the placing of Lampedona in Africa could also be read as a rejection of the representations of the violent defeat of American Amazons. Bartolomei Smeducci, in reaction to critiques of earlier "New" World poems, for instance, deliberately avoids scenes of violence by Vespucci and his crew against Indigenous Americans.

26. Rulers of the Kingdom of Mutapa, in the Zambezi valley, traded gold and ivory with the Portuguese. The local religion, Shona, has a single deity, Mwari.

27. For a comparison of depictions of Amazons in Diodorus Siculus and Herodotus, see V. Y. Mudimbé, *The Idea of Africa* (Bloomington, Indiana: University of Indiana Press, 1994), 82–92.

28. *L'America*, 159, canto 12, octaves 55–56. I have adapted the spelling, capitalization, and punctuation of the quotations in Italian.

29. Garavaglia, *Il mito delle Amazzoni*, 17.

30. "Esta, che non vestì femminea gonna/Dal dì che nacque, da straniera parte/Colà sen venne amazzona africana,/Prode guerriera al par d'ogni asiana." ("She, who had not worn feminine garb since the day she was born, came there [Monomotapa] from a foreign place, an African Amazon and as brave a warrior as any Asian Amazon"). Bartolomei, *L'America*, 158, canto 12, octave 53. Giovanni Boccaccio mentions the two first Amazon queens, Martesia and Lampedone, in *De mulieribus claris*. Giovanni Boccaccio, *Delle donne illustre*, trans. Giuseppe Bertussi (Florence: Giunti, 1606), 26–28. This particular edition includes further considerations of illustrious women by two authors, including added material on Amazons, a clear indicator of the interest in the subject of warrior women.

31. Giovanni Battista Ramusio, *Navigazioni e viaggi*, ed. Marica Milanesi. Vol. 2. (Turin: Einaudi, 1979), 337.

32. João dos Santos, *Ethiopia Orientale. L'Afrique de l'Est et l'océan Indien au XVIe siècle. La Relation de João dos Santos (1609)*, ed. Florence Pabiou-Duchamp (Paris: Chandeigne, 2011), 328.

33. Dos Santos, 228.

34. Filippo Pigafetta, *Relatione del reame di Congo e delle circonvicine contrade* (Rome: Bartolomeo Grassi, 1591), 73. Filippo Pigafetta's text is an account of the Portuguese Duarte Lopez's travels in West Africa from 1578 to 1587.

35. "Morta la Madre, mentre non succede/A lei l'impero del native regno,/La sorella maggior rimasta erede,/Dispettosa perciò n'arse di sdegno;/Quindi superba la materna sede/Nomò del suo valor teatro indegno,/E con ben cento, che compagne tenne/Al gran Monomotapa ella sen venne." ("With the death of her mother, the reign of her native kingdom was not accorded to her, since her older sister was the heir. Spiteful for that, she burned with indignation, and declared her maternal homeland a place unworthy of her valor. And along with one hundred companions, she went to the great Menomotapa"). Bartolomei, *L'America*, 159, canto 12, octave 59.

36. Fonte's unfinished epic poem is dedicated to Francesco I de' Medici, in commemoration of his marriage to Bianca Cappello. Unlike Lampedona, who remains a virgin and sacrifices herself to help the Tuscans, Risamante learns that her destiny is to give birth to Salarisa, a forebear of the Medici dynasty.

37. Clorinda is the daughter of the king of Ethiopia and a Black Christian queen, but is born white because, as the reason was given, she was conceived beneath a painting of Saint George.

38. "Mostra una mamma la fregiata pelle,/ Ma scompagnata, arsa mentr'altra reste." ("Her adorned skin reveals one breast, unaccompanied; one burnt off, while the other remains"). Bartolomei, *L'America*, 160, canto 12, octave 65.

39. Bartolomei, *L'America*, 163, canto 12, octave 97.

40. Bartolomei's epic poem as a whole reflects stylistically the influence of Marino and *marinisti* poets.

41. The racialization of Petrarchan tropes of female beauty in early-modern Italy has not yet been adequately addressed. For a discussion of Black beauty as reflecting religious

sanctity, see Erin Rowe's consideration of "brilliant blackness" in *Black Saints in Early Modern Global Catholicism* (Cambridge: Cambridge University Press, 2019), 170–205. Rowe's analysis provides compelling models for examining constructions of race in textual production after the Counter-Reformation.

42. Giambattista Marino, *Lira. Parte Terza* (Venice: Ciotti, 1638), 12. For an overview of the presence of Black Africans on the Italian peninsula in the early-modern period, see T. F. Earle and K.J.P. Lowe, eds., *Black Africans in Renaissance Europe* (Cambridge: Cambridge University Press, 2005).

43. Bartolomei, *L'America*, 160, canto 12, octaves 64 and 66.

44. Bartolomei, *L'America*, 228, canto 17, octaves 15–16.

45. Bartolomei, *L'America*, 235, canto 19, octave 60.

46. Bartolomei, *L'America*, 264, canto 19, octave 87.

47. Bartolomei, *L'America*, 269.

48. Bartolomei, *L'America*, 159, canto 12, octave 62. Again, Vespucci's expedition is presented as a Tuscan one, even if it is funded by the Portuguese. In the poem, Indigenous characters denounce directly Portuguese and Spanish violence in Africa and America, not Vespucci or his crew.

49. Bartolomei, *L'America*, 162, canto 12, octave 84.

50. Bartolomei, *L'America*, 162, canto 12, octave 93.

51. Lampedona conveys the king's suspicious attitude towards European visitors, mentioning those "scesi là dall'occaso uomini indegni:/a Mombazza e Quiloa n'arrecar danno,/ comparsi qua con prodigiosi legni,/E fer passaggio i rei pirati poi/che turbar gli africani, a' lidi eoi." ("Unworthy men came there from the West, bringing harm to Mombasa and Quiloa. They appeared here in large ships, and the evil pirates came to disturb the African and Indian shores"). Bartolomei, *L'America*, 162, canto 12, octave 92.

52. Bartolomei, *L'America*, 263, canto 19, octave 78. This echoes the king's words earlier in the canto: "Spiatrici malvagie in vista pie/Finte da' toschi lidi pellegrine. Langariche canaglie, che natie le loro rive loro abbandonar per fine/D'infestar gli africani, e gli'indi eoi, Ricchi di prede ritornando poi." ("Evil spies masquerading as pious, claiming to come from Tuscan coasts, Portuguese scoundrels who left their shores to infest Africa and the East Indies, returning rich from plundering"). Bartolomei, *L'America*, 235, canto 19, octave 56.

53. Bartolomei, *L'America*, 560, canto 40, octave 94.

54. Bartolomei, *L'America*, 560, canto 40, octave 97. Lampedona is described as an "alato spirto," "winged spirit," and because she represents glory, her wings evoke both classical precedents and an angelic figure.

55. The phrase evokes pagan temples, for example the temple of Venus in the *Aeneid*, "ubi templum illi,/ centumque Sabaeo ture calent arae" (I.416–417), ("where the temple and its hundred altars steam with Sabaean incense"). Virgil, *Eclogues. Georgics. Aeneid Books 1–6*, trans. H. Rushton Fairclough (Cambridge, MA: Loeb Classical Library, 1999) 290–1. Ludovico Dolce translates these verses as "un ricco tempio, e cento altari/fumano a lei di *sacri arabi odori*." *L'Enea di M. Lodovico Dolce* (Venice: Giovanni Varisco, 1567), 7 verso. My emphasis.

# PART II

# Gendering Identities

CHAPTER FOUR

# The Princess Nun

## The Familiar Letters of Suor Eleonora d'Este (1515–1575), Daughter of Lucrezia Borgia

GABRIELLA ZARRI
Translated by Giuseppe Bruno-Chomin

When Leonora Barbara was born on July 3, 1515, her mother Lucrezia-Borgia (1480–1519) was thirty-five years old, and—though mindful of her physical and spiritual well-being[1]—she must have already been weak from her continuous pregnancies. The newborn's survival was apparently of concern, since it was decided she should be immediately baptized, as reported by the Ferrarese chronicler Giovanni Maria Zerbinati: "Marti adì 3 luglio la illustrissima madama Lucretia Borgia nostra duchessa partorì una putta, e stava nelle stanze del giardino di Castel Vecchio, e fu battezata con prestezza in corte per dubbio di morte, e li fu posto nome Leonora e Barbara et la tene a batesimo madona Cassandra da Corezo compagna della duchessa"[2] ("On Tuesday the 3rd of July, the very illustrious lady Lucretia Borgia, our duchess, gave birth to a girl, in the garden rooms of Castel Vecchio. She was baptized at court in haste, for fear of her death, and given the name Leonora Barbara, and presented in baptism by the lady Cassandra da Correggio, the duchess's companion"). Leonora Barbara lived at court until the age of five. She was soon deprived of her mother's love. Several days after the birth of her little sister Isabella Maria, on June 15, 1519, Lucrezia "passò di questa vita . . . essendo di parto, e fu sepolta alle suore del Corpo di Cristo"[3] ("departed this life . . . having been in childbirth and was buried in the convent of the sisters of Corpus Domini"). Leonora Barbara was promptly entrusted to the nuns, for her care and education, and she was joined by Isabella Maria, presumably right after she was weaned.

Though current scholarship marks 1523 as the year in which Leonora Barbara entered the convent,[4] an informative letter, from the abbess at the time, indicates that the sisters had in fact been there since 1521. On March 7 of that year, Isabella Maria died. Two days later, Suor Lucida notified Isabella d'Este and poignantly described Leonora Barbara's grief. She also informed her of the tenderhearted decision by Duke Alfonso I (1476–1534) to reunite Lucrezia with her children—the infant Alessandro, born in 1502, who died a month after birth, and the second Alessandro, born in 1514, who died in 1516—in one tomb:[5]

> Noi per la Dio grazia ritrovarsi in assai bona valitudine e maxime la illustrissima dona Eleonora dela quale tucte noi siamo state stupite del corrode ha facto per la morte de la illustrissima sua sorelina, e per nula non voleva che noi la metessimo nela sepolture. Ma invero epsa signorina hera tanto bella così morta che proprio pareva uno anzolo come he. Ho inteso che l'è molto doluta ala excellentia del signore ducha. E benché credo la signoria vostra sapia come la prefata sua excellentia ne ha facto portare qua al monasterio nostro quelli due altri illustrissimi signorini che erano sepulto ali Anzolli. Et cusì inseme con la putina li havemo misse apresso ala illustrissima signora et perché era sua felice memoria ancora tuta intiera ecepto la testa ge havemo misse in braza la illustrissima signorina, cioè Isabella Maria.[6]

> We, by the grace of God, are in very good health, and especially the very illustrious lady Eleonora, whose reaction to her illustrious little sister's death astonished us all, and she did not want us to place her in the tomb. Verily the young lady was so beautiful in death she seemed an angel, as she is. I understand his excellency the duke is most aggrieved. And I believe your ladyship is aware that his excellency had the two young boys, previously buried in the Church of Santa Maria degli Angeli, brought to our convent. Together with the little girl, we placed them next to that most illustrious lady, as her body was intact save for the head, which we laid in the arms of the very illustrious young lady, Isabella Maria.

Could the young princess have attended that somber ceremony, during which the bodies of those children were returned to their mother? Lucrezia had anxiously awaited their births and grieved their deaths, as she wrote in letters to her in-laws, Francesco Gonzaga and his wife, Isabella d'Este.[7] Even if Leonora Barbara had not been permitted to observe, she would have, in the years that followed, sensed the presence of her mother within the convent walls, embracing her beloved sisters and the brothers—previously intombed in the Dominican Church of Santa Maria degli Angeli—whom she had never met. That motherly presence she could evoke daily, while walking the floor of the choir and the Church of Corpus Domini, where together, under a single tombstone, lay her grandmother Eleonora, her mother Lucrezia, her siblings, and later her father Alfonso.

Leonora Barbara's time at court was too brief to profit from the education and cultural refinement afforded to her older brothers under Lucrezia Borgia's attentive gaze. It was, however, enough to instill in the "illustrissima signorina" (very illustrious young lady) an awareness of ducal dignity and familial affection.

We know that Lucrezia had entrusted the education of her eldest son, Ercole, to the celebrated humanist Gian Giorgio Trissino. She conveyed her husband Alfonso's satisfaction with Trissino's undertaking and also asked if he could find the boy "un maestro di grammatica" (a Latin instructor).[8] This occurred on September 18, 1515, just two months after Leonora Barbara's birth. Trissino's educational approach is not revealed in their correspondence. And two of Lucrezia's letters from the following year indicate he was often away from court. Ercole's progress was nevertheless guaranteed by a tutor, who attested to his accomplishments: "a vostro contento vi advisamo come el suo preceptore sino adesso non potria restare di lui più satisfacto, né cum magiore speranza de reportarvi honore, et cum facilità, secundo che pensamo habiati anche inteso per sue lettere"[9] ("you will be pleased to know that thus far his tutor could not be more satisfied with him, nor have greater hope of bringing you honor, and effortlessly, as we believe you have also understood from his letters").

Leonora Barbara could not partake in this instruction. But her mother likely provided the rudiments of reading by surrounding her with educated young women and by telling edifying and exemplary stories. It was the Ferrarese convent of Corpus Domini, however, that became Leonora Barbara's training ground for a solid cultural and social education. Her arrival at the convent following her mother's death is confirmed by the attentive chronicler Zerbinati. In 1523, he relayed the important news that Duke Alfonso I had donated five properties to the Hospital of Sant'Anna to aid the Poor Clares of Corpus Domini and to support his young daughter. The reason the donation was made to the hospital, and not the convent, is explained by Zerbinati and is found in the original deed.[10] Since the Poor Clares had taken a vow of poverty, they were not permitted to own land. They could, however, receive alms:

> 1523 adì 23 luglio il signor duca nostro ha donato cinque possessioni con cinque vache e pecore cinquanta per possessione alle suore del Corpo di Cristo, nelle quali suore sono una figliola del duca d'età de 8 anni che ha nome Leonora et Barbara, la quale vi mandò il duca doppo la morte della duchessa sua madre per farla governare, le quali suore hanno da fare ogni dì overo ogni settimana limosine assai. Ma notta perché le suore non possono havere beni stabili, il duca ha datto le dette cinque possessioni all'Ospedale di Sant'Anna et il priore di Sant'Anna ha da governare dette cinque possessioni e dare ogni mese alle dette suore ducati trenta per fare la elemosina et per loro bisogno.[11]

> On 23 July 1523, our lord duke donated five properties, along with five cows and fifty sheep, to the sisters of Corpus Domini, to whose care he had entrusted his eight-year-old daughter, Leonora Barbara, following the death of her mother, the duchess. Each day, or rather each week, the sisters give abundant alms. Yet seeing as the nuns are not permitted to own land, the duke gave the five properties to the Hospital of Sant'Anna. And the prior of Sant'Anna is to tend to the land and give the said sisters thirty ducats each month for alms and to address their needs.

This confirms that the young princess entered the convent at age five to be "governata" (cared for) and educated, and the lavish donation made three years later indicates that she remained there. This decision to keep her there was perhaps made by her father, or it could have been Leonora Barbara's express wish, as attested by the famous physician Antonio Musa Brasavola, who had dedicated a written work to the princess-nun.[12]

It is well known that in the early-modern period, female honor—or rather, a girl's virginity—was tightly connected to the honor of her family and that parents thought the best way to protect daughters was to keep them home or send them to a convent to be brought up and educated. As a result, convents allowed even very young girls to enter. Beyond relying on convents to protect and educate their daughters, parents also chose this placement for another reason: many families could not afford to provide all of their daughters a dowry that was appropriate to their rank. Convents therefore tended to house young women of aristocratic or wealthy families, who secured a cell for them in which they could live with a *conversa* (a woman living in a monastery who has not taken vows and who could act as a servant) and with any nieces who might later enter. This happened most frequently in the oldest and most prestigious convents, where the girls professing vows belonged to the highest social echelons. The many convents in cities were of a variety of levels that corresponded to the wealth and social status of their residents.

The strong bonds that united families and female religious communities had the effect of transforming convents into what could be considered princely residences that offered healing and rest and a place to stay from time to time, or way stations during trips. In Italy, the use of the prince's apartment in male monasteries, such as the one used by Cosimo de' Medici in San Marco in Florence, or in female convents, like those used by Vittoria Colonna in Rome and Viterbo or by the Este family in Ferrara, was a privilege that was granted with approval through the pre-Tridentine period. After the Council of Trent (1545–1564), this practice was prohibited, even if we still find numerous exemptions, for example, in the case of Suor Eleonora d'Este.

The convent of Corpus Domini in Ferrara was not just the family mausoleum and place of healing and rest for Este duchesses, where they convalesced after childbirth or a lengthy illness. It was also the heart of the city's most refined nobility. The young girls who entered and professed could receive a suitable education and live in a convent with a reputation for great piety. The memory of the Caterina de' Vigri (1413–1463) lived on. The "saint" had been one of the convent's founders and a novice mistress for many years before being sent to Bologna to establish a new convent of the Poor Clares.[13]

Caterina de' Vigri was educated by her father's family and at the Este court. She could write, miniate, paint, play instruments, and compose poetry. She was also among the first women in Italy to write a book, which was printed just a few decades after her death.[14] Caterina transmitted the cultural heritage she had acquired to her community and newly professed sisters, along with a solid religious education.

What remained of Caterina's legacy at the Ferrarese convent? We know that, while in Ferrara, she had compiled a formulary of letters to serve as a model for properly relating with religious superiors, civil authorities, and benefactors. Among these letters were spiritual missives intended for young ladies who had recently arrived at the convent, or wished to enter it, persuading them to accept the Lord's call.[15] The formulary, which certainly had a practical function, could also be used for teaching and learning to write, as was the case at the Sforza court,[16] and likely also at the Este court. Caterina brought the formulary with her to Bologna, which was needed for this new experience, along with her "libro devoto" (holy book), which represented the summa of her spiritual teaching.[17] Caterina also brought the breviary she had personally copied and illuminated, which was used to teach younger nuns.[18] She also brought along a variety of books to spiritually nourish her fellow sisters,[19] as well as her viola to accompany songs of praise to the Lord.

We cannot, however, assume the Ferrarese convent had been stripped of its writings and assets. Though Caterina had left for Bologna with many of the "senior" sisters, some of whom were highly cultured, including Illuminata Bembo, the continuity of devout and educated women in Ferrara, distinguished by birth or reputation, must have profoundly influenced the community's cultural and spiritual character. When Leonora Barbara arrived at Corpus Domini, conditions were favorable for an excellent education, as will be shown below. I cannot be certain whether her confident grasp of Latin and Greek was acquired from older sisters at the convent or whether Leonora Barbara, who enjoyed certain privileges as a professed nun, made use of an external tutor. A musical education was perhaps easier to come by, since nearly all convents, especially those in Ferrara, had expert organists and could instruct the sisters and *educande* (convent boarders) in music and song.[20] Notwithstanding recurrent prohibitions, excellence in music could certainly be achieved through the use of external instructors. In Bologna, for instance, there were 150 nun musicians between the sixteenth and the eighteenth centuries.[21] And at the end of the sixteenth century, Modena would also be known for its nun musicians, when it became capital of the Este state.[22] We do not know if it was typical in the Ferrarese convent to perform comedies or other theatrical works for entertainment or during religious festivities, as Florentine nuns were famous for doing,[23] but it is certain that poetry recitation and liturgically inspired plays accompanied the celebration of religious investiture and profession.[24]

Thus with this limited information and many uncertainties, we leave the princess to her education and instead consider her "career" as a professed nun. Despite her early entry into Corpus Domini, Leonora Barbara made her profession in 1529, at the age of fourteen. She took the name Suor Eleonora, in memory of her paternal grandmother. This date is confirmed by Alfonso I's testamentary disposition from that same year, whereby he left a considerable sum of money to the convent, and his newly professed daughter, evidently in the form of a dowry.[25] To be sure, the Este princess enjoyed special privileges from the very beginning, chief among them the age at which she professed. If Caterina Vigri's memory were still alive, the Poor Clares of Ferrara would have been aware of her *Ordinazioni* (regarding the governance of the convent) in Bologna, where young women could only be accepted at age sixteen.[26] But in Suor Eleonora's case, there were even more noteworthy exceptions—to begin with, financial ones. Her father had left six thousand gold ducats for her personal use. These funds were to be administered by agents of the Hospital of Sant'Anna, who were required to pay the nun 900 lire annually. Alfonso I also charged his heir, Ercole II (1508–1559): "a provvederli per tutor il tempo della vita di essa Suora Eleonora de tutte quelle cose, siano di che sorte si vogliano essere, che serano per suo bisogno e honesti suoi apetiti, e secondo che li rechiederà e farà adimandare"[27] ("to provide that for the remainder of her life Suor Eleonora be afforded any and all things, of whatever nature they may be, that she shall need or desire, and according to which she requests and asks").

We would also like to know more about Suor Eleonora's living arrangements within the convent. In 1483, the sisters of Corpus Domini inherited a prestigious residence from Count Giovanni Romei, who came from an affluent merchant family.[28] His second wife, Polissena di Meliaduse, was an Este relation, and he had become Duke Ercole I's secret advisor. The Romei House, now a museum,[29] was adjacent to the convent; the year he died, Giovanni left the building to the Poor Clares. The sisters immediately incorporated the house into the convent, though some rooms were still occupied by Giovanni's widow.[30]

It was perhaps in that space—a prime example of fifteenth-century architecture—that Eleonora d'Aragona and Lucrezia Borgia stayed when they came to rest or to pray. And it was perhaps also in that part of the convent that Suor Eleonora established her apartment, later to be joined by her niece Lucrezia, the illegitimate daughter of her brother Ercole II and Diana Trotti.[31] The crown prince's eldest daughter, who had been lovingly accepted by his wife Renée de France (1510–1575)—who came to Ferrara in 1528—was sent to Corpus Domini to be looked after by her aunt. This likely took place in 1530 since, at the time of her death, in 1572, Suor Lucrezia had humbly served the convent for forty-two years.[32] On her tomb, she is praised with the words "moribus ac Sanctitate insignis"[33] (distinguished for conduct and sanctity) and is accorded the title "beata" (blessed) in the Franciscan Martyrology.[34]

The Romei house was equipped with a chapel and a study, as well as numerous rooms with fireplaces. During the sixteenth century, Cardinal Ippolito II (1509–1572) had the residence enhanced with frescoes and adornments, which

Figure 4.1. Courtyard of the Romei House (fifteenth century), incorporated into the Corpus Domini convent in 1483, where Suor Eleonora perhaps established her apartment. Wikimedia Commons, https://commons.wikimedia.org/wiki/File:Casa_romei,_cortile,_08.JPG.

made the *salone d'onore* (hall of honor) all the more majestic. By this time, the cardinal was without a residence in Ferrara. He had given the palazzo San Francesco, his paternal inheritance, opposite the convent, to his sister-in-law Renée. Whenever he passed through Ferrara during the course of his restless life, he would briefly stay in the beautiful fifteenth-century home, now part of the convent, where he could visit with his sister and niece.[35]

It is within the beautiful setting of the Romei house that we can envision the organ Suor Eleonora had decorated by Battista Dossi in 1537, as confirmed by a ledger recording the purchase of paints.[36] This instrument was accompanied by a harpsichord, painted by Tommaso da Treviso, for Suor Eleonora's personal use, and by an organ for the convent, adorned with carvings and paintings.[37] It was likely in this setting that concerts took place, captivating Cardinal Ippolito, who no doubt arranged meetings between his sister and the greatest musicians of the time. The princess was in fact a skilled performer. She may have also been a composer, as Laurie Stras has suggested with respect to an anonymous collection of motets, printed in Venice in 1543: *Musica quinque vocum: motteta materna lingua vocata.*[38]

Suor Eleonora had undoubtedly become an accomplished musician, having begun her musical studies at an early age. But her knowledge extended to other disciplines, and she cultivated a variety of interests. In addition to Latin and Greek, as previously mentioned, she was also well versed in the natural sciences. Aside from having been elected abbess at the young age of nineteen, Suor Eleonora was also, for a considerable time, the convent apothecary. In this role, she prepared medications for her fellow sisters. In convents, pharmaceutical knowledge was typically learned from senior officials and developed with practice and training. The custom of selling "medicamenti segreti" (secret medicines) or specialized products beyond the convent walls, for which various convents were renowned, must have greatly refined their preparation. The Dominican convent of San Pietro Martire in Bologna, for instance, was famous for an "unguento dorato" (golden ointment), which it shipped far and wide. And the convent of Corpus Domini, founded by Caterina Vigri, specialized in the preparation of a "cerotto," or ointment, "giovevole per le cadute" (beneficial for falls).[39]

Suor Eleonora was surely unsatisfied with being an "obedient" apothecary, merely fulfilling a role she had been assigned; she wanted to broaden her knowledge. We have no way of knowing if she recalled her mother's use of rhubarb.[40] But we do know she was acquainted with one of the most distinguished court physicians, whose services were used by both her father Alfonso I and her brother Ercole II: Antonio Musa Brasavola (1500–1555), the Ferrarese physician and naturalist. Brasavola was the author of a celebrated treatise on medicinal simples, printed in 1536.[41] Two years later, he published *Examen omnium syruporum quorum publicus usus est* (*An Examination of All Syrups for Common Use*),[42] which he dedicated to Suor Eleonora. From this dedication, we learn that the princess-nun regularly worked as an apothecary, had discussed syrups with Brasavola ("quum praecedentibus mensibus de syrupis inter nos sermo incidisset") ("when we had occasion to discuss syrups in these past months"), and was an expert in medications.[43] We also learn that her passion for work and study by no means detracted from her prayers. Brasavola, also known for his religious devotion and doctrine, in fact praised Suor Eleonora, whom he believed embodied the two exemplary models of female religious life: Martha and Mary. These typically contrasting symbolic representations of active and contemplative life are, in Brasavola's view, reconciled by Suor Eleonora. He maintains that she privileged the contemplative life but was also dedicated to the service of her fellow sisters, and that she voluntarily chose the contemplative life and had to overcome her father's initial reluctance. He reports that she always attended choir and prayed and that at night, while the nuns slept or labored, Suor Eleonora prepared medicines to aid her ailing sisters—thus called to her role like Martha. For Brasavola, her decision to remain at the convent was doubly praiseworthy: rather than marrying an illustrious prince, she chose to wed Christ, and she renounced becoming a duchess, empress, or queen, to partake in the joys of heaven and paradise.

Brasavola's dedication is of interest because it provides information about the Este princess's daily activities and cloistral life. But it also reveals a great deal about her knowledge and education. Indeed, we must assume she understood the Latin treatise and dedication, as well as the hexameter in Greek from the Pseudo-Phocilis embedded at the bottom of the text.

Little more can be known about Suor Eleonora's "secular" knowledge except for what little is revealed in the letters we will examine.[44] But another work by Brasavola, *La Vita di Iesù Cristo* (*The Life of Jesus Christ*), provides additional information about her religious and intellectual interests. This dense work, whose relevance to Este religiosity and Suor Eleonora I have emphasized on several occasions,[45] has largely been interpreted from a heterodox perspective. Gonatas Liboni, an exception to this trend, highlights the attention paid by Brasavola to one of the religious controversies of the time: the precept of fasting.[46] Adriano Prosperi has now contributed to a comprehensive view of the text, having undertaken the monumental task of compiling a critical edition.[47]

Apart from being a learned naturalist and an author of numerous scientific treatises, Brasavola was also deeply religious. His father initially urged him toward an ecclesiastic career, but he quickly abandoned this path to pursue his studies. The Ferrarese doctor had attained intimate knowledge of Savonarolian thought and embraced the Dominicans' moral vigor, disdain for abuse by the clergy, and concern for reforming the Church. He was also certainly familiar with the writings of Erasmus and the Northern European reformers, which he firmly refutes, as he does with the precept of fasting. He instead prefers models of Christian spirituality, including the Carthusian Ludolph of Saxony and Savonarola, whom he describes as blessed.

As Ercole II's personal physician, Brasavola was close to the Este court. But he was also in contact with the convent of Corpus Domini, where his sister, to whom he dedicates part of his work on the life of Christ, had professed and taken the name Teodora. Suor Eleonora turns to the esteemed naturalist for an explanation of Christ's life and to resolve doubts raised by conflicting preachers and confessors. This request forms the basis of a dialogue between the princess-nun and the naturalist—real or fictious—with which Brasavola opens his *Vita di Iesù Cristo*. The conversation takes place in the late 1530s, at a time when the Este court hosted preachers from different orders, reformers protected by Renée de France, and even Calvin himself.[48] I will not analyze the text here. However, I would like to stress the genuine cultural and religious interest displayed by Suor Eleonora. Her exploration of matters of faith and religious practices confirms that the princess-nun was able to reconcile the roles of Martha and Mary within the convent, as Brasavola observes, while also leading an extremely privileged life.

One of the privileges enjoyed by the princess concerned spiritual life and the observance of rules. Suor Eleonora was granted permission by Pope Paul III to recite the breviary of Francisco Quiñones, cardinal of Santa Croce, in her room, in the company of fellow sisters, and thereby satisfy her choral obligations. This permission was received by way of Cardinal Giorgio d'Armagnac, the French ambassador in Rome and her brother Ippolito's friend. She was also permitted to remove her habit during the summer and in the event of illness.[49] The granting of this privilege shows that Suor Eleonora's situation was by and large atypical. It confirms that she resided in her own apartment, had many lay sisters at her service, could lead a semiprivate life, and fulfill her choir obligations in her room. This papal concession is not, however, indicative of a relaxation of rules or noncompliance. Rather, it emphasizes a profoundly modern religious sensibility. The breviary of the Franciscan Cardinal Quiñones was the most liturgically advanced at the time: the entire Psalter was recited in a week; the main parts of the Holy Scriptures were read once a year; and daily recitations were approximately the same length. This breviary was commissioned by Clement VII, accepted by the Jesuits, and condemned by traditionalists. It did not receive approval from Paul IV and was ultimately replaced with the breviary of Pius V.[50] During the period it was in use, Suor Eleonora made a prudent and innovative choice.

Let us now return to the princess-nun's daily life. We have ascertained that her time was divided between choral prayer, or private recitation of the breviary—as required by rule—work as an apothecary—an obligation or labor of love—and music, for the liturgy and choir, but perhaps also for pleasant concerts before an audience. Part of Suor Eleonora's time was also spent in the convent parlor, where, like a titled duchess, she received petitions that she later forwarded to her brother the duke. This is particularly evident in letters sent to Ercole II. Because of these unique relationships, or others of a political and confidential nature, she was granted "ad personam" permission in 1537 by the Commissary of Cismontane Franciscan Observants to speak and negotiate with laypersons, even in secret and without witnesses.[51] This exemption was many times reaffirmed and reinforced by a special privilege granted during the final years of her life, to have a grate installed: "in qualunque luoco di detto Monasterio quale a essa Madre ne verrà più comodo; acciò che per iservitio suo possa detta R.da Ill.ma spedire if suoi daffari a detta Gratta, non potendo ella per la lunga sua indispositione andare a l'ordinario Parlatorio"[52] ("in whichever part of the convent is most convenient for the Reverend Mother, so that the Most Illustrious Reverend Mother can there tend to her affairs, as she is unable to visit the regular parlor, due to a prolonged illness"). This concession is dated June 16, 1571, four years prior to Suor Eleonora's death. Yet as the document attests, the Este princess had been ill for some time, which is also the reason why she was accorded various privileges. In 1556, for example, the provincial minister of Bologna granted Suor Eleonora the ability to leave the convent for a period, at the request of Duke Ercole II and her physicians. The time and place were not specified, but she could bring along "tre o ver' quattro di queste suore che la governano, presuponendo sempre che non habino fatto il votto de la clausura"[53] ("three or four of the sisters who care for her, provided they had not taken the vow of enclosure"). Sister Eleonora's illness must have indeed been serious, since she felt the need to draw up a will. The following year, Pope Paul IV gave her permission to bequeath her assets to one or more nuns at the convent and to have masses and offices said for her soul.[54]

It must be remembered that, aside from her father's inheritance, of which she could dispose "pro eius arbitratu" ("at her discretion"),[55] her brother Ercole II had left her "in testamento Mille Scuti d'oro di legato, solamente a beneficio e commodo suo"[56] ("one thousand gold scudi, solely for her benefit and comfort"). It also warrants noting that the convent and sisters benefitted as well. On May 22, 1571, Suor Eleonora was given permission by the minister general of the order to bequeath money to the nuns and for requiem masses after her death.[57] Notwithstanding the vow of poverty, the princess-nun could dispose of a considerable sum of money, which she invested, at least in part, in the convent or in carrying out her duties of office. On the basis of the letters sent to her brother, we can in fact assume she was mindful of financial matters.

The image of Suor Eleonora that we have reconstructed thus far, on the basis of external testimonies, can be completed and enriched by observing her own voice in correspondence with her family. I will here examine a sizeable number of letters at the Este Archive in Modena, addressed to her brother Ercole II and her nephew Alfonso II (1533–1597).

The letters signed by Suor Eleonora, and sent to her relatives, are contained in a single envelope, archivally arranged, and stored in two separate folders, which bear the name of the recipients. The first folder bears the inscription: "Eleonora d'Este (suor) di Alfonso I al fratello Ercole II 1530(?)–1552" ("Eleonora d'Este [sister] daughter of Alfonso I to her brother Ercole II 1530(?)–1552"); the second reads: "Eleonora d'Este figlia d'Alfonso I al nipote Alfonso II. 1571" ("Eleonora d'Este daughter of Alfonso I to her nephew Alfonso II. 1571").[58] There are a total of twenty-six letters addressed to her brother. The first sixteen have dates and are arranged chronologically from the year 1530 to the year 1552. The other ten letters are undated, with the exception of one to her brother, in which she grieves for the "caxo pericolosissimo occorso" ("most dangerous incident that occurred") and rejoices in his deliverance. They are separated from the others by a half sheet of green paper, upon which is written "senza data" (no date). Only two are addressed to her nephew, both written in 1571.

I will examine the letters to deepen our understanding of Suor Eleonora's life and education within the convent. And I will consider her status as a princess, with the aim of identifying, wherever possible, expressions of sentiment, esteem, and mutual aid among members of her family. But it is first necessary to chronologically contextualize her correspondence, which spanned a considerable number of years, albeit with varying regularity.

The date of the first letter—determined to be uncertain by the archivist—correctly reads 1530. The *superscriptio* (superscription) follows the conventional chancery formula: "Herculi Estensis Duci Dignissimo et fratri admodum Coll. mo" (Ercole d'Este Most Worthy Leader and Esteemed Brother); the destination is "Mantue vel ubi fuerit" (Mantua or wherever he may be); the *subscriptio* instead reads as follows: "Obsequentissima soror sor Eleonora Estensis manu propria subscripsit Celeriter" ("Signed in haste by Suor Eleonora d'Este your most obedient sister").[59] We can assume, on the basis of the designation "Duci dignissimo" (Most worthy leader), that Ercole, not yet a titled duke, was leader of a military outfit stationed in Mantua, or thereabouts. Since the prince was born in 1508, he was twenty-two or twenty-three years old at the time of this letter, whereas his sister was only fifteen. That Eleonora signs "Suor" (Sister) confirms that she took her vows before age sixteen—as mentioned above, contrary to Caterina Vigri's *Ordinazioni*—and that the Poor Clares of Ferrara followed different rules. By then, the young prince had been married to Renée de France for two years. He already had a daughter out of wedlock, who was destined, as has been said, to join her aunt in the cloister. Ercole II's first legitimate daughter, Anna, was born in 1531. But in the letters, there is only mention of the firstborn son in 1533. Neither their father's death, in 1534, nor Ercole II's succession are mentioned, and their brother Ippolito is named only once. The largest grouping of letters date from 1540 to 1552 and end seven years before the prince's death.

Though lacking in detail of family events and emotional ties, the letters reveal deep sentiments veiled behind deferential and formal language. The first missives sent by Suor Eleonora, while still a teenager, are particularly important in this regard. In a letter of March 27, 1530, for instance, she reluctantly writes to her brother: "io non harei ardire de scrivere . . ." ("I would not have the courage to write . . .") and addresses him as "Celsitudine" ("Highness"). She then acknowledges his many virtues, "è amatrice de pietade et misericordia che de la rigorosa iustitia" ("a lover of piety and mercy and of rigorous justice"), and is confident he cares for her "de vehemente amore e singolare dillectione" ("with ardent love and singular affection"). Another dateless letter appears to be written by a younger Suor Eleonora, wherein she addresses her brother as "Invittissimo" ("Most Indomitable"), "Illustrissima Signoria" ("Most Illustrious Lordship"), and "Eccellenza vostra" ("Your Excellency"), without neglecting to add "totto affectu" ("with total affection").[60] She continues to address her brother as "Your Excellency" in subsequent letters but with fewer signs of veneration and deference, which are replaced with a kiss on the hand.

The forms of salutation used by the princess-nun also indicate a notable shift in tone from formal to more confidential. She initially signs, "Obsequentissima soror sor Eleonora" ("Most obedient sister Suor Eleonora");[61] then "Servula et soror Eleonora" ("Servant and sister Eleonora");[62] "Devotissima servitrice sore Eleonora" ("Most devoted servant suor Eleonora");[63] "Sorella et Serva Sore Eleonora" ("Sister and servant Suor Eleonora");[64] and finally "Humile serva"[65] ("Humble servant"); "buona serva et sorella"[66] ("faithful servant and sister"); and all the more often, "Buona serva" ("faithful servant").

It is also worth mentioning a letter from 1533, in which the nun rejoices at the birth of Alfonso II, her brother's firstborn son: "Et vixitado con questa mia de gaudio piena la excellentia vostra, con la qualle applaudo et mi congratulo de la a se concessa masculina prole, per la cui quanta letitia la mente mia habia concepto, maxime per amore de V. S., im breve parole explicare nol potrei" ("I write to Your Excellency full of joy and to congratulate you on the birth of your son, which has brought me great happiness, especially because of my love for Your Excellency, which in few words I could not express"). She concludes the letter by sending her regards to his wife and the whole Este family, including her younger brother Francesco, and she appears somewhat saddened by the distance between them: "Quella si dignerà alla Illustrissima sua consorte racomandarme, applaudendo con lei della consolatione sua. Et ad ambe dui basio la mane. La Signoria Vostra etiam non li serà grave ex parte mea fare reverentia allo Excellentissimo Signore nostro padre et racomandarmi ad epso. Et similiter ricordarmi al Reverendissimo Monsignore fratello nostro et al signore don Francesco. Et in domino omnes bene ac felliciter valleant. Ex sacro monasterio Corporis Christi. Ferrarie"[67] ("You will please give my regards to your very Illustrious wife, whom I applaud and congratulate. And I kiss both your hands. Your Lordship will also please give my respects to our most Excellent father, to whom I commend myself. And also give my regards to our most Reverend brother and to *don* Francesco. And in God all things may be good and happy. From the holy monastery of Corpus Domini. Ferrara").

In another letter, Eleonora grieves for the danger that befell her brother and expresses joy at his escape. We are unable to contextualize this event since the letter is undated. But it is important to observe her concern for the prince's welfare, her regret at not being able to visit him, and her delight at his improved health:

> **Ill.mo e Excellentissimo Signore Fratello Osservantissimo**
> Non potendo presentialmente Vostra Signoria Illustrissima vixitare, come rechiederia il fraternale amore e dillectione che è tra nui, dunque per la presente mia quella vixito et saluto con ogni a me possibile reverentia basiandoli la mano, condolendomi quanto poscibile sia del caxo pericolosissimo occorso, il qualle mi è stato di tanta mesticia et gravissimo cordoglio che exprimere nol potrei. Ma rengratio il Clementissimo Idio se dignato liberare Vostra Excellentia da tanto pericolo. Et ha exaudito le prece che di continuo a sua Maestà Divina per quella si effondono

nel monastero nostro et molto più si augumentarano in rendere laude al Sommo Iddio de tanto dono et gratia consequita.[68]

**Most Illustrious, Excellent, and Observant Brother**
As I could not visit Your Most Illustrious Lordship in person, as would be required by the fraternal love between us, I come to you with this letter, with all possible reverence, and kiss your hand. And I very much condole with you for the most dangerous incident that occurred, which caused me great sadness and grief, such that I could not express. Yet I thank our most Merciful God who has deigned to deliver Your Excellency from such danger. His Divine Majesty has answered the prayers that continually flow forth from our convent, which shall be increased to render praise to God for the gift and grace obtained.

On another occasion, Suor Eleonora again conveys her happiness for the prince's "buon essere" (well-being) and for his visit to Ferrara; she rejoices, thanks God, and implores him to visit her soon.[69] But the cloistered princess's participation in the politics involving her brother and the Este state is primarily revealed in one letter. Suor Eleonora writes as follows regarding the recapture of Brescello, an important territory north of the Po, in a strategic location, coveted by many neighboring and foreign powers: "La buona nuova havuta della recuperazione di Bersello m' ha apportato infinito piacere et contentezza et tanto più maggior sodisfatione mi è stata quanto che l'Eccellentia Vostra si degni farmi favore di esserne avisata da lei et che mi tenga per quella vera e fidelissima serva ch'io le sono. Onde ne bacio le mani a Vostra Eccellentia ringraziandola quanto più posso. Con che facendo, humilmente mi raccomando alla sua desideratissima gratia pregando Nostro Signor Dio la conservi longamente"[70] ("The good news of the reconquest of Brescello has brought me infinite pleasure and contentment. And I am all the more gratified inasmuch as Your Excellency deemed me worthy of informing and considers me a true and faithful servant, as I am. Thus I kiss Your Excellency's hands and thank you profusely. And I humbly commend myself to your most desired graces and pray that God grant you long life").

We would also like to know whether the letters, the only extant writings by Lucrezia Borgia's daughter, disclose something about her erudition. In this case, the letters from her youth prove more significant. To begin with, they are personally signed. It was common practice in royal correspondence for a secretary to compose letters clearly and correctly. In convents, this task was entrusted to a chancery official, and Suor Eleonora's letters were penned by different individuals who alternated in this role. The letter dated March 27, 1530, for instance, was composed by a scribe and bears the princess's signature; it reads as follows: "Obsequentissima soror sor Eleonora Estensis manu propria subscripsit Celeriter"[71] ("Signed in haste by Suor Eleonora d'Este, your most obedient sister").

An examination of the two letters—owing much to Giovanna Murano's expertise[72]—reveals that the scribe used a basic and rather dignified chancery script, executed with strokes. The writing could be described as having formal ambitions, given the use of abbreviations (which are also decorative), uppercase letters (notably the "A" in the antepenultimate line), and the choice of punctuation (a colon in place of a period). It is safe to say, given the fluency and lack of errors and corrections, that the scribe was well educated and accustomed to writing.

Though the *subscriptio* is too brief for an in-depth analysis, Suor Eleonora's handwriting is certainly intriguing. She has a beautiful "Italian chancery" hand, executed with remarkable skill. Her script is characterized by small letters with elongated stems that end in additional strokes. This additional stroke, visible in the "p" of "subscripsit," is never used by the scribe. Suor Eleonora's uppercase "E" is also rather unique and may have been learned from her teacher, either at court or in the cloister.

The letters do not enable us to evaluate Suor Eleonora's writing skills, nor do they tell us much about her education and artistic interests. We can, however, make a number of observations. In her early letters, Latin expressions are more frequently interspersed with the vernacular. And in a letter of November 22, 1532, reference is made to Alexander the Great's generosity, which implies familiarity with Plutarch: "Ma lo exemplare vostro sia il Magnifico et famoso Alexandro che, essendo represo de uno munificentissimo dono che fece ad una ignobile persona, rispoxe che ad epso, che era Signore ditissimo, si convenia havere rispecto ex parte dantis, che era lui, et non ex parte recipientis, che era quello povero"[73] ("But may your example be the Magnificent and Famous Alexander who, when reproved for a very generous gift given to an ignoble person, replied that now, that he was very wealthy, it was fitting for respect to come from the giver, which was him, rather than from the receiver, who was poor"). Yet again, we have no way of knowing whether she was exposed to the tales of illustrious men during her childhood at court or whether these stories had also infiltrated the cloister. Nonetheless, they were certainly integral to the education of royals and complemented the method of teaching "per exempla" (by example), which also inspired the lives of saints. Thus a trace of secular culture could be found in Suor Eleonora, and it was undoubtedly shared within the convent.

The distinctive features that emerge most clearly from Suor Eleonora's correspondence are familial affection, respect for family dignity, political involvement—if not active engagement, then in the form of advice—and above-average knowledge. Suor Eleonora also supported her brother during periods of political friction and family conflict. This is evident from the care given to the duke's illegitimate daughter, Lucrezia. His legitimate daughters, Lucrezia and Eleonora, also permanently or temporarily resided in the convent, conceivably in their aunt's apartment, during the greatest moment of religious tension between Ercole II and his wife. In 1554, having prepared a Good Friday banquet, Renée sought to prevent her daughters from fulfilling the Easter obligation (that is, confession and communion during Mass). As a result, the duke took them from their mother and sent them to Corpus Domini, where his sister lovingly and spiritually cared for them.[74]

We have already seen that the convent of Corpus Domini in Ferrara was, in a way, an extension of the Este court: the family shrine, a place of care and repose for duchesses, a guest house for Cardinal Ippolito, and a refuge for young princesses. We would now like to know what the letters reveal about Suor Eleonora's demeanor toward her fellow sisters and the people who gravitated around the cloister. To be sure, her commitment to helping servants, friends, and the relatives of nuns constitutes the majority of requests forwarded to her brother.

Of the twenty-six missives Suor Eleonora sent to Ercole II, eighteen can be classified as letters requesting intercessions of different natures. Let us examine them more closely. On seven occasions, the princess-nun asks for a favor on behalf of a servant or friend, or she forwards a petition from an influential person, such as the princess of Molfetta, Isabella di Capua, wife of Ferrante Gonzaga, Count of Guastalla.[75] The petitions also concern interventions for prisoners[76] or individuals falsely accused of crimes.[77] On one occasion, Suor Eleonora asks that a house confiscated from a murderer be given to a poor servant with nowhere to stay.[78]

There are two particularly interesting instances in which Suor Eleonora intercedes for women in distress, toward whom she displays a particular emotional connection. One of these women was her brother Cardinal Ippolito's wet nurse, who, now widowed, was being harassed by her brother-in-law and subjected to violence:

> L'amore intenso porto a Madonna Angela dil Magro, Balia del Reverendissimo monsignore Cardinale nostro Fratello, fa ch'io hora a Vostra

> Illustrissima Signoria scrivendo cordialmente la racomandi a quella, a cui scio esserli noto tutto il caso suo circa il crudele et impio Giovanne suo cognato, che tutti vole occidere, ultra li molti oltragi ogn' anno l'ha facti, come credo Vostra Eccellenza sappi. Per tanto quella supplico per amor d'Idio et del Reverendissimo Fratello nostro, al qualle me rendo certa, prestando alla dita dona favore et aita li farà apiacer gratissimo, non lo voglia mancare, comettendo li sia facto ragione, et che per il futuro più non sia molestata né oppressa da questo suo adverso cognato. Unde quanto più posso anchor per amore mio prego et di gratia dimando la poverella Vidua la voglia haver per racomandata. Et io alla prefata Eccellentia humilmente di continuo mi racomando.[79]
>
> The great love for *Madonna* Angela dil Magro, our most Reverend brother the Cardinal's wet nurse, brings me to cordially write Your Illustrious Lordship and commend her unto you. I know the situation with her brother-in-law Giovanne is known. He wants to kill everyone, in addition to the many outrages he commits against her each year, as I believe Your Excellency is aware. Hence, I beseech you, for the love of God, and of our most Reverend brother, whom I am certain would be most appreciative and pleased by your helping this woman, that you not be remiss, and see that she receives justice, and in future is neither harassed nor oppressed by her hostile brother-in-law. For as much as my love yet enables, I pray and kindly ask that you help the poor widow. And I continue to humbly commend myself to Your Excellency.

The second woman who turns to Suor Eleonora for protection is kept anonymous in the princess's letter, conceivably to protect the lady who was unjustly accused and threatened by her husband. The nun forwarded the petition to her brother and asked that he fulfill the woman's request: "Drizzo la presente supplica a Vostra Illustrissima Signoria humilmente preghandola che per sua solita Clementia et per amor mio, voglia dignarsi haver per racomandata l'oratrice di questa, in farli gratia di quanto ella adimanda, comandando gli sia fatto ragione. Et non essere astretta ritornare col suo Consorte. Et di questo Vostra Eccellentia mi farà piacere singolarissimo, alla qual humilmente baciando la mane in sua buona gratia per sempre mi racomando"[80] ("I forward this petition to Your Most Illustrious Lordship and humbly pray that, with your usual mercy and love for me, you help the writer by fulfilling her request and order that she receive justice and not be compelled to return to her husband. With this Your Excellency will give me great pleasure, for which I humbly kiss your hand and commend myself forever to your good graces").

I would also like to stress that seven of the petitions sent by Suor Eleonora to her brother concern the relatives of nuns or *educande* at the convent. These individuals clearly placed their trust in the princess, who also served as abbess several times, and received consideration and sympathy in return. Of these petitions, only one is a request for a favor.[81] In most cases, a legal intervention was required: relief from false accusations, as previously mentioned; the release from prison of the father of two *educande*;[82] and the exoneration from a fine for an impoverished father of a nun with four daughters yet to marry:

> Essendo occorso uno caso et desgratia ad Antonio Maria de Nicolini contra sua voluntade, per el qualle he condennato come intendo scudi cento, del qualle caso scio la Excellentia Vostra n'è informata etiam per havere lui una sua strecta parente qua nel monastero nostro molto afflicta e tribulata. Per il che mossa a compassione io non posso fare che de core, quanto più scio e posso non preghi la Excellentia Vostra che, Amore Dei gratia, poi mio, voglia remettere tale condanasone al dicto Antonio Maria, et liberarlo, perché he persona da bene, ma povera e cargha de figlioli, mai harebe il modo di pagare tanti denari. Ha quattro figliole da maritare e dui figlioli, ali quali bisognaria andare mendicando. Unde di novo supplico ala Excellentia Vostra se digni et voglia tale gratia et apiacere concedermi, che me serà de summo contento.[83]
>
> A misfortune and disgrace have unwittingly befallen Antonio Maria de Nicolini, for which, I understand, he is sentenced to pay one hundred scudi. I know Your Excellency is informed thereof and he also has a close relative here in our convent who is most afflicted and troubled. Moved by compassion, I must wholeheartedly pray that, by your love for God and for me, Your Excellency overturn Antonio Maria's sentence and free him, since he is a good person, though poor and with many children. He has four daughters yet to wed and two little sons and would have to go begging. Thus I again implore Your Excellency to grant me this grace and favor, for which I would be most pleased.

These letters, in which Suor Eleonora intercedes with her brother on behalf of many others, seem sufficient to show the confidence that her fellow sisters and people connected with the convent had in the Este princess. They also display her singular dedication to them. We are thus able to take a further step toward understanding the world and the sentiments of the princess-nun. Yet to better understand her living conditions and her family, we must briefly reconsider her many privileges, and some additional letters.

Suor Eleonora's interactions with the relatives of nuns, servants, agents, and the convent's financial representatives, in an official capacity, justify her need to negotiate in the interest of the community or to address personal affairs. But in all likelihood, her conversations at the grate were not only limited to engaging in business or receiving petitions but also included political matters. We can reasonably conjecture that, aside from entrusting her with his daughters, in the periods of religious tension with his wife, Ercole II confided in his sister and asked for her help. For this reason, the privilege of being able to speak and negotiate with laypersons, even in secret and without witnesses—granted in 1537 by the Commissary of Cismontane Franciscan Observants and reaffirmed by several popes—appears to be justified. This privilege did not include friars, but the princess apparently obtained exemptions in their cases as well. In an undated letter to her brother, she refers to his order prohibiting friars from speaking to nuns without permission and asks for an exemption, as had been granted in the past.[84]

The management of finances and the duke's commitment to administering his sister's paternal inheritance all fall within the scope of familial and emotional rapports. In several letters, Suor Eleonora urges Ercole II to give her the amount set forth in their father's will. In April 1540, for instance, she requests 2000 lire needed to immediately repay a dept. She adds that if she does not get the money right away, there would be "tribolationi et . . . gran carico dell'honor mio"[85] ("great suffering and . . . burden upon my honor"). And at the end of the same year, she requests what she is due "per instrumento" ("as established in the notorial document").[86] On another occasion, Suor Eleonora asks her brother for five scudi for "certe Robbe quale ho tolto alla fiera" ("some things I got at the fair"). This somewhat enigmatic request implies that she left the convent. We know that Suor Eleonora could occasionally leave the cloister for health reasons or to visit other convents. Shopping at the fair, however, is not on the list of necessary or permitted excursions.

Though late in fulfilling his financial obligations, Ercole II is nevertheless considerate of his sister. He undertakes the task, for example, albeit without completion, of constructing or renovating her residence: "Prego quanto più posso che la Signoria Vostra se digni ordinar che sia fornita la mia fabrica già comintiata e doppoi lassata imperfecta acciò ch'io possa godermi il dono della Signoria Vostra et anchor levarmi da tanta incomoditade nella quale me retrovo. Et questo de gratia singolare humilmente a Vostra Excellentia racomandandomi basiandoli la mane"[87] ("I earnestly implore Your Lordship to order that the work begun on my residence, and left unfinished, be completed, so that I might enjoy Your Lordship's gift and also be freed from the very inconvenient state in which I find myself. And I humbly ask this of Your Excellency, commending myself unto you and kissing your hand").

Many years later, Duke Alfonso II, the nephew to whom Suor Eleonora wrote two letters the same year, proved to be more attentive than his father. He organized the relocation of his aunt and thirteen Ferrarese nuns to the convent of the Poor Clares in Carpi and afforded them every convenience:

> **Illustrissimo et eccellentissimo signor mio osservandissimo.**
> Per fare qualche parte di quel ch'io devo, vengo con questa mia a ringratiare infinitamente et a basciare la mano di Vostra Eccellenza delle molte commodità che per ordine di lei ho havuto in questo viaggio di Carpi, dove gionsi hier sera. Et mi conosco sommamente obligata, oltre a tante altre cause, del favore ricevuto in questa parte da Vostra Eccellenza, alla quale non possono corrispondere le forze mie con altri effetti, se non con supplicare Dio Nostro Signore che la conservi felice et pregando ben di cuore Vostra Eccellenza che si voglia ricordare a tempo di fare ch' io possa ritornare a servirla a Ferrara.[88]

> **My Most Illustrious, Excellent, and Esteemed Lord.**
> To do some small part of what I owe, I send this letter to infinitely thank you and kiss Your Excellency's hand for the many comforts you provided during this trip to Carpi, where I arrived yesterday evening. And I acknowledge myself supremely indebted, among other things, for this favor from Your Excellency, to which my strengths can only be summoned to beseech the Lord our God to keep you happy. And I wholeheartedly pray that Your Excellency will kindly remember to allow me promptly to come back to serve you in Ferrara.

It was January 1571. The previous winter, the city of Ferrara had been devastated by a severe earthquake, which had also struck the convent of Corpus Domini. The extensive renovations could not be carried out with the sisters in residence, and the Ferrarese nuns were transferred to other convents in the duchy and neighboring areas. The event was documented as follows in the records of the Carpi convent:

> Nota come il terramoto cominciò à tirare del 1570 adi 16 di Novembre, è ruinò delle quattro parti di Ferrara, le trè, et fino alli 13 di Decembre seguitava ancora sino ad'hora ch'è alli 9 di Febbraio del 1571.
>
> Nota come l'Ill.$^{ma}$ S.$^{ra}$ Leonora D'Este venne nel Monastero di S. Chiara di Carpi li 17 di Genaio, e fù del 1571 con tredeci Suore, doppo venne la Madre Suor Genevra, e Suor Olimpia ch'erano in numero 16.[89]
>
> Note how the earthquake began on the 16th of November 1570 and, of the four parts of Ferrara, destroyed three, and continued until the 13th of December up until now, which is the 9th of February 1571.
>
> Note how the very Illustrious Lady Leonora D'Este came to the Convent of Santa Chiara in Carpi on the 17th of January 1571 along with thirteen nuns. The Reverend Mother Genevra and Suor Olimpia arrived thereafter and there was a total of sixteen.

From another of Suor Eleonora's letters, we learn that her nephew Alfonso II even saw to the renovation of her rooms in Carpi.[90] We have no idea how long this compulsory relocation lasted. But we do know that Lucrezia Borgia's daughter—who outlived her brothers Ercole and Ippolito—died in her beloved Ferrara, just as she had desired, and was buried in the convent choir, next to her "blessed" niece Lucrezia.

After 1575, the year of her death, Suor Eleonora would be remembered by her convent sisters as a nun and a princess. She herself furnished the few words recorded on her tombstone: "Dom/ Eleonora/ Alphonsi Estensis/ et Lucretiae Borgiae/ Ferrariae Ducum filia/ Ordinis Divae Clarae/ Monialis Professa/ V. S. P."[91] ("Signora Eleonora, Professed Nun of the Order of St. Clair, daughter of Alfonso d'Este and Lucrezia Borgia, Dukes of Ferrara, commissioned her tombstone while still alive"). The tombstone rendered clear Suor Eleonora's desire to be included in the family mausoleum, even if her body would be buried in the internal nuns' choir, where professed sisters were buried. Little detail is offered about the princess, who distinguished herself above all for her learning and her devotion to her role as apothecary and who also stood out for her generosity toward the convent and her sisters. Her noble lineage was certainly a major factor in determining how she approached and experienced her religious profession and her long residence inside the walls of the convent—where she was welcomed not only with deference but presumably also with affection and gratitude.

Acknowledgments
With thanks to Giuseppe Bruno-Chomin (University of Pennsylvania) for providing the translation of this essay.

Notes

1. Patrizia Cremonini, "Il rabarbaro di Lucrezia Borgia e la lettera di frà Nicolò da Tossignano, custode di Terra Santa. Questione d'oriente, spezie, medici e commerci," *Quaderni estensi. Rivista* II (2010): 273–305, http://www.archivi.beniculturali.it/QE,2,2010.

2. Giovanni Maria Zerbinati, *Croniche di Ferrara: quali comenzano del anno 1500 sino al 1527*, ed. Maria Giuseppina Muzzarelli (Ferrara: Deputazione provinciale ferrarese di storia patria, 1989), 137.

3. Zerbinati, *Croniche di Ferrara*, 147.

4. Teodosio Lombardi, *Gli estensi ed il Monastero del Corpus Domini di Ferrara* (Ferrara: Industrie grafiche, 1980), 24; Laurie Stras, *Women and Music in Sixteenth-Century Ferrara* (Cambridge: Cambridge University Press, 2018), 30.

5. Lucrezia Borgia, *Lettere di Lucrezia Borgia: 1494–1519*, ed. Diane Ghirardo (Mantua: Tre Lune, 2020), 20–21.

6. Borgia, *Lettere di Lucrezia Borgia*, 641.

7. Borgia, *Lettere di Lucrezia Borgia*, 641. On September 19, 1505, in two separate letters, Lucrezia Borgia informed Francesco II Gonzaga and Isabella d'Este of Alessandro's birth: "uno bello figliolino maschio" ("a beautiful baby boy"), Borgia, *Lettere di Lucrezia Borgia*, 233. In response to Francesco II, on October 1 of that same year, Lucrezia affirmed that: "havemo inteso dil ben stare di vostra signoria et de la singulare consolatione presa dil nostro prospero et desiderato parto" ("We have learned of your lordship's well-being and great satisfaction from our favorable and desired birth"), Borgia, *Lettere di Lucrezia Borgia*, 236. On October 16, Lucrezia notified Francesco of Alexander's death: "per nostro debito le significamo che Illustrissimo nostro charissimo figliolino, essendo sta' agitato più volte da molti accidenti sopravenuti, questa matina sulle XIII hore è passato de questa vita. De che siamo in lachryme tanto tribolata et havemone tanto cordoglio quanto vostra signoria pote pensare, et sapemo che anche lei ne receverà summo dispiacere" ("as per obligation, we inform you that our most illustrious little son, having been overwrought many times by many misfortunes, departed this life at 1 o'clock. We are in tears and much aggrieved as your lordship can imagine and know that you too will have great sorrow"), Borgia, *Lettere di Lucrezia Borgia*, 249. On April 18, 1514, Lucrezia notified Isabella of the well-being of another son named Alessandro, who had just been born (Borgia, *Lettere di Lucrezia Borgia*, 526), but two years later, she sadly informed her brother-in-law Francesco II of the child's death: (" . . . è stato costretto questa nocte . . . render l'anima benedetta a nostro Signor Dio. El che non mediocremente me affligge, et ne sono restata con grandissimo dolor, et come ragionevolmente debbo per esser donna et matre" (". . . he was com-

pelled this night . . . to surrender his blessed soul unto our Lord God. This greatly pains me, and I remain with great grief, as is expected for my being a woman and mother"), Borgia, *Lettere di Lucrezia Borgia*, 549.

8. Borgia, *Lettere di Lucrezia Borgia*, 535. Lucrezia Borgia to Gian Giorgio Trissino, September 18, 1515.

9. Borgia, *Lettere di Lucrezia Borgia*, 545. Lucrezia Borgia to Gian Giorgio Trissino, June 1, 1516.

10. Duke Alfonso II's will, which provides for this donation, is dated March 25, 1520, and specifies that the donation will begin on the very day the document was drawn up, even if the document would not come into effect until a few years later. A copy thereof can be found in Teodosio Lombardi, *I francescani a Ferrara*, vol. 4, *I monasteri delle Clarisse: S. Guglielmo, Corpus Domini, S. Bernardino, S. Chiara* (Bologna: Grafiche Dehoniane, 1975), 161–166.

11. Zerbinati, *Croniche di Ferrara*, 158–159.

12. Gionata Liboni, "Imitare le sante donne. Medicina e religione in una lettera dedicatoria di Antonio Musa Brasavola a Eleonora d'Este," *Schifanoia* 40–41 (2011): 126.

13. Among the many works on Caterina de' Vigri and the Bolognese convent, see in particular *Caterina Vigri: la santa e la città: atti del Convegno, Bologna, 13–15 novembre 2002*, ed. Claudio Leonardi (Florence: SISMEL Edizioni del Galluzzo, 2004). On the Ferrarese convent of Corpus Domini, see *Dalla corte al chiostro: santa Caterina Vigri e i suoi scritti: atti della VI giornata di studio sull'Osservanza francescana al femminile: 5 novembre 2011*, eds. Pietro Messa and Filippo Sedda (Ferrara: Monastero Clarisse Corpus Domini, S. Maria degli Angeli, Assisi, 2013).

14. Caterina da Bologna, *Libro deuoto de la beata Chaterina bolognese de lordine* [*sic*] *dil seraphico San Francesco elqual* [*sic*] *essa lascio scripto de sua man propria*, Stampata in Bologna, per Zoa. Antonio de li Benedicti, 1500 a di 8. Mazo.

15. Gabriella Zarri, "Why Become a Poor Clare? Presenting the Observant Franciscan Life to Fifteenth-Century Women," in *Select Proceedings from the First International Conference on Franciscan Studies, The World of St. Francis of Assisi, Siena, Italy, July 16–20, 2015* (Siena: Betti Editrice, 2017), 217–223. This interesting manuscript, edited by Letizia Pellegrini, is in press (Rome: Edizioni di Storia e Letteratura) with the title *Intus ed Extra. Un formulario epistolare delle Clarisse bolognesi (seconda metà del XV secolo)*.

16. Monica Ferrari, *"Per non manchare in tuto del debito mio": l'educazione dei bambini Sforza nel Quattrocento* (Milan: Franco Angeli, 2000).

17. Caterina Vigri, *Le sette armi spirituali*, ed. Antonella Degl'Innocenti (Florence: SISMEL, Edizioni del Galluzzo, 2000).

18. Caterina Vigri, *Pregare con le immagini: il breviario di Caterina Vigri*, eds. Vera Fortunati and Claudio Leonardi (Florence: SISMEL Edizioni del Galluzzo, Bologna, 2004).

19. Caterina Vigri, *Laudi, trattati e lettere*, ed. Silvia Serventi (Florence: SISMEL Edizioni del Galluzzo, 2000).

20. Enrico Peverada, "Documenti per la storia organaria dei monasteri femminili ferraresi (secc. XVI–XVII)," *L'Organo. Rivista di storia organaria e organistica* 30 (1996): 119–193.

21. Craig A. Monson, "Ancora uno sguardo sulle suore musiciste di Bologna," in *I monasteri femminili come centri di cultura fra Rinascimento e barocco: atti del Convegno storico*

*internazionale: Bologna, 8–10 dicembre 2000*, eds. Gianna Pomata and Gabriella Zarri (Rome: Edizioni di storia e letteratura, 2005), 3–26.

22. Graziella Martinelli Braglia,"Musica claustrale e controriforma. Suor Sulpizia Cesis del monastero di San Geminiano," *Terra e Identità* 85, *Il Ducato* 46 (2018): 3–17; Braglia, "Donna Giulia Felice, figlia del Cardinale Alessandro d'Este. Una monaca musicista nel monastero di San Geminiano a Modena," *Atti e memorie della deputazione di storia patria per le antiche province modenesi* 11, no. 42 (2020): 175–207.

23. Elissa B. Weaver, *Convent Theatre in Early Modern Italy: Spiritual Fun and Learning for Women* (Cambridge, Cambridge University Press, 2002).

24. Gabriella Zarri, "Culture nel chiostro. Tra arte e vita," in *Artiste nel chiostro. Produzione artistica nei monasteri femminili in età moderna*, eds. Sheila Barker and Luciano Cinelli (*Memorie domenicane*, n. s., 46, 2015), 19–29.

25. Lombardi, *Gli estensi ed il Monastero*, 39–40.

26. Juri Leoni, "'A ciò che la regola nostra promessa meglio possiati observare.' Le ordinazioni delle Clarisse del Corpus Domini di Bologna," *Archivum Franciscanum Historicum* 109 (2016): 524.

27. Lombardi, *Gli estensi ed il Monastero*, 40.

28. Maria Teresa Sambin De Norcen, "Romei, Giovanni," in *Dizionario Biografico degli italiani*, 88, 2017, https://www.treccani.it/enciclopedia/giovanni-romei_(Dizionario-Biografico)/.

29. *Ferrara. Il Museo di Casa Romei guida alla visita*, ed. Andrea Sardo (Cinisello Balsamo: Silvana Editoriale, 2019).

30. *Ferrara. Il Museo di Casa Romei*, 9.

31. Luciano Chiappini, *Gli Estensi*, 3rd ed. (Varese: dall'Oglio editore, 1967), 258.

32. Lombardi, *Gli estensi ed il Monastero*, 61.

33. Lombardi, *Gli estensi ed il Monastero*, 55.

34. Lombardi, *Gli estensi ed il Monastero*, 61.

35. *Ferrara. Il Museo di Casa Romei*, 32; Mary Hollingsworth, *The Cardinal's Hat: Money, Ambition, and Everyday Life in the Court of a Borgia Prince* (Woodstock, NY: Overlook Press, 2004), which contains a number of inaccuracies. On the life of Ippolito II, see Lucy Byatt, "Ippolito d'Este," in *Dizionario biografico degli Italiani* 43 (1993): https://www.treccani.it/enciclopedia/ippolito-d-este_%28Dizionario-Biografico%29/

36. Peverada, *Documenti per la storia organaria*, 168.

37. Stras, *Women and Music*, 32.

38. Stras, *Women and Music*, 30–50.

39. *Abiti e lavori delle monache di Bologna: in una serie di disegni del secolo XVIII*, presentazione di Mario Fanti (Bologna: Tamari, 1972), 82; 76. On medicine in convents, see Gianna Pomata, "Medicina delle monache. Pratiche terapeutiche nei monasteri femminili di Bologna in età moderna," in *I monasteri femminili come centri di cultura fra Rinascimento e barocco: atti del Convegno storico internazionale: Bologna, 8–10 dicembre 2000*, eds. Gianna Pomata and Gabriella Zarri (Rome: Edizioni di storia e letteratura, 2005), 331–363; Katharine Park, *Secrets of Women: Gender, Generation, and the Origins of Human Dissection* (New York: Zone, 2006), 39–76; Sharon T. Strocchia, "The Nun Apothecaries of Renaissance Florence: Marketing Medicines in the Convent," *Renaissance Studies* 25, no. 5 (2011):

627–647; Sharon T. Strocchia, *Forgotten Healers: Women and the Pursuit of Health in Late Renaissance Italy* (Cambridge, MA: Harvard University Press, 2019).

40. See note 1.

41. Antonio Musa Brasavola, *Antoni Muse Brasauoli Ferrariensis Examen omnium simplicium medicamentorum, quorum in officinis vsus est, ad Illustriss. & sereniss. Principes Herculem Estensem Ferrarie Ducem et Renatam Gallam* (Rome: Antonii Bladi de Asula, 1536).

42. *Antonii Musae Brasauoli Ferrariensis Examen omnium syruporum, quorum publicus vsus est: ad illustriss. & pudicissimam virginem Elleonoram Estensem* (Venice: per D. Bernardinum Stagninum, 1538).

43. Liboni, *Imitare le sante donne,* 119–126, which also provides an ample bibliography on Brasavola. See also Liboni, "L' experimentum nella medicina pratica di Antonio Musa Brasavola," *Schifanoia* 50–51 (2016): 21–33.

44. Elissa Weaver, "Le muse in convento. La scrittura profana delle monache italiane (1450–1650)," in *Donne e fede. Santità e vita religiosa in Italia,* eds. Lucetta Scaraffia e Gabriella Zarri (Roma-Bari: Laterza, 1994), 253–276; in English translation as "The Convent Muses: The Secular Writing of Italian Nuns, 1450–1650," in *Women and Faith: Catholic Religious Life in Italy from Late Antiquity to the Present,* eds. Lucetta Scaraffia and Gabriella Zarri (Cambridge, MA: Harvard University Press, 1999), 129–143.

45. Gabriella Zarri, "Le istituzioni dell'educazione femminile," in *Le sedi della cultura nell'Emilia-Romagna. I secoli moderni. Le istituzioni e il pensiero,* ed. Adriano Prosperi (Milan: A. Pizzi, 1987), 84–109; now in Gabriella Zarri, *Recinti. Donne, clausura e matrimonio nella prima età moderna* (Bologna: Il Mulino, 2000), 145–200; Gabriella Zarri, *La religione di Lucrezia Borgia. Le lettere inedite del confessore* (Rome: Roma nel Rinascimento, 2006), 114–116.

46. Gionata Liboni, "Antonio Musa Brasavola sul digiuno: devozione, medicina e riforma della Chiesa," *I castelli di Yale online* 5, no.1 (2017): 41–87.

47. Antonio Musa Brasavola, *La vita di Iesu Cristo,* vol. 3, eds. Adriano and Anna Prosperi (Torino: Aragno, 2020).

48. Eleonora Belligni, *Renata di Francia (1510–1575): un'eresia di corte* (Turin: UTET, 2011); *Giovanni Calvino, Renata di Francia, Lealtà in tensione: un carteggio protestante tra Ferrara e l'Europa (1537–1564),* eds. Leonardo De Chirico and Daniel Walker (Caltanissetta: Alfa & Omega, 2009).

49. Lombardi, *I francescani a Ferrara,* 139.

50. Simon Ditchfield, *Liturgy, Sanctity and History in Tridentine Italy: Pietro Maria Campi and the Preservation of the Particular* (Cambridge: Cambridge University Press, 1995).

51. Lombardi, *I francescani a Ferrara,* 107.

52. Lombardi, *I francescani a Ferrara,* 112.

53. Lombardi, *I francescani a Ferrara,* 108.

54. Lombardi, *I francescani a Ferrara,* 109.

55. Lombardi, *I francescani a Ferrara,* 111–112.

56. Lombardi, *I francescani a Ferrara,* 113.

57. Lombardi, *I francescani a Ferrara,* 114.

58. Eleonora d'Este (suor) di Alfonso I al fratello Ercole II 1530(?)–1552; Eleonora d'Este figlia d'Alfonso I al nipote Alfonso II 1571 (Archivio di Stato di Modena [Modena, Italy], Cancelleria. Carteggio tra Principi Estensi, b. 154 [hereafter cited as ASMo]).

59. ASMo, Suor Eleonora to her brother Ercole II, letter of March 27, 1530.

60. ASMo, Suor Eleonora to her brother Ercole II, undated letter.

61. ASMo, Suor Eleonora to her brother Ercole II, March 27, 1530.

62. ASMo, Suor Eleonora to her brother Ercole II, November 27, 1533.

63. ASMo, Suor Eleonora to her brother Ercole II, November 5, 1537.

64. ASMo, Suor Eleonora to her brother Ercole II, undated.

65. ASMo, Suor Eleonora to her brother Ercole II, July 30, 1539.

66. ASMo, Suor Eleonora to her brother Ercole II, May 9, 1540.

67. ASMo, Suor Eleonora to her brother Ercole II, November 22, 1533.

68. ASMo, Suor Eleonora to her brother Ercole II, undated letter, cited above.

69. ASMo, Suor Eleonora to her brother Ercole II, July 30, 1539.

70. ASMo, Suor Eleonora to her brother Ercole II, October 13, 1552.

71. ASMo, Suor Eleonora to her brother Ercole II, March 27, 1530.

72. In particular, see the edited volume "Autographa," 2.1, entitled *Donne, sante e madonne: (da Matilde di Canossa ad Artemisia Gentileschi)*, ed. Giovanna Murano (Imola: La mandragora, 2018).

73. Suor Eleonora to her brother Ercole II, November 22, 1533, b. 154, Cancelleria. Carteggio tra Principi Estensi, ASMo.

74. Chiappini, *Gli Estensi*, 260.

75. Suor Eleonora to her brother Ercole II, February 3, 1544, b. 154, Cancelleria. Carteggio tra Principi Estensi, ASMo.

76. ASMo, Suor Eleonora to her brother Ercole II, May 9, 1540.

77. ASMo, Suor Eleonora to her brother Ercole II, September 20, 1549.

78. ASMo, Suor Eleonora to her brother Ercole II, undated letter.

79. ASMo, Suor Eleonora to her brother Ercole II, June 9, 1539.

80. ASMo, Suor Eleonora to her brother Ercole II, undated letter.

81. ASMo, Suor Eleonora to her brother Ercole II, undated letter.

82. ASMo, Suor Eleonora to her brother Ercole II, May 9, 1540, and undated letter.

83. ASMo, Suor Eleonora to her brother Ercole II, undated letter.

84. ASMo, Suor Eleonora to her brother Ercole II, undated letter.

85. ASMo, Suor Eleonora to her brother Ercole II, April 26, 1540.

86. ASMo, Suor Eleonora to her brother Ercole II, December 7, 1540.

87. ASMo, Suor Eleonora to her brother Ercole II, undated letter.

88. ASMo, Suor Eleonora to her nephew Alfonso II, January 18, 1571.

89. *Memoriale* II, *ad diem*. Archivio del Monastero di Santa Chiara di Carpi. On the convent and its history, see *Le Clarisse in Carpi. Cinque secoli di storia XVI-XX*, vol. 1, *Saggi*, ed. Gabriella Zarri (Reggio Emilia: Fondazione Cassa di Risparmio di Carpi, 2003); *Le Clarisse in Carpi. Cinque secoli di storia XVI-XX*, vol. 2, ed. *Testi*, Anna Maria Ori (Reggio Emilia: Fondazione Cassa di Risparmio di Carpi, 2003). Many thanks to Anna Maria Ori for providing me the transcription of the cited document.

90. Suor Eleonora to her nephew Alfonso II, September 29, 1571, b. 154, Cancelleria. Carteggio tra Principi Estensi, ASMo.

91. Vivens Sepulcrum Posuit o Viva Sibi Posuit

CHAPTER FIVE

# A Christian Romance for Married Women

## Marriage, Female Spirituality, and the Pursuit of Saintliness in Antonia Pulci's *Rappresentazione di Santa Guglielma*

EMANUELA ZANOTTI CARNEY

An accomplished author of *sacre rappresentazioni* and *laude*, Antonia Tanini Pulci (1452/54–1501)[1] holds a position of particular importance in Renaissance studies. Through both her dramatic works and her lived experience, Pulci made a significant contribution to the development of female spirituality in Renaissance Florence and promoted a spiritual ideal conceived by a woman for a female public. Throughout her literary career, Pulci devoted special attention to issues that were relevant to the women of Florence. This interest is clearly manifested in the *rappresentazioni* she published in Florence in the last decade of the fifteenth century. What follows is intended as a contribution to our understanding of how Pulci's dramatic works, under the guise of entertainment, guided women—forced to choose between marriage and convent and yearning for "un'altra vïa" ("another path") to spiritual fulfillment—toward novel forms of religious association and alternative paths to Christian perfection and even holiness.

Pulci's life and works took place in a cultural and devotional context marked by an intense female piety that was characterized by affectivity, penitential ascetism, devotion to the Passion, and supernatural experiences. Women's spiritual needs and expectations found expression in novel forms of devotion: the increasing female participation in religious roles was paralleled by a dramatic growth in the number of recognized female saints, most notably married women.[2] In the dramatic arena, the *sacre rappresentazioni* (religious plays in rhyming octaves) of Quattrocento Florence responded to this cultural and spiritual environment by privileging models of female sanctity, virgin martyrs, chaste widows, and holy married women.[3] Recognized for their educational and catechetical role and deemed especially suitable for the construction of models of behavior directed to the laity, *sacre rappresentazioni* were an integral part of the Florentine cultural landscape at the time of Pulci's writing.[4] As part of a body of devotional literature in the vernacular that "attempted both to channel, construct, and contain feminine spirituality,"[5] *sacre rappresentazioni* played an important role in the life of women at a time when clerical writers, itinerant preachers, and lay humanists alike were anxious to control increasingly literate female audiences. In the vast corpus of fifteenth-century religious drama, Pulci's sacred plays stand out, for she deliberately spoke to the experiences of contemporary female audiences and promoted models of holiness that, transcending the limitations traditionally associated with their gender, emboldened women to be spiritually and socially independent from male authority.

As I have discussed elsewhere,[6] for instance, in her play *Santa Domitilla,* Pulci presents a virgin model of female holiness predicated on the refusal of marriage and motherhood, and, polemically drawing from the writings of clerical and contemporary humanist sources, she forcefully challenges the centrality of the conjugal family and the prescribed gender roles of female submission that were the cornerstones of patriarchal society. A similar strategy is at work in the *rappresentazione di Santa Guglielma,* the sacred drama under consideration in the present essay. While the cultural values and the devotional responses encouraged by *sacre rappresentazioni* for their audiences by and large reflected and endorsed prevailing attitudes toward the virtues of submission and obedience that were deemed appropriate for married women, I would argue that in *Santa Guglielma,* the Florentine playwright purposefully uses gendered representations drawn from secular and religious sources to underscore the moral implications and transformative potential of a woman's obedience and patient suffering at the hands of her husband. Thus, the first task of this essay is to examine Pulci's clever employment of adaptation and reinterpretation of didactic sources and legendary materials in order to illustrate how, in her skillful hands, the dramatic adaptation of the Guglielma legend tradition becomes a privileged *locum* for crafting strategies to gain women spiritual freedom from the wifely obligations and marital submission underpinning both the ideology and the daily practices of the Florentine patriarchal family.

An accomplished playwright, Antonia Pulci emerged as a powerful literary figure in Quattrocento Italy.[7] Born to a mercantile Florentine family of modest social standing, she became a member of the Florentine aristocracy in 1470 through her marriage to Bernardo Pulci, an accomplished writer in Latin and the vernacular and the brother of the more famous Luigi, author of the epic poem *Morgante*. Widowed in 1488 and childless, Antonia returned for a time to her paternal home, where she embraced a spiritual life of penitence and prayer, becoming an *ammantellata*, a member of the Augustinian third order. A spiritual leader and a patron of the arts, she commissioned a chapter in the Church of San Gallo, where she wished to be buried, and with the money of her dowry, she founded Santa Maria della Misericordia, a female religious community, whose prioress she became in 1500, a year before her death in 1501. Conversant with the writings of the Church Fathers and the works of the humanists alike, Pulci's literary references to vernacular genres like *cantari*, prose legends, lyric poetry, and epic poems are indicative of her participation (and the participation of at least part of her audience) in the literary culture of her time.[8] An accomplished practitioner of writing, though not the exceptional female writer in Medicean Florence, Pulci holds the distinction of possibly being the first Italian female author to see her works published "through the printing press."[9]

At a time when women were denied access to institutionalized clerical and civic authority, Pulci effectively used dramatized lives of female saints as a platform from which to enter the public domain, to shape contemporary sociosexual and religious discourse on "Woman," and to empower women to shape their own spiritual vocation. Putting female agency and spiritual capital front and center, the Florentine playwright's body of work sought to renegotiate normative assumptions about gender and to redefine gender constrictions and medieval power relations, thus strengthening women's private and collective spiritual identity.

While Pulci dramatizes the theme of a virgin martyr's spurned nuptials in *Santa Domitilla*, in *Santa Guglielma* she shifts to the sanctification of the couple through marriage and the reconciliation of matrimony with the construction of holiness.[10] In *Santa Guglielma*, chaste marriage and voluntary enclosure in the hermitage, not virginal martyrdom, allow Guglielma the spiritual freedom that a forced marriage had denied her. The discussion on the role played by spiritual marriage in *Santa Guglielma* is indeed another focus of the present essay. Drawing from Dyan Elliott's seminal work on spiritual marriage in the Middle

Ages and from Bryce's perceptive reading of *Santa Guglielma*, I follow Bryce's lead and explore further her initial observations that that " the ideal indirectly presented in the play is one of spiritual marriage in the context of extreme ascetism."[11] I argue that, addressing the concerns of married women who felt that the loss of their virginal status, their wifely obligations, and their worldly households irremediably prevented them from emulating the holy models of virgin saints' lives, Pulci sets forth spiritual marriage as an alternative female religious practice for women caught between coerced marriages and the desire for chastity. I also suggest that accommodating the experience of married laywomen within a broadening understanding of holiness, the play underscores the potential for female piety to sanctify family and community through chaste matrimony and arguably encourages women forced into unwanted marriages to explore their own version of religious vocation and become advocates for spiritual marriage, a potentially subversive initiative that threatened male authority and the hierarchy of the sexes.

The rubric of *Santa Guglielma* refers to it as a sacra *rappresentazione* and provides details of the name, sex, and social status of the author, who is identified as Mona Antonia, wife of Bernardo Pulci.[12] Redacted before 1488 (the year of Bernardo's death),[13] *Santa Guglielma* appeared in the two-volume incunable collection published intermittently between 1483 and 1490 by Antonio Miscomini, a Florentine printer close to the Medici milieu.[14] An edition of the play was later issued in Florence by the printer Bartolomeo de Libri circa 1495, following a second publication of the anthology by Miscomini sometime before his death in 1495.[15] We have scant information on whether the play was ever staged or whether it was meant for voiced performance; as it was printed in a collection that was meant to circulate among the laity, it was likely intended as reading material.[16] *Santa Guglielma* met with the favor of contemporary audiences. The most popular of Pulci's *rappresentazioni* collected in the anthology, it was published at least thirty-three times between 1490 and 1640, its female authorship notwithstanding.[17] Centered on a married noblewoman's spiritual quest for *una vïa vera e perfetta* ("a true and perfect path") to live out her religious vocation, a leitmotif that Pulci developed to varying degrees in three of her plays, *Santa Guglielma* is, as I have suggested elsewhere, part of a trilogy with *Santa Domitilla* and *Distruzione di Saul e il Pianto di Davit*, each play commemorating a different form of female holiness—the virgin martyr, the married woman, and the widow. Taken together, these plays offer a uniquely feminine perspective on issues of spiritual salvation, marriage, and female autonomy, and they ought to be viewed as Pulci's personal and artistic answer to the prevailing *ad status* literature of her day.[18]

In *Santa Domitilla,* Pulci celebrates a virgin martyr of the early Church and argues at length in favor of the superiority of chastity to the married life. The monastic ideal of renunciation of all physical and affective ties made it difficult for married women to attain the ideal of Christian perfection.[19] In *Santa Guglielma,* she commemorates the life of a married "santa viva" (or living saint)[20] of sorts and promotes a model of female sanctity active in the world and accessible to married women. While we have no conclusive proof that this particular play was written at the request of women nor that it was meant for a female audience, be it a community of nuns, a household of laywomen who had professed a life of celibacy, or a reading community of devout married women,[21] I would argue that the hagiographical pattern of Guglielma's story seems particularly suited to the lived experiences of Florentine women who had to confront parental pressure to marry against their will. Like most married female saints, Guglielma had her childhood desire to remain chaste thwarted by a coerced marriage.

More legend than hagiography, the story of Santa Guglielma is rendered in an atmosphere, with images and a language strongly reminiscent of those commonly found in the courtly literature of the time, emphasizing the love, the beauty, and the genteel demeanor of the protagonist. The narrative subject itself was far from original: the unjustly persecuted but faithful queen, falsely accused of sexual debauchery by a spurned suitor, and whose innocence after numerous travails is finally vindicated, was a traditional *topos* in medieval literature.[22] The *rappresentazione* dramatizes the story of Guglielma, the ever-obedient daughter of the King of England, forced to marry the newly converted Hungarian king. Though she had vowed to remain a virgin and live her life as a bride of Christ, the young Guglielma consents to the marriage arrangements in obedience to her parents. Welcomed by her spouse with promises of blissful love, Guglielma persuades him to leave on a pilgrimage to the Holy Land. While the king is away, his lustful brother attempts to seduce Guglielma. Sternly rejected, he accuses Guglielma of immoral behavior. Upon his return, the king, enraged by his wife's alleged debauchery, condemns her to death. Guglielma escapes with the help of her executioners and wanders in the desert, where the Virgin Mary and two angels appear in a vision to comfort her. Guglielma receives from the Virgin a ring and miraculous thaumaturgic powers. As God's reward for her faith, Guglielma is granted the authority to confess and to heal repentant sinners with the sign of the Cross. After many travails, Guglielma finds refuge in a monastery, albeit refusing to take religious vows. News of her miraculous deeds reaches the Hungarian court. The king sets off for the monastery with his brother, now afflicted by leprosy as divine punishment for his false accusations, and asks Guglielma, whom he does not recognize, to heal his sick brother. Guglielma heals her brother-in-law after he publicly confesses his sins, and reveals her true identity. Restored to her royal position, Guglielma follows her spouse home. Back in Hungary, the king abdicates and withdraws from the world and, accompanied by his wife and his brother, leads a life of penance in a hermitage.

In Italy, the story of Guglielma, a saint of dubious origins and ambiguous spiritual affiliations,[23] had been commemorated in at least a *cantare*,[24] attributed to Bernardo Pulci, and a prose legend, popular in Northern and Central Italy at the time Pulci wrote her play.[25] Drawing on the *topoi* and the language of gendered relations so pervasive in "ad status" literature, Antonia Pulci deftly adapts and amplifies the narrative content of the prose legend, imbuing the popular story of a saintlike married woman with new spiritual and social significance.

While *Santa Domitilla* is singularly replete with arguments in favor of virginity and the superiority of the virgin life, in *Santa Guglielma*, the preferability of the virginal life to matrimony is summarily dealt with. As Guglielma protests against her proposed betrothal, the king dismisses her concerns that sexuality and marriage are insurmountable obstacles to spiritual attainments. Albeit recognizing that virginity and mystical marriage to Christ are a worthy ideal ("Che la verginità sia degna cosa/ a questo ignun non è che contradica" ["A worthy condition is virginity, / Of course, this no one will deny"]),[26] the king paradoxically restates Guglielma's wishes for a holy life, declaring that it is through suffering the burdens of marriage rather than through physical virginity that the holiness of a woman's life can be more clearly evinced: a wife behaving modestly while "nel mondo" ("in the world") and striving "nella fé di Iesù" ("in the faith of Jesus Christ") is all the more pleasing to God, an argument popularized by Antonino da Firenze, among others.[27]

In this exchange on the honorable state of marriage, Pulci alludes to contemporary debates on the preeminence of the "natural" state of matrimony over celibacy, its attendant benefits for the state, and its sacramental value within the Church. Preaching about the spiritual benefits of lifelong virginity and ascetic renunciation, patristic commentators had warned Christian women of the evils of marriage and sexuality and had established an ascetic hierarchy of spiritual perfection that ranked women according to their status (virgin, widows, and married women). Viewing spiritual fulfillment and family life as incompatible states, the Church Fathers refused to elevate marriage to the level of consecrated virginity, thus denying married women, polluted by sexual intercourse, access to the angelic purity of the virginal life and its hundredfold rewards in Heaven.[28] By the time of Pulci's writing, however, the Church had established the sacramental grace of matrimony, had recognized that marriage was a "natural" social contract, and had promoted a positive evaluation of conjugal love and parenthood.[29] These shifting ideologies gave rise to a vast body of pastoral literature that sought to regulate marriage and reshape family morality on a wide array of topics, ranging from domestic relationships and the "conjugal debt"[30] to issues related to the upbringing of children and household management. No longer deploying a scathing antimarital rhetoric on the vexations of wedlock, the clergy began promoting the benefits of matrimony: sanctioned by God at Creation, marriage was deemed a social institution of paramount importance in furthering the Church's mission.[31] However, Church positions on matters of sexuality and female submission to male authority remained ambiguous, as sexuality and domestic obligations still barred married women from achieving spiritual perfection.[32]

Italian humanists, meanwhile, considered celibacy unnatural, viewed marriage as both an affective and an economic partnership, and defended the conjugal family as "the pivotal social institution" upon which the survival of the Florentine republic rested.[33] Concerned with matrimonial strategies and with discussing the function of marriage and the role accorded to each spouse within the family structure, fifteenth-century lay writers such as Leon Battista Alberti and Francesco Barbaro did not debate whether virginity was a state superior to that of matrimony; they centered their discussions on the virtues to be sought in wives and how to train a young wife to administer the house with prudence and vigilance.[34] Both clerical and lay figures discussing matrimony and female autonomy within marriage strove to preserve gender boundaries and made female obedience to male authority a central tenet of their educational theory, further inscribing women into subordinate roles within the socio-sexual hierarchy of the family.

It is precisely with this patriarchal discourse that Pulci seeks to engage, and it is the language of gendered relations and stereotypes so pervasive in the didactic literature of the time that she purposefully employs in *Santa Guglielma*.

In his *De uxoria,* or "On Wifely Duties," a tract dedicated to Lorenzo de Medici the Elder and written on the occasion of his nuptials to Ginevra Cavalcanti in 1416, the Venetian humanist Francesco Barbaro stresses the importance of choosing a wife "who is a virgin well-endowed with virtue, charm, a noble lineage, whose great wealth the entire world indeed admires but whose chastity, constancy, and prudence all men of goodwill esteem highly."[35] Similarly, in Pulci's play, the King of Hungary instructs his ambassadors to search far and wide for a noble wife "adorna di costumi e d'onestate" ("graced with chastity and habits good").[36] Echoing Barbaro's instructions, Guglielma's parents admonish her to remember the virtues and obligations deemed essential for a good wife: Guglielma should be respectful of her spouse ("reverente" in the original), wise in speech, chaste and devout in her actions, merciful and kind to all her subjects, mindful of her parents, zealous in charity, and fearful of God.[37]

Conversant with clerical sources and humanist writings on virginity, marriage, and the role of women within the family, Pulci was familiar with the narrative legend tradition of Guglielma, though we have no proof that she worked directly with the extant fifteenth-century prose version of the legend, composed by the Ferrarese friar Antonio Bonfadini.[38] Nonetheless it is to Bonfadini's prose narrative that I will refer in discussing the striking adaptation Pulci made to the legend tradition, as she wove didactic sources and contemporary issues of gender and spirituality into the dramatic text.

In one remarkable adaptation of the prose material, Pulci skips altogether the second iteration of the slandering, the fall from high status, and the reinstatement pattern that is typical in the narrative tradition of the persecuted queen.[39] While this could indeed be a dramatic necessity, I would argue that the playwright strategically manipulates the narrative tradition to reinforce the moral and spiritual lessons she intended to convey to her contemporary audiences, while also addressing issues that were part and parcel of the lived experiences of her female public. Pulci's most striking innovation in relation to the legend is the distinctive emphasis she places on the themes of female obedience and women's submission to fathers and husbands, widespread *topoi* in the contemporary writings of clerical and lay authors alike. A central construct in her *rappresentazione,* these themes are virtually absent in the legend. Both the legend and the play open with a search for a bride and a marriage stipulation, as the King of England tries to persuade Guglielma to forgo her vow of virginity and wed the King of Hungary. In the legend, Guglielma is portrayed as a "national heroine"[40] called to continue the royal tradition of activism in the evangelization of faraway territories, the establishing of religious houses, and the funding of charitable institutions. The author of the prose narrative is careful to emphasize the missionary aspect and the momentous achievements of such a pious undertaking: in Bonfadini's depiction of female sanctity, Guglielma's self-sacrifice—understood as forced renunciation of a life of virginity—engenders the spiritual salvation of the newly converted Hungarian people.[41]

In the play, however, the emphasis on the proselytizing strategy of conversion is missing. Using Guglielma's desire for virginity coercively, the king frames his discourse within a narrow domestic dimension, couched in a language of domestic obligations and moral duties: Guglielma can fulfill her spiritual vocation by strengthening her newly converted husband's faith.[42] The king's exhortation is consistent with the teachings of contemporary preachers, who stressed a wife's role in maintaining a devout Christian household. The Franciscan friar Bernardino da Siena insisted on the moral obligation of women to care for the spiritual well-being of their spouses: "Today is a time in which wives have to instruct their husbands, since in general the women of Florence have more of God than men."[43] Similarly, Cherubino da Siena, reflecting on the salvific potential of domestic female piety ("molte volte si salva lo marito iniquo e malvagio per la moglie buona e pietosa" ["many times is an unjust and wicked husband saved by a good and pious wife"]), preached that God had granted wives a spiritual role as "helpmates" (*aiutorio*) of their husbands.[44] By underscoring the domestic scope of Guglielma's ordeals, Pulci signals early on that it is within the theater of the family that new forms of "martyrdom" become accessible to pious women.[45]

Female obedience and submission to male authority was a main concern of humanists as well, who hailed obedience as the most important virtue to be cultivated in a woman. For Barbaro, obedience is a wife's master and companion, "nothing more important, nothing greater can be demanded of a wife than this."[46] Drawing from the writings of the ancients, he recounts the admirable words of a Spartan woman as a model to be imitated by Florentine wives: "when I was a girl I learned to obey the dictates of my parents, and now I realize that it is best to follow the wishes of my husband if I want to be what I ought to be."[47] This rhetoric of female obedience to fathers and husbands, so inimical to notions of female agency, figures prominently in the play, yet it is virtually absent in the prose narrative. As mentioned earlier, in the prose legend Guglielma takes an active role in her decision to marry and, at first, withholds her consent. It is only after receiving clerical assurances that it is God's will that she wed for the sake of a newly formed community of believers that the young princess agrees to the betrothal. In the play, however, Pulci deliberately emphasizes the coercive role that parental pressure plays in Guglielma's decision to marry, portraying Guglielma as a powerless victim of patriarchal hierarchies she is unable and unwilling to contest. When the queen enjoins her daughter to assent to their demands, Guglielma, addressing her father as "maestate" and "signor" ("your majesty" and "my lord"), acknowledges her gendered obligation to obedience:

Per non esser a voi disubidiente
io voglio a tanti prieghi aconsentire,
benché disposta fussi la mia mente
vergine e casta vivere e morire.
Benigno padre mio, giusto e clemente,
né debbo o posso a te nulla disdire:
se così piace alla tua maestate,
signor, sia fatto la tua volontate.

To not be disobedient to you,
I wish to yield to prayers so pressing, yet
My mind has been resolved to be a maid,
A virgin chaste to live and chaste to die.
My kindly father, merciful and just,
For that I can't refuse you, and should not,
If it's so pleasing to your majesty,
My lord, then let your will be done by me.[48]

With words modeled, almost verbatim, on the Lord's Prayer, she then submits to the king's request: "My lord, then let your will be done by me," a reminder to Pulci's audiences that in the "natural" hierarchy underpinning Florentine family structure, the law of obedience to fathers took precedence over religious inclinations and that, in Marsilio Ficino's words, fathers were a "second God" whose divine commands were to be obeyed with reverence and fear.[49]

Pulci again places Guglielma's obedience front and center at the betrothal, when the king celebrates the submissive nature of his daughter: though determined to serve Christ, Guglielma had granted his prayers, "pur volendo ubidir come figliuola" ("an obedient daughter she would be").[50] While mentions of Guglielma's spiritual inclinations testify to her chaste nature, the emphasis on her obedient nature might be intended to reassure her spouse: primed to be a docile and respectful daughter, the young bride would very likely be agreeable to subjecting herself to the authority of a husband. In praising the willing obedience of Giannozzo's wife, Leon Battista Alberti makes a similar argument: "Rispuose e disse che aveva imparato ubidire il padre e la madre sua, e che da loro avea comandamento sempre obedire me, e pertanto era disposta fare ciò che io gli comandassi" ("She replied and said that she had learned to obey her mother and father, and that they had instructed her to always obey me, and therefore she was willing to do whatever I commanded her").[51] Such exhortations to wifely obedience were also pervasive in the matrimonial literature popularized by the clergy. In his *Regole della vita matrimoniale,* Cherubino da Siena instructed women to emulate Sara, the biblical paradigm of female obedience, and to address their spouses reverently and humbly as "messere" and "signore," for that was the will of God.[52] In his *Regola del governo di cura familiare,* Giovanni Dominici reminded Bartolomea degli Obizzi that the absolute power of husbands over their wives was divinely ordained as a consequence of Eve's disobedience and that wifely obedience is both punitive and redemptive.[53]

Interested in the political function of marriage, humanist thinkers insisted on the central role played by a submissive wife in maintaining social harmony and civic peace.[54] Barbaro emphasized a wife's obligation to obey her husband, stating that "a wife must agree to the first principle that she does not disagree with her husband on any point." For the humanist, "If [a wife] is to perform her duty of maintaining and securing peace and quiet in her marriage, then nothing should more occupy her mind than the need in all matters to assent to her husband."[55] This is a lesson Guglielma seems to have internalized well, as she vows herself to utter submission to her husband's wishes: "Altro non vo' se non ch'io chiego grazia/ch'i' facci, signor mio, tua voglia sazia" ("I wish naught else—unless I ask for grace/ That I, my lord, may here perform your will").[56] It is this language of obligation pervasive in *ad status* literature and this terrestrial chain of command that binds married women to their husbands that Pulci brings forcefully to the fore, as when Guglielma's father reminds the Hungarian ambassadors that "Guglielma ha' ubidire il suo signore: [. . .] Quanto gli par, di lei disponga e quando" ("Guglielma' s duty is to obey her lord/ [. . .] Let him/ Direct her when and as he will").[57] Perceived as an extension of God's will, the saintly heroine's obedience to her husband's authority is never in doubt. Addressed as "Guglielma mia, sempre ubbidiente" ("my ever-obedient Guglielma") by her spouse, Guglielma is forced to leave behind the monastery where she had taken refuge:"Dilette suore mia, poi ch'a Dio piace/ che questo sposo mio debba seguire, [. . .] con ch'io credetti viver e morire. [. . .] a me bisogna a' sua prieghi ubidire ("Belovèd sisters mine, since God is pleased/ That this my husband I accompany, [. . .] With you, I'd thought to live, had planned to die. [. . .] But his requests, I am obliged to heed."[58] Her favor with God publicly acknowledged and her spiritual authority firmly established, Guglielma still remained subject to her husband's will.

While hagiographic narratives of female saints were traditional tools in molding women and while Pulci carefully portrays her holy heroine as conforming to the norms of the Florentine ideology of marriage, *Santa Guglielma* is not, despite appearances, a dramatized manual of conduct aimed at regulating women's social behavior and reinforcing prescriptive norms about female submission to male authority. Drawing on the *topoi* and the language of gendered relations pervasive in conduct manuals and domestic treatises penned by clerical and humanist writers of her time, Pulci reinterprets the current debate on the role of women in the family to explore ways for women, who are trapped in a marriage and seek to quench their desire for spiritual fulfillment, to transition to a new vocation ("or altra vïa mi convien cercare" ["another path I must expect to seek"] a wretched Guglielma anxiously laments).[59] Bravely repudiating the traditional conjugal family, Pulci puts forward with originality the penitential ideal of spiritual marriage for her female audience, a call to women to advocate for intramarital chastity[60] as both a way to actualize their yearnings for a deeper, more intimate relationship with God and as a "stepping stone to freedom"[61] within marriage.

A prominent feature of late medieval female piety, lay chastity was inextricably tied to the penitential ethos and the devotional practices promoted by the mendicant orders and by popular reformers such as San Bernardino da Siena, Bernardino da Feltre, Fra Mariano da Genazzano, and Girolamo Savonarola in their repeated calls for the spiritual and social renewal of the Florentines.[62] Powerful among laypeople of Quattrocento Florence, the penitential ideal was a defining feature of female sanctity and women's religious practices at the time of Pulci's writing.[63] Indeed, an examination of Pulci's many adaptations and amplifications of the prose legend reveal her programmatic effort to imbue the dramatic text with the penitential ethos. Given the rapidly rising number of contemporary laywomen seeking to commit to penitential practices as "a way of life,"[64] it is hardly surprising that, in a *rappresentazione* arguably intended for a female audience, Pulci is careful to underscore the association of women's holiness with the hallmarks of penitential piety (chastity, humility and obedience, devotion to the Passion, patient suffering, asceticism, and supernatural experiences), spiritual *topoi* that are conspicuously undeveloped in the prose narrative.

A careful examination of the play reveals that all trappings of a female vocation to intramarital chastity and the ascetic life are cleverly woven into the dramatic text. First, Guglielma's story clearly conforms to the pattern of hagiographic narratives of chaste married saints: a childhood desire to remain chaste, thwarted by a coerced marriage, is a common feature in the *Vitae* of female saints who initiated chaste unions.[65] Indeed, in the later Middle Ages, saints' lives were traditionally associated with the circulation of models of spiritual marriage: while familial examples and contemporary saints were compelling models in shaping the vocation for chastity, hagiographical models of spiritual marriage were internalized by the laity through widespread circulation of saints' *Vitae*.[66] Furthermore, "wedding-night proselytism" and devotion to the Passion of Christ are common traits in the lives of pious matrons who successfully initiated a chaste union.[67] Pulci develops the penitential *topos* of the Passion in a long "pastoral" speech uttered by Guglielma after her wedding feast. Approaching the temple with her spouse, Guglielma looks upon a crucifix and "dice molte cose della vita e passione di Cristo" ("says many things about the life and passion of Christ"):[68] so convincing is her preaching, that the king experiences something of a mystical experience (his mind "a complemplar resta sospeso" [is "fixed in contemplation"]) and presumably forgoes all bodily desires, given that he "né altro brama o cerca la mia mente" ("neither seeks nor yearns for anything") other than traveling to the Holy Sepulcher to visit the place where Christ's body "fu disteso in croce per salvar l'umana gente" ("hung upon the cross to save the human race"),[69] possibly a nod to their unconsummated union and to the mutual conversion to chastity that awaits the couple at the end of the play.

Another striking addition Pulci makes to the dramatic text is Guglielma's lengthy denunciation of the physical and spiritual wretchedness brought about by wedlock and by the dutiful obedience to father and spouse, an explicit indictment of the burdens of marriage consistent with advocacy for chaste unions. Awaiting her execution with trembling and fear, Guglielma bitterly laments that torture and death are the "delizie e somme feste" ("solemn celebrations and delights") meted out by a "crudo sposo" ("cruel spouse") she never once failed to please ("Ah crudo sposo, come hai sentenziato/ colei che a te non fe' mai fallimento?/Per premio sarò data a tal supplicio, / sì come Isach al santo sacrificio" ["Ah, cruel spouse, why have you sentenced her/ Who never once has disappointed you?/As my rewards, I am given to the fire/Like Isaac, offered on the holy pyre"]). It is, however, to the "dolce padre" ("sweet father"), who had sent her "in perdimento" ("to perdition"), that Guglielma addresses most of her poetic grievances: although she had vowed to remain "pura e casta" ("pure and chaste") and to renounce all "mondane spoglie" ("wearisome and worldly spoils"), she had agreed to marriage only out of filial obedience, against "tutte le mie voglie" (her "every wish"). Coerced to remain in a world "pien d'ogni martire" ("filled with every pain"), she was now condemned to bear "grieve pesi" ("such heavy grief") and end her life "in pianti e 'n doglie" ("in weeping and in woes").[70] Rendered in images and a language imbued of penitential spirituality, wifely suffering at the hands of a persecuting husband is also evoked to emphasize the saint's patience and humility.[71] Indeed, the torture meted out by husband and father functions as a backdrop against which the saintly heroine can show off her exceptional virtues of submission and long-suffering obedience, traditional *topoi* in the hagiographic narratives of married saints' lives.[72] Guglielma's bitter disappointment with earthly love highlights the fallacious value of obedience directed to terrestrial relationships; her direct connection with biblical paradigms of obedience and patient suffering such as those of Isaac (but also those of Job and Daniel) also signifies the moral superiority of suffering when obedience to a spouse is humbly carried out as submission to the will of God.[73] The penitential afflatus of her extreme denunciation of all secular values (the "wearisome and worldly spoils" she so abhorred) seems to also suggest that the experience of suffering at the hands of a husband was to be understood by married women as a stage toward their spiritual perfection in imitation of Christ's suffering.

Pulci significantly amplifies the narrative again in relation to the prose legend, by circling back to Guglielma's quest to forge a new spiritual vocation for herself, a *via vera e perfetta* ("true and perfect path") to female spiritual perfection, immediately after her denunciation of the folly of obedience to male authority, which had prevented her from embracing the penitential life she had yearned for from youth.[74] Wandering alone in a desert, her heart ablaze with love for God, Guglielma pledges to serve her new bridegroom Christ and "her" mother Mary ("Tutta la mia vita servire intendo / a te, mio Sposo, e mia madre Maria/ fa' che sia meco" ["And I intend, my Spouse, to serve you all/ My life and let my mother Mary be with me"]), a vow of chastity conspicuously absent in the prose legend.[75] While earlier Guglielma had questioned a conception of mundane love that engenders fruitless suffering, here she promotes mystical union with Christ as the ideal marriage.[76] In renouncing the familial relationships that had prevented her from pursuing a religious vocation and from joining a more gratifying celestial family, Guglielma signaled to married women that celestial union with Christ as bridegroom was preferable to a mortal spouse and that they too, after obediently submitting to male demands, could at last gain independence from the authority of husbands and enjoy a mature union with Christ through the superior state of chaste marriage.[77] Indeed, while it is true that the late Middle Ages saw a significant increase in the number of married saints, it was by renouncing sexuality and the married life and by embracing the ascetic life that these holy figures achieved sanctity.[78]

A strong penitential afflatus also permeates the opening and closing stanzas, with its emphasis on suffering, humility, obedience and the characteristic call to reject all worldly values, a sentiment clearly dear to Antonia Pulci, for we find a similar, if only more feverish, urging for *contemptus mundi* in *Santa Domitilla*. In the prologue, the *angelo annunziatore* draws a parallel between the crucified Jesus and Guglielma, between his Passion and the prolonged miseries (*affanni*) endured by Gugliema as she wandered in the world (*peregrina*) until she was restored ("ristorata"), like Job, to her previous exalted state as queen. The penitential ideal and the didactic purpose of the play are reintroduced, and more fully developed, in the closing stanza. Urging all those still embroiled in the secular world (*selva errante*) to repudiate the world's allurements as elusive folly and turn to God in all humility, the angel proclaims the salvific function of penitential suffering, whose eternal reward will be in Heaven ("Felice chi nel mondo è tormentato / per viver poi nel ciel sempre beato" ["Ah, they are happy whom the world's oppressed, / For they'll live on in heaven, ever blest"]).[79] It is worth noting that, by situating Guglielma's wanderings not in the dark woods of the prose legend but in the religious landscape of the desert wilderness, Pulci further emphasizes the interiority and penitential character of her heroine's sanctity and signifies the rigorous path of renunciation and salvation from sin that Pulci meant to encourage for her audience, if not for herself.[80]

The widely held belief that patient suffering, penitential asceticism, and chastity earn the saint heavenly rewards is confirmed supernaturally through visions.[81] No sooner has Guglielma vowed herself to chastity than she experiences angelic encounters, and the Virgin Mary herself appears to praise Guglielma for her unwavering faith, her obedience, and her patience in adversity. As a reward, Guglielma receives intimate reassurances about her state, becomes the recipient of divine favor, and is endowed with thaumaturgic powers and the authority to confess repentant sinners, a supernatural affirmation that the saint had achieved a high state of spiritual perfection and was on the right path to forge a new vocation for herself.[82]

At the end of the play, upon his return to Hungary, the king invites his courtiers to embrace a life of renunciation, poverty, prayer, and discipline in what is a remarkable paean to the penitential ideal:

Questo ermo sarà il mio regal palazo,
questi cilicci fien le riche veste,
queste caverne fien nostro solazo,
le discipline fien l'ornate veste.
O mondo falso, o stolto, o cieco, è pazzo
chi delle tue delizie si riveste!
Adio, vi lascio, umana pompa e gloria,
e tu, Signor, mi mostra la vittoria.

This hermitage my royal palace will
Become, let these hair shirts be my rich clothes,
These caverns, let them be our solace, and
Let us array ourselves with the marks of whips.
O false, O foolish world, O blind, one who
Arrays himself in your delights is mad!
Farewell, I leave you, pomp and human glory,
And, Lord, may you show me the victory![83]

This is arguably the most startling adaptation of the prose legend. In the prose narrative Guglielma and the king return to Hungary, where they glorify God by lavishly endowing monasteries and churches. Guglielma continues to performs miracles and is commended for her great sanctity; the couple, however, do not renounce their worldly powers. In the play, on the contrary, Guglielma, the king, and his brother divest themselves of all mundane affiliations and enter a hermitage together, where they embrace the austerities of the penitential life.

Such striking adaptation of the prose material clearly points to a penitential model of spiritual sanctification for married women underpinned by the notion of conjugal chastity: as humility and obedience to God surpass virginity as criteria for sanctity, chaste marriages emerge as the other path to spiritual perfection and even holiness.[84] The story of the long-suffering Guglielma fulfills St. Paul's hope of unified salvation of husband and wife, as Guglielma converts her husband to both faith and chastity: this is the ultimate sign of her success, a success she achieves through her own unquestioning obedience.[85] As her spouse shifts from master to companion in service, Guglielma moves from a position of submission to one of equality: freed of familial responsibilities, the ever-obedient Guglielma obtains at last to embrace the penitential ethos of renunciation and to live out the vocation to chastity she had aspired to from youth.

In *Santa Guglielma,* marriage is thus cast as a divinely ordained investment in salvation of which patient suffering, utmost humility, and total submission to male authority were sine qua non conditions. In this perspective, no longer deemed as a stumbling block in a woman's spiritual progress, marriage and subordination to a husband could be presented as an integral part of a married woman's progress toward a mature spiritual vocation.[86] Against the persecution of fathers and husbands, Pulci deployed the story of Guglielma's Job-like obedience, suffering, and reinstatement to reassure married women that God loves and rewards chaste and obedient wives as much as virgin maids.[87]

Denied secular authority because of her gender, Guglielma gains spiritual authority through her exemplary display of steadfast obedience to father and husband—a submission interpreted as obedience to God's will—and through her humility. As her spiritual authority ripples through society, the ever-obedient Guglielma becomes a model of conjugal sanctity, a community healer, a mediator of supernatural protection, a corporate intercessor, and an agent of salvation, thus defying traditional gendering of spiritual authority. Her privileged relationship with God offers Guglielma the visibility women traditionally lacked, allows her to publicly take on a religious and social role, and ultimately empowers the saintly heroine to negotiate positions of spiritual and social independence for herself, thus turning upside down dominant hierarchies of power relations and gender expectations.

Patterned after a long list of married female saints that had initiated intramarital chastity, Guglielma's tale can thus be taken to exemplify the spiritual journey of contemporary married women toward a new spiritual vocation that, arising from their childhood desire for the virginal life and in keeping with the penitential philosophy of the day, embraced the notion of spiritualized marriage as a model for marital union. One is bound to wonder, however, whether the story of Santa Guglielma, with its emphasis on female obedience and submission, should be interpreted as a tale of female empowerment or female subjugation, as encouraging women's potential for subversion or as reinscribing female submission to male authority. In her work on Margery Kempe, Sarah Beckwith warns that hagiographic narratives could be deployed to reinforce social norms and to pressure young women into marrying.[88] Pointing to the "precarious balance between subversion and subservience"[89] in the lives of chaste female saints, Beckwith argues that such narratives, by equating "victimisation, passivity, subjection with femininity" and by "underpinning that subjection with a heavenly guarantor," rather than subverting oppressive social hierarchies, effectively contribute to perpetuate patriarchal discourse.[90] For Dyan Elliott, however, the model of spiritual marriage was largely a female initiative and should be taken as a woman's "affirmative choice;"[91] chaste cohabitation offered women unparalleled opportunities to participate in the penitential movement and to engage in austere models of ascetism, and as such, it enabled women to gain autonomy from male control and to enjoy greater freedom of movement;[92] furthermore, the hagiographic narratives of chaste saints emboldened women who construed spiritual marriage as a mechanism to bridge social expectations and spiritual aspirations.[93] I would argue that Pulci provided models of female chastity that shaped women's aspirations and that inspired them to take steps toward social autonomy and spiritual independence; and that Guglielma's story of spiritual progress and transition to chastity and the penitential life could be read by a female public as a "stepping stone to freedom."[94]

I would like to suggest that Pulci's dramatized hagiography of a chaste married woman might have also functioned as a conduit to express contemporary women's social distress and religious dissent.[95] While this argument needs further elaboration elsewhere, I would like to briefly touch on it with a few examples taken from the play. To begin with, eschewing the prevailing clerical and humanistic view on the goodness of matrimony and the importance of the conjugal family for the state, Pulci does not guide the behavior of pious women toward a model of spiritual affirmation that conformed to, and was functional within, the patriarchal society of Renaissance Florence; rather, she puts forth a more radical, spiritualized model of marriage, suggesting that release from sexual duties is a first step for married women toward renunciation of the world and entry into unconventional, loose modes of spiritual affiliations that better served female piety and that placed women beyond male control.[96] A "transgressor" for having entered "into the male territory of authorship,"[97] Pulci scatters hints of "subversion" across the dramatic text. Guglielma finds her own authentic voice and speaks out in distress precisely when she denounces an oppressive patriarchal social system that forces girls to forgo their childhood vow of virginity in the name of strategic matrimonial alliances. While in the legend Guglielma achieves the nominal conversion of her spouse yet fails to transition to chastity, Pulci advocates for her heroine a more extraordinary example of piety and a rigorous ascetic path to spiritual perfection that demanded renunciation of all worldly values, at a time and in a city aflame with calls for social and spiritual renewal. The noninstitutional orientation of Guglielma's piety and the disappearance from the dramatic text of any reference to the *servi di Dio* (who play a deciding role in the legendary heroine's decision to marry) could also be taken to suggest both spiritual dissent and an inclination to eschew clerical control. Even more extraordinary is the model of female holiness Pulci selects for her play. While we have no proof that Pulci was familiar with the cult of the historical Guglielma, her authorial choice is nonetheless intriguing. A controversial saint, the historical Guglielma was first venerated as the "Incarnation of the Holy Spirit for the salvation of women,"[98] and posthumously declared a heretic. Like Pulci's fictional heroine, she held great spiritual authority, performed miracles, lived chastely (as a widow), and performed great works of charity. Considering the transgressive example of Pulci's dramatic heroine—a healer, a confessor, and a visionary unencumbered by a male confessor—we might speculate that Pulci might have made her authorial selection to dismiss the idea that women, barred from institutional forms of power, were incapable of holding positions of social and spiritual authority and perhaps even to express her own aspirations for spiritual leadership, which she was able to actualize only after the death of her husband. It is also worth noticing that while promoting models of female holiness, Pulci sets forth male examples of social renunciation as well. The Hungarian king's decision to publicly renounce wealth and social status and to reject reproduction and family responsibilities would have entailed significant social and political consequences: by entering into a chaste union and by embarking on a life of prayer and penance, he willingly forgoes his duties to govern and to secure the royal lineage by producing an heir. In Quattrocento Florence, where marriage and family were the cornerstone of civic ethics and the foundation of the city's socio-economic and political order, *Santa Guglielma* delivered a potentially subversive political message of social dissent that encouraged Florentine men, whose main responsibility was to increase the family,[99] to take a radical step and to leave Florentine's society most cherished institution behind.[100]

While chastity made the marriage holier, the clergy discouraged married women from the pursuit of spiritual marriage, for release from sexual activities subverted gender constructions and allowed women to gain autonomy from their husbands.[101] Husbands, likewise, feared that excessive piety might induce wives to disobey them, thus eluding women's obligations of submission to their authority.[102] In promoting chastity in marriage as a path to female sanctity, Antonia Pulci thus emboldened women to seek out a female spiritual vocation that challenged patriarchal authority at home and in society.

Notes

1. I will not repeat here what has been written elsewhere. Elissa Weaver has done the seminal archival research on Pulci's life and works. See her introduction to Antonia Pulci, *Saints' Lives and Bible Stories for the Stage: A Bilingual Edition*, ed. Elissa B. Weaver, trans. James W. Cook (Toronto: Centre for Reformation and Renaissance Studies, 2010); Elissa B. Weaver, "Antonia Pulci e la sacra rappresentazione al femminile," in *La maschera e il volto. Il teatro in Italia*, ed. Francesco Bruni (Venice: Fondazione Giorgio Cini: Saggi Marsilio, 2002); Elissa B. Weaver, "Antonia Tanini (1452–1501), Playwright, and Wife of Bernardo Pulci (1438–1488)," in *Essays in Honor of Marga Cottino-Jones*, eds. Laura White, Andrea Fedi, and Kristin Phillips (Fiesole: Edizioni Cadmo, 2003), 23–37; Emanuela Carney, "Antonia Pulci's *Rappresentazione di santa Domitilla* and the Defense of Virginity in Quattrocento Florence," in *Scenes from Italian Convent Life: An Anthology of Theatrical Texts and Contexts*, ed. Elissa B. Weaver (Ravenna: Longo Editore, 2009), 11–36 and attendant bibliography; Judith Bryce, "Adjusting the Canon for Later Fifteenth-Century Florence: The Case of Antonia Pulci," in *The Renaissance Theatre: Texts, Performance, Design*, ed. Christopher Cairns (Aldershot, UK: Ashgate, 1999), 133–134; Judith Bryce, "'Or altra *vïa* mi convïen cercare': Marriage, Salvation and Sanctity in Antonia Tanini Pulci's Rappresentazione di Santa Guglielma," in *Theatre, Opera, and Performance in Italy from the Fifteenth Century to the Present: Essays in Honour of Richard Andrews*, eds. Brian Richardson, Simon Gilson, and Catherine Keen (Leeds: The Society for Italian Studies, 2004). Modern editions of Pulci's plays are found in Alessandro D'Ancona, *Sacre rappresentazioni dei secoli XIV, XV e XVI* (Florence: Successori Le Monnier, 1872), 3: 208–234; *Teatro del Quattrocento: sacre rappresentazioni*, ed. Luigi Banfi (Turin: Utet, 1963), 533–577; *Sacre rappresentazioni fiorentine del Quattrocento*, ed. G. Ponte (Milan: Marzorati, 1994), 69–98.

2. The bibliography on the subject of female spirituality in the late Middle Ages and the proliferation of new modes of women's religious affiliations is vast. For a brief, yet excellent, introduction to the topic see Caroline Walker Bynum, "Religious Women in the Later Middle Ages," in *Christian Spirituality: High Middle Ages and Reformation*, ed. Jill Raitt (New York: Crossroads, 1987), 127–139; on the rise of women saints and the characteristics most often associated with female holiness during this period, see Donald Weinstein and Rudolph M. Bell, *Saints and Society: The Two Worlds of Western Christendom, 1000–1700* (Chicago: The University of Chicago Press, 1986), 220–238.

3. Carney, "Antonia Pulci's *Rappresentazione*," 23 and n. 42.

4. There exists an extensive bibliography on the "sacre rappresentazioni." See at least the fundamental studies done by Nerida Newbigin, *Making a Play for God: The Sacre Rappresentazioni of Renaissance Florence* (Toronto: Centre for Renaissance and Reformation

Studies, 2021); Nerida Newbigin, "Antonia Pulci and the First Anthology of Sacre Rappresentazioni (1483?)," *La Bibliofilia* 118, no. 3 (2016); Nerida Newbigin, *Feste d'Oltrarno: Plays in Churches in Fifteenth-Century Florence* (Florence: Leo Olschki, 1996). See also Cesare Molinari, *Spettacoli fiorentini del Quattrocento: contributi allo studio delle sacre rappresentazioni* (Venice: Neri Pozza, 1961); Paola Ventrone, *Gli araldi della commedia: teatro a Firenze nel Rinascimento* (Ospedalettto [Pisa]: Pacini Editore, 1993); Paola Ventrone, "Per una morfologia della sacra rappresentazione fiorentina," in *Teatro e culture della rappresentazione: lo spettacolo in Italia nel Quattrocento*, ed. Raimondo Guarino (Bologna: Il Mulino, 1988), 195–225.

5. Sarah Beckwith, "A Very Material Mysticism: The Medieval Mysticism of Margery Kempe," in *Medieval Literature: History, Criticism and Ideology*, ed. David Aers (New York: St. Martin's Press, 1986), 37.

6. Carney, "Antonia Pulci's *Rappresentazione*," 11–36.

7. For full biographical information, see Pulci, *Saints' Lives*, 5–30, and note 1 above.

8. On Antonia Pulci's comparatively advanced literacy, see Carney, "Antonia Pulci's *Rappresentazione*," 15–16. See also Pulci, *Saints' Lives*, 2 and note 2; Bryce, "Adjusting the Canon," 134; Weaver, *Convent Theatre*, 240. On women's literacy in fifteenth-century Florence, see at least Judith Bryce, "Les Livres des Florentines. Reconsidering Women's Literacy in Quattrocento Florence," in *At the Margins: Minority Groups in Premodern Italy*, ed. Stephen J. Milner (Minneapolis: The University of Minnesota Press, 2005), 133–161; Sharon Strocchia, "Learning the Virtues: Convent Schools and Female Culture in Renaissance Florence," in *Women's Education in Early Modern Europe: A History, 1500–1800*, ed. Barbara J. Whitehead (New York: Garland, 1999), 3–46; Christiane Klapisch-Zuber, "Le chiavi fiorentine di Barbablù: L'apprendimento della lettura a Firenze nel XV secolo," *Quaderni Storici* 57 (1984): 765–792; Maria Ludovica Lenzi, *Donne e madonne: L'educazione femminile nel primo Rinascimento italiano* (Torino: Loescher, 1982); Virginia Cox, *Women's Writing in Italy, 1400–1650* (Baltimore: Johns Hopkins University Press, 2008), 1–36.

9. Newbigin, *Making a Play for God*, 37, and Newbigin, "Antonia Pulci," 337. Weaver argues that Antonia Pulci was "if not the first, certainly one of the first women writers to have sent her work to press," sharing such distinction only with the humanist writer Cassandra Fedele. Pulci, *Saints' Lives*, 2 and n. 2. Lucrezia Tornabuoni was another notable woman writer associated with Medicean Florence. However, Lucrezia's literary production circulated in manuscript form. See Lucrezia Tornabuoni, *Poemetti sacri*, ed. Fulvio Pezzarossa (Firenze: Olschki, 1978); Lucrezia Tornabuoni de' Medici, *Sacred Narratives*, ed. and trans. Jane Tylus (Chicago: University of Chicago Press, 2001).

10. On marriage as a "theater of sanctification" of the couple and its redemptive potential on family and community see Duncan Robertson, *The Medieval Saints' Lives: Spiritual Renewal and Old French Literature* (Lexington, KY: French Forum, 1995), 234–239, 247–249.

11. Dyan Elliott, *Spiritual Marriages: Sexual Abstinence in Medieval Wedlock* (Princeton, NJ: Princeton University Press, 1995); Bryce, "'Or altra vïa," 31-32.

12. On Antonia and Bernardo Pulci, see George Ulysse, "Un Couple d'écrivains: les sacre rappresentazioni de Bernardo et Antonia Pulci," in *Les femmes écrivains en Italie au Moyen ge et à la Renaissance*, ed. George Ulysse (Aix-en-Provence: Publications de l'Université de Provençe, 1994), 177–196.

13. Weaver suggests that Antonia Pulci's plays were set in type while Bernardo was still alive, since Antonia appears, in both *Santa Domitilla* and *Santa Guglielma*, as "lady Antonia, wife of Bernardo Pulci," which indicates she had not yet become a widow; see Weaver, in Antonia Pulci, *Saints' Lives*, 22–23. Newbigin dates the collection to before the year 1484, "Antonia Pulci," 344. Dávid Falvay suggests that Pulci wrote her play in the 1470s, in "Il mito del re ungherese nella letteratura religiosa del Quattrocento," *Nuova Corvina: rivista di italianistica* 20 (2008): 60. More recently, Newbigin has argued that 1483, the date that appears on the first page of the first volume of the Miscomini anthology, should be taken as the year of publication. See Newbigin, *Making a Play for God*, 440.

14. Newbigin safely attributes the two-volume anthology of religious plays to the press of Antonio Miscomini and argues that Antonia Pulci was responsible for compiling the collection and that the "modestly elegant" anthology was likely meant as a joint tribute to Lucrezia Tornabuoni and Lorenzo de' Medici. Noting that Bernardo and Antonia Pulci are the only authors whose names appear in the anthology, Newbigin also points out that the plays are closely connected to the Florentine youth confraternity of the Purification and were meant for the advancement of boys; additionally, she suggests that the couple's involvement with the confraternity dated from early in their married life. Newbigin, *Making a Play for God*, 440–443. *Making a Play for God*, Newbigin's seminal work on the Florentine "rappresentazioni," appeared after this study was completed.

15. Newbegin, "Antonia Pulci," 345; Weaver, in Antonia Pulci, *Saints' Lives*, 2–3. See also Paola Veltrone, "Acting and Reading Drama: Notes on Florentine *sacre rappresentazioni* in Print," *Journal of Early Modern Studies* 8 (2019): 74.

16. Carney, "Antonia Pulci's *Rappresentazione*," 15; Veltrone, "Acting and Reading Drama," 71–73. Veltrone notes that the textual arrangement and choice of fonts made the anthology highly suitable for reading. Weaver points out that there is scant surviving evidence of staged performances by nuns, *Convent Theatre*, 99–100 and n. 9. Judith Bryce notices that Lucrezia Tornabuoni expected her poems to be read or read aloud. See her "Vernacular poetry and mystery plays," in *A History of Women's Writing in Italy*, eds. Letizia Panizza and Sharon Wood (Cambridge: Cambridge University Press, 2000), 13.

17. Anna Pullia and Dávid Falvay, "La Sacra Rappresentazione Fiorentina di Santa Guglielma, Regina d'Ungheria," in *Sul filo di ragno della memoria. Studi in onore di Ilona Fried*, eds. Franciska d'Elhoungne Hervai and Dávid Falvay (Budapest: ELTE, 2012), 235. On the "sacre rappresentazioni" safely attributed to Antonia Pulci, see Weaver, in Antonia Pulci, *Saints' Lives*, 4; Weaver, *Antonia Tanini*, 32–34 and n 35, 39, and 40; Weaver, *Convent Theatre*, 103.

18. Carney, "Antonia Pulci's *Rappresentazione*," 12–13. By "ad status" literature, I am referring to a vast body of didactic works (pedagogical tracts, manuals of conduct, sermons, pastoral letters, etc.) written for the spiritual development and moral edification of women. Directed to female audiences and aimed at the social and religious disciplining of women in each different stage of life, these prescriptive texts were geared toward particular categories of women, grouped according to their sexual status (as virgins, widows, and married women) or according to their social roles (daughter, mother, wife, widow, or nun). See Gabriella Zarri, "Christian good manners: spiritual and monastic rules in the Quattro- and Cinquecento," in *Women in Italian Renaissance Culture and Society*, ed. Letizia Panizza

(Cambridge: Legenda, 2000), 77; Gabriella Zarri, ed. *Donna, disciplina, creanza cristiana dal XV al XVII secolo. Studi e testi a stampa* (Rome: Edizioni Storia e Letteratura, 1996).

19. Antonella Degl'Innocenti "Spose e madri nell'agiografia medievale," in *Religione domestica: Medioevo, età moderna* (Caselle di Sommacampagna: Cierre, 2001), 9–10.

20. I am referring here to those charismatic women who established their reputation for holiness as "living saints" during their lifetimes by virtue of their visionary experiences, revelations, prophecies, and miracle-working powers. On this typology of female sanctity and the prominent social, cultural, and political role "sante vive" played in Italy in the period between the last decade of the fifteenth century and the middle of the sixteenth century, see the groundbreaking work by Gabriella Zarri, *Le sante vive. Profezie di corte e devozione femminile tra '400 e '500*, (Torino: Rosenberg & Sellier, 1990).

21. On the reading communities of devout women within the Medici family and the textual practices of lay women's religious associations, see Bryce, "Livres," 147–48 and n.90.

22. On the "accused queen" narrative tradition, see Nancy Black, *Medieval Narratives of Accused Queens* (Gainesville: University Press of Florida, 2003). On the intersection of hagiography and courtly romance, see Robertson, *Medieval Saints' Lives*, 200–204. I will return to this aspect of the play in a future study.

23. There is no mention of a Santa Guglielma in the *Acta Sanctorum* or other martyrologies. We have historical documentation on the existence of a Guglielma da Milano (d. 1281/1282), who was venerated by her followers as the "True God and Holy Spirit." On the historic Guglielma and the hagiographical amplifications of her story, see Marina Benedetti, "Di Regine, Sante e Eretiche. Su Guglielma e sulla Recente Storiografia," *Reti Medievali Rivista* 19, no. 1 (2018): 211–230, doi: 10.6092/1593-2214/5535; Benedetti, *Io non sono Dio. Guglielma di Milano e i Figli dello Spirito Santo* (Milan: Biblioteca Francescana, 1998); Benedetti, *Milano 1300: I processi inquisitoriali contro le devote e i devoti di santa Guglielma*, ed. Marina Benedetti (Milan: Libri Scheiwiller, 1999); Patrizia Maria Costa, *Guglielma la Boema. L'"eretica" di Chiaravalle* (Nuove Edizioni Duomo: Milano, 1985); Grado Giovanni Merlo, "Guglielma la Boema: Tra santità ed eresia al femminile," in *Eresie ed eretici medievali* (Bologna: Il Mulino, 1989), 113–18; Luisa Muraro, *Guglielma e Maifreda Storia di un'eresia femminista* (La Tartaruga Edizioni: Milano, 1985); Barbara Newman, "The Heretic Saint: Guglielma of Bohemia, Milan, and Brunate," *Church History* 74, no. 1 (2005): 8–9; Newman, "Woman Spirit, Woman Pope," in *From Virile Woman to WomanChrist: Studies in Medieval Religion and Literature* (Philadelphia: University of Pennsylvania Press, 1995), 182–223.

24. Bernardo was drawing from a Latin source, the thirteenth-century *Speculum Historiale* of Vincent de Beauvais. See Paola Casciano, "Il cantare di santa Guglielma," in *Editori ed edizioni a Roma nel Rinascimento*, ed. Paola Farenga (Roma: Roma nel Rinascimento, 2005), 28. In Bernardo's "cantare," Guglielma is Empress of Rome, one of the two distinct archetypes of the "accused queen" narrative tradition (see Black, *Medieval Narratives*, 2). Both legend and "rappresentazione" share striking similarities with the Empress of Rome story.

25. For the textual transmission of the legend, see Zsuzsa Kovacs, "La leggenda di santa Guglielma, figlia del Re d'Inghilterra e donna del re d'Ungheria," *Rivista di studi ungheresi* 9 (2010): 29–31; Pullia and Falvay, "Rappresentazione fiorentina," 240–241. I have consulted

the text published by Giuseppe Ferraro, *Vite di S. Guglielma regina d'Ungheria e di S. Eufrasia vergine romana scritte da frate Antonio Bonfadini* (Bologna: G. Romagnoli, 1878).

26. Octave 10. The Italian original and English translation come from Pulci, *Saints Lives*, 152–53.

27. Octave 10, 152–153. On spiritual marriage as a "psychological placebo" and a coercive device as pious women faced a forced marriage, see Elliott, *Spiritual Marriages*,12.

28. For a fuller discussion on the Church Fathers' position on virginity and matrimony, see Carney, "Antonia Pulci's *Rappresentazione*," 23–31 and attendant bibliography. Elizabeth A. Clark, "Dissuading from Marriage: Jerome and the Asceticization of Satire," in *Satiric Advice on Women and Marriage: From Plautus to Chaucer*, ed. Warren S. Smith (Ann Arbor: University of Michigan Press, 2005), 155.

29. Silvana Vecchio, "The Good Wife," in *Silences of the Middle Ages*, ed. Christiane Klapisch-Zuber (Cambridge, MA: Harvard University Press, 1992), 105–106.

30. A cornerstone of medieval Canon law regulating marriage and the sexual relationship of spouses, the concept of conjugal debt refers to the notion that both husband and wife, by virtue of being married, had a mutually binding obligation to engage in sexual intercourse when one spouse demanded it.

31. Vecchio, "The Good Wife," 128–132.

32. Vecchio, "The Good Wife," 132.

33. Francesco Barbaro, *The Wealth of Wives: A Fifteenth-Century Marriage Manual*, ed. and trans. Margaret L. King (Toronto: Iter Academic Press, Arizona Center for Medieval and Renaissance Studies, 2015), 6.

34. Pulci fiercely challanged the ideology of marriage and the prevailing misogyny of humanist writers in *Santa Domitillla*. See Carney, "Antonia Pulci's *Rappresentazione*," 32–35.

35. I have consulted Francesco Barbaro, "On Wifely Duties," in *The Earthly Republic: Italian Humanists on Government and Society*, eds. Benjamin G. Kohl and Ronald G. Witt, trans. Benjamin G. Kohl (Philadelphia: University of Pennsylvania Press, 1978), 227.

36. Pulci, *Saints Lives*, octave 4, 148–149.

37. Pulci, *Saints Lives*, octave 16, 156–157. See also Vecchio, "The Good Wife,"105.

38. On Pulci's presumed access to manuscript material, in and beyond Florence, see Bryce, "'Or altra *vïa*," 25.

39. On the four-part plot structure that characterize tales of accused queens, see Black, *Medieval Narratives*, 2.

40. On this type of female saint, see Michael Goodich, "The Contours of Female Piety in Later Medieval Hagiography," *Church History* 50, no. 1 (March 1981): 26.

41. On saintly queens as "domestic proselytizers," see Jane Tibbetts Schulenburg, "Female Sanctity: Public and Private Roles, ca. 500–1100," in *Women and Power in the Middle Ages*, eds. Mary Carpenter Erler and Maryanne Kowaleski (Athens: University of Georgia Press, 1988), 105. Nancy Black suggests that "the adoption of an idealized queen who chooses to remain in the world" can be construed as an attempt by fifteenth-century authors to put forth new models of female devotion, while also appealing to wider audiences (see Black, *Medieval Narratives*, 139).

42. For examples of this practice, see Elliott, *Spiritual Marriages*, 218.

43. I owe this reference to Nirit Ben-Aryeh Debby, *Renaissance Florence in the Rhetoric of Two Popular Preachers: Giovanni Dominici (1356–1419) and Bernardino da Siena (1380–1444)* (Turnhout, Belgium: Brepols Publishers, 2001), 146.

44. Cherubino da Siena, *Regole della Vita Matrimoniale di Frate Cherubino da Siena*, eds. Francesco Zambrini and Carlo Negroni (Bologna: Romagnoli-dall'Acqua, 1888), 24.

45. On the family as a "theater" where the saint can enact new types of martyrdom, see Robertson, *Medieval Saints' Lives*, 211.

46. Barbaro, "Wifely Duties," 193.

47. Barbaro, "Wifely Duties," 193.

48. Pulci, *Saints Lives*, octave 11, 152–153.

49. I owe the reference to Marsilio Ficino to Francis W. Kent, *Household and Lineage in Renaissance Florence: The Family Life of the Capponi, Ginori, and Rucellai* (Princeton, NJ: Princeton University Press, 1977), 47.

50. Pulci, *Saints Lives*, octave 12, 154–155.

51. *I libri della famiglia*, eds. Ruggiero Romano and Alberto Tenenti (Turin: Einaudi, 1969), 266. Translation is mine.

52. Cherubino da Siena, *Regole*, 18–19.

53. Giovanni Dominici, *Regola del governo di cura familiare: compilata dal beato Giovanni Dominici* (Florence: A. Garinei, 1860), 87.

54. Vecchio, "Good Wife," 109.

55. Barbaro, *Wealth of Wives*, 99.

56. Pulci, *Saints Lives*, octave 17, 158–159.

57. Pulci, *Saints Lives*, octave 14, 156–157.

58. Pulci, *Saints Lives*, octave 97, 220–221.

59. Pulci, *Saints Lives*, octave 59, 192–193.

60. Elliott (*Spiritual Marriages*, 4) defines spiritual marriage as a chaste cohabitation in the context of licit marriage.

61. Elliott, *Spiritual Marriages*, 264.

62. Elliott, *Spiritual Marriages*, 256, 196–198. On the reformers' calls for a moral renewal of the city, see Alison Brown's introduction to Anne Borelli et al., *Selected Writings of Girolamo Savonarola: Religion and Politics, 1490–1498*, ed. Donald Beebe (New Haven, CT: Yale University Press, 2006), xvi; on Bernardino da Siena's and Savonarola's social and moral criticism, see also Michael Mullett, *Popular Culture and Popular Protest in Late Medieval and Early Modern Europe* (London: Croom Helm, 1987), 123–148.

63. A witness of the spiritual crisis in Florence, Antonia Pulci might have proved highly receptive to Savonarola's penitential message and calls on the need for repentance and spiritual reform of the city. While a discussion on female spirituality and Christian ways of life as put forth in Antonia Pulci's plays, analyzed in the context of—and in comparison with—Girolamo Savonarola's program of spiritual and moral reform of women, is beyond the scope of this study and warrants further research, a few preliminary observations can be made here. Although the Dominican friar's message of spiritual renewal and moral perfection had found admirers among the members of the Laurentian circle and the Florentine intellectual elite to which Antonia Pulci belonged, there seems to be no documentary evidence that Antonia Pulci had direct contact with Savonarola nor that she was among

his followers (and indeed, it was from Fra Mariano da Genazzano, a longtime foe of Savonarola's, that Antonia Pulci took the habit of the Augustinian *ammantellata*). One could speculate that Antonia Pulci might have been among those few "poor women" who heard Savonarola preach the Lenten sermons in the Basilica of San Lorenzo during his first stay in Florence from 1482 to 1487 or that she was familiar with the Advent sermons Savonarola delivered at the convent known as "Le Murate," where Annalena de' Tanini—Antonia's sister and the dedicatee of Bernardo Pulci's *Passione del nostro Signor Gesù Cristo*—was a nun. On Fra Mariano da Genazzano, see Weaver, in Antonia Pulci, *Saints Lives*, 26 and n. 77. On Savonarola's dwindling audience during his first time in Florence, see Lauro Martines, *Fire in the City: Savonarola and the Struggle for the Soul of the Renaissance* (Oxford: Oxford University Press, 2006), 17. On Bernardo's dedication of the *Passione* see Weaver, in Antonia Pulci *Saints' Lives*, 13 n. 31. While Savonarola deemed women to be morally weaker and intellectually inferior to men, he believed in the spiritual equality of sexes and in women's potential in the redemption and salvation of the world. Convinced that women could contribute greatly to the reform movement in Florence and to his program of universal renovation, he was willing to grant Florentine women an unprecedented role in their self-reform, as well as in legislative affairs. See Lorenzo Polizzotto, "Savonarola, Savonaroliani e la riforma della donna," in *Studi savonaroliani*, ed. Gian Carlo Garfagnini (Florence: Edizioni del Galluzzo, 1996), 229–232 and n. 7; see also Polizzotto, "When Saints Fall Out: Women and the Savonarolan Reform in Early Sixteenth-Century Florence," *Renaissance Quarterly* 46, no. 3 (1993): 486–490; F. William Kent, "A Proposal by Savonarola for the Self-Reform of Florentine Women (March 1496)," *Memorie domenicane*, n.s.,14 (1983): 335–341. Tamara Herzig points out that Savonarola, however, strongly encouraged women to conform to prescribed gender roles and cautioned them against developing any familiarity with "spiritual women," for they harbored the devil in their hearts. See Tamara Herzig, *Savonarola's Women: Visions and Reform in Renaissance Italy* (Chicago and London: The University of Chicago Press, 2008), 15–18 and n. 16. Concerned with the spiritual guidance of women, the charismatic Dominican preacher attracted a large female audience who flocked to hear his sermons, and he addressed the moral and spiritual needs of his lay and religious female audiences in several vernacular works, a programmatic effort to treat topics that were relevant to women in different stages of life that emerges from Antonia Pulci's plays as well, as I suggested elsewhere. Infused with a deep *contemptus mundi*, his sermons and devotional works reverberated with a call for a return to the poverty and simplicity of the primitive Church and emphasized inner devotion and inward reflection, traits he arguably shared with Antonia Pulci's dramatic heroines, and possibly with Antonia herself. On Savonarola's devotional works aimed at a female readership, see Herzig, *Savonarola's Women*, 16. On the Dominican friar's *contemptus mundi*, see Mullett, *Popular Culture and Popular Protest*, 131–134. On the importance Savonarola placed on inner spirituality and private meditation at home, see Brown's "Introduction," in Borelli et al., *Selected Writings*, xviii. The yearnings for a moral *renovatio* and the return to the true way of Christian life, which emerge in Savonarola's apostolate and in Antonia Pulci's plays, were shared by a large swath of the Florentine population, as millenarian expectations swept through the city. As Donald Weinstein points out, the year 1484 was not only the year that Savonarola experienced a sudden prophetic illumination in the monastery of San Giorgio in Florence; it was also widely regarded as the year of apocalyptic expectations, the highly anticipated "annus mirabilis" that would harbinger profound religious reform. See Donald Weinstein, *Savonarola and Florence: Prophecy and Patriotism in the Renaissance* (Princeton, NJ: Princeton University Press, 1970), 85–88. These widespread millenarian expectations of a universal renewal might have also affected the composition of Antonia Pulci's plays and the decision to see them published in print in 1483–1484. Indeed, both preacher and playwright seem to have understood from early on in their "literary" career the groundbreaking role of the printing press in the dissemination of devotional works and in the campaign for moral and spiritual reform. On Savonarola and the printing press, see Paola Ventrone, "Fra teatro libro e devozione: sulle stampe di sacre rappresentazioni fiorentine," *Annali di storia moderna e contemporanea* 9, (2003): 272–273. 265–313; on Antonia Pulci's early adoption of the new technology, see Newbigin, *Making a Play for God*, 440. Antonia Pulci's critique of humanistic culture and its ideology of marriage in *Santa Domitilla* echoes the thundering chorus of penitential preachers who condemned the worldliness and paganism of classical culture. On Pulci's attack on the ideology of marriage espoused by the humanists, see Carney, "Antonia Pulci's *Rappresentazione*," 31–34; on Savonarola's rejection of classical culture and of the Renaissance cult of antiquity, see Donald Weinstein, *Savonarola: The Rise and Fall of a Renaissance Prophet* (New Haven, CT: Yale University Press, 2011), 3–6.

64. André Vauchez, *The Laity in the Middle Ages: Religious Beliefs and Devotional Practices*, trans. Margery J. Schneider (Notre Dame, IN: Notre Dame University Press, 1993), 122.

65. Elliot, *Spiritual Marriages*, 211.

66. Elliott, *Spiritual Marriages*, 216.

67. On wedding-night conversion of the unbelieving husband, see Elliott, *Spiritual Marriages*, 218.

68. Pulci, *Saints Lives*, octave 20, 160–161.

69. Pulci, *Saints Lives*, octaves 20–24, 160–165.

70. Pulci, *Saints Lives*, octaves 40–42, 176–179.

71. Richard Kieckhefer, *Unquiet Souls: Fourteenth-Century Saints and Their Religious Milieu* (Chicago: The University of Chicago Press, 2004), 55.

72. Elliott, *Spiritual Marriages*, 228. On the "ideology of suffering" espoused by hagiographic narratives and secular romances see Brigitte Cazelles, *The Lady as Saint. A Collection of French Hagiographic Romances of the Thirteenth Century* (Philadelphia: University of Pennsylvania Press, 1991), 74–75.

73. On Job as biblical model of patience and obedience for medieval saints, see Kieckhefer, *Unquiet Souls*, 59.

74. Pulci, *Saints Lives*, octave 15, 156–157.

75. Pulci, *Saints Lives*, octave 49, 184–185. On the domestication of female mysticism through the use of images in which the female mystic is encouraged to see herself as mother, wife, and daughter of Christ, see Beckwith, "Material Mysticism," 46.

76. Cazelles (*Lady as Saint*, 75–76) discusses the "fictional" value of suffering for terrestrial love in courtly romances vs. the "didactic and redemptive" value of suffering offered to God of hagiographic romances.

77. However, to be valid, a female vow of chastity needed the husband's consent. See Elliott, *Spiritual marriages*, 155.

78. Degl'Innocenti, "Spose e madri," 22.

79. Pulci, *Saints Lives*, octave 106, 228–229.

80. On female contemplative piety, penitential practices, and patronage at the Medici court, see Stefanie Solum, *Women, Patronage, and Salvation in Renaissance Florence: Lucrezia Tornabuoni and the Chapel of the Medici Palace* (Farnham and Burlington, VT: Ashgate Publishing, 2015), 213–253; on the penitential afflatus of the play, see Bryce, "'Or altra *vïa*," 30–31.

81. On the connection between patient suffering, humility, devotion to Christ's passion, supernatural experiences, and celestial rewards see Kieckhefer, *Unquiet Souls*, 50–72.

82. On medieval perceptions of female sanctity and the prominence of supernatural powers and penitential ascetism in the lives of female saints, see Weinstein and Bell, *Saints and Society*, 220–238. Elliott points out that mysticism was the preserve of saintly laywomen, the majority of whom were married (*Spiritual Marriages*, 234); according to Weinstein and Bell, married women used mystical experiences as tools to develop a new vocation for themselves (*Saints and Society*, 234–235).

83. Pulci, *Saints Lives*, octave 105, 226–227.

84. On the topic of chaste marriage, see Vecchio, "Good Wife," 133. On the sanctifying function of chastity in marriage and the spiritual progress of couples, see Degl'Innocenti "Spose e madri," 19–27. On saints' "widening circles of redemption" see Robertson, *Medieval Saints' Lives*, 249; on holiness "despite" marriage, see Bryce, "'Or altra *vïa*," 29–30.

85. Elliott, *Spiritual Marriages*, 255.

86. According to Elliott, marriage was not "an interruption" in a woman's "spiritual career"; on the contrary, for the woman coerced to marry "both sexual activity and subordination to the husband were the sine qua non which shaped her mature religious vocation" (*Spiritual Marriages*, 231). See also Weinstein and Bell, *Saints and Society*, 235.

87. On the shifting hierarchies of virginity and the married state, see Elliott, *Spiritual Marriages*, 239–241.

88. Beckwith, "Material Mysticism," 46–47, 52; Elliot, *Spiritual Marriages*, 12, 264.

89. Beckwith, "Material Mysticism," 37.

90. Beckwith, "Material Mysticism," 54.

91. Elliott, *Spiritual Marriages*, 209.

92. Elliott, *Spiritual Marriages*, 264, 256, 253.

93. Elliott, *Spiritual Marriages*, 216.

94. Elliott, *Spiritual Marriages*, 264.

95. I am adapting this expression from Sarah Beckwith, who speaks of female mysticism as a "vital form of religious distress and dissent." See her "Material Mysticism," 40.

96. On women's predilection for non-institutional modes of spiritual affiliations, see Caroline Walker Bynum, "Women's Stories, Women's Symbols: A Critique of Victor Turner's Theory of Liminality," in *Anthropology and the Study of Religion*, eds. Frank Reynolds and Robert Moore (Chicago: Center for the Scientific Study of Religion, 1984), 116–117; Elliott, *Spiritual Marriages*, 208–210.

97. Bryce, "Vernacular Poetry," 31.

98. Newman, "The Heretic Saint," 31. Newman is citing from the *Annales Colmarienses maiores* ad 1301, MGH Scriptores 17 (Hannover: Hahn, 1861), 226.]

99. On the civic expectations and moral obligations placed upon Florentine men, see Paola Tinagli, "Womanly Virtues in Quattrocento Florentine Marriage Furnishings," in *Women in Italian Renaissance Culture and Society*, ed. Letizia Panizza (European Humanities Research Centre, University of Oxford, 2000), 265–267.

100. Antonia Pulci was not alone in rejecting the Renaissance cult of the conjugal family. Savonarola, for example, stood in favor of the well-being of the wider community over the primacy of an individual's obligations to satisfy familial ambitions of social advancement through marriage. Resisting the claims of his own family, Savonarola had entered the Dominican order against his parents' objections and was a stalwart champion of an individual's free choice between a religious way of life and marriage; the Dominican preacher even advocated that women should be freed from the marriage bond, should they desire to enter the religious life. See Mullett, *Popular Culture and Popular Protest*, 127–30; see also Weinstein, *Savonarola: The Rise and Fall*, 9–15.

101. Elliott, *Spiritual Marriages*, 4–5.

102. Elliott, *Spiritual Marriages*, 245, 259–60.

CHAPTER SIX

# Maestre Pie Venerini and Filippini

## Instituting Public Education for Women in Seventeenth- and Eighteenth-Century Lazio

JENNIFER HARAGUCHI

On October 24, 1716, Pope Clement XI and eight cardinals visited the *Maestre Pie* (pious women teachers), a community of laywomen-teachers in Rome, founded by Rosa Venerini (1656–1728).[1] The pope's celebrated visit was memorialized in a painting,[2] and multiple accounts record him as saying that Venerini's schools—where *zitelle* (unmarried laywomen) taught reading and Christian doctrine to girls—were a blessing for Rome and the surrounding areas and that they were doing more good for the city than even the seminaries of young men.[3] One of Venerini's biographers, Andrea Girolamo Andreucci (1684–1771), similarly relayed the visit, adding that the pope wanted these schools in every diocese, because he believed that communities that supplied medical doctors for the "salute dei corpi" ("health of physical bodies") should also provide for the "salute delle anime" ("welfare of souls").[4] A study of Venerini's schools makes clear that Clement XI was applauding post-Tridentine efforts to disseminate Christian doctrine among the lay population, to teach women how to be good educators in the home, and to implement rigorous moral discipline.[5]

The pope was assuredly pleased that Venerini's schools provided an alternative experience for the daughters of impoverished families, who were often constrained to work in the fields alongside young men of loose morals.[6] Indeed, Andreucci reported that Venerini's schools had such an impact on society as to eliminate the practice of raucous bonfire parties in the countryside, where

Figure 6.1. Maestre Pie Venerini and Pope Clement XI. Reproduced with permission by the Congregazione delle Maestre Pie Venerini, Via Giuseppe Gioachino Belli 31, Rome.

young men and improperly dressed young women spent the whole night dancing and singing. Similarly, Venerini's teachings put an end to the revelry at funeral gatherings, where everyone enjoyed carousing around the casket.[7] Venerini's schools were so successful, in fact, that Father Antonio Baldinucci (1665–1717), a popular Jesuit priest who preached in 30 dioceses and 448 missions surrounding Frascati and Viterbo, was often heard saying, "Basta una Scuola Pia per riformare un paese" ("It only takes one of these Pious Schools to reform a village").[8]

Because Venerini's schools fostered such significant improvements in moral and social behavior, the top Church hierarchy proposed that Venerini, and later her assistant, Lucia Filippini (1672–1732, sixteen years her junior), establish additional schools and hire more teachers throughout the small villages surrounding Lago Bolsena, a volcanogenic lake located about one hundred kilometers from Rome.[9] In these first attempts to institute public education for women in Rome and the surrounding countryside, Venerini and Filippini were celebrated by some and derided by others. Yet today, even though many of their schools still exist across the world, not much is known about the pioneering efforts of these two educators. Approximately forty years ago, in his fundamental study of primary education in Italy from the sixteenth to the nineteenth centuries, Guerrino Pelliccia made a brief mention of Venerini's and Filippini's schools.[10] A year later, Sira Serenella Macchietti published a book on these first public institutions of learning for women in the Lazio region.[11] The present study expands on the work of Pelliccia and Macchietti by drawing more extensively on the *Positio* of both Venerini and Filippini—large tomes of transcribed documents prepared by the Sacra Congregazione dei Riti for the beatification proceedings of Venerini (1943) and Filippini (1923).[12] It also relies heavily on Andreucci's biography of Venerini, Francesco Di Simone's biography of Filippini,[13] and Pietro Bergamaschi's biography of Cardinal Marcantonio Barbarigo (1640–1706), who encouraged and supported Filippini.[14]

Through a consideration of social and cultural details not mentioned in previous studies, my work argues for the importance of recognizing that devout laywomen—such as *terziarie*, *pinzochere*, and Maestre Pie, who often lived in all-female lay communities[15]—were not anomalies in the early-modern period and that clergy supported and validated their cause.[16] I demonstrate that ecclesiastical leaders provided substantial support for Venerini's and Filippini's initiatives to establish public institutions of learning for women outside the convent, regardless of the difficulties these schools created by destabilizing social and religious norms and class and gender hierarchies. Venerini's and Filippini's schools encountered aggressive opposition by townspeople because they challenged the societal notion that unmarried middle-aged women, who were neither nuns or tertiaries nor under the direct authority of an enclosed convent or a spouse, could not live on their own and serve a vital role in the community, managing institutions of learning for girls and women of all classes in society. Furthermore, at least one clergy member expressed his disapproval when Venerini made frequent appearances with civic and religious leaders to ask for support and funding for her schools, and certain ecclesiastical leaders were quick to seek condemnation of Filippini's method of instruction on mental prayer.

Notwithstanding these rebukes, Venerini and Filippini forged ahead, successfully instituting over forty schools in the villages surrounding Lago Bolsena[17] and experimenting with new and unusual pedagogical practices, with the help of male leadership who recognized their unique capabilities: Venerini was supported by Ignazio Martinelli of the Compagnia di Gesù, and Filippini had the backing of Cardinal Barbarigo, bishop of Montefiascone and Corneto, of the

Padre Pii Operai.[18] While this essay points to some of the distinctions between the two religious orders, which influenced both women and ultimately may have led Venerini to break away from Filippini, my primary focus is to demonstrate that negotiation and collaboration took place between clergymen and these two women, which opened up possibilities for the acceptance of a female apostolate and a professional career for women as teachers and administrators who moved freely about the countryside to attend to their duties.[19]

Venerini's and Filippini's schools are cases that prove that the seventeenth- and eighteenth-century Church hierarchy sanctioned and promoted widespread education for women in self-determining institutions. I refer to the institutions that Venerini and Filippini founded as "schools" because that is what Clement XI and others at the time called them.[20] Throughout the early-modern period, institutions such as these were often called "conservatories" or "congregations," but I believe that the specific references here to "schools" signals a change in the way that Venerini's and Filippini's institutions were uniquely viewed, not as mere shelters for unmarried girls but as centers of spiritual and intellectual learning first and foremost, followed by training in the domestic arts (sewing, knitting, lace making).[21] This education was intended to meet the post–Tridentine Church's objective of preparing women for their duties in the home or convent, yet these schools presented remarkable paid opportunities for laywomen to provide significant work in their communities as pedagogues, recruiters, fundraisers, accountants, bookkeepers, artisans, advisers, spiritual leaders, custodians of girls, and social workers, even in the face of public criticism, disapproval by some religious leaders and charges of apostasy by others.

Venerini's schools were among the first public schools in Italy for girls of all classes between the ages of six and fourteen.[22] Supported by Church funds, the schools offered an unconventional (and free) educational opportunity to girls whose only chance at formal education previously was in the convent as *educande* (boarders). Venerini and her assistant Filippini, who later formed separate institutions and a distinctive curriculum of her own, were not bound by solemn vows, nor were they required to follow traditional rules of enclosure.[23] Thus, they were free to establish both day and boarding schools for girls in various villages and to offer popular evening classes to adult women (in Filippini's case, often to an overflow audience who had to sit in the stairwell),[24] in which they learned Christian doctrine and openly discussed solutions to social issues pertaining to women.

While the public schools Venerini and Filippini founded cannot be compared to those of today, they offered novel aspects that are still characteristic of modern public education: full-time instruction; breakfast and snacks (the girls went home for lunch and at the end of the day if they were not boarders); and a comprehensive education (providing instruction in practical, cultural, and spiritual matters—reading, writing, singing, simple math, household management, spinning, sewing, and lace making, in addition to religion). The schools were free of charge and widely promoted, and the curriculum was oriented toward a girl's future within her family and community. Furthermore, Venerini and Filippini sought to bridge the gap between public and private instruction by encouraging their day school students to return to their homes in the evening and share with their families what they were learning.[25] Cardinal Barbarigo found that this type of informal instruction in the home, led by the girls themselves, was instrumental in dispelling pernicious habits that were building up in the community. He praised this unique way of training "tante maestrine domestiche" ("so many little domestic teachers"), whose teaching in the home, he believed, had the capacity to solve many of the problems of an entire diocese.[26]

For centuries, convents served as the primary institutions of learning for girls who enrolled there as boarders under strict enclosure. In the late 1530s in Milan, however, there was another option for women's education, albeit on a smaller scale: confraternities began offering general instruction to children in reading and writing—on Sundays and holidays—with a focus on religious and moral issues; priests and parents volunteered as their teachers. While called *Scuole della Dottrina Cristiana* (Schools of Christian Doctrine), they were not schools per se but simple meetings held in church buildings. Supported by Pius IV, the *Scuole* made their way to Rome in 1560, where classes were taught on Sundays to numerous boys and girls in separate spaces.[27] In these lessons, the children learned how to read and write from a sixteen-page primer called the *Summario*, a text that presented the alphabet, the sign of the cross, Latin prayers ("Pater Noster," "Ave Maria," "Credo," "Salve Regina"), the Ten Commandments, the Seven Sacraments, the five bodily senses, the four cardinal virtues, and a number of precepts, hymns, and prayers.[28] According to Christopher Carlsmith, "The Schools [of Christian Doctrine] present an intriguing paradox: driven and staffed by laymen and laywomen, yet engaged in training boys and girls in catechism and rudiments of faith."[29] The Counter-Reformation Church was beginning to realize that literacy and the spread of Christian doctrine was not going to happen without the help of the lay community.

In the early seventeenth century, Church leadership enlarged the scope, the extent, and the duration of education for girls, especially for those of the lower classes who could not afford the dowry required of convents.[30] Ecclesiastical leaders recognized the value of institutional education in a noncloistered environment as a way to keep girls out of the fields, off the streets, and in a place where they would learn Christian doctrine and marketable skills that would help reform society. Since the confraternal schools taught children only on Sundays and holidays, ecclesiastical leaders promoted the formation of day and boarding schools—*collegi, scuole,* or *conservatori*. These institutions were not third-order monastic communities, and their teachers were not nuns or tertiaries.[31] Because they focused on developing ethics and morals through literacy as well as *lavori femminili* (women's work),[32] they differed from those conservatories whose primary purpose was simply to house girls *in serbanza* (for safekeeping) until they were married or joined the convent.[33] These new schools, with a central focus on public women's education, were located throughout Italy: the Collegio della Beata Vergine, founded in Cremona in 1610 by Lucia Perotti, with the assistance of the Jesuit priest Giovanni Melina;[34] Il Conventino and La Quiete, established in Florence in 1628 and 1650, respectively, by Eleonora Ramirez di Montalvo, with the support of the Jesuit father Cosimo Pazzi;[35] and the schools of the Maestre Pie, founded by Rosa Venerini (the first, founded in Viterbo in 1685) and Lucia Filippini, with the backing of the Jesuits and the Padre Pii Operai.[36]

Another example of an institution of learning created only for girls outside the convent was the Scuole Pontificie (Pope's Schools), founded by Girolamo Farnese in 1655 during Alessandro VII's papacy, which offered free tuition for students and a modest stipend from the pope's steward for teachers. However, the Scuole Pontificie—where "il santo timor di Dio e l'arti domestiche" ("a holy fear of God and domestic arts") were taught—focused for the most part on lavori femminili, with the primary objective that girls would learn some type of needlework to supplement their family's income.[37] Literacy was not an essential part of the curriculum in these institutions. According to Angela Groppi, schools for girls in Rome outnumbered schools for boys, but their emphasis was on needlework rather than on learning how to read.[38] Teachers were required to be married, but they were not expected to know how to read; in fact, it was rare that reading was even taught.[39] Of the forty Scuole Pontificie, Pelliccia notes that only two in 1676 actually taught girls how to read; in 1695, five did.[40]

In contrast to the Scuole Pontificie, the Scuole delle Maestre Pie, or Scuole Pie,[41] founded by Venerini and Filippini, provided much more than a curriculum centered on lavori femminili. Their first aim was to teach girls how to read for the purpose of learning and understanding Bellarmino's *Dottrina cristiana* (*Christian Doctrine*); the teachers often taught the girls while they were doing their lavori femminili, which Andreucci defined as knitting, sewing, and bobbin lace making.[42] Second, and for those students "più capac[i]" ("more capable"), the teachers taught them how to write, but in a separate space so they would not distract the others.[43] They also offered instruction in prayer—both vocal and mental—and taught their young charges how to recite the Acts of Faith, Hope, and Charity.[44] According to the *Regole* (Rule), the Maestre Pie of Montefiascone and Corneto were advised to teach the girls how to read "libri buoni e santi" ("good and holy books").[45] Bergamaschi reports that Barbarigo opened a library in every school, which included the *Meditazioni* of various authors: Spinola, da Ponte, Pietro d'Alcantara, and Ranieri. The library also contained copies of the following, which all were encouraged to read: Francesco di Sales's *I Trattenimenti*; Crispino's *La Scuola di S. Filippo Neri* and Scupoli's *Il Combattimento spirituale*; the works of Granata; Segneri's *Il Cristiano istruito*; the *Vite* of Francesca Farnese, Caterina da Siena, Chiara di Montefalco, and Villana; the *Esercizi spirituali* of Maestro de Marinis; and Pinamonti's *Cibo dell'anima*.[46] One of Venerini's pupils, Maria Cecilia Baij (1694–1766), praised Venerini's methodology, reporting to her biographer that she herself, at seven years of age, "dicev[a] benissimo l'officio della Madonna e leggev[a] perfettamente" ("said the Office of the Madonna very well and read perfectly").[47]

Venerini and Filippini presented opportunities for women to work outside the home as Maestre Pie, where they could make careers of teaching traditional subjects—Christian doctrine, the lives of the saints—as well as unconventional disciplines like history, geography, and basic arithmetic.[48] Remarkably, the Maestre Pie also carried out important assignments previously conducted by men of the priesthood: delivering sermons (sometimes even in church), leading others in the Ignatian Spiritual Exercises, and calling on families in a pastoral way to help them through their difficulties.[49] Venerini's teachers were required to be *zitelle* (single women) without ties to a spouse or children and without responsibilities in the home.[50] Two teachers were paid an annual salary of eighteen *scudi*, three *rubbia di grano*, and ten *barili* of wine, which Andreucci admits was "una tassa . . . leggiera" ("a modest wage").[51] Recognizing how meagerly the teachers were paid, Cardinal Barbarigo bought, rented, and renovated houses for Filippini's schools and purchased a plot of land on which they could cultivate grain and harvest grapes to make wine.[52] He also gave each school fifteen *giuli* of his own money every month, in addition to wine, oil, and black twill for the teachers' clothes.[53]

Venerini's and Filippini's teachers would have been an unusual sight among communities of people who were accustomed to seeing adult women either in the convent or living under the protection of a spouse, parents, or relatives. One cardinal sought to clarify the uncommon nature of this kind of school as a "domus saecularis, mulieres partes saeculares, quamvis sub pio instituto viventes" ("secular place, where the women, although residing in a pious institution, are still secular").[54] The Church formally recognized pious communities like those of Venerini and Filippini, where women did not takes vows or observe enclosure, when in 1616 the Congregation of Bishops and Regulars listed them as "congregations" instead of "convents."[55] While the Church sanctioned these schools and they filled a need in society, the Maestre Pie still faced much public opposition from those who were not willing to accept the fact that women teachers could live in places outside the jurisdiction of men and make independent decisions.

Contemporaneous reports indicate that many thought Venerini's first school in Viterbo was full of bad omens: one of Venerini's biographers records that Venerini's assistant Porzia Bacci got sick and had to return home, an event viewed by many as a sign that the school would certainly fail; others believed that this incident proved that the school was full of tuberculosis. In another village, at Ronciglione, a man who was said to be possessed of the devil shouted loudly around town, "If that school comes here, all hell will break loose!"[56] This man's statement seemed to presage what happened next: when Venerini's teachers first arrived in town late at night to set up their school, they found their accommodations were cold, and they were given hardly any food; in the days to follow, the townspeople yelled and threw things at them as they walked through the streets. Someone shot a musket (arquebus) at them through the window of their house; while the musket balls missed them, they hit and damaged a credenza in their lodging. Then, someone set fire to the main entrance of their school, which filled with smoke. Finally, it was said that the devil himself pushed a servant down the stairs, severely injuring her head and neck. Andreucci believed it was in fact the devil who was trying to get the Maestre to leave.[57] In the communities of Viterbo and the surrounding regions, people were apprehensive about this new opportunity for women to reside in places where enclosure was not strictly enforced and where they had a measured amount of freedom outside of patriarchal control.

The townspeople further complained that Venerini's and Filippini's female students were not learning how to perform the customary work required of them; that they were spending all their time in prayer; that the teachers admitted only those girls who had silk dresses; and that they allowed men inside their institutions late at night.[58] When families stopped sending their girls to Filippini's schools so they could work instead in the fields to supplement their family's income, Cardinal Barbarigo sought to draw them back by supplying each school with a substantial amount of hemp fiber that the girls could spin while listening to their lessons, thus learning important moral and religious principles while earning money toward their dowries.[59] In an attempt to persuade villagers of the importance of educating women, ecclesiastical leaders also intervened in other ways. Cardinal Urbano Sacchetti, bishop of Viterbo, explained to the local priests, citing Cardinal Gaetano, that women had the right to receive more education than what was available to them through the standard catechism classes offered on Sundays. Sacchetti quoted to them Acts 2:18—"upon my servants indeed and upon my handmaids will I pour out in those days of my Spirit, and they shall prophesy"[60]—teaching the local congregations that the Lord's spirit is felt through instruction, imparted not only to men but also to women.[61]

Alessandro Mazzinelli, the rector of Cardinal Barbarigo's Seminario in Montefiascone, also sought to define and to justify this new type of school. In his *Istruzione per regolamento delle scuole della Dottrina Cristiana*, a 1717 revision of the rule Cardinal Barbarigo had established for the teachers of Filippini's schools, Mazzinelli stated that the Maestre Pie practiced "un terzo stato di vita" ("a third way of life")—offsetting the two customary options of wife and nun—that "un[isce] i doveri della vita religiosa con i travagli della vita secolare" ("unites the duties of the religious life with the work of a secular life").[62] Mazzinelli explained that these schools were noteworthy because they assumed "una sorte di vita in cui, senza essere ristrette dai chiostri né impegnate nel secolo, godano le prerogative di ambedue questi stati, senza provarne i discapiti" ("a type of life where, without being confined to the cloister or absorbed in the world, they enjoy the privileges of both these positions, without experiencing any of the disadvantages").[63] According to Mazzinelli, the Maestre Pie were returning to a way of living that early Christian women enjoyed: "Né questa sorte di vita è nuova, poiché è quella che le vergini cristiane conducevano nei primi secoli della Chiesa, quando ancora non erano istituti né i monasteri né i chiostri. Le caste pose del Signore vivevano in mezzo al mondo e la sola virtù ed il rispetto portato alle loro persone serviva di difesa alla loro innocenza; dividendo santamente il loro tempo fra la contemplazione, il culto di Dio e l'assistenza che prestavano al prossimo, non erano oziose nella solitudine né dissipate negli offici della loro carità"[64] ("Neither is this way of life new since it is the same that the Christian virgins led in the first centuries of the Church when monasteries or cloisters did not yet exist. The chaste spouses of the Lord lived in the midst of the world, and the unique virtue and respect reflected in their demeanor served as a defense of their innocence; dividing their time in a holy manner between contemplation, the worship of God, and the assistance they lent to their neighbor, they were not idle in seclusion nor consumed by their charitable duties"). Mazzinelli (and possibly Barbarigo as the original author of this text) believed that the Maestre Pie were restoring an ideal way of existence, thus finding middle ground between the active and the contemplative lives.

With the support of spiritual directors who recognized that female leadership could have a transformative influence on society, Venerini's and Filippini's schools endured social criticism and even a split in leadership. Venerini and Filippini parted ways not just to divide and conquer[65] but also because of fundamental differences in pedagogical methods within the leadership of separate religious orders. Filippini served as Venerini's assistant in Viterbo and the surrounding areas, until Cardinal Barbarigo asked her to take over the school Venerini had founded in Montefiascone (with enrollment starting at forty students, including some of the children's mothers). The cardinal called Filippini's schools the "pupilla degli occhi suoi" ("apple of his eye")[66] and financially supported any girl who wanted to matriculate.[67] Filippini's biographer Andreucci recalls an experience when the girls of one of Filippini's schools were returning from Mass and encountered a group of boys playing bocce. One of the boys, the son of the governor, approached one of Filippini's girls and cleaned his muddy bocce on her apron. When the cardinal found out about this, he threw the boy in jail for a time and then sent him and his father to live elsewhere.[68]

Barbarigo and Martinelli supported Filippini's and Venerini's fundamental differences in pedagogy and even in the governing of their schools. Barbarigo declared that Filippini, as the *elemosiniera* (treasurer), was to have full control over the financial dealings of her institutions and provided her with vouchers to give to the baker, the merchants, and the shopkeepers in exchange for necessary goods.[69] Concerning Venerini's many duties—interacting with local authorities, bishops, parish priests, and benefactors—it was believed that Martinelli served only an advisory role and did not intervene: "Egli peraltro, da uomo prudente, ebbe cura di non sovrapporsi alla Fondatrice e di lasicarle quindi la necessaria libertà: così era la Venerini che presentava ai Comuni domande e suppliche per l'ammissione delle maestre e per le relative sovvenzioni; era la Venerini che trattava anche con vescovi e prelati, ed era la Venerini che, sentito il parere del Padre, dava alle sue figlie le ultime decisioni: in una parola il P. Martinelli consigliava, indirizzava, sorreggeva la Fondatrice, senza però diminuirne l'autorità presso le sue figliole"[70] ("Among other things, as a wise person, he was careful not to overshadow the foundress and to give her accordingly the necessary freedom: thus, it was Venerini who presented requests and petitions to the municipal offices for the acceptance of teachers and the requisite funding; it was Venerini who also interacted with bishops and prelates; and it was Venerini who, having heard Martinelli's view, made the final decisions for her girls. In a word, it was Father Martinelli who advised, directed, and supported the foundress, but without diminishing any of her authority with regard to her dear girls"). In fact, when Martinelli was transferred to Loreto, Venerini was left entirely in charge of the school in Viterbo. Both Marangoni and Andreucci point out that Venerini appeared energized during the period in which Martinelli was in Loreto (1691–95) and that she went about visiting bishops of the surrounding dioceses to see if they would open other schools on the basis of the model of the Viterbo school. Venerini's new spiritual director, Girolamo Moirani, however, considered this type of active proselytizing a temptation and tried to discourage her from doing it.[71]

Venerini made frequent appearances at the municipal offices to ask for public funds so that her schools would not be obligated to charge tuition. In Soriano, for example, on March 19, 1707, Venerini made a request to Tullio Politi, the governor, in her role as "Istitutrice delle Scuole Pie a pro' del sesso femminino" ("Foundress of the Scuole Pie on behalf of the feminine sex"). The governor then wrote an appeal to his cabinet, stating that the funds would be "una piccola ricompensa rispetto alle fatiche che fanno dette Maestre, in educare le ragazze" ("a little reward considering the efforts these Maestre make in educating girls"). Two years later, the Maestre Pie of Soriano received four scudi a year for their lodging.[72] It is highly probable that Venerini's initiative served as an example for the Maestre Pie of Ronciglione, who made a similar petition to the Consiglio del Comune on August 1, 1723, to request funding; they subsequently received twenty scudi a year.[73]

It turns out that Filippini's methods were more popular with the girls than were Venerini's. According to Cardinal Barbarigo's biographer Pietro Bergamaschi, Filippini's charisma attracted many followers, as she went around town with a cross and a companion who rang a bell to encourage girls to come to her school.[74] One of Filippini's biographers, Francesco Di Simone, relates that one of her first students in Rome, who later became a Maestra Pia in Montefiascone, made the following statement about Filippini: "Mi venne tanta voglia di stare con lei (sono sue proprie parole) che piangeva [*sic*] acciocché i miei parenti mi facessero stare con essa. Sembravami ella una santa; e mi piaceva tanto l'esercizio della scuola, e l'orazione che dava, che n'ero impazzita. Per tal cagione, non lasciai giammai di andare a scuola; ed anche qualche sera io vi restava [sic] a dormire con mio molto contento"[75] ("I had such a desire to be with her [these are her own words] that I cried so that my relatives would let me stay with her. She seemed like a saint to me; and I liked the training at the school so much, and the prayers that she gave, that I was crazy about all of it. For that reason, I never missed going to school; and also, some nights I was very happy to stay there to sleep").

Di Simone gives examples of Filippini's well-received practice of heroic asceticism, which included girls begging to lie on the ground and kiss the feet of those who trampled over them. Other types of self-punishment included girls willingly offering their faces to be slapped or publicly asking for forgiveness and making crosses on the floor with their tongues.[76] Cardinal Barbarigo's biographer writes that Filippini encouraged the girls to make heavy wooden crosses to drag around for penance, to climb the stairs on their bare knees, simulating the devotion of pilgrims at the *scala santa* (holy stairway), to eat disgusting food or to lick the wounds or vomit of others, and to let Filippini cut off their eyelashes. These acts of self-mortification would not have been permitted in a Jesuit congregation, of which Venerini was a part, as her schools were under the jurisdiction of Father Ignazio Martinelli of the Compagnia di Gesù.[77]

Filippini's emphasis on self-mortification may have been guided by her own natural inclination, but it also seems to have been driven by the spiritual orientation of the Padre Pii Operai, distinct from that of the Jesuits, in practicing a "regola severa, spirito austere, zelo esuberante, pietà soda, ma con manifestazioni esterne secondo il genio meridionale e con una tinta di rigorismo spagnuolo" ("strict rule, austere spirit, exuberant zeal, firm piety, but with outward expressions similar to the southern way and with a shade of Spanish rigor").[78] Moreover, Filippini's teaching and practice of self-mortification and *orazione mentale* (mental prayer) were directly aligned with the methods of the Padre Pii Operai, many of whom were examined for heretical tendencies by Church authorities. In 1707, when Filippini spent a few months in Rome to establish another school of Maestre Pie, she too was suspected of following the principles of the heretical movement Quietism, especially in the manner of leading others in mental prayer. She decided to return to Montefiascone and asked Venerini to take her place as the director at the school in Rome.[79] To avoid upsetting the girls, Filippini left the school in secret late one night, and when the girls woke up the next morning, they discovered that Venerini was their new superior. Biographers report that Venerini insisted on changing the way Filippini was doing things. The girls did not like Venerini's methods and began to leave the school. After only three months, the pope's almoner, Pompilio Bonaventura of the Padre Pii Operai, suggested that Venerini return to Viterbo and Filippini to Rome.[80]

Filippini's emphasis on extreme self-mortification and mental prayer led to accusations of heresy, notwithstanding the support she received from Cardinal Barbarigo and Bishop Tommaso Falcoia (1663–1743).[81] After the first denunciation in 1707, Filippini was again accused in 1711 in Todi for the "novità dei suoi esercizi mentali" ("newness of her mental exercises").[82] Finally, in 1719, she was examined for practices in her schools that were similar to Quietism, Jansenism, and Molinism (Molinos had published his *Guía espiritual* in Rome in 1675).[83] However, in the end Filippini was found not guilty. The vicar Nicola Ranieri testified on July 6, 1719 that he observed Filippini (thirty-five years old, "di aspetto mediocre" ["of mediocre appearance"]) and a teacher, Santa (twenty-six or twenty-seven years old, "di bello aspetto" ["with a beautiful appearance"]), in Scansano performing mental prayer, with women in one room and men and priests in another, for eight hours a day for the eight days the authorities were there examining their case; the only unusual thing that happened during that time was that some women fainted, and the vicar thought they had fainted because it was too hot and there were too many women in the room.[84]

Filippini's and Venerini's schools still exist and thrive today in Italy and various parts of the world,[85] but with one very important change. In 1941, Venerini's Maestre Pie accepted binding vows and convent rules. By contrast, Filippini's followers take pride in the fact that they are not nuns but remain to this day

Figure 6.2. Statue of Lucia Filippini, Saint Peter's Basilica, Rome. Photograph taken by Jennifer Haraguchi, included with her permission.

pious laywomen-teachers who have chosen their vocation without constraint and who make conscious efforts to rededicate themselves daily to their work. Because they are not bound by monastic rules and are free to leave their congregation at any time, their commitment, as one of the Maestre Filippini in Montefiascone told me, is perhaps stronger and more devoted to their founder's aims.

Both Lucia Filippini and Rosa Venerini have been canonized: Filippini in 1930 and Venerini in 2006. But it is the more radical leader—Filippini—who has been recognized with the highest of public honors by the Catholic Church. In the nave of St. Peter's Basilica stands a thirteen-foot marble statue of Filippini with a young female student at her side in one of the upper recesses on the left, designed by the artist Silvio Silva. This rendition of Filippini is one of only thirty-nine statues (ten of which are women) placed between the mid-eighteenth century and the mid-twentieth century in the niches of the nave, the apse, and the transepts (the ancient bronze statue of Peter brings the count to forty).[86] These statues—depicting Saints Benedict, Francis, Dominic, Angela Merici, and Teresa di Gesù, for example—represent the most important founders of religious orders and congregations of the Catholic Church since the Middle Ages.[87] Although the last of these sculptures was put in place in 1954—well before Venerini was even declared a saint—Filippini's statue remains as a distinguished reminder that the early-modern Church sanctioned and promoted unconventional educational practices with women at the helm.

Twenty years ago, Gabriella Zarri called attention to the widespread prevalence in early-modern society of the *terzo stato* (third status), whereby those who did not marry or enter the convent adopted a life of prayer and community service, while residing in their homes or in all-female communities.[88] Zarri argued convincingly that this third position was a recurrent option in early-modern Italy, yet many scholars have continued to view the presence of devout laywomen—especially those who resided in all-female communities—as a rare departure from the two primary vocational options of wife and nun. Because scholarship of the past thirty years has prioritized all-female communities that capitulated to pressure from Church authorities to renounce their lay status, historians have perpetuated the notion of a commanding patriarchal rule[89] that prohibited those institutions from surviving independently, as their founders had wished. While some semiautonomous groups of women were eventually constrained to a cloistered existence, the current tendency to claim that the Church was reluctant to permit such lifestyle arrangements has tainted our view, leaving us with the impression that there was no room for exception and innovation.[90] By concentrating our efforts on the recovery of documents that illuminate the powerful leadership role that early-modern women assumed in public institutions of learning, we will discover greater collaboration between ecclesiastical leaders and women and more important responsibilities for women than were previously thought.

Notes

1. Two of Venerini's biographers record different dates for the pope's visit. This discrepancy has been resolved in Sacra Rituum Congregatio, *Romana seu Viterbien. Beatificationis et canonizationis Servae Dei Rosae Venerini, fundatricis Magistrarum Piarum quae ab eius cognomine nuncupantur († 1728), Positio super virtutibus ex officio compilate* (Roma: Typis polyglottis Vaticanis, 1943), 316–317. I am pleased to have my article included in this special volume in honor of Elissa Weaver, whose teaching, research, and publications have been fundamental to my own; she generously introduced me to the work of the Florentine educator and writer Eleonora Ramirez di Montalvo and her seventeenth-century lay conservatories, which set me on the path to research additional educational initiatives for women outside the convent throughout early-modern Italy.

2. This painting is on display in the corridor of the main administrative building and school of the Maestre Pie Venerini in Rome on Via Giuseppe Gioachino Belli 31.

3. Clement XI's words were recorded as such: "Con queste Scuole . . . ci santificherete Roma, e noi saremo aiutati a soddisfare alle proprie obbligazioni. Ci ricordiamo di ciò che ci disse il Signor Cardinale Barbarigo, Vescovo di Montefiascone; quando era vivo ci diceva, che ricavava più frutto da queste Scuole di zitelle, che dei giovani del Seminario" ("With these schools . . . you will sanctify Rome and help us fulfill our own obligations. Let us remember what the signor Cardinal Barbarigo, bishop of Montefiascone, said to us; when he was alive he would say to us that more benefits were drawn from these schools of zitelle than from the young men in the Seminary") (Giuseppe Antonio Patrignani, *Menologio di pie memorie d'alcuni religiosi della Compagnia di Gesù* [Venezia: 1730], in Sacra Rituum Congregatio, *Romana seu Viterbien,* 104). Unless otherwise indicated, all translations are mine.

4. Andrea Girolamo Andreucci, *Ragguaglio della vita della serva di Dio, Rosa Venerini, Viterbese Institutrice delle scuole e Maestre Pie (1732),* in *Le vite delle due Maestre Pie Rosa Venerini e Lucia Filippini* (Roma: Stamperia della S. Congr. De Propag. Fide, 1868), 88.

5. For more on the concept of education and moral discipline as a tool of the Counter-Reformation, see Ottavia Niccoli, "Creanza e disciplina: buone maniere per i fanciulli nell'Italia della Controriforma," and Gabriella Zarri, "Disciplina regolare e pratica di coscienza: le virtù e i comportamenti sociali in comunità femminili (secc. XVI–XVIII)," in *Disciplina dell'anima, disciplina del corpo e disciplina della società tra medieovo ed età moderna,* ed. Paolo Prodi (Bologna: Il Mulino, 1994), 929–963 and 257–278; see also the essays in Gabriella Zarri, ed., *Donna, disciplina, creanza cristiana dal XV al XVII secolo: studi e testi a stampa* (Roma: Edizioni di Storia e Letteratura, 1996).

6. The city council in the town of Caprarola spoke of this precise concern when its members agreed to set aside ten scudi a year to rent a building where Venerini could open a school for the daughters of destitute families (*Memoriale dei padri di famiglia, 12·dicembre 1711,* in Sacra Rituum Congregatio, *Romana seu Viterbien,* 214–215). See also note 8 below. The historian Marina Caffiero states that the territory of Corneto (today, Tarquinia) attracted many seasonal workers, since it served as one of the primary sources for Rome's grain supply (*Religione e modernità in Italia, secoli XVII–XIX* [Pisa: Istituti Editoriali e Poligrafici Internazionali, 2000], 117, 184).

7. Andreucci, *Ragguaglio della vita,* 33–34. In the preface to his biography of Venerini, Andreucci states that he writes not only as a historian but also as a reliable witness to the life and times of Venerini. He was twenty-eight years her junior.

8. Francesco Maria Galluzzi, *Vita del P. Antonio Baldinucci* (Roma: 1720), in Sacra Rituum Congregatio, *Romana seu Viterbien,* 327–328. According to Galluzzi, Baldinucci expressed concern that defenseless young women were frequently compelled to work in the fields in the company of libidinous men. See also Celestino Testore, "Baldinucci, Antonio, beato," in *Enciclopedia Cattolica,* vol. II (Città del Vaticano: Ente per l'Enciclopedia Cattolica e per il Libro Cattolico, 1949), 735.

9. In 1684, at twenty-eight years of age, when Venerini was deciding if she wanted to profess solemn vows, the Jesuit Ignazio Martinelli encouraged her to establish a lay school for girls instead, where she could do more good for the community than if she lived a cloistered existence (see Sacra Rituum Congregatio, *Romana seu Viterbien,* 45; Andreucci, *Ragguaglio della vita,* 16–17; and Patrignani, in Sacra Rituum Congregatio, *Romana seu Viterbien,* 99). With the approval of Cardinal Urbano Sacchetti, on August 30, 1685, Ven-

erini opened her first school, free for lower-class girls, in Viterbo. In 1692, Cardinal Barbarigo asked Venerini to open another school in Montefiascone (Sacra Rituum Congregatio, *Romana seu Viterbien*, xxxv).

10. Guerrino Pelliccia, *La scuola primaria a Roma dal secolo XVI al XIX: L'istruzione popolare e la catechesi ai fanciulli, nell'ambito della parocchia e dello "Studium Urbis," da Leone X a Leone XII (1513–1829)* (Roma: Edizioni dell'Ateneo, 1985), 407–411. Pelliccia does not mention Sira Serenella Macchietti's article, which appeared eight years previously: "Le scuole delle Maestre Pie: esperienze di educazione femminile e popolare nel '600," *Pedagogia e vita* 38 (1977): 633–646.

11. Sira Serenella Macchietti, *Rosa Venerini all'origine della scuola popolare femminile: l'azione educativa del suo istituto dal 1685 ad oggi* (Brescia: Editrice La Scuola, 1986).

12. Sacra Rituum Congregatio, *Romana seu Viterbien*, 1943; and Sacra Rituum Congregatio, *Romana seu Faliscodunen. Beatificationis et canonizationis Ven. Servae Dei Luciae Filippini, fundatricis atque Antistitae Instituti Magistrarum Piarum ab eius cognomine nuncupatarum, Positio super virtutibus compilate* (Roma: Typis polyglottis Vaticanis, 1923).

13. Andreucci's 1732 biography of Venerini and Francesco Di Simone's 1732 biography of Filippini are both reprinted in *Le vite delle due Maestre Pie Rosa Venerini e Lucia Filippini* (Roma: Stamperia della S. Congr. De Propag. Fide, 1868).

14. Pietro Bergamaschi, *Vita del Servo di Dio Card. Marc'Antonio Barbarigo Vescovo di Montefiascone e Corneto*, vol. II (Roma: Tipografia Poliglotta Vaticana, 1919). Cardinal Barbarigo was well known for having established in Montefiascone the Seminario Montis Falisci et Corneti, a prestigious institution that provided instruction for young men whose teachers came from the Sorbonne in Paris and other universities in Rome. The Seminario contained a printing press and a rich library with books in Latin, Greek, Hebrew, and Asian languages (see *Il Cardinale Marco Antonio Barbarigo e il suo tempo: catalogo e mostra*, eds. Fabio Fabene and Lydia Saraca Colonnelli [Montefiascone: Chiesa di S. Andrea, Saloni di rappresentanza della Banca Cattolica, 2006], 24–25, 29, 49–50).

15. "Terziarie" (tertiaries) were considered third-order mendicants who, like "pinzochere," lived a spiritual and service-oriented life outside of the convent, taking simple (not solemn) vows. These lay sisters had various names: "bizzoche," "monache di casa," "oblate," "vestite," "mantellate," "dimesse," "converse," and so on. See G. Rocca, "Terz'ordine," in *Dizionario degli Istituti di Perfezione*, eds. Guerrino Pelliccia and Giancarlo Rocca, vol. IX (Roma: Edizioni Paoline, 1997), 1042–50; and R. Guarnieri, "Pinzochere," in *Dizionario degli Istituti di Perfezione*, vol. VI (Roma: Edizioni Paoline, 1980), 1722–1750.

16. In her review of Alison Weber's 2016 edited volume *Devout Laywomen in the Early Modern World*, Merry Wiesner-Hanks states "that devout laywomen were everywhere and that continuing to view them as anomalies is imposing a judgment that they and the communities in which they were embedded did not share" (*The Sixteenth Century Journal* XLVIII, 1 [Spring 2017]: 259–261).

17. At the time of her death in 1728, it was reported that Venerini, with Filippini's help, had established over forty schools in seven dioceses (Sacra Rituum Congregatio, *Romana seu Viterbien*, xxxv).

18. The nicknames given to the teachers clearly indicate that they were supervised by different orders with distinct pedagogical philosophies. Venerini's teachers were known

as "Maestre Pie Gesuite" or "Gesuitesse," whereas Filippini's teachers were recognized as "Maestre Pie del Cardinal Barbarigo" or "Maestre Pie Operaie." It was not until the nineteenth century that they were called "Maestre Pie Venerini" and "Maestre Pie Filippini" (Sacra Rituum Congregatio, *Romana seu Viterbien*, xxxvi).

19. On negotiation and collaboration between devout laywomen and clergy, see Jodi Bilinkoff, *Related Lives: Confessors and Their Female Penitents, 1450–1750* (Ithaca, NY: Cornell University Press, 2005); see also Barbara F. Diefendorf, "Rethinking the Catholic Reformation: The Role of Women," in *Women, Religion, and the Atlantic World (1600–1800)*, eds. Daniella Kostroun and Lisa Vollendorf (Toronto: University of Toronto Press, 2009), 31–59.

20. See note 3 above.

21. For more on institutions of relief for poor women and girls (e.g., conservatories, foundling homes, and orphanages), see Nicholas Terpstra's works: *Abandoned Children of the Italian Renaissance: Orphan Care in Florence and Bologna* (Baltimore: The Johns Hopkins University Press, 2005); *Lost Girls: Sex and Death in Renaissance Florence* (Baltimore: The Johns Hopkins University Press, 2010); *Cultures of Charity: Women, Politics, and the Reform of Poor Relief in Renaissance Italy* (Cambridge, MA: Harvard University Press, 2013).

22. For the purposes of this article, I define "public" schools as lay institutions of learning distinct from convents and open to day students as well as boarders. While these schools were often called "secular" in their day (to distinguish them from convents), we should not consider them as secular by our modern definition, since they were heavily religious. Unlike convents that required a dowry, Venerini's and Filippini's schools did not charge fees or require a dowry, were heavily subsidized by the Church, and at times requested additional financial assistance from the local government.

23. They were not constrained by solemn and binding vows (and the consequences that come with breaking them), but they made private promises to themselves nonetheless to observe the rules of chastity, obedience, and humility: "Le maestre non fanno voti ma li osservano come se li facessero volontariamente, senza obbligo" ("The teachers do not take vows but they keep them as if they took them voluntarily, without compulsion") (*Regole per le maestre pie dell'Istituto della serva di Dio Rosa Venerini, ricavate dalla vita, dalla relazione e dai manoscritti della medesima* [Roma: 1837]).

24. Bergamaschi, *Vita del Servo di Dio Card. Marc'Antonio Barbarigo*, 58.

25. See Mario Presciuttini, "Santa Lucia Filippini, catechista," *Rivista lasalliana: trimestrale dei fratelli delle scuole cristiane* 4, anno XLVI (1979): 305. It is likely that Venerini and Filippini imitated the "schools" of Christian Doctrine that also encouraged students to return home to teach their parents and relatives. See Guerrino Pelliccia, "Nuove note sulla educazione femminile popolare a Roma nei secoli XVI–XVII," *Quaderni* 1 (1980): 296–297 n 4.

26. Bergamaschi, *Vita del Servo di Dio Card. Marc'Antonio Barbarigo*, 72.

27. For more on the Schools of Christian Doctrine, see Christopher Carlsmith, *A Renaissance Education: Schooling in Bergamo and the Venetian Republic, 1500–1650* (Toronto: University of Toronto Press, 2010), 145–59; and Guerrino Pelliccia, *La scuola primaria*, 27–50.

28. Christopher Carlsmith, "The Three Rs: Education in Early Modern Rome," in *A Companion to Early Modern Rome, 1492–1692*, eds. Pamela M. Jones, Barbara Wisch, and Simon Ditchfield (Leiden: Brill, 2019), 500–514.

29. Carlsmith, *Renaissance Education*, 46.

30. Perhaps the Church was also responding to a demand to provide more for the education of girls than what the Schools of Christian Doctrine could offer, at least in Bergamo, where Carlsmith notes that "by 1610 females constituted the majority of participants in the Schools of Christian Doctrine in Bergamo, with twice as many female teachers and thirteen hundred more girls enrolled than boys" (Carlsmith, *Renaissance Education*, 152).

31. Patrignani wrote that the teachers of Venerini's schools were not "Monache" ("nuns") or "terziarie" ("tertiaries") but "secolari in abito nero positivo e civile" ("laywomen in unmistakable secular, black dress") (in Sacra Rituum Congregatio, *Romana seu Viterbien*, 100).

32. Women's work consisted of spinning, sewing, knitting, embroidery, lace making, and the like.

33. For information on these institutions, see Gabriella Zarri, *Recinti: Donne, clausura matrimonio nella prima età moderna* (Bologna: Il Mulino, 2000), 196; and Angela Groppi, *I conservatori della virtù: Donne recluse nella Roma dei Papi* (Rome: La Terza, 1994).

34. See Massimo Marcocchi, "Le origini del Collegio della Beata Vergine di Cremona, istituzione della Riforma Cattolica (1610)," *Annali della Biblioteca Statale e Libreria Civica di Cremona* 24 (1973): 7–156.

35. On Eleonora Ramirez di Montalvo and her conservatories, see my article "Convent Alternatives for Rich and Poor Girls in Seventeenth-Century Florence: The Lay Conservatories of Eleonora Ramirez di Montalvo (1602–59)," in *Devout Laywomen*, 255–275.

36. I have excluded the most obvious examples of educational initiatives for early-modern women—Angeliche, Orsoline, Gesuitesse—because they lost their lay status early in their establishment.

37. The number of Scuole Pontificie was reduced to thirty in 1659 and twenty-seven in 1664; however, in 1695 the Scuole numbered fifty institutions, with sometimes as many as seventy students per school, some of whom paid admission (Pelliccia, *La scuola primaria*, 402–405).

38. Angela Groppi, "Lavoro e proprietà delle donne in età moderna," *Il lavoro delle donne*, ed. Angela Groppi (Bari: Editori Laterza, 1996), 136–337.

39. While it was not requisite that teachers were literate, someone in the school was expected to know how to read ("Ciascheduna scuola habbia una maestra, che sia donna di nota bontà, e sappia leggere o tenga una che sappia leggere" ["Each school should have a teacher, a woman who is known for her goodness, and she should know how to read or have an assistant who knows how to read"] [Pelliccia, *La scuola primaria*, 402]).

40. Pelliccia, *La scuola primaria*, 395–417. Pelliccia mentions other schools outside the convent, such as the Scuole delle Convittrici del Bambino Gesù, which were established in 1659 as religious comunities of oblate (406). He also recognizes the Orsoline and the Gesuitesse, which, while they may have started out as lay congregations, were later required to profess solemn vows; the Gesuitesse were eventually suppressed in 1630 (398–399). Additionally, see Guerrino Pelliccia, "Scuole di catechismo e scuole rionali per fanciulle nella

Roma del Seicento," *Ricerche per la storia religiosa di Roma* 4 (1980): 237–268, in which the author provides details about other public and private initiatives organized by local parishes to have laywomen teach Christian doctrine to children, often for free or in exchange for whatever payment parents could afford. See also Sacra Rituum Congregatio, *Romana seu Viterbien*, xxix–xxx.

41. Venerini's schools were called Scuole Pie because they were free of charge; so too were the Scuole Pie founded for young men by Giuseppe Calasanzio, but the fact that both sets of institutions did not require fees appears to be the only connection between Venerini and the Scolopians. By adopting an identical name, Venerini may have merely been alluding to practical reasons rather than to methodology. However, there was some hesitancy to call Venerini's schools Scuole Pie: Pope Urban VIII declared in 1630 that only the schools of the Padri Scolopi could be called as such. Still, Venerini used the term in a manuscript, "Nota degli esercizi che si fanno ogni venerdì nelle Scuole Pie," and the denomination was later changed by the Scolopian priest Rodolfo Brasàvola di San Girolamo when this manuscript was published (see Sacra Rituum Congregatio, *Romana seu Viterbien*, 335–336).

42. ". . . quivi si devono dalle scolare apprendere vari lavori donneschi, che s'insegnano, cioè far calzette, cucire, far merletti a piombino, e simili" ("in the schools they should learn various types of women's work that are taught there, namely, how to knit, sew, make lace with bobbins, and other similar work") (Andreucci, *Ragguaglio della vita*, 71). The girls were not allowed, however, to weave on a loom or spin silk, because these jobs were considered too noisy and would distract them from learning. Similarly, embroidery and drawing (except for small projects) would require too much concentration and were not conducive to learning (*Regole per le maestre pie*).

43. Andreucci, *Ragguaglio della vita*, 71.

44. Andreucci, *Ragguaglio della vita*, 51–52.

45. Bergamaschi, *Vita del Servo di Dio Card. Marc'Antonio Barbarigo*, 77–78.

46. Bergamaschi, *Vita del Servo di Dio Card. Marc'Antonio Barbarigo*, 50–51.

47. Pietro Bergamaschi, *Vita della serva di Dio Donna Maria Cecilia Baij* (Viterbo: Agnesotti, 1923), 16, in "Il dono di Santa Rosa Venerini a M. Cecilia Baij," by Suor Eliana Massimi, MPV, in *M. Cecilia Baij e le altre donne in ricerca di Dio nel Settecento viterbese*, eds. Nadia Togni and Annamaria Valli (Viterbo: Graffietti, 2018), 43.

48. Macchietti, "Le scuole delle Maestre Pie," 638.

49. Caffiero, *Religione e modernità*, 119.

50. Venerini excluded widows, who she believed would have difficulty adjusting their expectations and living habits, as well as tertiaries, whose vocation required additional responsibilities, although she made some exceptions for the latter: "non sono al caso per tal ministero, conforme alla sua idea, le vedove, perché assuefatte al governo delle loro case, non sanno accomodarsi al modo di vivere, richiesto in questo ministero" ("widows are not suited for such an office, according to [Venerini's] plan, because they are accustomed to being in charge of their own houses and do not know how to adjust to the way of life that this office requires") (Andreucci, *Ragguaglio della vita*, 63).

51. Andreucci, *Ragguaglio della vita*, 52–53. According to John Henderson (*Florence Under Siege: Surviving Plague in an Early Modern City* [New Haven, CT: Yale University Press, 2019], xiv–xv), 1 gold scudo = 1 fiorino = 7 lire (1 lira = 20 soldi) = 140 soldi. Thus,

Venerini's two teachers were paid 18 scudi per year, or 1,260 soldi each. Henderson points out that the average wage of a skilled worker (master mason) in 1630–33 Florence was 40 soldi per day, and of an unskilled worker, 25 soldi per day. Working six days a week, the unskilled Florentine worker would have made 7,800 soldi per year, a much greater sum than what the Maestre Pie earned. A rubbia was the equivalent of about 8–9 kilograms (see "Rubbio," *Grande dizionario della lingua italiana*, vol. XVII [Torino: Unione Tipografico-Editrice Torinese, 1994, 194–195].

52. Bergamaschi, *Vita del Servo di Dio Card. Marc'Antonio Barbarigo*, 45–50.

53. Andreucci, *Ragguaglio della vita*, 53. A giulio was a silver coin, minted by Giulio II in 1504; it was of little value, about 10 baiocchi, or 6 cents (see "Giulio," *Grande dizionario della lingua italiana*, vol. VI [Torino: Unione Tipografico-Editrice Torinese, 1994, 881] and "Baiocco," *Grande dizionario della lingua italiana*, vol. I [Torino: Unione Tipografico-Editrice Torinese, 1994, 948]).

54. Giovanni Battista de Luca, *Theatrum veritatis et justitiae, sive Decisivi discursus per materias*, Liber 14, I, *De Regularibus et monialibus* (Venetiis, apud Paulum Balleonium: 1706), in "Il dono di Santa Rosa Venerini a M. Cecilia Baij," by Suor Eliana Massimi, MPV, in *M. Cecilia Baij e le altre donne in ricerca di Dio nel Settecento viterbese*, eds. Nadia Togni and Annamaria Valli, (Viterbo: Graffietti, 2018), 46 n 7.

55. See G. Lesage, "Congregazione religiosa," *Dizionario degli Istituti di Perfezione*, vol. II (Roma: Edizioni Paoline, 1975), 1559–1572.

56. The "uomo indemoniato" is reported to have said, "Oh adesso quel prete tratta con Rosa di mettere qua la scuola, ma se ci verrà, s'ha da scatenare l'Inferno" ("Oh now that priest is working with Rosa to set up a school here, but if it comes here, all hell will break loose") (Andreucci, *Ragguaglio della vita*, 35).

57. Andreucci, *Ragguaglio della vita*, 37.

58. Andreucci, *Ragguaglio della vita*, 40–41.

59. Bergamaschi, *Vita del Servo di Dio Card. Marc'Antonio Barbarigo*, 54.

60. Angela M. Kinney, ed. and trans. *The Vulgate Bible: The New Testament, Douay-Rheims Translation*, vol. VI (Cambridge: Harvard University Press, 2013), 619.

61. Andreucci, *Ragguaglio della vita*, 42–43.

62. Alessandro Mazzinelli, *Istruzione per regolamento delle scuole della Dottrina Cristiana delle Maestre Pie Filippini* (1717) (Viterbo: Tipografia AEMME Grafica, 1994), 16.

63. Mazzinelli, *Istruzione*, 16.

64. Mazzinelli, *Istruzione*, 15–16.

65. Together they founded about forty schools in the villages surrounding Lago Bolsena. There are conflicting reports from early biographers (Andreucci and Di Simone) as to who actually established these schools, with each biographer presenting either Venerini or Filippini as the founder (see Sacra Rituum Congregatio, *Romana seu Viterbien*, 120). From 1699 to 1707, schools were also opened in the dioceses of Viterbo, Tuscania, Bagnoregio, Sutri, Nepi, Civita Castellana, Orte, and Gallese (see Sacra Rituum Congregatio, *Romana seu Viterbien*, xx).

66. Andreucci, *Ragguaglio della vita*, 54; Patrignani, in Sacra Rituum Congregatio, *Romana seu Viterbien*, 101; and Marangoni, *Vita del servo di Dio Cardinal Marcantonio Barbarigo*, in Sacra Rituum Congregatio, *Romana seu Viterbien*, 156.

67. Bergamaschi, *Vita del Servo di Dio Card. Marc'Antonio Barbarigo*, 51.

68. Bergamaschi, *Vita del Servo di Dio Card. Marc'Antonio Barbarigo*, 53; Andreucci, *Ragguaglio della vita*, 54.

69. Bergamaschi, *Vita del Servo di Dio Card. Marc'Antonio Barbarigo*, 60.

70. Sacra Rituum Congregatio, *Romana seu Viterbien*, 47.

71. Sacra Rituum Congregatio, *Romana seu Viterbien*, 130–131.

72. Sacra Rituum Congregatio, *Romana seu Viterbien*, 210–212.

73. Sacra Rituum Congregatio, *Romana seu Viterbien*, 218–219.

74. Bergamaschi, *Vita del Servo di Dio Card. Marc'Antonio Barbarigo*, 59.

75. Francesco Di Simone, *Della vita della serva di Dio Lucia Filippini, Superiora delle Scuole Pie (1732)*, in *Le vite delle due Maestre Pie Rosa Venerini e Lucia Filippini*, 66–67 (Roma: Stamperia della S. Congr. De Propag. Fide, 1868), 66–67.

76. Di Simone, *Della vita della serva*, 64–65.

77. Bergamaschi, *Vita del Servo di Dio Card. Marc'Antonio Barbarigo*, 37–38. The "Positio" draws the conclusion on the basis of two biographies of Venerini (Andreucci and Di Simone) that the self-mortification methods of the Padre Pii Operai would never have been permitted in the Jesuit schools (Sacra Rituum Congregatio, *Romana seu Viterbien*, 253).

78. Sacra Rituum Congregatio, *Romana seu Viterbien*, 127.

79. Sacra Rituum Congregatio, *Romana seu Viterbien*, 250–251.

80. Sacra Rituum Congregatio, *Romana seu Viterbien*, 251–252; Di Simone, *Della vita della serva*, 62–66. Martinelli urged Venerini later to return to Rome to establish her own schools; in 1713, Venerini founded a school there, with others following until her death in 1728 (Sacra Rituum Congregatio, *Romana seu Viterbien*, 274).

81. Falcoia, also a Pio Operaio, helped Filippini draft the "Costituzioni" for her Maestre Pie. Falcoia was examined for quietist tendencies but seems to have been wrongly accused of heresy. See O. Gregorio, "Falcoia, Tommaso," in *Dizionario degli Istituti di Perfezione*, vol. III (Roma: Edizioni Paoline, 1976), 1386–1387.

82. Angelo Biondi, *Le Maestre Pie Filippini nella Maremma Sovanese dal '700 al '900: Una Istituzione anticipatrice dell'educazione alle donne* (Grosseto: Laurum Editrice, 2003), 105 n 51.

83. Some high-ranking Padre Pii Operai had been accused of Molinism and Quietism and were examined by the Inquisition: Antonio Torres, Pier Matteo Petrucci, and Don Ludovico Sabbatini. See Mafaldina Rocca, *Una luce nella chiesa: Santa Lucia Filippini (1627–1732) Fondatrice delle Maestre Pie Filippini* (Roma: Brossura, 1969), 68; and Carlo Salotti, *La Beata Lucia Filippini: Fondatrice e Superiora dell'Istituto delle Maestre Pie Filippini* (Roma: Casa Generalizia delle Maestre Pie Filippini, 1926), 287.

84. "Summarium additium," 4–6, in Sacra Rituum Congregatio, *Romana seu Faliscodunen*. See also Salotti, *La Beata Lucia Filippini*, 290–91. The practice of mental prayer for eight hours a day for eight days follows the pattern of a standard Ignatian retreat, where penitents, once a year, perform the Spiritual Exercises for a limited period of time.

85. For more on the Maestre Pie Filippini and their presence worldwide, see http://www.pontificioistitutompf.it/. In 1942, the Maestre Pie Venerini counted sixty-two institutions with 429 nuns and two novitiates (see Sacra Rituum Congregatio, *Romana seu Viterbien*, xxxix; and https://maestrepievenerini.it/dove-siamo/).

86. One nineteenth-century visitor, the French writer Stendhal, had a negative reaction to these statues. Describing St. Peter's Basilica, he said, "Elle est ornée de grosses statues de saints de treize pieds de proportion. Saint-Pierre est si beau, qu'on oublie leur laideur. [. . .] Presque toutes les statues placées dans Saint-Pierre sont ridicules" ("[The basilica] is adorned with huge statues of saints, thirteen feet in size. Saint Peter is so beautiful that you forget how ugly they are. [. . .] Almost all the statues placed in Saint Peter's are ridiculous") (Virgilio Noè, *I santi fondatori nella basilica vaticana* [Modena: Panini, 1996], 9).

87. Noè, *I santi fondatori*. Among the figures represented are Benedetto, Francesco, Domenico, and ten women—Angela Merici (Orsoline), Francesca Saverio Cabrini (Missionarie del Sacro Cuore), Francesca Romana (Oblate di Tor de' Specchi), Giovanna Antida Thouret (Suore della Carità), Giuliana Falconeri (Servi di Maria), Lucia Filippini, Luisa de Marillac (Figlie della Carità di San Vincenzo d' Paoli), Maddalena-Sofia Barat (Dame del Sacro Cuore), Maria di Santa Eufrasia Pellettier (Nostra Signora di Carità), and Teresa di Gesù (Carmelitani Scalzi).

88. See Zarri, "The Third Status," in *Time, Space and Women's Lives in Early Modern Europe*, eds. Anne Jacobson Schutte, Thomas Kuehn, and Silvana Seidel Menchi (Kirksville, MO: Truman State University Press, 2001), 181–199.

89. Often cited is Pio V's papal bull "Circa pastoralis" (May 29, 1566), which in theory compelled tertiaries who lived in all-female communities to take solemn vows and to observe the rules of enclosure; however, recent scholarship has determined that its enforcement was inconsistent (see Alison Weber, "Introduction, Devout Laywomen in the Early Modern World: The Historiographic Challenge," in *Devout Laywomen in the Early Modern World*, ed. Alison Weber [London: Routledge, 2016], 5).

90. Some notable departures are Katherine Jane Gill, "Penitents, Pinzochere and Mantellate: Varieties of Women's Religious Communities in Central Italy, c. 1300–1520," (PhD diss., Princeton University, 1994); Claudio Paolocci, ed., *Congregazioni laicali femminili e promozione della donna in Italia nei secoli XVI e XVII*, Atti della giornata di studio in occasione del quarto centenario delle Medee, Genova, 3 giugno 1994 (Genova: Associazione Amici della Biblioteca Franzoniana, 1995); and Liise Lehtsalu, "A Welcome Presence: The Custodial Activities of Third Order Women Religious in Seventeenth- and Eighteenth-Century Italy," *Journal of Early Modern History* 22 (2018), 19–66.

PART III

# Gendering Sanctity

CHAPTER SEVEN

# The State of Grace in the *Libro del Cortegiano*

MICHAEL SHERBERG

Consistent with its Platonism, the *Libro del cortegiano* obsesses over questions of transcendence, ranging from the mundane to the sublime. It maps out how to transcend the limits attendant to one's birth, how to overcome situational challenges, how and when women might breach gender norms, how the courtier might magnify his role, and how to transcend the limits of old age and access divine love. Baldesar Castiglione's masterpiece is a quintessential work of escapist fiction, because it is all about means of escape. The impulse to evasion has its origins in the tortured body of the duke, beset by the gout that will kill him. That body is at once alive and dysfunctional, a daily reminder of mortality whose disturbing proximity the courtiers mitigate at night by cloistering themselves with the duchess and playing games, including the featured game of "formar con parole un perfetto cortegiano" ("depicting in words a perfect courtier").[1]

This game, proposed by Federico Fregoso, opens onto an extended digression whose final purpose is to explain the exalting power vested in the duchess.[2] For if the duke's body denotes mortality, the duchess's body signifies immortality. Fregoso indeed prefaces his proposal by acknowledging the merits of the duchess, "la qual sola con la sua divina virtú basteria per levar da terra al cielo i piú bassi spiriti che siano al mondo" ("together with her divine virtue, [is] capable of transporting the meanest spirits from earth to heaven").[3] This phrase finds echo in Pietro Bembo's final discourse on love, which he describes as an all-unifying force that mediates between the human and the divine and that enables us to "levandone da terra esser ammessi al convivio degli angeli" ("soar above the earth to join the feast of the angels").[4] The etymological figure, which runs through the text to connect the start of the game to its conclusion, is not casual. The love object that triggers this process is of course the beloved lady, of whom the duchess is paradigmatic, the focus of an erotic desire that is intensified, thanks to woman's fundamental inscrutability. The entire process of describing the perfect courtier, then, constitutes an extended meditation on power and empowerment centered, yes, on an ideal male, but as a subdiscourse to a prior question about women and power.[5]

This essay proposes to look at the *Cortegiano* through a lens that centers women in the text rather than effacing them. Given the amount of textual space that the book devotes to men and their self-fashioning, it is easy to see women as marginal figures in it. Another reader, Valeria Finucci, has argued that the *Cortegiano* also undertakes to transcend the presence of the female. While I agree with many of her points, which rely on a psychoanalytic model, I remain less convinced that woman is made to vanish from the text, as she claims. Finucci reads Emilia Pia's final gesture, in which she gently tugs on Bembo's robe lest he levitate, as "partly demystif[ying] this otherworldly discourse, but it may be yet another demonstration that women are too intellectually unsophisticated to appreciate philosophical and theological arguments."[6] Dante, among others, would surely disagree. I would argue, instead, that Emilia Pia's gesture is sublimely subversive, in that it serves to remind Bembo of the limits of men's claim to an intellectual monopoly within the court, as their discursive power has no real impact in a court space ruled by women. In other words, she reminds Bembo that this is all a game, sanctioned by women, and that in its social organization, this court must account for the power of women. It is perhaps because of this that we see evidence among the men of concern about gender identity, as if the model offered by women threatens men's sense of who they are. In the pages that follow, I shall offer some examples of this problem at work.

Emilia's intervention at the end of Bembo's speech also serves to remind readers of the presence of a frame in the book. Indeed, so all-encompassing is the discourse of the perfect courtier, as flagged even in the book's title,[7] that it can be easy to overlook the frame, reminiscent to that of the *Decameron*.[8] Notwithstanding Castiglione's claims to the contrary, the book's structure owes a debt to Boccaccio. As in the case of the *Decameron*, the introduction of a frame troubles the text's engagement with principles of mimesis. On the one hand, the discursive performances of the various courtiers are arguably mimetic, akin to the act of storytelling in the *Decameron*. On the other, the extent to which the content of those performances, i.e., the prescription for a perfect courtier, is mimetic comes into question precisely because the frame secures it as art.[9] As constituted, the frame tale of the *Cortegiano* links the text to a history recent enough to be knowable, but also marked by an idealized distancing that equates that history to something more akin to myth.[10] In turn, this frame relegates its proleptic, normative content to an ideal future that the defects of the present render impossible.[11] If Urbino reached a near-Edenic perfection under Guidobaldo's father, Federico da Montefeltro, the son's own toxic presence has so damaged the court that it requires imaginative restoration under the guidance of Elisabetta and her entourage. Far from eradicable, then, the duchess becomes the conduit through which the courtiers can imagine a better future, one in which their rhetorical power will become real.

Castiglione locates his meditations on questions of transcendence in a Renaissance court, with its own unique values, norms, and modes of expression. While our author distances himself rhetorically from the effort to codify this culture by assigning the task to various historical personages whom he locates at Urbino at the time of the game to describe the perfect courtier, he nevertheless positions himself at the forefront of the effort to record it. The record of this game survives, thanks first to the excellent memory of one of its audience and to Castiglione's transcription of that person's record, and second to Castiglione's timely rescue of the text from possible publication of an unauthorized scribal copy in Naples and his own authorized first edition.[12] By publishing his account, Castiglione shows how the printing press can save the word from mutilation and death.[13]

The record of events is not limited to its insistent normativity about the courtier's role, it also involves the implementation of a lexicon so novel that Castiglione feels impelled to define many of its words. His interest in the vernacular extends beyond the familiar pages about the question of the language; he understands that he is adding pages to the Italian dictionary generated by court culture. Among his newly defined words are *la sprezzatura, la bellezza, la gloria, la virtù, il vicio, il detto, l'arguzia, la burla, il bischizzo, faceto, maligno,* and *l'ignoranza*.[14] Many of these words, five hundred years later, seem not to require a definition, a reflection in turn of the enduring impact of Castiglione's contribution to the Italian lexicon. He further understands, importantly, that language is polysemous, and he ruminates on the implications of ambiguity. At one point, he has Bernardo Bibbiena say, "Spesso si dice ancor una parola, nella quale è una nascosta significazione lontana da quello che par che dir si voglia" ("Often, too, we use a word in which there is a hidden meaning quite remote from the one we seem to intend").[15] That hidden distance can be either synchronic or diachronic, as we shall see. It is also the space of irony, as Bibbiena makes clear in the examples he offers.

In some cases, Castiglione lays a word on his table and, perhaps in a nod to its stubborn polysemy, offers a sort of nondefinition of it. This is the curious case of *la grazia,* curious because *la grazia* is the keyword of keywords, the confluence point of Castiglione's whole theory of the courtier, "the most important term of value in the *Courtier.*"[16] It is also, not surprisingly, a keyword in the discourse of gender that subtends Castiglione's theory. By its ordinariness it stands in contrast to its novel sibling, the untranslatable *sprezzatura,* with which it has an intimate connection. In the political and cultural economy of the *Cortegiano, la grazia* begets *la grazia.*[17] Federico Fregoso makes this clear early in Book Two, when he takes up the topic assigned to him the night before by Emilia, "in qual modo e maniera e tempo il cortegiano debba usar le sue bone condizioni, e operar quelle cose che 'l Conte ha detto che se gli convien sapere" ("how and in what manner and when the courtier should put his good qualities into use and practice those things which the Count said it was right for him to know").[18] While much of Book Two expands on his basic point, he summarizes his answer as follows: "Onde, consentendo con le opinioni sue, ed oltre al resto circa la nobilità del cortegiano e lo ingegno e la disposizion del corpo e grazia dell'aspetto, dico che per acquistar laude meritamente e bona estimazione appresso ognuno, e grazia da quei signori ai quali serve, parmi necessario che e' sappia componere tutta la vita sua e valersi delle sue bone qualità universalmente nella conversazion de tutti gli omini senza acquistarne invidia. . . ." ("So, agreeing with the Count's opinions, including those he gave concerning the courtier's noble birth, talents, physical constitution and graceful appearance, I say that to be praiseworthy and highly thought of by everyone, and to secure the goodwill of the rulers whom he serves, the courtier should know how to order his whole life and to exploit his good qualities generally, no matter with whom he associates, without exciting envy").[19] Whereupon two important points emerge. First, *la grazia* is a function of *aspetto,* appearance, and not of *corpo,* the body. It is therefore a quality that men may share with women, but with the caveat, as I shall detail later, that in their expression of it, men do not appear to be *like* women. Second, the courtier must deploy all these qualities in conversation for the purpose of earning esteem from his peers and *grazia* from his lords. The two relations differ, with the *signore* capable of delivering more than peers do.

*La grazia* is therefore not merely an aesthetic quality; it also has a political function, in interactions both with other courtiers and with the duke and duchess. Curiously enough, however, while we are looking at these two different uses of the word here, critical attention—and the implicit invitation to define the word—has fallen frequently on the former. In a 1983 essay, Eduardo Saccone reviewed the aesthetic and the political definitions. I cite two important examples adduced by Saccone. Eugenio Garin says of *grazia* that "non è che 'fior di bellezza', ossia verace e compiuta bellezza, è il sensibilizzarsi, e manifestarsi nel moto corporeo di un moto spirituale" ("is it nothing other than the 'flower of beauty,' in other words, true and complete beauty, and the awareness of a spiritual movement and its manifestation in bodily movement").[20] Late in Book Four, Bembo tells his audience that "'l bono e 'l bello a qualche modo [sono] una medesima cosa" ("in some manner the good and the beautiful are identical"), making specific reference to "questa graziosa e sacra bellezza" ("this gracious and supreme beauty") of the natural world.[21] Elsewhere he speaks of "grazia di bello aspetto" ("good looks"), and he defines *la bellezza* as "la faccia piacevole, allegra, grata e desiderabile del bene" ("the pleasant, gay, charming and desirable face of the good").[22] In other words, *la grazia* informs beauty but is not beauty itself. Unlike Garin, Bembo makes no mention of a relationship between *la grazia* and movement. Anthony Blunt, also cited by Saccone, likewise does not consider a kinetic aspect: "Grace, therefore, is that extra quality which is added to the more solid 'properties' and 'conditions' which can be acquired by precept. Grace . . . cannot be learnt; it is a gift from Heaven; and it comes from having a good judgement."[23] Blunt's definition is as ambiguous as Castiglione's own; indeed, it pretty much repeats what the text says, while raising new questions. Common to both definitions, in any event, is the insistence on the spiritual quality of grace and its resistance to definition. You know it when you see it, but that does not mean you can say what it is.

The *Vocabolario della Crusca* offers two definitions of *la grazia* that correspond to the two instantiations in Castiglione. The first references the Latin *venustas*: "bellezza di che che sia, e avvenentezza d'operare, che alletta, e rapisce altrui ad amore" ("the beauty of something, and attractiveness in comportment, which entices and enraptures someone else to love"). This is the *grazia* that the perfect courtier must display, as well as the *grazia* of the beloved lady. The dictionary traces the second definition to the Latin *gratia* : "amore, e benevolenza del superiore inverso lo 'nferiore, favore" or "concessione di cosa richiesta a superiori, o gran personaggi" ("love, and benevolence of a superior toward an inferior, favor; the concession of something requested from superiors, or great personages").[24] This is the earthly, political *grazia* that characterizes the relationship between perfect courtier and duke. The element common to both is *amore*, love. *La grazia* is both the bewitching capacity to enamor and a sign of the love felt by the other who is so enamored.

In the arena of self-fashioning, therefore, *la grazia* manifests itself in aspect and behavior. In courtier-duke relations, it hovers somewhere between favor and privilege (for Saccone, "acceptance, recognition, praise, and favor"[25]) and, I would argue, forgiveness—a forgiveness for being human, for our fallen state. And yet, in explicit terms, Castiglione remains cautious, at one point having Cesare Gonzaga offer a circumlocution that makes *la grazia* sound a little like salt: it is "un condimento d'ogni cosa, senza il quale tutte l'altre proprietà e bone condicioni sian di poco valore" (I.24, "a seasoning without which all other attributes and good qualities would be almost worthless"). Here we can discern another possible reason for Castiglione to avoid a precise definition: in his mind, *la grazia* behaves not like a noun but rather like a modifier; it is the sparkle on the shoe rather than the shoe itself, an adaptive quality that turns the mundane into a shiny object. It is a noun without substance, the animating feature of everything it inhabits. It is the beautiful soul made visible, and the attention that the beautiful soul draws.[26]

We can trace the convergence of these two terms, *venustas* and *gratia*, historically as well. Not coincidentally, perhaps, that convergence also marks one of the singular moments in the history of *grazia* as transaction. We appear to have a *terminus ante quem* for it in the Latin vulgate of the New Testament, in the late fourth century or thereabouts. The notion of *gratia* is in fact the sine qua non of both the incarnation of Jesus and the birth of Christianity. The incarnation represents an ideal case of what Morello da Ortona calls, late in Book Four, "Il generar . . . la bellezza nella bellezza con effetto . . . [i.e.] il generar un bel figliolo in una bella donna" ("this engendering of beauty in beauty . . . the begetting of a beautiful child in a beautiful woman"), a result that he deems paradigmatically transactional.[27] This event centers on the angel Gabriel's oft-quoted words to Mary in Luke 1. The angel uses the word *gratia* twice in the Vulgate, first at 1.28, saying "Ave gratia plena" ("Greetings, favored one": literally, "Hail, one is who full of grace"), and then at 1.30, "Ne timeas, Maria: invenisti enim gratiam apud Deum" ("Do not be afraid, Mary, for you have found favor with God").[28] In the former case, Gabriel may be using *gratia* as a synonym for *venustas*, whereas in the latter example, he appears to hew to the *Vocabolario della Crusca*'s second definition. Translations, beginning with the King James Version, rely on the English "favor," though with decidedly flattening effect. For example, when the angel describes Mary as "gratia plena," he does not specify whether she was full of *gratia* before she became pregnant, in which case her pregnancy would have been a consequence of that, or whether her being full of *gratia* means that she *is* pregnant, which would make Jesus himself synonymous with *gratia* as reciprocation. In other words, we cannot know whether her *gratia* is coterminous with her fetus or independent of it, though it is likely both. Luke's second use of *gratia* suggests that it originates with God, taking the form of the little gift she is hosting in her uterus. If in fact the *gratia* of which Mary is *plena* is the same *gratia* that comes from God, then Mary has received from God, not just in her uterus but also in her person, the divinity, the same eternal life to which Augustine refers. The scene in Luke thus condenses a meditation on the relationship between the material and the immaterial that lies at the core of Christian theology: the ways in which God becomes visible and creates a humanity that transcends mortality.

The suggestion that Mary realizes full grace in the incarnation finds support in Plato. In the *Timaeus*, we learn about the four kinds of living things, one divine and three mortal: the heavenly race of gods, then birds, sea creatures, and land animals. The singular god created the heavenly race of gods and, Timaeus explains, distributed them throughout the universe: "He spread the gods throughout the whole heaven to be a true adornment for it, an intricately wrought whole."[29] Another translation reads as follows: "distributing them over the whole circumference of heaven, which was to be a true cosmos or glorious world spangled with them all over."[30] In a literal sense, the gods appear to be stars, but beyond that Plato is talking about how divinity makes itself visible—as light—and about the brightening effect of the divine presence in the universe. The heavenly race of gods, in other words, appears to us as immaterial light; by illuminating other objects, they remain not unto themselves but always in relation to other things, which benefit from their presence.

Castiglione's notion of grace weaves together these two threads, the Platonic notion of how divinity makes the universe sparkle and the Christian notions of *gratia* embedded in the New Testament. His Platonism finds expression in Bembo's remark that beauty is "un raggio divino" ("a ray of the supernatural") and that it is best appreciated as detached from the body, which is subject to decay: "godasi con gli occhi quel *splendore*, quella *grazia*, quelle *faville amorose*, i risi, i modi e tutti gli altri piacevoli ornamenti della bellezza" (IV.62; italics mine, "he should . . . enjoy with his eyes the radiance, the grace, the loving ardour, the smiles, the mannerisms and all the other agreeable adornments")[31]. Grace here enhances beauty, which transcends the corporeal and points to the divinity. Relationally, the beholder finds himself in a position inferior to the beheld, who possesses divine qualities that he lacks. In its Christian expression, however, the relations are flipped, with the beholder, God, in a position superior to that of the beheld, Mary. Neoplatonism effectively reverses the Christian hierarchy, imagining a grace that does not simply inhere in the subject but is also something the subject can receive from above. The Christian notion of grace thus builds on the aesthetic foundation of Neoplatonism to install a political relationship. This is where the notion of grace as forgiveness enters the picture. As we know, God's recognition of Mary's grace, or alternatively his decision to infuse her with it, has a salvific purpose of rescuing fallen humanity from its first tragic error. Mary's pregnancy and the birth of the son of God therefore represent the resetting of a lost order, what we might term the order of subservience, the human race's recognition of God's superiority. Castiglione fuses the classical with the Christian precisely because his version of humanism seeks to mediate these binary but interrelated cultural legacies.[32]

Castiglione could not ignore the iconic status of Mary as an embodiment of grace. Images of the Annunciation were ubiquitous by his time, and their commonality suggests that the association of grace with femininity had become something of an anchor to late medieval and Renaissance culture. As early as Simone Martini, artists made the association explicit, sometimes painting Gabriel's words of annunciation on a scroll or a banner issuing from his mouth. While the referent of "gratia plena" remains unclear, the effect is to locate grace in Mary, in a woman's body. The *Cortegiano* itself records a certain anxiety about how to account for the gendered history of *gratia / grazia* in a text and a culture that wants to assign it also to men. The count cautions against a grace that veers into effeminacy, drawing narrow parameters within which grace and masculinity can successfully coexist. Early in the discussion, the count replies to a coy question from Bibbiena about his own body, affirming that Bibbiena's appearance is "gratissimo e piacere ad ognuno, avvenga che i lineamenti d'esso non siano molto delicate; ma tien del virile, e pur è grazioso" ("very agreeable and pleasing to all, even if your features are not very delicate, though then again you manage to appear both manly and graceful").[33] This leads the count to specify that the courtier should be "non cosí molle e feminile come si sforzano d'aver molti" ("not so soft and feminine as so many try to do"), not one of those who work too hard on their hair and eyebrows and who appear so "tenere e languide" ("effeminate and languid") as to suggest that they want to be women.[34]

This is an early inflection point in Castiglione's discussion of *grazia*. It should come as no surprise perhaps that Castiglione has Bibbiena raise these questions, as he was known to be sodomitically inclined, to use the parlance of the day, so Castiglione is painting him not just as determinedly self-conscious but also as voicing a key question, whether a man can display *grazia* without appearing to be gender aberrant. The count's observations here, his judgment not just of Bibbiena but also of men who veer into effeminacy, reflects a norm of masculinity according to which the male body should find a way to incorporate an effeminizing grace, while remaining identifiably masculine. Bibbiena succeeds in this. Castiglione's Italian here is emphatic: the count says that Bibbiena's appearance "tien del virile, e pur è grazioso," has something manly about it, and *yet* is graceful (my emphasis). Bibbiena's own sexual proclivities are therefore not problematic as long as he does not behave in a way aimed at inviting the sexual interest of other men, but he would do that if the infusion of grace tipped him into effeminacy.

We are thick in the weeds of gender norms here, and the discourse of gender appears to have ambushed the discussion, with Bibbiena's body serving as its locus. The count had attempted to forestall this question by declaring grace a gift of nature: "voglio che sia in questa parte fortunato, ed abbia da natura non solamente lo ingegno e bella forma di persona e di volto, ma una certa grazia e, come si dice, un sangue, che lo faccia al primo aspetto a chiunque lo vede grato ed amabile; e sia questo un ornamento che componga e compagni tutte le operazioni sue e prometta nella fronte quel tale esser degno del commerzio e grazia d'ogni gran signore" ("I would have the courtier favored in this respect, too, and receive from Nature not only talent and beauty of countenance and person but also that certain air and grace that makes him immediately pleasant and attractive to all who meet him, and this grace should be an adornment informing and accompanying all his actions, so that he appears clearly worthy of the companionship and favour of the great").[35] To the extent that it is nature that endows men with grace, grace becomes an acceptable component of masculinity. The tipping point comes at a time when men strike a pose that is unacceptable, not just because it is obvious but also because it is incompatible with being biologically male and with the associated the norms of masculinity. The purpose of this type of affectation is not entirely clear, and the count limits himself to saying that it becomes more pronounced around men of power: "e quanto piú si trovano con la natura, come essi mostrano desiderare di parere ed essere, omini di grado, tanto piú usano tai termini" ("And the more they find themselves in the company of men of rank, the more they carry on like that").[36] Even Barberis, in his edition of the dialogue, remains uncertain of Castiglione's meaning here: "Come se, per apparire gentiluomini, di fronte alla crudezza dei modi delle persone di umile condizione, si dovesse assumere un atteggiamento languido, distante dalle fatiche dell'uomo comune" ("As if, in order to appear to be gentlemen, in the face of the crude behavior of people of low rank, one needed to assume a languid posture, distant from the efforts of the common man").[37] Barberis's phrasing is cautiously speculative and focuses on the possibility that this behavior is an affectation aimed at appearing to belong to the leisure class. What he does not explain, however, is what being men who affect a devotion to leisure has do with being effeminate in a way that compares to courtesans or even common prostitutes ("le più lascive e disoneste femine del mondo" ["the most wanton and dissolute creatures imaginable"][38]), and why what appears to be deliberately seductive behavior should become supercharged in the presence of powerful men.

In other words, the count's analysis of Bibbiena's appearance locates itself at the unsurprising intersection of gender and sexual identity that in turn says something about the courtier and *grazia*. Men who take too much interest in their own appearance, preening like women, do not simply cross the border into effeminacy but do so in a way that makes them appear to want to seduce other men. The problem lies not with homosexuality per se—Bibbiena is, after all, a welcome member of this group of courtiers—but with appearing to be like a woman and wanting to occupy a woman's social and, by extension, sexual position. In other words, men may be homosexuals, but they should not be passive, penetrated homosexuals, because to be so would be to associate themselves with women, and therefore with the inferior sex. The courtier must learn to deploy his natural charm—recall that *grazia* has a relationship with the Latin *venustas*—for purposes not of sexual seduction but of political seduction. The relationship between subordinate and superior may thus be implicitly erotic, but it can never be overtly sexual.

The interlaced discourse of gender and *grazia* does not end with this part of the discussion. It makes an unexpected return later in the dialogue, in a context that affords the new discussants an opportunity to reinforce the importance of unaffected grace, while also underscoring the unique challenges of courtiership. Theirs is a brief discussion of religious women and male clerics, both of whom are compared to the courtier. To advance the analysis, the discussant, Giuliano de' Medici, turns to a different courtly space, which he describes not on the basis of lived experience but more in a flight of the imagination. That alternative space is the convent.

To understand the role of the convent in the dialogue's rhetorical economy, some context is necessary. Several chapters into Book Three, a debate breaks out over whether women are inferior or equal to men. Resident misogynist Gaspare Pallavicino provocatively affirms, citing "omini sapientissimi" ("very learned men"), that the birth of a woman is "difetto o error della natura e contra quello che essa vorrebbe fare" ("a mistake or defect, and contrary to Nature's wishes").[39] Nature, apparently not being able to control every outcome, appears to be subject to the whims of fortune. Women, Gaspare asserts, are born "a sorte" and "per caso," by luck or chance, like a blind man or a cripple; being a woman is therefore tantamount to having a disability. He also claims, I would argue disingenuously, that this is not a reason to hate women or disrespect them—we should just acknowledge their defects and limitations.

There ensues a lot of arcane Aristotelian back-and-forth about women's nature, so much so that Emilia finally interrupts Giuliano, who argues in defense of women, begging him to speak "di modo che siate inteso" ("that you can be understood"), a telling intervention that reminds the men to use language accessible to women.[40] Overall, the encounter seems to be staged so that Giuliano can refute any theoretical argument by which women are inferior to men. He begins his defense by accepting the predicate that women would prefer to be men, but he denies the reason attributed to them: "Le meschine non desiderano l'esser omo per farsi più perfette, ma per aver libertà e fuggir quel dominio che gli omini si hanno vendicato sopra esse per sua propria autorità" ("The poor creatures do not wish to become men in order to make themselves more perfect but to gain their freedom and shake off the tyranny that men have imposed on them by their one-sided authority").[41] The defense, while condescending toward women ("le meschine"), exposes how men's claims to authority over women rest entirely on the premise, advanced by men, that men are perfect humans and women, who live enslaved to them, are not. More telling perhaps is his assertion that men claim to rule women by *their own* authority. Absent here, quite surprisingly, is a natural-law claim that men's authority to rule over women derives from God.

Pallavicino remains obstinate in his insistence that women are inferior to men, a claim that can only be perplexing to the duchess and Emilia, who bear witness to this dispute. It seems clear that what is at stake is the question of the basis of the duchess's authority, which admittedly is not her sex but her proximity by marriage to the duke. Giuliano's point remains valid: men have historically arrogated power unto themselves, constituting a hierarchical authority that allows the transfer of power to women under certain circumstances. The after-dinner arrangements in the palace of Urbino do not implode, because everyone knows that the duchess's authority derives from the duke, who retains the power to punish insurrectionists. Giuliano understands all of this perfectly well, and he participates in a project that acknowledges the duke's position at the apex of power. The case of the convent, to which I now turn, serves as a reminder that men's power is by no means absolute, because there are places in the world where they do not rule; rather, God does.

As part of his defense of women, Giuliano spends quite a bit of time rehearsing examples of their virtuous behavior. Before he gets there, however, he decries a general problem: namely that many stories of women who follow the example of the Virgin Mary remain untold. These women demonstrate *constanzia,* constancy, helpfully defined a few pages later as "la ostinazione che tende a fine virtuoso" ("Obstinacy that produces virtuous acts"), and *scienzia,* knowledge.[42] We do not know their stories, he claims, because "le meschine"—note his repeated use of this word—"stanno chiuse senza quella pomposa superbia di cercare appresso il vulgo nome di santità, come fanno oggidì molt'omini ipocriti maledetti" ("the poor creatures are shut away and do not have the ostentatious pride to seek a reputation for sanctity in the world, as do so many damned hypocrites among the men of today").[43] From the diatribe that follows, it is clear that Giuliano is talking about men of the cloth, not all men. However, it should be equally clear that the clerics are straw men, and Giuliano's long-winded attack on them serves as a convenient distraction from his initial point that cloistered women live in a place where they do not have to seek approval. They live in God's court, not the ducal court, and they live free of pressure because, like Mary, they are chosen for grace; they do not have to earn it.

The men of the cloth who do not live in God's court also do not necessarily enjoy natural grace. In a description that rivals Panfilo's account of ser Ciappelletto in the *Decameron,* Giuliano provides a bill of particulars about corrupt friars: they make fun of the simple-minded, they falsify wills, they cause stress in marriages, they use enchantments, they attempt to corrupt women, and they provoke fraternal strife. Most tellingly, perhaps, they use their bodies in ways that sound vaguely reminiscent of the effeminate men the count had critiqued in his discussion with Bibbiena: "Altri senza vergogna si dilettanto d'apparer morbidi e freschi, con la cotica ben rasa e ben vestiti; ed alzano nel passeggiar la tonica per mostrar le calze tirate e la disposizion della persona nel far le riverenzie" ("Others shamelessly delight in appearing dainty and gay, with their bristles well scraped, and wearing fine clothes; and as they pass they lift their habit to display their neat hose, and bow here and there to show what fine figures of men they are").[44] They are, in other words, too studied about their appearance. This sentence shares two features with the count's assessment of affected men: first, a pair of effeminizing adjectives, "morbidi e freschi" (earlier: "molle e feminile," "tenere e languide"), and second, a focus on performance (earlier: how affected courtiers behave around men of power). There are, as well, important differences: the effeminate courtier offers himself to powerful men, while the preening friar seeks to establish his superiority over those he meets. Both seek the gaze but for different reasons.

Both types of men are in turn guilty of a kind of pride manifested in their self-fashioning. Augustine helps explain. In *On Grace and Free Choice,* he comments on Paul's claim in Ephesians 2:9 that grace "is not from works, lest anyone be filled with pride": "He said 'not from works' as if they existed for you as yours from yourself, but rather as these things for which God fashioned you—that is, for which he created and formed you."[45] In other words, first, it is not up to persons to fashion themselves, for God has already done so. Second, pride comes from thinking that your positive qualities come from you, rather than as gifts from God. Humility then would be the ability to accept oneself within the limits imposed by nature and not to strive for more. Both affected courtiers and affected friars err through a display that attempts to substitute for any natural grace, which is the only authentic kind, and thus they announce themselves as more gifted than they truly are.

Back to the nuns. The comparison of virtuous women to nuns involves not only gender but also setting. To be sure, nuns have an extraordinary example in the Virgin, who, in addition to being a woman, was singularly endowed with *grazia*. The Marian example is one of surrender to God's will, with no expectation of recompense beyond what is offered: "'Ecce ancilla Domini: fiat mihi secundum verbum tuum'" (Luke I.38).[46] Mary's acceptance of God's gift signals also an acceptance that he recognizes her as worthy. By Giuliano's account, nuns make a similar pledge of commitment to service, with the difference that they live at a remove from the world and from any audience. Castiglione sharpens this point by offering up two different models of the cloister, the religious cloister of nuns and the lay cloister of the Urbino court. The game of describing the perfect courtier takes place in a liminal space, not the holy space of a church but rather a mobile space sanctified by the divine presence of the duchess: she draws the group to her wherever she is.[47] This space resembles the cloister in its removal from a world marked by signs of temporality and, by extension, mortality. The ritual of the game inverts natural time; the courtiers spring to life as soon as the duke goes to bed, "dopo cena assai per tempo se n'andava a dormire" (I.4, "always retired to his bedroom soon after supper"), the duke's retirement foreshadowing his coming death.[48] The fourth night's conversations extend all the way to dawn, and the group suspends only upon seeing "la luce che incominciava ad entrar per le fissure delle finestre" ("the light that was beginning to come in through the clefts of the windows").[49] It is almost as if dawn breaks the spell and returns time to its regular order, complete with its reminders of mortality. Unlike the world of the religious cloister, however, where women and men live apart, the lay cloister of the duchess's space is insistently coeducational and filled with performances given over to men.[50]

There are of course problems with Giuliano's argument. Most concerningly, his characterization of the cloistered life appears to be wholly invented: he offers no evidence that he actually knows what he is talking about. He also assumes that nuns are content with their lot and harbor no earthly ambitions or desires. Multiple examples clarify that they do in fact have earthly ambitions, but cloistered women confront barriers that can be well-nigh insurmountable.[51] Those barriers involve not just the enclosure of the cloister but also forced monachization, which consigns young girls who later develop worldly ambitions to the very state of unfulfilled desire that Giuliano attributes to them. Nevertheless, Giuliano's logic establishes a marked difference between the faux cloister of the Urbino court and the real cloister that houses nuns. The former remains subject to all the pressures and ambitions that necessitate and reward the acquisition of *grazia* on the part of the courtier, while the latter is a place of privilege where transcendence does not need to be taught or attempted, because the nun's vow creates it. In the world of the court, where performance is all, grace offers the chimera of transcendence, always conditional, never guaranteed.

The discourse of *grazia* in the *Cortegiano* thus brings various gender-related tensions to light. These involve, first off, the effeminizing effects of *grazia* on men, who must accept the fact that in order to be their best selves, they must mediate characteristics that they share with women and that potentially undermine the norms of masculinity. Staving off any gender cross-contamination in turn staves off any creeping effeminization of a court in which women hold significant power, and who by doing so demonstrate characteristics typically associated with men. The source of this confusion, as well as various efforts to address it, lies in the rotting body of the duke and his historical failures, which catalyzes a series of shifts that heighten the level of gender uncertainty at court. The game of describing the perfect courtier reflects a rage to order personified by the speakers who advance each topic and who must resist voices that undermine their efforts by asking questions, introducing exceptions, and subtly dismantling the predicates of their arguments. What remains unclear as the dialogue ends is whether, even if the men succeed in imposing their ideal order, they can also erase the lessons about gender and power that this period of disorder has taught everyone.

Notes

1. I cite from Castiglione, *Il libro del Cortegiano*, ed. Walter Barberis (Turin: Einuadi, 1998), by book and chapter number (here, I.12). Here and throughout, translations are taken from Castiglione, *The Book of the Courtier*, trans. George Bull (New York: Penguin Books, 1981).

2. So great is the duchess's power, in fact, that Castiglione locates her magnetism specifically in her. The group gathers at night wherever she is and not in a specific, predetermined spot; Castiglione characterizes that spot as an "albergo della allegria" ("inn of happiness"); the contentment they feel in her service comes about "ogni volta che al conspetto della signora Duchessa ci riducevamo" (I.4, "whenever we came into the presence of the Duchess"). She unites them, he continues, in "una catena che tutti in amor tenesse uniti" ("between us a bond of affection so strong").

3. Castiglione, *Il libro del cortegiano*, I.12.

4. Castiglione, *Il libro del cortegiano*, IV.70. The reference to the "convivio degli angeli" may allude as well to the conversations recorded in the book, which happen regularly "dopo cena," (after dinner), not unlike those of Plato's *Symposium*.

5. Of the six games proposed, three directly address questions of love, while one focuses on the mystery of the letter S that the duchess wears on her forehead. Fregoso's proposal appears to decenter the duchess—"lasciando ancor i meriti della signora Duchessa" (I.12, "leaving aside the merits of the Duchess")—but it is perhaps more accurately read as a sign of the enduring tension between men and women at this court.

6. Valeria Finucci, *The Lady Vanishes: Subjectivity and Representation in Castiglione and Ariosto* (Stanford, CA: Stanford University Press, 1992), 71.

7. Castiglione's title captures a striking ambiguity in his use of the preposition "di," which functions here as both a genitive and an objective genitive: *The Courtier's Book*, and *The Book of (about) the Courtier*. It is thus both a prescriptive handbook for the courtier and a descriptive book about the courtier.

8. On the relationship between the *Cortegiano* and the *Decameron*, see Stephen Kolsky, "The *Decameron* and *Il Libro del Cortegiano*: Story of a Conversation" (*Heliotropia* 5 [2008]: 1–17).

9. Richard Lanham makes this point well: "If we come to *The Courtier* with a serious referent reality then, and a serious referent self, we shall find a narrative carefully prepared and consistently sustained as a game, a rhetorical contest. The behavior *within* the game is completely rhetorical, of course. Pose, not central self, victory not truth, pleasure not improvement, prevail. Pleasure is the presiding deity" (Richard Lanham, *The Motives of Eloquence: Literary Rhetoric in the Renaissance* [New Haven, CT: Yale University Press, 1976], 147–148).

10. Castiglione worked hard on this problem through his various drafts, incorporating important sources. For a detailed analysis, see Uberto Motta, *Castiglione e il mito di Urbino. Studi sulla elaborazione del "Cortegiano"* (Milan: Vita e Pensiero, 2003), 69–168. Lanham has called this effect "almost a 'faction,' a fiction from real life, halfway between life and art" (*The Motives of Eloquence*, 145).

11. Castiglione's strategies to create distance are multiple and include his own professed absences from the Urbino court at the time of the game. In addition, he positions the game of describing the perfect courtier as part of another game, proposed by Emilia: "'ch'ognun proponga secondo il parer suo un gioco non piú fatto; da poi si eleggerà quello che parerà esser piú degno di celebrarsi in questa compagnia'" (I.6, "each one of us should suggest some game he likes that has not been played before; and then the choice will be made of the one that seems worthiest of us"). The group includes members of the papal court who have remained behind after their colleagues, and the pope himself, have decamped for Rome. The duchess's assignment to Emilia of the choice of a game, which she turns into a game about gaming, is of a piece with the *Cortegiano*'s overall strategy of investing after-hours legal authority in women. Finucci terms their role "hardly more than ceremonial" (*The Lady Vanishes*, 18), but such a claim ignores the fact that the duchess's authority is final and absolute. I believe that David Quint more accurately captures the dynamic: "The political homology that structures and unifies the book aligns the court lady not with the disempowered courtier, but with the prince who has power over him—they have become one and the same in the person of the Duchess" (David Quint, "Courtier, Prince, Lady: The Design of the *Book of the Courtier*," *Italian Quarterly* [2000]: 185–186).

12. Castiglione explains the genesis of the book in Alfonso Ariosto's request "ch'io scriva qual sia, al parer mio, la forma di cortegiania piú conveniente a gentilomo che viva in corte de' príncipi" (I.1, "that I should describe what, in my view, is the form of courtiership most appropriate for a gentleman living at the Courts of princes"), implying that at least one person has recognized his unique qualifications for this project. Consistent with the overall rhetorical strategy of the book, however, he distances himself from his material: "benché io non v'intervenissi presenzialmente per ritrovarmi, allor che furon detti, in Inghilterra, avendogli poco appresso il mio ritorno intesi da persona che fidelmente me gli narrò, sforzerommi punto, per quanto la memoria mi comporterà, ricordarli" (I.1, "Even though I did not take part in them in person, [being in England when they were held], they were faithfully reported to me soon after my return by someone who was present, and I shall endeavor to reproduce them as accurately as my memory allows"). As Amedeo Quondam has

detailed (see Part I of *Questo povero Cortegiano*), the compositional process was anything but linear, despite Castiglione's claims to the contrary. Another aspect here, however, involves the privileging of the role of the secretary over that of the author, consistent with Castiglione's sense of his courtly role.

13. Castiglione writes that he rushed the book into print to prevent it from appearing in a wounded state: "In ultimo seppi che quella parte del libro si ritrovava in Napoli in mano di molti; e, come sono gli omini sempre cupidi di novità, parea che quelli tali tentassero di farla imprimere. Ond'io, spaventato da questo periculo, diterminaimi di riveder súbito nel libro quel poco che mi comportava il tempo, con intenzione di publicarlo; estimando men male lasciarlo veder poco castigato per mia mano che molto lacerato per man d'altri" ("Al reverendo ed illustre Signor don Michel de Silva," *Il libro del Cortegiano*, 5). "Eventually I discovered that the part of the book concerned had found its way into the hands of many people in Naples; and since men are always eager for something new, it appeared that they would try to have it printed. I was so alarmed by this threat that I at once made up my mind to revise what little I could in the time available with the intention of publishing it myself, in the belief that it would do less harm to let the work be seen only slightly corrected by my own hand rather than badly mangled by others"). Readers will recall that Vittoria Colonna, having obtained from Castiglione a good chunk of the book, had had it copied and distributed.

14. Boccaccio defines "l'ira," in the *Decameron* IV.3.4: "un movimento subito e inconsiderato, da sentita tristizia sospinto, il quale, ogni ragion cacciata e gli occhi della mente avendo di tenebre offuscati, in ferventissimo furore accende l'anima nostra" ("a sudden, thoughtless impulse, which, set in motion by a feeling of resentment, expels all reason, plunges the mind's eye into darkness, and sets our hearts ablaze with raging fury").

15. Castiglione, *Il libro del cortegiano*, II.81.

16. Joseph Anthony Mazzeo, *Renaissance and Revolution: The Remaking of European Thought* (New York: Pantheon Books, 1965), 146.

17. See Quint: "In return for their devotion, the courtier and lover expect from their prince and lady the reward that the *Courtier* from its very beginning (1.1) calls 'grazia.' The term covers both the more general favor—'quella universal grazia'—of the prince and of other nobles and ladies (2.17; 4.5), and the specific mercenary favors which the prince may grant the courtier but for which the astute courtier will rarely, almost never ask (2.18; 2.19)" ("Courtier, Prince, Lady," 186).

18. Castiglione, *Il libro del cortegiano*, I.55.

19. Castiglione, *Il libro del cortegiano*, II.7.

20. Cited in Eduardo Saccone, "Grazia, Sprezzatura, Affettazione in the Courtier," in Castiglione: The Ideal and the Real in Renaissance Culture, eds. Robert W. Hanning and David Rosand (New Haven, CT: Yale University Press, 1983), 138.

21. Castiglione, *Il libro del cortegiano*, IV.59.

22. Castiglione, *Il libro del cortegiano*, IV.56 and IV.58.

23. Saccone, "*Grazia, Sprezzatura, Affettazione*," 97–98.

24. *Vocabolario degli Accademici della Crusca*. Venice: 1612. https://www.Vocabolario.sns.it.

25. Saccone, "*Grazia, Sprezzatura, Affettazione*," 45–67.

26. Thus, as Ita Mac Carthy points out in her recent study, the discussants struggle to define it, and Ludovico da Canossa finally changes the subject to talk about "la sprezzatura" instead. (Ita Mac Carthy, *The Grace of the Italian Renaissance* [Princeton, NJ: Princeton University Press, 2020], 52).

27. Castiglione, *Il libro del cortegiano,* IV. 63. Morello makes his point in response to Bembo's claim that the courtier's treatment of his beloved will cause her to be "dolce e affabile" (IV.62, "charming and affable," and as disposed to "compiacergli" (please him) as he is toward her: "compiaccia ed onori con ogni riverenzia la sua donna" ("with the greatest reverence the lover should honor, please and obey his lady"). He deems this a "molto piú chiaro segno ch'ella amasse l'amante compiacendolo di questo, che di quella affabilità che voi dite" (IV.63, "a far clearer sign that she loved her lover if she pleased him in this than if she treated him merely with the affability you mention").

28. Translations are from *The New Oxford Annotated Bible, New Revised Standard Version,* ed. Michael D. Coogan (New York: Oxford University Press, 2010).

29. Plato, *Timaeus,* trans. Donald J. Zeyl (Indianapolis: Hackett, 2010), 26.

30. Plato, *Timaeus,* trans. Benjamin Jowett, in *The Collected Dialogues,* eds. Edith Hamilton and Huntington Cairns, 1151–1211 (Princeton, NJ: Princeton University Press, 1985), 1169.

31. Castiglione, *Il libro del cortegiano,* IV.62.

32. Here I disagree principally with Saccone's approach to this problem, inasmuch as he limits himself to classical definitions of "la grazia" while ignoring the Christian legacy.

33. Castiglione, *Il libro del cortegiano,* I.19.

34. Castiglione, *Il libro del cortegiano,* I.19.

35. Castiglione, *Il libro del cortegiano,* I.14.

36. Castiglione, *Il libro del cortegiano,* I.19.

37. Castiglione, *Il libro del Cortegiano,* 49 n 5.

38. Castiglione, *Il libro del cortegiano,* I.19.

39. Castiglione, *Il libro del cortegiano,* III.11.

40. Castiglione, *Il libro del cortegiano,* III.17. The infraction is a grave one. As far back as *La vita nuova,* writers have insisted on using the vernacular because of its accessibility for women. Italian literature's capacity to speak to women is well documented and includes not just Dante but Boccaccio as well. Giuliano's recourse to a semantic field that excludes women, scholasticism, suggests that even within the borders of the vernacular, there are ways in which insensitive men can exclude women from the conversation, which under the present circumstances—the men are there to entertain the women, after all—is beyond the pale. It is curious, however, that Castiglione assigns this fault to Giuliano, who after all is the most vigorous defender of women's interests at this point. He appears to be suggesting that even the most ardent philogynist can harbor unacknowledged biases.

41. Castiglione, *Il libro del cortegiano,* III.16.

42. Castiglione, *Il libro del cortegiano,* III.23.

43. Castiglione, *Il libro del cortegiano,* III.20.

44. Castiglione, *Il libro del cortegiano,* III.20.

45. Augustine, *On the Free Choice of the Will, On Grace and Free Choice, and Other Writings,* ed. and trans. Peter King (Cambridge: Cambridge University Press, 2010), 141–184, 157.

46. The narrative records that at first Mary is perplexed, "turbata est in sermone ejus, et cogitabat qualis esset ista salutatio" (Luke I.29), but then accepts the gift of insemination. Michael Baxandall has written about how Renaissance painting recorded these different responses in Mary (Michael Baxandall, *Painting and Experience in Fifteenth-Century Italy: A Primer on the Social History of Pictorial Style* [Oxford: Oxford University Press, 1988], 51–56).

47. This notion of mobile holiness goes all the way back to the perambulations of the Ark of the Covenant in the Old Testament, as the Israelites traversed the desert for forty years. The Tent of Meeting, the holy structure that surrounded the Ark, could be erected wherever the Ark was. It was not associated with a single place.

48. Castiglione, *Il libro del cortegiano*, I.4.

49. Castiglione, *Il libro del cortegiano*, IV.73. The other nights run late, but apparently not quite as late. On the first night, the group ends "poiché l'ora è tarda" ("since the night was now far gone") (I. 56), and they go off to bed, so in theory there is still time for sleep. On the second night, there are no clear indications, except that they will reconvene the next day "a bon'ora" ("at an early hour") (II.100), promptly. At the end of the third night, the duchess anticipates that "aspettando insino a domani aremo piú tempo" ("we shall have more time if we wait till tomorrow") (III. 77) for what remains to be said, and then after sending everyone away she "si ritrasse nella stanza sua piú secreta; e ognuno si fu a dormire" (she "withdrew to her bedroom. And everyone went off to sleep"). This last remark distinguishes the duchess's bedroom from the rooms where she holds court, reinforcing the liminal nature of the latter: they lie between the public rooms ruled by the duke and her most private space.

50. While women rule, the men outnumber them: "súbito giunti alla presenzia della signora Duchessa, ognuno si ponea a sedere a piacer suo o, come la sorte portava, in cerchio; ed erano sedendo divisi un omo ed una donna, fin che donne v'erano, ché quasi sempre il numero degli omini era molto maggiore; poi, come alla signora Duchessa pareva si governavano" (I.6: "as soon as anyone came into the presence of the Duchess he would take his place in a circle, sitting down wherever he wished or wherever he happened to find himself; the group was arranged alternately one man and one woman, as long as there were women, for invariably they were outnumbered by the men. Then the company was governed according to the wishes of the Duchess"). The group thus strives to integrate by gender, but in a telling inversion of the demographics of the *Decameron*'s "brigata," even though there are more men than women, they must submit to a woman's authority. One is left to wonder whether, in this inversion, Castiglione had intuited something that is common knowledge today, namely that there are more women than men in the world but that somehow men find ways to be in charge.

51. A near-contemporary work by a nun, Beatrice del Sera's *Amor di virtù* (1548), allegorizes this very dilemma. See Weaver's introduction in Beatrice del Sera, *Amor di virtù* (Ravenna: Longo, 1990, 46–53), for this reading.

CHAPTER EIGHT

# Singing Women, Saint Cecilia, and Self-Fashioning in Seventeenth-Century Rome

COURTNEY QUAINTANCE

Two images, considered together, offer an intriguing starting point for this investigation of the self-fashioning strategies of seventeenth-century singing women. The first is an engraved portrait of Margherita Costa, born in Rome at the turn of the seventeenth century, an accomplished singer and one of the most prolific and published women writers of her generation.[1] The portrait, created by the Florentine etcher and draftsman Stefano della Bella, appeared on the frontispieces of two of Costa's earliest publications: *La chitarra,* dedicated to the grand duke of Tuscany Ferdinando II de' Medici in 1638, and *Lettere amorose,* dedicated to Ferdinando's brother Giovan Carlo de' Medici in 1639.[2]

Enclosed within an ornamental, scrolled cartouche, Costa regards the viewer with a composed and solemn expression, her mouth closed and unsmiling.[3] Her hands are folded in front of her chest. She wears a gown of what looks to be brocade, draped in heavy folds, and a high-necked chemise. Her facial expression, her posture, and her matronly gown signal decorum and respectability. At first glance, it would be easy to assume that the image makes no reference to Costa's musical talents. But a closer look reveals the tools of her trade scattered beneath the cartouche: a haphazard arrangement of baroque guitars, wind instruments of various shapes, and vocal music part books, draped open as if they have been set down in midperformance.

The visual composition in della Bella's portrait echoes—intentionally or not—that of Raphael's influential altarpiece, *The Ecstasy of Saint Cecilia,* painted

Figure 8.1. Stefano della Bella, *Portrait of Margherita Costa* (c. 1638), etching on paper. Rijksmuseum, Amsterdam.

over a century earlier. Cecilia, at the center of the painting, holds an *organetto* (portative organ); curiously, the instrument is upside-down, and several of its pipes are falling to the ground. Cecilia directs her gaze upward, as she listens to the choir of angels perched on the clouds at the top center of the picture. At her feet, on the bare earth in the bottom foreground of the painting, lies a jumble of discarded musical instruments. A viola da gamba is angled to the left and toward the viewer. In della Bella's etching of Margherita Costa, the headstock and the neck of a baroque guitar emerge at a similar angle, perhaps echoing Cecilia's discarded viola da gamba. Margherita looks at the viewer rather than at the heavens—she is a poet, not a saint, after all—but the open book hovering directly above her head, its fanned pages supported by the ornate architectural scrolls of the cartouche that encircles the portrait, recalls the musical scores held by Cecilia's singing angels.

I begin with these two images—a portrait of a seventeenth-century singer and a sixteenth-century altarpiece representing a musical female saint—not to argue for a direct relationship between them, but instead to use them as a starting point for thinking about the complexities of self-fashioning for singing women during the seventeenth century, a watershed period for music history and one that saw major shifts in norms and proscriptions regarding women's speech and song. One of the most important of these developments was the emergence of opera at the beginning of the century, which brought with it new opportunities and new visibility for women singers. Another significant cultural force was the climate of religious reform in the wake of the Council of Trent, which intensified concerns regarding the potential dangers of literature, music, and art to lead the faithful astray but which also encouraged reflection on how the arts could be used for spiritual growth. Also of particular significance for representations of singing women was the aftermath of the exhumation in 1599 of Saint Cecilia's incorrupt body under the high altar of her church, the Basilica di Santa Cecilia in Trastevere—one of the most documented exhumations in history. This very public event sparked new interest in the figure of Saint Cecilia and reinvigorated her cult. Over the course of the seventeenth century, representations of Cecilia, whether visual or literary, increased dramatically.[4] As opera flourished and women singers moved into the public eye, Cecilia was increasingly depicted as actively making music and sometimes—if rarely—in the act of singing. In the essay that follows, I consider how these three factors—the rise of opera, social and political changes in the wake of religious reform, and new interest in Cecilia as the patron saint of musicians—intersected,

Figure 8.2. Raphael, *Estasi di Santa Cecilia fra i Santi Paolo, Giovanni Evangelista, Agostino e Maria Maddalena* (c. 1518), Bologna, Pinacoteca Nazionale di Bologna. Photo: Fondazione Federico Zeri.

and how they impacted not only how women singers were represented and received but also how the singers themselves fashioned their own public images.

## Cecilia and the Musical Body in the Sixteenth and Seventeenth Centuries

The origins of Cecilia's association with music can be traced to a brief passage in the sixth-century *Passio S. Caeciliae*.[5] As the *Passio* recounts, Cecilia, a noble Roman maiden, had pledged to remain a virgin as a sign of her devotion to God, despite her arranged marriage to the pagan Valerian, who would later convert to Christianity. On the day of the wedding, "while instruments were playing, Cecilia sang in her heart to God alone, "Let my heart and my body remain undefiled, lest I be ashamed.'"[6] This brief anecdote became the basis for the responsory for Cecilia's feast day and was also used for motet settings by composers such as Lasso, Marenzio, and Palestrina.[7] As Lucia Marchi has argued, the text highlights the contrast between the festive music played by the instruments at Cecilia's wedding and Cecilia's spiritual, silent music heard by God alone.[8]

Although Cecilia was represented with the organ as early as the thirteenth century, it was not until the sixteenth century that her status as patron saint of music and musicians would be firmly established. Raphael's *Ecstasy of Saint Cecilia*, finished by 1518, was an important visual model for the representation of Cecilia's association with music, codifying her rejection of worldly music in favor of spiritual music, as illustrated by her upturned eyes. In Raphael's altarpiece, the choir of angels hovering in the clouds, toward which Cecilia gazes with rapt attention, symbolizes the celestial music that only she seems to hear, while the instruments scattered at her feet—which include a tambourine, two kettledrums, a triangle, and a pair of cymbals—symbolize the worldly music that she has renounced.[9]

Raphael's painting was commissioned by the Bolognese patrician Elena Duglioli dall'Olio for a chapel dedicated to Cecilia in the Church of San Giovanni in Monte.[10] The choice of subject was not casual: Elena modeled her own life after that of Cecilia, resolving to remain a virgin at a young age and convincing her own husband to join her in a vow of lifelong chastity. During her lifetime and beyond, music was an important part of Elena's reputation as a mystic and holy woman. Contemporary biographers recount that she was known for her frequent ecstatic visions, during which she was reported to hear "celestiali concerti" (celestial concerts) and even to have spoken and sung with the angels.[11] Upon Elena's death, she was buried in the chapel where Raphael's altarpiece had been hung, as she had wished.[12] Through Cecilia's image, Elena made visible her own saintlike chastity, as well as her uncommon capacity to perceive celestial music and to use music as a vehicle for communication with the divine. While her beatification would not be confirmed until 1828, Elena was widely regarded as a modern-day Cecilia during her lifetime and was venerated as a saint by many after her death in 1520.

A century after Elena's death, Cecilia's cult was flourishing. But her association with music and her status as a model for feminine devotion became ever more complex over the course of the seventeenth century. In 1599, Cecilia's miraculously incorrupt body was rediscovered under the high altar of her church in Trastevere during renovations led by Cardinal Paolo Camillo Sfondrati, in preparation for the Jubilee of 1600. Cesare Baronio, an eyewitness to the discovery and exhumation of the body, recorded his impressions in meticulous detail:

> And we saw (a thing worthy of admiration) not the body lying supine in the tomb, as usual, but instead, the supremely chaste virgin rested on her right side, as if she were lying in bed, with only her knees bent, to signal her modesty, almost giving the impression that she was sleeping rather than dead, in such a way that we all immediately perceived the truth of her virginity precisely because of the composed position of her body, so that (another admirable thing), nobody, despite observing with curiosity, dared touch that virginal body.[13]

The news of the marvelous discovery soon spread, and all of Rome came to see Cecilia's body, which had been laid out in the basilica, where it was displayed for over a month. The crowd was so large, and so eager to catch a glimpse of the saint, that at one point the cardinals had to call in the Swiss Guard to keep the situation under control.[14] To commemorate the occasion, Cardinal Sfondrati commissioned the Roman sculptor Stefano Maderno to carve a statue of the saint. The statue was installed beneath the high altar of the basilica, where it still lies today. An inscription in the pavement, in the voice of the cardinal, reminds the viewer that the statue reproduces Cecilia's body exactly as it was found in 1599: "Behold the likeness of the most holy virgin Cecilia, which I saw myself lying intact in the tomb. This same likeness, in precisely the same position of her body, I have portrayed for you in this marble."[15]

Figure 8.3. Stefano Maderno, *Santa Cecilia,* Basilica di Santa Cecilia in Trastevere, Rome. Photograph taken by Courtney Quaintance, included with her permission.

These descriptions of the theatrical spectacle of Cecilia's body and the statue that reproduced it offer another window into the ways in which seventeenth-century viewers reacted to the new presence of performing women on the stage. On the one hand, Maderno's statue is a visible response to the reform of religious sculpture that was gaining traction in Rome at the turn of the century. Estelle Lingo has argued that Maderno's statue is "the idol knocked down," commissioned by Cardinal Sfondrati as a "counter-argument to the most damning of the perceptions of sculpture, its close association with the idol."[16] At the same time, the cardinal's detailed, almost obsessive description of Cecilia's body as a visible manifestation of modesty and virginity also reveals concerns regarding how and why the female body can be displayed and represented. In that sense, I would argue, seventeenth-century concerns regarding the representation of the body in religious sculpture can be linked to worries about women singers, whose bodies were on display. The body, whether in church or on stage, could be dangerous.

The undertow of these concerns changed the way in which Cecilia was represented and received, especially as women singers moved into the public eye. If in the sixteenth century, Raphael's Cecilia was seen as an unambiguous representation of spiritual music making, by the seventeenth century, Cecilia's relationship to music had become more complex. In 1550, Giorgio Vasari praised Raphael's *Saint Cecilia* as spiritual ecstasy made visible. The instruments scattered at Cecilia's feet, which appeared "non dipinti, ma vivi e veri" ("not painted, but true to life and real"), were for Vasari proof of Raphael's incredible technical ability.[17] Just half a century later, the presence of those realistic and worldly instruments, even in a religious painting, required clarification. In his description of Raphael's painting, the organist and music theorist Adriano Banchieri ventriloquizes Cecilia, imagining that she is preaching directly to the instruments as she casts them off: "Gitene, gitene suoni, canti, & voi tutti mondani piaceri alla gran madre antica, che io altro non bramo solo essere assignata nella santissima Cappella Musicale tra quei Musici, & Organisti elletti vittoriosi gli quali concertano continoamente avanti il mio dolcissimo sposo IESÙ santo, santo, santo!"[18] ("Away with you, tunes, songs, worldly pleasures! Go back to your ancient mother, earth! I desire nothing else but to have a place in the holiest of choirs and to make music continually before my sweetest spouse, Jesus, singing Holy, Holy, Holy!")

The poet, classics scholar, and theologian Bartolomeo Beverini, in his *Vita di Santa Cecilia* (1663), was careful to point out that while Cecilia was known for having been "dilettata del canto, e della musica" ("delighted by singing and by [instrumental] music"), she was certainly not to be interpreted as a worldly musician.[19] Beverini annotated Cecilia's potentially compromising musical proclivities with an admonition against "l'abuso di cantare nelle case Cristiane canzoni lascive" ("the violation of singing lascivious songs in Christian homes").[20] There Beverini instructs that children should be taught to follow Cecilia's example—that is, they should learn to sing and play exclusively sacred music. Secular music, on the other hand, should not be tolerated in the Christian home, because "canzoni oscene, e profane, e piene di vezzi, e di spasimi" ("obscene, profane songs, full of affectation and tremors") are like "veleno dolce" ("sweet poison"), gradually corrupting the hearts and souls of listeners.[21] For Beverini, writing at the height of opera's popularity, the specter of the lascivious female singer seems to lurk in the shadows, ready to steal the show from his spiritual Cecilia at any moment.

## Singing Women and the Stage in the Seventeenth Century

As opera became ever more popular, and ever more profitable, women singers moved into the limelight as never before. But in a culture that associated public display with promiscuity, women's new prominence on the stage was cause for concern. The first public opera theater opened its doors in Venice in 1637, with Maddalena Mannelli, the wife of the composer Francesco, in the title role of Andromeda. Women shared the stage with men in Venice, Florence, Bologna, and other Italian urban centers, where, as Beth Glixon has shown, some women singers were paid as much as or more than their male colleagues.[22] In Rome, however, the presence of women in private or public theaters—whether on the stage or in the audience—was officially frowned upon and closely monitored by church authorities.[23] This meant that women singers usually performed in private settings, often providing musical entertainment for literary or social gatherings. Less often, they sang in fully staged productions put on by Roman and foreign aristocrats in their homes.[24]

The crusade against women's participation in the theater (whether as actresses, singers, or both) waged by the Jesuit Giovanni Domenico Ottonelli offers insight into larger worries about the potential disruptive power of women singers.[25] In 1646—at the height of Margherita Costa's career—Ottonelli devoted an entire book to the dangers of women's voices: *Della pericolosa conversazione con le donne, o poco modeste, o ritirate, o cantatrici, o accademiche* (*On the Dangers of Conversing with Women, Whether They Be Immodest, Religious, Singers, or Academicians*).[26] In the chapter that focuses on *cantatrici*, Ottonelli argues that the experience of watching and listening to a singing woman is particularly dangerous to men's souls because it engages not only one but two senses—sight and hearing: "La vista della Donna molte volte è privatione della vista di Dio; e la faccia femminile, troppo considerata, troppo infiamma la mente all'Impudicitia: ma quando all'aspetto di Donna si aggiunge di più la soavità della voce, e del canto; dite pure, che le anime di molti deboli di Spirito corrono pericolo d'incorrere in una peste spirituale, & homicida."[27] ("Many times, the sight of a woman equals deprivation of the sight of God, and the female face, if one considers it for too long, inflames the mind to immodesty. But, when to a woman's physical aspect is added the sweetness of her voice, and the sweetness of song; you can surely say that souls of many who are weak in spirit run the risk of catching a spiritual and deadly plague.")

In another lengthy volume focused on the uses and abuses of theater, *Della christiana moderatione del theatro* (*On the Christian Moderation of Theater*), Ottonelli returned to the dual danger of a woman's body and voice in his argument that *comiche* (comic actresses, who often sang during their performances) should be banned from the stage: "Poiche queste femminelle ordinariamente sono belle, lascive, e hanno venduta l'onestà; e con i movimenti, e gesti di tutto il corpo, e con la voce molle, e soave, con il vestito, e leggiadria a guisa di Sirene incantano, e trasformano gli uomini in bestie"[28] ("Because these little females are usually beautiful and lascivious, and have sold their chastity; and, with the way they move and those gestures they make with their entire bodies, and with their sweet, melodious voices, and with their costumes and their grace, just like the Sirens, they enchant men and transform them into beasts").

Ottonelli was an extremist, even among his fellow reformers, but the idea that a singer's particularly potent affective power came from the double impact of her bodily and vocal presence was a common thread in seventeenth-century discourse, reflecting larger concerns about the representation and display of the body—especially when that body was female. A particularly vivid example of this concern can be found in Filippo Picinelli's *Mondo simbolico*, an emblem book first published in 1653. Picinelli's "Mondano" (worldly gentleman) resolves to adopt the basilisk (a mythological serpentlike monster that could kill with its gaze) as his personal emblem, hoping that the image of the creature will protect him from the seductive gaze and siren song of a beautiful singing woman he cannot seem to forget: "Un Mondano, osservando, che questo perniciosissimo animale offende, e col fiato pestifero, o sia col fischio, ed anco con la malignità dello sguardo, ne fece un imagine, segnata con le parole: E DA GLI OCCHI, E DAL CANTO, e ciò per inferire ch'egli doveva procedere con questa doppia circospettione, e cautela, per non soggiacere alla forza, & energia efficace di bella cantatrice"[29] ("A worldly gentleman, observing that this most pernicious animal wounds both with its pestiferous breath, that is, its hiss, and also with its malevolent gaze, made an image of it, inscribed with the words: FROM HER EYES, AND FROM HER SONG, from which we can infer that he needed to proceed with this double circumspection and caution, in order not to succumb to the potency and efficacious energy of a beautiful female singer").

A woman singing on stage, then, posed a potential double threat to her audience, who could be drawn in by both her gaze and her song. For many female singers, performances on stage were important sources of income publicity and patronage. But the same performances could also be used as evidence against a singer's reputation for decency and modesty. The tension between stage singing and moral reputation is exemplified by the mixed reactions to the performances of Margherita Costa and her sister Anna Francesca in 1647 in Paris, where they sang in the lavish production of *L'Orfeo* (music by Luigi Rossi on a libretto by Francesco Buti) organized at the court of Anne of Austria by the Italian-born prime minister of France Giulio Mazzarino.[30] As the courtier Nicholas Goulas recounted in his memoirs, one of the female opera singers (unnamed, but likely one of the Costas) had become a favorite of the queen, who enjoyed her beautiful singing voice as well as her charm. The gossip at court was that the queen's favorite was known for having "vend[u] sa beauté en Italie" ("sold her beauty in Italy").[31] As Goulas reported with obvious delight, when the queen asked Anna Colonna—a guest at court along with her husband Taddeo Barberini—if she had ever invited the singer to her palace in Rome, an outraged Donna Anna responded that "Si elle y fut venue, je l'aurois fait jeter par les fenestres!" ("If she had come, I would have had her thrown out through the windows!").[32]

## Costa and the Bandit: From Medici Florence to Barberini Rome

In 1644, three years before she would sing at the French court for the queen, Margherita Costa published the sacred poem *Cecilia martire*.[33] Written in *ottava rima*, the poem tells the story of Cecilia's martyrdom, death, and burial in four *canti*. Costa dedicated the work to Francesco Barberini, cardinal nephew of the reigning Pope Urban VIII; it was her first and only religious work, as well as her first and only work to be published in Rome, her native city. From the 1630s to 1641, when she published her comedy *Li buffoni*, Costa's energies and publications had been focused on cultivating the support of the Medici clan in Florence. But by 1644, as she worked to finish *Cecilia martire*, she had changed course and was seeking to reestablish her ties with the Barberini and to return to Rome, her native city. She had a pressing reason for this sudden change of scene: his name was Tiberio Squilletti, a one-time bandit, also known as Fra Paolo, who was in the service of the grand duke of Tuscany, Ferdinando II de' Medici, by 1637.[34]

The details of Costa's relationship with Squilletti have largely been avoided by modern scholars, perhaps out of justified concern that to revive the story of her relationship with a man with such a notorious past is to reinforce the moralistic critics of the nineteenth century, who saw Costa's relationship with Squilletti as proof that she was a loose woman whose life was titillating but whose literary and musical career was of little importance. My purpose here, instead, is to offer an account of Costa's relationship with Squilletti that is based on archival evidence rather than relying on the slurs of Costa's contemporaries. In doing so, I mean to illuminate the social context for Costa's poem on Saint Cecilia in particular and for her writing and singing career more generally.

Costa and Squilletti may have already been living together in Florence in September of 1639, when Squilletti's criminal past caught up to him and he was stabbed in the neck by a hired thug and almost bled to death. It was probably this traumatic event that Costa dramatized in her poem, "Tirsi trafitto" ("Tirsi Stabbed"), published the same year.[35] The poem is, of course, a work of fiction, but the story it recounts is based on details that are present in the archival documentation of the trial of Squilletti's would-be assassin, one Sinibaldo Contucci, condemned to death by the Grand Duke Ferdinando II de' Medici and executed by public hanging less than two months later.[36] The basic storyline of Costa's poem accurately reproduces the circumstances of the attack as they are recounted in the archives: the gaping wound in Tirsi's/Squilletti's neck ("dal ferro nella gola aperto il mira" ["she sees his neck split open by the knife"]), his return to health at the hands of skilled doctors sent by "il gran Fernando" ("the Grand Duke Ferdinando II"), and the punishment of the "empio" ("evil man") who attacked Tirsi by the "gran Re Toscano" ("great Tuscan King," another reference to Ferdinando II).[37]

By 1640, Squilletti was acting as a literary agent of sorts for Costa. In a letter to Leopoldo de' Medici, the youngest of the grand duke's three brothers, Squilletti thanked the prince "del favore che mi fece in agiustare a stampare un'opera di Margherita Costa" ("for the favor that [he] did for me of preparing a work of Margherita Costa's for print").[38] Along with the letter, Squilletti sent a copy of Costa's drama, *La flora feconda* (1640), promising to "a voce rendergliele duplicate di queste, quando sarà stampata la opera sua" ("double these thanks in person when the work is printed").[39]

The next year, what security Costa and Squilletti had managed to find in Florence was interrupted when another plot was hatched to assassinate Squilletti. A certain Camilla Perugina wrote directly to advise Costa that two brothers in Florence had been offered large sums of money to kill Squilletti by a "Gran Prencipe" ("Great Prince") in Rome. Swearing Costa to secrecy, Perugina warned: "V[ostra] S[ignoria] faccia guardare bene l'amico Fra' Paolo perché hanno detto questi, che, se non potranno averlo altrove, che lo macellaranno nel Palacio del Sig Gran Duca" ("Your Ladyship, make sure that your friend Fra' Paolo is well-guarded, because these men have said that if they cannot find him elsewhere, they will butcher him in the Palace of his Lordship the Grand Duke").[40]

Shortly thereafter, Squilletti received an anonymous letter with the troubling suggestion that his Medici patrons were involved in the plot against him.[41] The plot was even thicker than it seemed, however. Another letter, addressed to the grand duke, reports that it is none other than Cardinal Antonio Barberini who wants Squilletti dead and that he has promised to pay an additional 3000 scudi upon receiving Squilletti's severed head.[42] I have not yet been able to establish who was behind the plot to kill Squilletti, although the answer is probably hidden somewhere in the copious archival documentation in Florence. Whatever the truth of the matter was, Costa and Squilletti seem to have felt it was time to get back into the good graces of the Barberini and to leave Florence behind for Rome.

By February of 1644, as chronicled by the Roman diarist Giacinto Gigli, Margherita Costa had used her social capital and connections to the Barberini to arrange for Squilletti's absolution by the pope, thus allowing the ex-bandit to safely enter Rome.[43] Costa, described by Gigli as a "famosa meretrice" ("famous prostitute"), had also declared her intentions to become a penitent, and "il Cardinale Barberino, il quale ha grandissimo gusto quando sente che un peccatore o peccatrice si vuol ridurre a penitenza, l'ha ajutato e favorito" ("the Cardinal [Francesco] Barberini, who takes supreme delight in hearing that a male or female sinner wants to become a penitent, helped and favored her").[44] Upon his arrival in Rome, Fra Paolo was met with carriages and hosted by Taddeo Barberini at Palazzo Barberini al Monte di Pietà; the Barberini brothers provided Squilletti with a stipend of 100 scudi per month ("30 from Taddeo, and 70 from Francesco").[45] All of Rome was scandalized by this news; more so by the talk that the Barberini were planning to grant Squilletti a canonicate at San Pietro.[46]

Squilletti's life in the lap of Barberini luxury did not last even a year. Pope Urban VIII, who on January 5, 1644, had indeed absolved Squilletti of all his previous sins, died in July of the same year.[47] The new pope, Innocent X, from the rival Pamphilj family, began to investigate the Barberini for financial corruption, and the balance of power in the city shifted abruptly. In the end, it turned out that Squilletti's suspicion of his former patron Ferdinando II de' Medici was warranted: on December 18, 1644, on Ferdinando's orders, Squilletti was ambushed by armed guards and promptly locked up in the Bargello prison in Florence, where he would die at the age of 81 in 1677.[48] The only thing that kept him from trying to kill himself, according to a (probably romanticized) account written after he died, was to remind him of "la cara sua Checca [*sic*]

Costa, che estremamente desiderava che egli vivesse, per corroborazione di che fu necessario mostrarli un anello che essa teneva in dito" ("his dear Checca [i.e., Margherita, who was often confused with her sister during her lifetime], who greatly desired that he might live, and to corroborate that [desire], it was necessary to show him a ring that she wore on her finger").[49]

At the end of the nineteenth century, Gigli's account of the exploits of Fra Paolo and Margherita Costa was trotted out as part of a debate regarding whether Costa was a courtesan. According to the nineteenth-century scholar Costantino Arlìa and many others following in his wake, the answer was a definitive yes.[50] Although many modern scholars seem to agree with that assessment, I would suggest that a more fruitful question is not whether Margherita Costa was a courtesan but why Costa and so many other women singers were routinely viewed as such. Indeed, as we saw above, for seventeenth-century audiences and commentators, the line between singer and prostitute was especially blurry when a woman's body, along with her voice, was displayed on stage, whether that stage was private and princely or public and commercial.

## Embodying Cecilia

Costa's choice of Cecilia as protagonist in her bid for Barberini patronage was strategic on many levels. Cecilia, after all, was the most Roman of saints, believed to have been born and martyred in the second century on the very land where her church, the Basilica di Santa Cecilia in Trastevere, was located. Like Cecilia, Margherita was a native Roman. In addition, Margherita had close ties to Cecilia's home neighborhood of Trastevere. For a time, she owned a vineyard nearby, just outside of Porta Portese and next to the now-demolished Villa Massimo.[51] And in her will of 1635, she asked to be buried in the church of S. Francesco a Ripa, about five minutes by foot from Santa Cecilia.[52] Margherita's *romanità* seems to have been an important part of her public image: she published all of her works, except for the final one, under the byline "Margherita Costa Romana." In the dedication to Francesco Barberini that prefaces the 1644 edition of *Cecilia martire*, Costa deftly highlights the provenance she shares with Cecilia. At the same time, she modestly acknowledges the saint's divine perfection and her own worldly imperfection: "Nata in Roma ho stimato convenevole dedicare all'Eminenza Sua il Martirio della Romana Cecilia, acciò quanto in me non vaglio tutto meriti in lei, che puotè meritare il Cielo" ("Born in Rome myself, I thought it appropriate to dedicate to Your Eminence the Martyrdom of Roman Cecilia, so that she who was worthy of Heaven might make up for all that is not worthy in me").[53]

Another thing that Costa and Cecilia had in common, of course, was music. Costa was an opera singer; Cecilia was well-established by the middle of the seventeenth century as the patron saint of music and musicians. Already in 1585, Sixtus V established by papal bull a guild for professional musicians, the Congregazione dei Musici sotto l'invocazione della Beata Vergine e dei Santi Gregorio e Cecilia (Congregation of Musicians under the Invocation of the Blessed Virgin and Saints Gregory and Cecilia), still operating today as the Accademia Nazionale di Santa Cecilia. In 1624, Urban VIII issued a brief giving the Congregazione dei Musici total control over music printing in Rome, as well as over music education in the city.

During Urban VIII's papacy, Urban and his nephews Francesco, Antonio, and Taddeo Barberini were the most important patrons of music and spectacle in Rome.[54] Costa would have understood her talents as a singer were the way to Barberini hearts. She would also have known that as a woman who sang on the public stage, she would have to display her singing body with care. It was precisely her status as a "donna pubblica" ("public woman") that made it inappropriate for Costa to cast herself directly as Saint Cecilia.[55]

In 1619, Arcangela Paladini, a Medici singer, had done just that, playing the role of Saint Cecilia in a staged compline service for Grand Duchess Maria Magdalena and her children. But Arcangela Paladini was no public woman; she performed exclusively in court settings—never on the public stage—and her body and reputation were closely surveilled by her patroness, the grand duchess. According to the librettist Jacopo Cicognini, who was present at the performance, Arcangela performed the role of Cecilia so well that the audience almost believed the saint herself had appeared before them:

> Ma, quello ch'io non voglio né debbo tacere, fu l'ammirabile stupore che lasciò negli animi di ciascuno la Signora Arcangela Paladini Brohomans, la quale con sì graziosa, e devota maniera rappresentò con l'attione, e col canto Santa Cecilia, che se è lecito il dirlo, credo che ciascuno in quel punto credesse, che quella stessa gloriosa Vergine fosse apparita in quel santo Oratorio a chiamarne al Paradiso, perciocchè non solo col suono di voce veramente angelica, ma con gesti e movimenti sovrahumani

Figure 8.4. Tomb of Arcangela Paladini, Santa Felicita, Florence, detail. Photograph taken by Courtney Quaintance, included with her permission.

> esprimeva le parole, e concetti spirando tal'hora da gli occhi sollevati in alto purissimi raggi d'humiltà, e devozione.[56]
>
> But what I neither want nor can keep silent was the admirable awe left in the souls of each of us by the Signora Arcangela Paladini Brohomans, who with such a graceful and devout manner represented Saint Cecilia through action and through song, that, if it is appropriate to say so, I believe that each of us at the time believed that the glorious virgin herself had appeared in that holy oratorio to call us to Paradise, because not only with truly angelic sound of her voice, but also with extraordinary gestures and movements, she expressed the words and conceits, emitting at times from her raised eyes the purest rays of humility and devotion.

When Arcangela died at only twenty-three, the grand duchess commissioned a monumental tomb for her, located under the portico of the Medici church of Santa Felicita. In the center, a portrait bust depicts Arcangela, her head chastely covered. To the left, a woman who represents Painting appears to be sleeping, her brushes and palette in her lap, alluding to Paladini's skills as a painter. To the right, an allegory of Music plays the harp, her upward gaze reminding us of Saint Cecilia, who sang in her heart to God alone. The epitaph on the tomb describes Paladini as "innocent in celestial singing, the Tuscan Siren, the Italic muse."[57] When Paladini performed the role of Cecilia, her voice and her body transmitted not danger but purity; she was perceived—at least by Cicognini—as a conduit of the divine.

## Singing Statues

Unlike Paladini, Margherita Costa, perceived by many of her contemporaries as a *donna di malavita* ("woman of ill-repute"), could not literally inhabit Saint Cecilia's singing body. Instead, she could offer to her Barberini patrons a literary Cecilia: a vehicle meant to appeal to their ideals of erudition and of music as a means for spiritual enlightenment. In the dedicatory letter to Francesco Barberini that precedes the poem, Costa makes a bold rhetorical move, casting herself as the famous singing colossus of Memnon, one of a pair of ancient statues in the Theban Necropolis.[58] Like the statue, which produced sound when it was warmed by the morning light, Costa's songs are inspired and then supported by her patron Francesco, here cast as a noble ray of light emanating from Pope Urban's Barberini sun.[59] "Anzi se la Statua di Mennone figliuolo dell'Aurora tocca dalla luce del Sole apprendeva il suono, io, che seguace sono di Febo, mi confido in virtù del suo chiarissimo nome sciogliere il Canto; E perché V.[ostra] Eminenza è gran raggio del Vaticano Sole Barberini, auguro all'opra mia nobile splendore d'Immortal vita.[60] ("Indeed, if the statue of Memnon, son of Aurora, began to make sounds when touched by the light of the sun, I, a follower of Phoebus, trust in the virtue of your most illustrious name to unfurl my song; and because Your Eminence is a noble ray of the Barberini Sun of the Vatican, I hope my work will be granted the noble splendor of immortal life").

Costa's reference to the singing colossus would not have been lost on Francesco Barberini, who was intensely interested in the art and archeology of Egypt.[61] The so-called Colossi of Memnon were built in honor of the Pharoah Amenhotep III, who ruled during the eighteenth dynasty. But after an earthquake damaged the northern colossus in 27 B.C., the statue began to emit a sound—described variously as a human wail, a song, or an eerie whistle or screech—at daybreak, when the first rays of the sun warmed its stone body. The singing statue was interpreted by early visitors as Memnon, the son of the dawn-goddess Eos (Aurora to the Romans), who died on the battlefield of Troy; the statue's cries were Memnon's response to his mother's grief. The ancient tourists who came to see the statue left inscriptions on its base recording their reactions; it inspired a flood of texts and poems beginning in the first century CE and continued to be a source of fascination for early-modern European travelers and scholars. Through the erudite metaphor of the singing statue, Costa deftly transcends—even if only rhetorically and fleetingly—the problematic associations of her female body. Taking on the ancient, stone body of the fallen warrior, she inhabits her role as celebrated singer, while keeping her distance from seventeenth-century notions of proper feminine comportment that associated women's performances with the promiscuity and danger of the earthly siren.

Another ancient colossus is featured in the engraving that immediately follows Costa's dedicatory letter and its literary image of the singing fallen warrior Memnon. This time, the colossus is a female warrior-goddess: Dea Roma, the personification of the city of Rome. The visual image of Dea Roma echoes and reinforces Costa's erudite self-presentation as the statue of Memnon in her dedication, transforming the singing male colossus from Egypt into a distinctly Roman and female presence, whose songs are in celebration of the victories of the Barberini family.

This version of Dea Roma appears to be an invention of the engraver (perhaps with Costa's involvement) rather than a representation of an existing statue, although her pose and attributes recall images of the same goddess on the reverse of ancient Roman coins.[62] Like her ancient ancestor, the seventeenth-century representation of the goddess wears a plumed helmet and poses atop a triumph of discarded armor and weapons, her foot resting on a sphere that symbolizes terrestrial domination. In her right palm, she holds a statuette of the winged goddess of victory; in her left hand, she displays a shield decorated with the three bees of the Barberini family arms. Inscribed on her pedestal are the words "MELLEO SAECULO URBANO" ("the honeyed age of Urban"), a flattering allusion to Urban VIII's accomplishments during his reign as pope.

## Saint Cecilia and Urban's Rome

The statue dominates a distinctly seventeenth-century architectural *capriccio*. On the left is the Basilica of Santa Cecilia in Trastevere; on the right, the church

Figure 8.5. Unknown artist, engraving representing Dea Roma with the churches of Santa Cecilia in Trastevere and Sant'Urbano alla Caffarella in the background. In Margherita Costa, *Cecilia martire* (Rome: Mascardi, 1644). Houghton Library.

of Sant'Urbano alla Caffarella, which is located off the Appia Antica, nowhere near Trastevere. The visual presence of these two buildings anchors Costa's poem in its specific Roman context and emphasizes her connections to her patrons. The image of Cecilia's titular church recalls the rediscovery of her body there in 1599 and reminds us that in both Cecilia's *Passio* and Costa's poem, Cecilia had been martyred on that very spot. The image of Sant'Urbano in Caffarella is a tribute to the extensive restoration of the church that Francesco Barberini had spearheaded in the 1630s. His interest in the church was part of a larger project to document and to restore early Christian art and architecture.[63] Originally a Roman temple, the church was dedicated in the tenth century to Saint Urban (Pope Urban I from A.D. 222 to 230). Saint Urban's church was of particular interest to the Barberini family for the obvious reason that he was the pope's eponym. In her text, Costa deftly assigned the restorations of the church an allegorical, Christian meaning: "le predittioni delle lodi del Pontefice Urbano VIII, che ristorar deve il Tempio di S. Urbano, sono i meriti dell'honore, il quale in terra per le buone opere si acquista" ("the predictions of praise for Urban VIII, who will restore the Church of Saint Urban, symbolize the honor, which on earth one acquires through good works").[64]

Urban's hagiography had always been entwined with that of Cecilia. In Cecilia's *Passio*, Urban baptizes Cecilia's husband Valerian and his brother Tiburtius, before they are martyred, and he consecrates Cecilia's house, on her request, as a church. The connections between Urban and Cecilia were made visible in the eleventh-century frescoes decorating the interior of the church, which featured episodes from the lives of both saints. As part of his project to document early Christian imagery, Francesco Barberini had the artist Antonio Eclissi make watercolor copies of the frescoes in Sant' Urbano, as well as those in Santa Cecilia in Trastevere.[65] In her version of Cecilia's legend, Costa capitalized on the Barberini family's particular interest in both saints. While Urban does not speak a word in Cecilia's *Passio*, in Costa's poem he is given a starring role as Cecilia's spiritual guide and interlocutor.

The second engraving represents a scene from Cecilia's martyrdom, echoing the title of Costa's poem as well as its content. Here Cecilia kneels in front of a Roman fountain, her head already crowned with rays of divine light, as the burly executioner draws his sword and prepares to strike. Winged putti fly down from the top left, carrying the martyr's palm and Cecilia's attributes (the portative organ and the crown of flowers), defeating the demons on the right. In the background, a woman looks on and weeps, flanked by two Roman sol-

Figure 8.6. Unknown artist, engraving representing Saint Cecilia kneeling in prayer, as her executioner draws his sword. In Margherita Costa, *Cecilia martire* (Rome: Mascardi, 1644). Houghton Library.

diers. The man with the bald head, the mustache, and the beard on the far right is probably Cecilia's pope, Urban I. To my eye, his features bear a striking resemblance to those of Urban VIII as he appears in contemporary painted and sculpted portraits. The miniature portrait of Urban VIII would have further emphasized the parallels between the first Urban and his seventeenth-century Barberini namesake, skillfully emphasized by Costa in her text, a hymn to Barberini power.

## Cecilia Sings: In Defense of Singing Women

Costa's poem does more than praise the good Christian leadership of her patrons. Through the voice of her literary Cecilia, Costa defends singing women, appropriating and then reversing concerns about the disruptive and dangerous power of the female voice that became increasingly common in the seventeenth century, as women singers like Costa gained status and prominence on the stage. As we saw earlier, Ottonelli had likened women singers to basilisks, warning that they could destroy men's souls with their eyes and their voices, and Picinelli's worldly gentleman had created an emblem to protect him from the seductive gaze of his *bella cantatrice*. A scene in Costa's poem between Cecilia and her would-be executioner deftly responds to and reverses the trope of women's dangerous gazes and voices. After Almachius has unsuccessfully attempted to suffocate Cecilia to death in her bathhouse, he sends an executioner to finish her off with his sword. But when the executioner arrives, he is blinded by the divine light that emanates from Cecilia's gaze, and he is unable, momentarily, to follow through on his deadly orders. He cries out: "Ahi lasso, e chi sarà che vaglia/ contro costei, che d'alta gratia splende, e con la luce l'altrui luci offende" ("Alas, who can ever win against this woman, resplendent with divine grace, capable of wounding the eyes of others with the light of her own eyes")?[66]

If the eyes of Ottonelli's singers could elicit lascivious thoughts and sinful behavior, the eyes of Costa's Cecilia are instead capable of stopping evildoers in their tracks. As the cowed executioner continues to contemplate Cecilia's face and gaze at her "lumi splendenti" (shining eyes), he hears heavenly music, which awakens in him "novi timori" (renewed fears).[67] At first the music, played by invisible angelic musicians, is in praise of Cecilia, but soon the saint herself begins to play the organ.[68] Finally, she begins to sing, warning the executioner that human audacity and pride will never win in a contest against the Creator of the

Universe. As her song finishes, she reminds the executioner that "Regnar Pluto non può, dove Dio posa" ("Pluto cannot reign in God's presence").[69]

This is a crucial moment in the poem: the executioner is almost won over by the sweetness of the music, a scene that emphasizes music's potential power to incite good rather than evil. But as the executioner ponders the question of whether he should refuse his orders to kill Cecilia, he is assailed by demons, who incite him to doubt the heavenly musical vision he has been granted. Then, following the lead of Ulysses, who stopped up the ears of his men so that they could resist the temptations of the Sirens, the executioner resolves to close his own ears to Cecilia's "canti infidi" ("treacherous songs").[70] He denounces Cecilia's music as "falsa magia" ("false magic") and resolves to execute her: "Cedi misera il collo, e ancisa prova,/ Se 'l tuo splendor, se 'l tuo cantar ti giova" ("Give me your neck, wretched woman! And when you are killed, you'll see if your splendor and your singing can save you!").[71] The executioner raises his sword and strikes three blows to Cecilia's neck. He is first amazed, and then terrified, when he realizes that even his sword cannot kill her. Eventually, even Pluto, the ruler of the underworld, must grudgingly concede that his powers of darkness are no match for Cecilia's songs.[72]

I read Costa's executioner as a cipher for the seventeenth-century listener-turned-critic. Unable to perceive the potential of a woman's voice as a vehicle for closeness to and knowledge of the divine, some critics and commentators reacted with violence. This violence was not only literary in nature, as a chronicle of "Frustature di diverse cantarine e donne di malavita" ("public whippings of various singers and other disreputable women") in Rome during the 1630s demonstrates.[73] One of these singers was Barbara Rasponi, also known as "La Castellana," who was publicly whipped and then exiled to Naples as a result of her performances at the private residence of the Spanish ambassador in Rome—a punishment that was probably intended to discipline the ambassador as much as his singer.[74] There is no documentary evidence that Costa herself experienced such violence directly, but for a stage singer like Costa, whose financial and social stability (and personal safety) depended on the support of powerful patrons, the possibility of punishment must have been a realistic concern—especially in the early 1640s, when she was uncertain of Medici support and attempting to make the move to Rome in the wake of the attempts on Tiberio Squilletti's life.

As Costa sought to reestablish contact with her Barberini patrons in Rome, perhaps the executioner's challenge to Cecilia—"Let's see if your singing can save you!"—was foremost in her mind. Costa's poem is composed in *ottava rima*, appropriate for her sacred subject. And yet the poem has an operatic feel: as far as I am aware, the presence of the mythological ruler of darkness Pluto, along with his demons and furies, as Cecilia's primary opponent is original to Costa. Spectacular battles between the forces of good and evil were a common element in the plots of opera librettos of the period, which often contained mythological elements alongside religious characters and stories. Costa's Cecilia is not quite an operatic diva—Costa is too skillful to fall into that trap in a poem addressed to a cardinal—but she is a prima donna of sorts, with operatic characteristics.

If in her *Passio*, Cecilia is said to sing only "in her heart, to God alone," in Costa's poem, Cecilia's voice takes center stage. In her dramatic death scene, God himself sends the angels to sing their praises of Cecilia and to offer her divine comfort through their heavenly music.[75] As Cecilia lays dying, Urban arrives—in the manner of an operatic leading man—to comfort her. She offers an impassioned monologue repenting for her sins and asking for his guidance—her exit aria (although she speaks [*dice*] rather than sings, if we read the text literally). In the end, Cecilia's singing does save her soul, if not her body. As she lays dying in his arms, Urban urges Cecilia to keep singing in heaven:

Snoda, regia donzella, al nume amato
Le tue note felici, e'n vago canto
Sciogli gratie a colui, che t'ha creato,
E spiega ne' tuoi detti il sommo vanto.[76]

Unfurl, regal maiden, for your beloved deity,
Your happy notes, and in your lovely songs
Offer thanks to the one who created you,
And with your words, make plain his supreme virtue.

## Embodying the Singing Goddess

Urban VIII died in July of 1644, less than a year after Costa's *Cecilia martire* was published. The new Pamphilj pope, Innocent X, ran the rest of the Barberini family out of town, charging them with financial corruption. The three Barberini nephews, Antonio, Francesco, and Taddeo, took refuge in Paris at the court of Anne of Austria, under the shelter of their old friend Giulio Mazzarino, who had just been appointed prime minister of France. When Margherita and Anna Francesca Costa arrived in Paris in late December of 1646, summoned by Mazzarino to sing in Luigi Rossi's *L'Orfeo,* they found the Barberini clan still in residence there.

In the wake of the success of the opera, Margherita turned once again to the figure of Saint Cecilia to reaffirm her relationship with the Barberini clan. Costa's *La Tromba di Parnaso* (1647) includes a poem addressed to Antonio Barberini, who had certainly heard the opera. As the rubric declares, the poem was written to thank Antonio for his gift of a golden chain and to accompany her own gift of a copy of her *Cecilia martire.*[77] Remarkably, the opening lines of the poem cast Costa not as Cecilia but instead as the goddess Juno—the role she had played in *L'Orfeo*—to Barberini's Jupiter. "Io pendo da te . . . degno Giove," ("I am bound to you . . . worthy Jupiter,") she declares, evoking a well-known episode from Homer's *Iliad,* in which Jupiter punishes Juno for her cruelty to Hercules by suspending her from a golden chain with two anvils attached to her feet.[78] As Juno, Costa pays the role of willing prisoner to Antonio, who has enchained not only her neck but her heart, with his golden gift. The metaphor casts Antonio as the wealthy and all-powerful patron who has bound Margherita to him, as the god Jupiter bound his consort Juno. At the same time, by assuming the guise of Juno in her poem, Margherita could evoke for her patron the experience of the performance, during which she sang the role of Juno, as he listened and watched in the audience. Yet it is telling that in the closing lines of her poem to Antonio Barberini, Costa sheds her Juno costume to align herself once more with Cecilia, the singing saint—perhaps a more socially acceptable avatar in negotiations with a cardinal. Just as Saint Urban watched over Saint Cecilia, Costa's literary Cecilia will defend the Barberini name from attack. In return, she asks only that the Barberini family offer her their protection: "E se nei Barberini ella [Cecilia] si loda/ In lei l'honor de' Barberini goda" ("And if Cecilia glories in praising the Barberini, let the Barberini glory in praising her").[79]

Margherita Costa's deft transformation from singing saint to pagan goddess and back again, as she sought support from the Barberini clan, highlights the ways in which Saint Cecilia's body became a flashpoint for representation of singing women in the seventeenth century, whether as an example of music's power to move its listeners closer to the divine or as a mediator between earthly sirens and their powerful patrons. Over the course of the seventeenth century, as the new art form of opera provided more opportunities for women singers to be seen and heard in public, Cecilia was increasingly represented in the act of making music, and sometimes even in the act of singing. But against the backdrop of Counter-Reformation concerns and the moralist antitheater crusade that aimed to exclude women from the stage, even as Cecilia could be seen as a mediator between the spheres of heavenly and earthly music, a professional female singer like Margherita Costa had to tread carefully when aligning herself with the singing saint. If in her *Cecilia martire*, Costa's Pope Urban I had urged Cecilia to "unfurl her happy notes," Costa was careful to present herself as a singer and poet in service to the Barberini in her dedication to Francesco: "io intanto freno le voci per snodare i canti, e profondamente la Sacra sua Porpora riverisco" ("meanwhile, I will stop talking so as to unfurl my songs, in deep reverence to your sacred scarlet [Cardinal's hat]").[80]

Notes

1. On Costa's life and publications, see Martino Capucci, "Costa, Margherita (Maria Margherita)," in *Dizionario biografico degli italiani* (Rome: Istituto della Enciclopedia italiana, 1984). https://www.treccani.it/enciclopedia/margherita-costa_(Dizionario-Biografico)/; Natalia Costa-Zalessow, "Margherita Costa," in *Seventeenth-Century Italian Poets and Dramatists* (Farmington Hills, MI: Gale Publishing, 2008); Natalia Costa-Zalessow, ed., *Voice of a Virtuosa and Courtesan: Selected Poems of Margherita Costa* (New York: Bordighera Press, 2015); Virginia Cox, *Women's Writing in Italy, 1400–1650* (Baltimore: Johns Hopkins University Press, 2008); Margherita Costa, *The Buffoons, a Ridiculous Comedy: A Bilingual Edition*, ed. and trans. Sara E. Dìaz and Jessica Goethals (Toronto: Iter Press, 2018). On Costa's literary production, see Jessica Goethals, "The Bizarre Muse: The Literary Persona of Margherita Costa," *Early Modern Women* 12, no. 1 (2017): 48–72; Jessica Goethals, "The Patronage Politics of Equestrian Ballet: Allegory, Allusion, and Satire in the Courts of Seventeenth-Century Italy and France," *Renaissance Quarterly* 70, 4 (2017): 1397–1448. On Costa's *Lettere amorose*, see Luca Piantoni, "*Le lettere amorose* (1639) di Margherita Costa tra sperimentalismo e 'divertissement,'" *Studi secenteschi* 59 (2018): 33–51.

2. Margherita Costa, *La chitarra della signora Margherita Costa romana, canzoniere amoroso* (Frankfurt: Daniel Wastch, 1638); Margherita Costa, *Lettere amorose della signora Margherita Costa romana* (Venice: s.n., 1639). For the frontispiece of *Lettere amorose*, the inscriptions were removed and replaced with a laurel wreath and other foliate decorations, but the portrait of Costa was reused, unchanged. In lieu of the portrait reproduced in Figure 1, the copy of *La chitarra* held at the Bancroft Library of the University of California at Berkeley contains a different portrait made by an unknown artist, which I do not discuss here. This second portrait appeared in most copies of another of Costa's poetry collections, *Lo stipo* (Venice: 1639). For reproductions of all three frontispieces, see Costa-Zalessow, *Voice of a Virtuosa and Courtesan*, 16–18. For more on the 1638 portrait, see the introduction by Sara Dìaz and Jessica Goethals, in Costa, *The Buffoons*, 6–7. On portraits of seventeenth-century singers, including Margherita, her sister Anna Francesca Costa, and Leonora

Baroni, see Amy Brosius, "'Il suon, lo sguardo, il canto': The Function of Portraits of Mid-Seventeenth-Century *Virtuose* in Rome," *Italian Studies* 63, no. 1 (2008): 17–40.

3. Della Bella's preliminary sketch of the portrait is held at the Gabinetto Disegni e Stampe at the Uffizi (n. 623 O). For the argument that in the printed etching Costa's expression is "meno bonario e più arguto" (less good-natured and more witty) than in della Bella's sketch, see Sandro Bellesi, "I ritratti delle sorelle Costa di Cesare Dandini e Stefano della Bella," in *Con dolce forza: Donne nell'universo musicale del Cinque e Seicento*, ed. Laura Donati (Florence: Polistampa, 2018), 71. A presumably unpublished version of the 1638 frontispiece (probably a proof), now held at the Rijksmuseum, contains a version of the portrait that appears closer to della Bella's sketch than to the published version; the face is longer, the hair is dressed more loosely, and the expression is softer, suggesting that Costa preferred the more authoritative (if less appealing) expression to accompany her publications. See Stefano della Bella, *Portrait of Margherita Costa*, etching on paper, 179 × 130 mm, Amsterdam, Rijksmuseum, https://www.rijksmuseum.nl/nl/collectie/RP-P-OB-34.305. In 1681, Filippo Baldinucci included a "Ritratto al naturale di Margherita Costa" (portrait from life—or as if from life—of Margherita Costa) among the works of della Bella that is probably the portrait in question. See Baldinucci, *Notizie de' professori del disegno da Cimabue in qua*, 6 vols. (Florence: Santi Franchi, 1681), 1:231.

4. On visual representations of Cecilia, see Lisa Festa, "Representations of Saint Cecilia in Italian Renaissance and Baroque Painting and Sculpture" (PhD diss., Rutgers University, 2003). On literary publications dedicated to Cecilia in the seventeenth century, including Margherita Costa's *Cecilia martire*, see Jessica Goethals, "The Singing Saint: The Martyrdom of Saint Cecilia in Seventeenth-Century Literature and Theatre," *Women Language Literature in Italy/ Donne Lingua Letterature in Italia* 2 (2020): 43–61. For an important discussion of the *Rappresentazione di Santa Cecilia vergine e martire*, a convent play by the Benedictine nun Cherubina Venturelli that appeared in at least six printed editions from 1612 to 1685, see Elissa B. Weaver, *Convent Theatre in Early Modern Italy: Spiritual Fun and Learning for Women* (Cambridge: Cambridge University Press, 2007), 216–227.

5. For information on the dating of the *Passio* and some of its sources, see Hippolyte Delehaye, *Étude sur le légendier romain: Les saints de Novembre et de Décembre* (Brussels: Société des Bollandistes, 1936), 74–75, 78–80.

6. *Passio*, 196, cap. 3: "Venit dies, in quo thalamus collocatus est et cantantibus organis illa in corde suo soli Domino decantabat, dicens: fiat cor meum et corpus meum immaculatum ut non confundar." Cited and translated in Thomas Connolly, *Mourning into Joy: Music, Raphael, and Saint Cecilia* (New Haven, CT: Yale University Press, 1994), 63 n 9.

7. See Lucia Marchi, "For Whom the Fire Burns: Medieval Images of Saint Cecilia and Music," *Recercare* 27, 1–2 (2015): 7 n 4.

8. Marchi, "For Whom the Fire Burns," 7.

9. On Raphael's painting, see Stanisław Mossakowski, "Raphael's 'St. Cecilia': An Iconographical Study," *Zeitschrift für Kunstegeschichte* 31, no. 1 (1968); Connolly, *Mourning into Joy*; Nico Staiti, "'L'estasi di Santa Cecilia e quattro santi' di Raffaello: Riflessioni su pittura e musica," *Il saggiatore musicale* 8, no. 2 (2001): 177–192.

10. For Elena Duglioli dall'Olio's biography, see Marina Romanello, "Duglioli, Elena," in *Dizionario Biografico degli Italiani* (San Zeno Naviglio: Treccani, 1992). On Duglioli and

the painting, see Regina Stefaniak, "Raphael's *Santa Cecilia*: A Fine and Private Vision of Virginity," *Art History* 14, no. 3 (1991): 345–371; Gabriella Zarri, "L'altra Cecilia: Elena Duglioli Dall'Olio," in *Le sante vive: Profezie di corte e devozione femminile tra '400 e '500* (Turin: Rosenberg & Sellier, 1990).

11. Mossakowski, "Raphael's 'St. Cecilia': An Iconographical Study," 4.

12. Mossakowski, "Raphael's 'St. Cecilia,'" 2.

13. Cesare Baronio, *Annales Ecclesiastici* 9 (1601), 862: "Visebaturque (quod admiratione dignum erat) non ut assolet, in sepulchro resupinum positum corpus, sed ut in lecto iacens honestissima virgo supra dextrum cubare latus, contractis nonnisi ad modestiam genibus, ut dormientis imaginem redderet potius quam defunctae, ipso ita ad insinuandam omnibus virginalem verecundiam composito situ corporis; adeo ut (quod aeque mirandum) nemo quamuis curiosus inspector, ausus omnino fuerit virgineum illud detergere corpus." Cited and translated into Italian in Alessia Lirosi, "Il corpo di Santa Cecilia (Roma, III-XVII secolo)," *Mélanges de l'École française de Rome: Italie et Méditerranée modernes et contemporaines* 122, no. 1 (2010): 50–51 n 166. English translation mine.

14. On the rediscovery of Cecilia's body, see Lirosi, "Il corpo di Santa Cecilia (Roma, III-XVII secolo)," 5–51. For a description of the crowds that came to see the body in 1599, necessitating the Swiss Guard's intervention, see page 27.

15. On Maderno's statue, see Estelle Lingo, *Mochi's Edge and Bernini's Baroque* (London: Harvey Miller, 2017), 48, 51–52. For a translation of the inscription, see page 49.

16. Lingo, *Mochi's Edge and Bernini's Baroque*, 48–49.

17. Vasari's complete description of the painting reads: "Evvi una Santa Cecilia che, da un coro in cielo d'Angeli abbagliata, sta a udire il suono, tutta data in preda alla armonia, e si vede nella sua testa quella astrazzione che si vede nel viso di coloro che sono in estasi; oltra che sono sparsi per terra instrumenti musici che non dipinti, ma vivi e veri si conoscono, e similmente alcuni suoi veli e vestimenti di drappi d'oro e di seta, e sotto quelli un ciliccio maravaglioso" ("In it is a S. Cecilia, who, entranced by the choir of angels on high, stands listening to the sound, wholly absorbed in the harmony; and in her countenance is seen that abstraction which is found in the faces of those who are in ecstasy. Scattered about the ground, moreover, are musical instruments, which have the appearance of being, not painted, but real and true; and such, also, are some veils that she is wearing, with vestments woven in silk and gold, and below these, a marvellous hair-shirt"). Giorgio Vasari, *Le vite de' più eccellenti pittori, scultori, ed architettori*, 2 vols. (Florence: Giunti, 1568); Giorgio Vasari, *Lives of the Most Eminent Painters, Sculptors & Architects*, trans. Gaston du C. du Vere (London: Macmillan & The Medici Society, 1912–1914), 229–230.

18. Adriano Banchieri, *Conclusioni nel suono dell'organo* (Bologna: Gio. Rossi, 1609), 4–5. Translation mine. Cited in Connolly, *Mourning into Joy*, 15–16.

19. Bartolomeo Beverini, *Vita di S. Cecilia vergine e martire descritta dal padre Bartolomeo Beverini della Congreg. della Madre di Dio, con alcune annotationi historiche, e morali* (Lucca: Iacinto Paci, 1663), 119.

20. Bartolomeo Beverini, *Vita di S. Cecilia vergine, e martire descritta dal padre Bartolomeo Beverini*, 119.

21. Bartolomeo Beverini, *Vita di S. Cecilia vergine, e martire descritta dal padre Bartolomeo Beverini*, 120.

22. Beth Glixon, "Private Lives of Public Women: Prima Donnas in Mid-Seventeenth-Century Venice," *Music & Letters* 76, no. 4 (1995): 509–531; Beth Glixon, "*La sirena antica dell'Adriatico*: Caterina Porri, a Seventeenth-Century Roman Prima Donna on the Stages of Venice, Bologna, and Pavia," in *Musical Voices of Early Modern Women: Many-Headed Melodies*, ed. Thomasin LaMay (Aldershot: Ashgate, 2005), 211–238.

23. I have found no evidence to support the oft-repeated claim that in 1588 Pope Sixtus issued a ban forbidding women to appear in public theaters in Rome and the Papal States. This incorrect assumption seems to have its roots in the misinterpretation of evidence brought to light in the nineteenth century by Alessandro Ademollo. See Alessandro Ademollo, *Una famiglia di comici italiani nel secolo decimottavo* (Florence: C. Ademollo, 1855), XXXI. Instead, what Sixtus did in 1588, as reported in an "avviso di Roma" of that year, was to grant the Accademica dei Desiosi a license to perform in Rome, but only "senza donne" (without women). A few years later, in 1593, Sixtus issued another license to the Desiosi, specifying that no women were to attend the performances ("che non vi vadano donne"). For the 1593 license and further discussion of the lack of evidence for a papal ban, see Giulia De Dominicis, "I teatri di Roma nell'età di Pio VI," *Archivio della Società romana di storia patria* 46 (1922): 74–76.

24. See Margaret Murata, "Why the First Opera Given in Paris Wasn't Roman," *Cambridge Opera Journal* 7, no. 2 (July 1995): 95–96.

25. On Ottonelli as a "guerilla engaged in combat against the theater and especially against the role of women in it," see Joseph Connors, "Chi era Ottonelli?," in *Pietro da Cortona: Atti del convegno internazionale, Roma-Firenze 12–15 novembre 1997*, eds. Christoph L. Frommel and Sebastian Schütze (Milan: Electa, 1998), 21–27.

26. Giovanni Domenico Ottonelli, *Della pericolosa conversatione con le donne, o poco modeste, o ritirate, o cantatrici, o accademiche* (Florence: Luca Franceschini & Alessandro Logi, 1646).

27. Ottonelli, *Della pericolosa conversatione con le donne*, 440.

28. Giovanni Domenico Ottonelli, *Della christiana moderatione del theatro, libro primo* (Florence: Luca Franceschini and Alessandro Logi, 1648), 80.

29. The story of the worldly gentleman and his cantatrice is found in a short section on the symbolic meanings of the basilisk in Filippo Picinelli, *Mondo simbolico, o sia Università d'imprese scelte, spiegate, ed'illustrate con sentenze, ed eruditioni sacre, e profane* (Milan: Francesco Mognaga, 1653), 238. Cited and translated in Elena Laura Calogero, "'Sweet alluring harmony': Heavenly and Earthly Sirens in Sixteenth- and Seventeenth-Century Literary and Visual Culture," in *Music of the Sirens*, eds. Lynda Phyllis Austern and Inna Narodistskaya (Bloomington: Indiana University Press, 2006). My translation differs slightly from that of Calogero.

30. On the 1647 *L'Orfeo*, and especially its relevance to the Barberini family, who were in Paris for the performance, see Frederick Hammond, "Orpheus in a New Key: The Barberini Flight to France and the Rossi-Buti *L'Orfeo*," in Frederick Hammond, *The Ruined Bridge: Studies in Barberini Patronage of Music and Spectacle 1631–1679* (Sterling Heights, MI: Harmonie Park Press, 2010), 153–190.

31. Nicolas Goulas, *Mémoires de Nicolas Goulas: 1643–1648*, vol. 2 (Paris: Librairie Renouard, 1879), 212.

32. Goulas, *Mémoires de Nicolas Goulas: 1643–1648*, vol. 2, 213.

33. Margherita Costa, *Cecilia martire poema sacro di Margherita Costa romana, all'Emin.mo Prencipe Francesco Card. Barberino, Vicecancelliero di Santa Chiesa* (Rome: Mascardi, 1644).

34. "Il Capitano Tiberio Squilletti" appears among the "provisionati" ("people supported financially") of Ferdinando II de' Medici, beginning in 1637. Florence, Archivio di Stato di Firenze, Camera del Granduca, 19. For a nearly contemporary account of Squilletti's long and storied life, see "Vita e morte di Tiberio Squilletti, detto comunemente Fra Paolo (1677)," in *Le prigioni più rinomate d'Italia* (Florence: Jacopo Grazzini, 1854).

35. Margherita Costa, *La selva dei cipressi: opera lugubre di Margherita Costa romana* (Florence: Massi & Landi, 1640), 188–205.

36. The Medici archive holds a thick file labeled "Capitano Tiberio Squilletti" and consisting of thirty folders of documentation of Squilletti's relations with the Medici court, various plots to murder him, and letters from Squilletti to Ferdinando II, among others (Florence, Archivio di Stato di Firenze, Miscellanea Medicea, 504). For the details of Tiberio Squilletti's stabbing in 1639, see especially Fasc. 1, "Processo per il ferimento del capitano Tiberio Squilletti per mano di Sinibaldo Contucci" ("Investigation regarding the wounding of Captain Tiberio Squilletti by the hand of Sinibaldo Contucci"), and Fasc. 4, "Processo contro Sinibaldo Contucci condannato alla forca come feritore del capitano Tiberio Squilletti" ("The case against Sinibaldo Contucci, sentenced to the gallows as the wounder of Capitan Tiberio Squilletti").

37. Costa, *La selva dei cipressi*, 189, 202–205.

38. Tiberio Squilletti to Leopoldo de' Medici, Florence, November 24, 1640: Florence, Archivio di Stato di Firenze, Mediceo del Principato 5561, c. 606. Squilletti's role in Costa's literary career may be part of the reason why some sources assert incorrectly that he was the true author of some of Costa's works. See, for example, the seventeenth-century manuscript by Anton Francesco Marmi, "Zibaldone di diverse notizie letterarie, e storiche raccolte per lo più dagli eruditissimi discorsi del Sig:re Antonio Magliabechi . . ." (Florence, Biblioteca Nazionale di Firenze, MSS VIII, 8, 6, parts II and III); this manuscript contains many other inaccuracies regarding Costa's life.

39. Tiberio Squilletti to Leopoldo de' Medici, Florence, November 24, 1640. Archivio di Stato di Firenze, Mediceo del Principato 5561, c. 606. Cited in Paola Barocchi and Giovanna Gaeta Bertelà, eds., *Collezionismo mediceo e storia artistica*, vol. 3, *Il Cardinale Giovan Carlo, Mattias e Leopoldo 1628–1667* (Florence: SPES, 2005), 380.

40. Camilla Perugina to Margherita Costa, from Rome, January 19, 1641. Florence, Archivio di Stato di Firenze, Miscellanea Medicea 504, fasc. 6, fols. 9–10.

41. Anonymous to Tiberio Squilletti, January 30, 1641. Florence, Archivio di Stato di Firenze, Miscellanea Medicea 504, fasc. 8, fols. 1–2.

42. Antonio Fancelli to Ferdinando II de' Medici, January 12, 1641. Florence, Archivio di Stato di Firenze, Miscellanea Medicea 504, fasc. 6, fols. 2–3.

43. "Finalmente havendo amicitia di una certa Margarita Costa famosa meretrice, la quale anco era amica di uno, il quale poteva assai con i Barberini, con questi mezzi ottenne di poter venire a Roma, pentito come egli diceva delli suoi misfatti per ottenere dal Papa l'assolutione" ("Finally, due to his friendship with a certain Margherita Costa, a famous prostitute who was also the friend of a man who had great influence with the Barberini,

with these means he was able to obtain permission to come to Rome, having repented, as he said, of his misdeeds to gain absolution from the Pope"). Giacinto Gigli, *Diario romano (1608–1670)*, ed. Giuseppe Ricciotti (Rome: Tuminelli, 1958), 242.

44. Gigli, *Diario romano (1608–1670)*, 242.

45. "Fu ben vero, che venne a Roma fra Paolo famoso ladrone, et assassino facinoroso, et fu ricevuto con incontro di carrozze, et menò cariaggi, et andò ad alloggiare in casa di D. Taddeo Barberino al Monte della Pietà, e quivi fu honorato, et andava in carrozza con D. Taddeo con maraviglia di tutti.[. . .] Questo è certo che D. Taddeo gli dà trenta scudi il mese, et il Card. Barberino settanta" ("It is really true that Fra Paolo, the famous thief and violent murderer, came to Rome, and he was met with carriages, bringing baggage, and he went to stay at the house of Don Taddeo Barberini at the Monte della Pietà, and there he was honored and went around in the carriage with Don Taddeo to the wonder of all [. . .]. It is certain that Don Taddeo gives him thirty *scudi* a month, and Cardinal [Francesco] Barberini, sixty"). Gigli, *Diario romano (1608–1670)*, 242.

46. "Et è fama che gli sarà dato un Canonicato di S. Pietro." Gigli, *Diario romano (1608–1670)*, 242.

47. There are three copies of Pope Urban's brief absolving Squilletti (dated January 5, 1644) in his file in the Medici archive in Florence: Archivio di Stato di Firenze, Miscellanea Medicea 504, fasc. 29, fols. 1–15.

48. For details of Squilletti's capture, see Florence, Archivio di Stato di Firenze, Miscellanea Medicea 504, fasc. 15, fols. 1–11. For an account of Squilletti's time in prison and his death, see "Vita e morte di Tiberio Squilletti, detto comunemente Fra Paolo (1677)."

49. "Vita e morte di Tiberio Squilletti, detto comunemente Fra Paolo (1677)," 612. The author refers to Margherita Costa as "Checca," confusing her with her sister, Anna Francesca.

50. See Costantino Arlia, "Un bandito e una cortigiana letterati," *Il bibliofilo* 2, no. 8–9 (1881): 164–66.

51. "La mia vigna che ho fuora della porta di Portese accanto alli Massimo." "Testamento di Margherita Costa," Rome, Archivio di Stato di Roma, Notai dell'Auditor Camerae, Testamenti, busta 82, fol. 345r.

52. "Et quando verrà il caso della mia morte il mio cadevere sia seppellito nella chiesa di S. Francesco a Rippa." "Testamento di Margherita Costa," Rome, Archivio di Stato di Roma, Notai dell'Auditor Camerae, Testamenti, busta 82, fol. 343r.

53. Margherita Costa, dedication to Francesco Barberini, in Margherita Costa, *Cecilia martire poema sacro di Margherita Costa romana*, n.p.

54. On the Barberini family as music patrons, see Frederick Hammond, *Music and Spectacle in Baroque Rome* (New Haven, CT: Yale University Press, 1994); Hammond, *The Ruined Bridge: Studies in Barberini Patronage of Music and Spectacle 1631–1679*; Margaret Murata, *Operas for the Papal Court (1631–1668)* (Ann Arbor, MI: UMI Research Press, 1981); Virginia Christy Lamothe, "The Theater of Piety: Sacred Operas for the Barberini Family (1632–1643)" (PhD diss., University of North Carolina at Chapel Hill, 2009).

55. In 1645, a Modenese ambassador described Margherita and her sister Anna Francesca as "donne assai diffamate e pubbliche" ("very infamous and public women") in his dispatch from Rome. Modena, Archivio di Stato di Modena, Ambasciatori d'Italia, Roma

243, August 30 1645, n.p. Cited in Amy Brosius, "'Il suon, lo sguardo, il canto': *Virtuose* of the Roman Conversazioni in the Mid-Seventeenth Century" (PhD diss., New York University, 2009), 106.

56. Jacopo Cicogni to Ottavio Corsini, April 22, 1619, in *Versi Sacri*, 59–62: Cited and translated in Lisa Goldenberg Stoppato, "Arcangela Paladini and the Medici," in *Women Artists in Early Modern Italy: Careers, Fame, and Collectors*, ed. Sheila Barker (Turnhout: Brepols, 2016), 86 n76. My translation differs slightly from that of Stoppato.

57. The full inscription reads: "Arcangela Paladinia—Ioannis Broomans Anturpiensis uxor—Cecinit hetruscis regibus, nunc canit Deo—Vere Palladinia quae Palladem acu—Apellem coloribus Cantu aequavit musas—Obiit an suae aetatis XXIII—die XVIII Octobris MDCXXII—Sparge rosis lapidem coelesti innaxia cantu—Thusca jacet sirem; Itala muta jacet" ("Arcangela Palladini, the wife of Jan Broomans of Antwerp, sang for the rulers of Etruria [i.e., Tuscany], and now sings for God. A true paladin, who equaled Pallas Athena in needlework, Apelles in painting, the muses in singing, died at the age of 24 on 18 October 1622. Place roses on this stone where, innocent in celestial singing, lies the Tuscan siren, lies the muse of Italy"). Cited and translated in Lisa Goldenberg Stoppato, "Arcangela Paladini and the Medici," 85.

58. On the statues, the inscriptions left by ancient visitors, and the poems and descriptions they inspired, see Patricia A. Rosenmeyer, *The Language of Ruins: Greek and Latin Inscriptions on the Memnon Colossus* (New York: Oxford University Press, 2018).

59. Urban VIII adopted the sun (usually represented as a round face emanating rays of light; the sun on the Barcaccia fountain in Piazza di Spagna is one of the many examples that can still be seen today) as his personal emblem, along with the three bees of the Barberini family arms.

60. Dedicatory letter from Margherita Costa to Francesco Barberini, in Margherita Costa, *Cecilia martire poema sacro di Margherita Costa romana*, n.p.

61. It was Francesco Barberini who arranged for the Jesuit scholar Athanasius Kircher to have a position at the Collegio Romano, to benefit from Kircher's knowledge of Egyptian hieroglyphs. On Kircher's relationship with the Barberini, see Ingrid D. Rowland, *The Ecstatic Journey: Athanasius Kircher in Baroque Rome* (Chicago: The University of Chicago Press, 2000); Daniel Stolzenberg, *Egyptian Oedipus: Athanasius Kircher and the Secrets of Antiquity* (Chicago: The University of Chicago Press, 2013).

62. Dea Roma shared many attributes with Athena/Minerva. For a recent discussion of Roma's iconography, see Lillian Joyce, "Roma and the Virtuous Breast," *Memoirs of the American Academy in Rome* 59/60 (2014): 1–49.

63. On Sant'Urbano in Caffarella, see Kirstin Noreen, "Sant'Urbano alla Caffarella, Rome: The Reconstruction of an Ancient Memorial," *Memoirs of the American Academy in Rome* 47 (2002): n.p.

64. "Allegoria: Canto Quarto" ("Allegory of the Fourth Canto"), in Costa, *Cecilia martire poema sacro di Margherita Costa romana*, n.p.

65. The copies are now in the Biblioteca Apostolica Vaticana, MS Barb.lat. 4402.

66. Margherita Costa, *Cecilia martire poema sacro di Margherita Costa romana all'Emin.[entissi]mo Prencipe Francesco Card.[inale] Barberino, Vicecancelliero di Santa Chiesa* (Rome: Mascardi, 1644), 49.

67. Costa, *Cecilia martire poema sacro di Margherita Costa romana*, 49.

68. "La Diva all'hor su risonanti legni, /c'han di concave canne ordini industri, / con le dita trascorre . . ." ("The diva, then, runs her fingers over the resonant pieces of wood, worked into concave orders of pipes"). Costa, *Cecilia martire poema sacro di Margherita Costa romana*, 50.

69. Costa, *Cecilia martire poema sacro di Margherita Costa romana*, 51.

70. "Sù, sù, timido core, ardito ancidi/ Costei, che tanto in contrastarti vale,/ Chiudi l'orecchie al suono, a i canti infidi,/ E 'l colpo avventa qual cadente strale" ("Come on, timid heart, boldly kill/this woman so valiant in her fight against you,/ Close your ears to the music, to the treacherous songs,/ and strike the blow like a falling arrow"). Costa, *Cecilia martire poema sacro di Margherita Costa romana*, 58.

71. Costa, *Cecilia martire poema sacro di Margherita Costa romana*, 59.

72. "Io, che ne' bassi Regni inalzo il vanto/ Contr'ogni spirto fortemente atroce, / Ad una Vergin ceda, e co 'l suo canto/ Ella stingua il furòr de la mia foce. /E Pluto io sono[. . .] ("Am I, the one who in the underworld lifts up my boasting cries against the strongest, most atrocious spirits, truly conceding to a virgin? And is she, with her songs, extinguishing the fury that flows from my maw? Am I not Pluto")? Costa, *Cecilia martire poema sacro di Margherita Costa romana*, 66.

73. Rome, Biblioteca Apostolica Vaticana MS Urb.lat. 1647, fol. 545r.

74. For Barbara's story, see "Frustatura di una Cantarina chiamata Barbara Rasponi detta la Castellana per aver recitata in un opra fatta fare dal Amb.[asciatore] di Spagna" ("Whipping of a singer named Barbara Rasponi, called the Castellana, for having performed in an opera put on by the Spanish Ambassador"), in Rome, Biblioteca Apostolica Vaticana MS Urb.lat. 1647, 547r—549r [=548r].

75. "Da l'alte sfere de le stelle intanto/ Scendon' à gara gli Angeli festosi,/ E con lieta armonia di dolce canto/ Scaccian de' venti i turbini nembosi,/ Spiegano di Cecilia il nobil vanto" ("From the celestial spheres of the stars, meanwhile, the joyous angels descend, vying with one another, and with the happy harmony of their sweet songs, they chase the whirlwinds of clouds away on the breeze"). Costa, *Cecilia martire poema sacro di Margherita Costa romana*, 82.

76. Costa, *Cecilia martire poema sacro di Margherita Costa romana*, 95.

77. Costa's poem, titled "All'Eminentissimo Principe Antonio Cardinale Barberino, per un dono di una catena d'oro mentre le presenta il suo poema di Santa Cecilia con alcune ventaglie" ("To the Most Eminent Prince Antonio, Cardinal Barberini, for the gift of a gold chain, while presenting to him her poem on Saint Cecilia, with some fans"), is found in Margherita Costa, *La tromba del parnaso* (Paris: Sebastian Craimoisy, 1647), 68–72.

78. Costa, *La tromba del parnaso*, 69. The punishment of Juno is described in the *Iliad*, Book XV.

79. Costa, *La tromba del parnaso*, 71.

80. Costa, dedication to Francesca Barberini, in *Cecilia martire poema sacro di Margherita Costa romana*, n.p.

CHAPTER NINE

# "Polemics That Might Seem Spiteful in Heaven"

## Female Spiritual Authority in Arcangela Tarabotti's *Paradiso Monacale*

MEREDITH K. RAY AND LYNN LARA WESTWATER

The Venetian nun and feminist writer Arcangela Tarabotti (1604–1652) was the author of seven widely circulated works, most of them overtly polemical in nature, that contested the raison d'état that led both secular and ecclesiastical leaders to sacrifice the needs of women to advance their own power.[1] The religious life was forced upon Tarabotti, who called convents prisons because of the number of women who lived in them unwillingly in strict cloister, though they had no religious vocation.[2] Tarabotti's attack on forced monachization, a practice she depicted as a conspiracy by Church and State against women and a violation of the will of God, underpins virtually all her works, from the searing *La semplicità ingannata* (*Innocence Deceived*), which earned a spot on the Index of Prohibited Books in 1661, to the seemingly more conventional pages of *Paradiso monacale* (*Convent Paradise*) [1643], the centerpiece of her devotional writings. Tarabotti, who describes in *Paradiso monacale* her struggle to come to terms with enclosure, draws a clear line between free and forced vocations.

Though she was a fierce critic of the institutionalized abuses against women within the Church, she nevertheless embraced certain doctrinal aspects of Catholicism, especially the intercession of Jesus Christ and the Virgin Mary and the centrality of free will, and highlighted in particular the role of female saints in the history of the Church. Tarabotti wrote yearningly of the mystical marriage between voluntary nuns and Christ that she herself found always out of reach, and she saw no contradiction between her religious and secular writings. Indeed, her focus on highlighting the centrality of women's contributions in Church history and safeguarding women's interests within its institutions was part of her broader advocacy for women, from defending their access to education and their well-being within marriage to demanding their protection from abuse by family and state, as well as by Church. In keeping with the spirit of reform-minded women before her, such as Saint Catherine of Siena (1347–1380)—in whose example she found inspiration, though by no means equivalency—Tarabotti sought to use her status as a woman religious to claim authority to speak about matters beyond the cloister. Such efforts required a complex and nuanced rhetorical project that plays out throughout Tarabotti's oeuvre. She interweaves discourses of gender and devotion to create an activist feminist spirituality that distinguishes itself for its scope and radicalism.

While Tarabotti's iconoclastic polemics have been the focus of increasing interest from scholars, particularly in her most openly controversial works such as *Inferno monacale* (*Convent Hell*) and *La tirannia paterna* (*Paternal Tyranny*, her original title for *La semplicità ingannata*), her use of positive female exemplars in Church history to support and strengthen her arguments has received far less attention.[3] Yet in many of her works—and most notably in *Paradiso monacale*—Tarabotti draws on the authority of female saints, in particular that of the Virgin Mary, to bolster her sweeping critique of the social, political, and religious mechanisms that combined to oppress women. In their unassailable virtue and devotion, such figures offer a clear rebuke to male criticism and mistreatment of all women. Tarabotti also offers these models in implicit contrast to the figure of Eve, whose rebellious role in the creation story was used to malign the female sex.[4] Alongside Mary stand other exemplars of female spirituality, such as Clare of Assisi, Catherine of Prato, and, notably, Catherine of Siena, whom Tarabotti mentions frequently. As Tarabotti writes in *Paradiso monacale*, these women are central to God's order on earth and in heaven, inspiring others to follow their path: "O quante anime seguendo la traccia de loro esempi, arricchirono se stesse del Cielo, & il Cielo di se stesse. Sono innumerabili le Religiose che con gli splendori della Santità hanno illuminata la Chiesa" ("Oh, how many souls, following in the footsteps of their example, enriched themselves with heaven, and enriched heaven with themselves? The number of nuns who have illuminated the Church with the splendor of sanctity is limitless").[5]

Tarabotti seizes upon these figures to further the prowoman polemics that always subtend her writing, noting that it is "superfluous" to name all such illustrious female models,

> . . . poiché io so di poter dire, senza incontrare oppositione veruna, che se gli huomini con le loro solite maldicenze asseriscono che in ogni affare le donne diano negli eccessi, che negl'interessi di Religione e negli esercitij d'attioni divote e sante [le donne] oprano con eccessive ardenze & inimitabili bontà, poiché le astinenze, mortificationi, e penitenze vengono da loro pratticate con ogni pontualità, e rigore.

> . . . for I know I can say, without anyone contradicting me (since men with their usual slanderous tongues assert that women are excessive in everything they do) that women engage in devotional and holy practices and actions with excessive ardor and unrivalled goodness, for they practice abstinence, mortifications, and penitence with the utmost precision and rigor.[6]

Tarabotti makes it clear, however, that she praises the religious life only for women who seek and embrace it. Female saints such as Catherine of Siena (who rejected her parents' desire that she marry and instead remained at home as a Dominican tertiary) are embodiments of the life religious, freely chosen: "O quanto meglio fora il persuaderle alla santità e religione con gli esempi che con le parole e con la forza!" ("Oh, how much better it would be to urge [women] toward holiness and the religious life by means of role models than through words and force!").[7] Tarabotti's own situation was nearly the polar opposite: forced into the convent at thirteen, she envied her secular counterparts who could look forward to the festivities associated with a worldly wedding and to what she perceived as the privileged life of married women, as she details in *Inferno monacale*.[8] Only true women religious, Tarabotti notes in *La semplicità ingannata*, "si dovrebbero serrar fra sacre mura" ("should be locked up behind holy walls")[9]; her struggle to accept her own cloistered status marks virtually all her writings.

After a brief review of Tarabotti's use of female religious figures across her works, this essay will examine how the writer, seeking in *Paradiso monacale* to embrace her status as a nun and to use it as a foundation upon which to assert authority in religious as well as political matters, calls upon two icons of female Christian spirituality, Catherine of Siena and—most pervasively—the Virgin Mother (a central figure in Catherine's own mystical story) in order to claim a divine endorsement of her controversial sociopolitical thought. In all her works, whether overtly polemical or intimately spiritual, these models of female sanctity lend weight to Tarabotti's efforts to advocate broadly for women's interests, while also providing a framework in which she can come to terms with her own enclosure and inner spiritual struggle. While the example of Catherine of Siena serves as a sometimes-unacknowledged backdrop that allows Tarabotti to assert agency over her experience of forced monachization and to critique social, political, and religious structures, the figure of Mary functions as an explicit and deliberate presence in Tarabotti's works, particularly in *Paradiso monacale*, where the nun engages in a sustained dialogue with this most authoritative of female religious figures. Tarabotti's unique use of both figures finally comes into sharper focus through comparison to the approach of her contemporary in Venice, Lucrezia Marinella (1571–1653), a secular writer who published several popular saints' lives, including works devoted to both Catherine and Mary.

## Female Saints in Tarabotti's Works

By making her 1643 literary debut with *Paradiso monacale*, Tarabotti signaled her intention to use the female religious experience as literary subject matter, while at the same time foregrounding her authority in religious matters as a nun. The use of the devotional genre, widely accepted as appropriate even for cloistered women, softened the boldness of Tarabotti's entree into the public literary sphere, even as she made an explicit bid for fame with an elaborately produced volume studded with encomiums from contemporary writers (see Figure 9.1).[10]

Even more prominent than these impressive literary testimonials was Tarabotti's dedication of the volume to Patriarch Federico Corner (1579–1653), Venice's highest ecclesiastical official. This dedication, which added a political dimension to the work by touting Tarabotti's powerful connections, while at the same time underscoring her religious devotion, harmonized with the rest of the volume's carefully orchestrated presentation. The work engages extensively with iconic figures of the Christian tradition, male and female—Saints Augustine, Benedict, and Francis figure prominently, alongside Mary Magdalene, Clare of Assisi, Catherine of Alexandria, Scholastica, and others—while also providing an elaborate intertextual web of allusions to biblical and religious sources. However, Tarabotti reserves the bulk of her attention not only for her spiritual bridegroom, Christ, but for the Virgin Mary. In this she

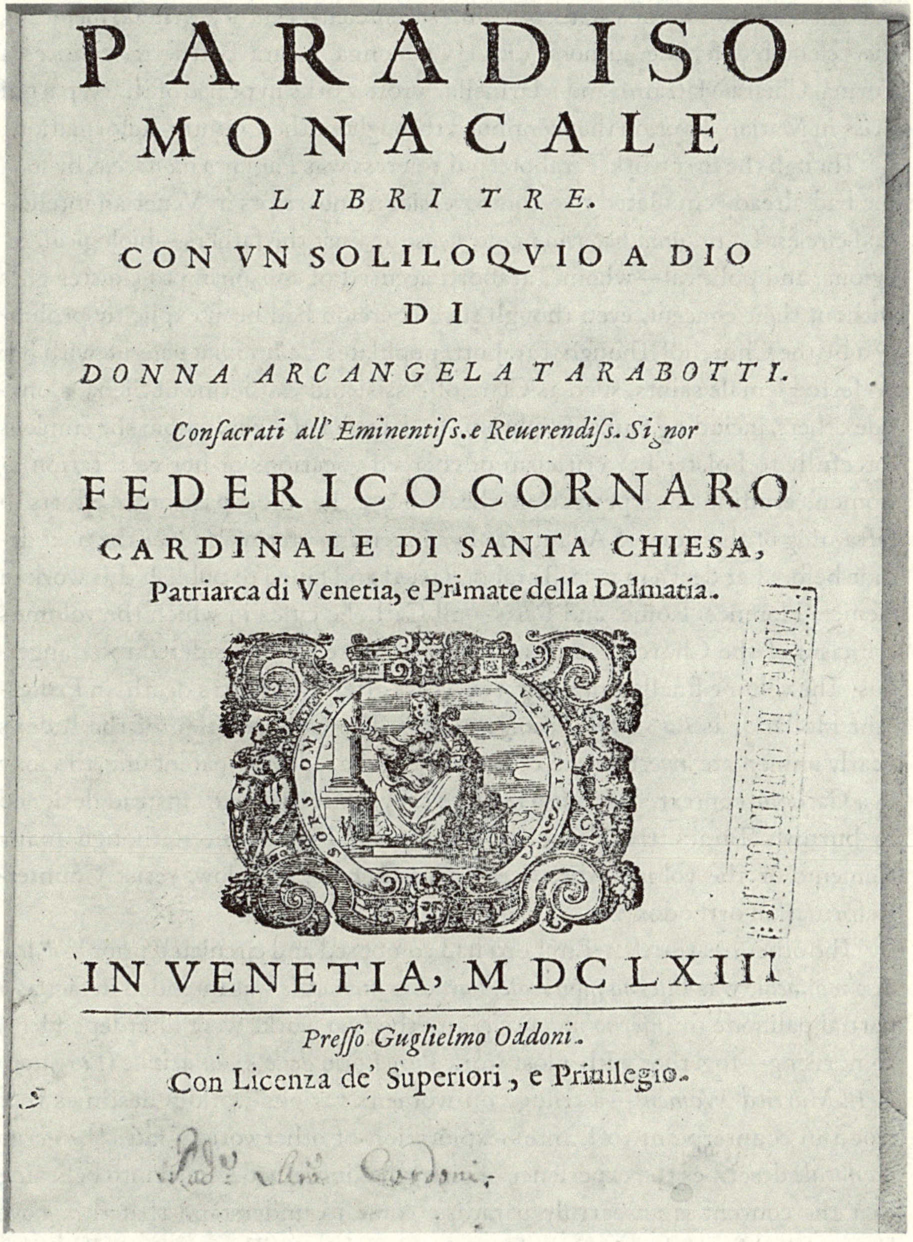

PARADISO

MONACALE

*LIBRI TRE.*

CON VN SOLILOQVIO A DIO

DI

*DONNA ARCANGELA TARABOTTI.*

*Consacrati all' Eminentiss. e Reuerendiss. Signor*

FEDERICO CORNARO

CARDINALE DI SANTA CHIESA,

Patriarca di Venetia, e Primate della Dalmatia.



IN VENETIA, M DCLXIII

*Presso Guglielmo Oddoni.*

Con Licenza de' Superiori, e Priuilegio.

Figure 9.1. Title page of Arcangela Tarabotti's *Paradiso monacale* (1643). With permission of the Comune di Padova—Assessorato alla Cultura.

was not alone: numerous sixteenth- and seventeenth-century writers, including the celebrated female authors Vittoria Colonna, Laura Battiferra, Francesca Turina, Chiara Matraini, and Marinella, wrote works in praise of Mary, part of a rise in Marian devotion that continued throughout the Counter-Reformation.

Though the first work Tarabotti put to press was *Paradiso monacale*, by 1643 she had already circulated two controversial manuscripts in Venetian intellectual circles. *La tirannia paterna* made a case against the fathers—biological, religious, and political—whom Tarabotti accused of conspiring to cloister girls without their consent, even though such coercion had been explicitly prohibited by the Church.[11] Though Tarabotti populates *La tirannia paterna* with her preferred female saints, such as Clare of Assisi and Catherine of Siena, alongside others, including Saints Euphronia and Teresa of Avila, whom she employs forcefully to bolster her criticism of coerced vocations or her celebration of women's erudition and perfection, she dedicates her most passionate efforts to reframing of the story of Adam and Eve in feminist terms.[12] Over the next decade before her death in 1652, Tarabotti tried and failed to publish this work in Venice, Florence, Rome, and Paris—all Catholic cities in which the volume's criticism of the Church and of monastic practice was considered too dangerous. The volume finally came out, two years after Tarabotti's death, in Protestant Holland, as *La semplicità ingannata*.[13] The Congregation of the Index's nearly immediate investigation of the work underscores its patent unorthodoxy in a Catholic context.[14] *Paradiso monacale*, by contrast, seems instead designed to burnish Tarabotti's Catholic religious credentials, even though many elements of the volume, discussed in further detail below, resist Counter-Reformation orthodoxy.

The other treatise that Tarabotti had composed and circulated prior to *Paradiso monacale* was *Inferno monacale*. *Paradiso monacale* was intended in fact as a partial palinode to *Inferno monacale*, and the two works were interdependent, comprising—together with a lost work *Purgatorio delle malmaritate* (*Purgatory of Ill-Married Women*)—a trilogy on women's various worldly destinies that stood in counterpoint to Dante's exploration of otherworldly fates.[15] *Inferno monacale* describes the experience of girls who, initially deceived into believing that the convent is an earthly paradise, come to understand that they have been tricked into taking a vow of perpetual enclosure. The convent, filled with unwilling nuns who lack a true spiritual vocation, therefore becomes a veritable hell on earth, where desperation abounds and vice flourishes. Notably, *Inferno monacale* draws primarily on secular sources such as Dante's *Inferno*, and

Tarabotti's most extensive biblical allusion here is to Jeremiah—the "weeping prophet" considered the author of Lamentations. Tarabotti did not even attempt to put *Inferno monacale* to press, either because she recognized that the work's focus on the rampant sinfulness in monasteries was even more explosive than *La tirannia paterna*'s denouncement of forced monachization or because she worried that *Inferno monacale* portrayed women—and specifically women religious, the necessary protagonists of this sorrowful tale—in an unflattering light.

After keeping a tight focus on the life of women religious in the first three works that she wrote, Tarabotti changed tack, publishing a work in 1644 that made it clear that she did not intend to limit herself only to religious subject matter. The work, titled *Antisatira* (*Antisatire*), defended women against the charges of vanity and frivolity lodged by a Sienese writer.[16] As Elissa Weaver writes, Tarabotti was "unrelenting in her criticism of [her adversary's] discourse and of the attitudes he expresses regarding women."[17] She not only answered this author by defending women's right to luxury on the basis of their natural superiority but also broadened the scope of the debate to denounce the numerous injustices women face in a patriarchal society, including their lack of access to education and the double standards that condoned in men certain behaviors that were condemned in women. The work makes few mentions of religious figures, though the Virgin Mary herself is invoked in her capacity as "avocata della terra appresso Dio" ("earth's advocate before God").[18] As the *Antisatira* widened Tarabotti's purview beyond religious literature, she denied her ambition by publishing under her initials only and by feigning that she did not want to see the work in print.[19]

Tarabotti spent the rest of the 1640s composing a variety of works, some devotional and some secular, while she built up a vast network of correspondents throughout Italy and into Northern Europe. Tarabotti was able to advertise her impressive contacts with the publication in 1650 of her *Lettere familiari e di complimento* (*Letters Familiar and Formal*).[20] Tarabotti's 256-letter volume is stunning when we consider that Venetian nuns were nominally prohibited from corresponding with anyone outside their family. Though the *Lettere* frequently underscores Tarabotti's own status as a nun, the volume is markedly secular in tone and intent, relying far more on literary references than religious ones and displaying Tarabotti's skill in a popular vernacular genre considered a hallmark of success for a writer.[21] However, in a bid to satisfy censors, Tarabotti justified the publication of this work by accompanying it with *Le lagrime di*

*Arcangela Tarabotti per la morte dell'illustriss[ima] signora Regina Donati* (*Tears of Arcangela Tarabotti for the Death of the Most Illustrious Lady Regina Donati*), a semidevotional work about a deceased convent sister who is described in distinctly hagiographic terms.[22] In *Le lagrime*, Tarabotti models her friend's "vita" on the female saints' lives that were important source materials for her other works; in Tarabotti's account, Regina Donati conforms to the sort of Catholic orthodoxy that Tarabotti struggles with herself and that she elsewhere undercuts with her representation of female saints. Tarabotti's Donati resembles Mary and even Christ in her perfection,[23] comparisons that are often implicit (Regina, for example, is presented as a model of obedience); explicitly, Tarabotti also compares Donati to important male saints, including King David, Job, and Francis of Assisi, and calls her "a modern, most formidable Judith."[24] Though Tarabotti used this slim encomiastic volume to encircle the secular letters that it accompanied with a religious halo, it in fact did little to change the overall worldly thrust of the *Lettere*.[25]

In 1651 Tarabotti published the last of her works she would see in print, *Che le donne siano della spetie degli uomini* (*Women Belong to the Same Species as Men*), under a loosely veiled pseudonym.[26] The work responded to a heretical tract, originally circulated in Latin and published in Italian in Venice in 1647, that asserted that women lacked souls. As with the *Antisatira*, Tarabotti felt compelled to publish a general defense of women in response to an attack. But Tarabotti's tone is entirely at odds with the *Antisatira*'s more jocular style; in battle with a heretic, Tarabotti adopts a more aggressive stance, frequently depicting her adversary as an animal. In the unusual, and perhaps uncomfortable, position of defending Catholic orthodoxy against an adversary who undercuts a major premise of Christianity (that all humans have souls) and who mocks Catholics as "papists," Tarabotti underscores the importance of women in the Bible, and particularly female saints such as Catherine of Siena (herself authorized, Tarabotti notes, by the power and blessing of the Virgin Mary), in upholding the sacraments of the Church.[27]

Finally, in addition to *Paradiso monacale*, the works in which Tarabotti presumably engaged most extensively and deliberately with female saints are a corpus of three lost manuscripts, mentioned in her *Lettere*: *La via lastricata per andare al cielo* (*The Paved Path to Heaven*), *Contemplationi dell'anima amante* (*Contemplations of the Loving Soul*), and *Luce monacale* (*Convent Light*), all composed before 1650. Judging from their titles and the brief comments she makes about them in her *Lettere* (she advises a friend that, of all her works, these alone may safely be printed), these manuscripts were devotional in nature, but they may have been marked by the same unconventional approach to female spirituality that is on display in *Paradiso monacale.*[28] Because these works are no longer extant, *Paradiso monacale* remains the richest territory for exploring Tarabotti's strategic use of female religious figures in her work.

## Tarabotti and Catherine of Siena: A Model for Female Power within the Church

If Tarabotti turns to a corps of female saints for inspiration throughout her works, the figure of Catherine of Siena (1347–1389), appears to hold special resonance. Singled out for praise even in the most openly polemical of Tarabotti's works, such as *Inferno monacale* and *Che le donne siano della spetie degli uomini,* and named on six occasions in *Paradiso monacale,* Catherine was a powerful model who combined exemplary spiritual devotion, lived out on her own terms, with decisive interventions in the political and religious landscape of medieval Italy. Adept at managing tropes of gender and devotion, Catherine's virginity and self-imposed asceticism allowed her to occupy a unique position of authority: as Thomas Luongo notes, she stood "at the center of international politics," but participated in "worldly affairs only by being apart from the world."[29] This combination of spiritual and secular authority made Catherine a touchstone for Tarabotti, who was determined that her own condition of enclosure in Sant'Anna should not prevent her from condemning injustice and corruption in the world, from forced monachization to sexual violence. Tarabotti sought to balance impassioned critique of Church, State, and social institutions with the religious devotion that was required of nuns. As detailed in *Paradiso monacale,* she yearned for but struggled to find the intimate mystical connection to Christ that was Catherine's hallmark, but she freely used her pen to speak out against corruption and injustice, as Catherine did. And, like Catherine, Tarabotti saw Mary as a powerful figure, at once mother and teacher, uniquely capable of blessing her spiritual union with her son.

St. Catherine's story and legacy would have been familiar to Tarabotti through a variety of channels, both religious and literary—from Raymond di Capua's hagiographical account of her life *Legenda maior* (*Life of St. Catherine of Siena*), which had numerous reprints up to the Seicento, including Ambrogio

Caterino Politi's vernacularization *Vita miracolosa della serafica S. Catherina da Siena* (1524), to the account published by Marinella in 1624, *De gesti heroici, e della vita meravigliosa della serafica S. Caterina*.[30] Though Catherine was born in Siena, Tommaso d'Antonio da Siena, known as "Caffarini," established a scriptorium in Venice devoted to producing hagiographical works for Catherine to help bring about her canonization (which occurred in 1461). Caffarini's efforts, which also highlighted Catherine's literary importance as a prolific writer of letters and as the author of a *Dialogo* (*Dialogue*) with Christ, made the Veneto a center of Catherine devotion, and it was the Venetian editor Aldo Manuzio who published the first edition of Catherine's collected *Epistole* (*Letters*) in 1500, thus inserting her prominently into the canon of vernacular literature.[31] Tarabotti, who authored her own volume of letters in 1650, was undoubtedly familiar with Catherine's literary significance, and she and her convent sisters would have also learned about Catherine through prayer and liturgy.

Among various key episodes from Catherine's story, repeated in the many accounts of her life, some likely stood out for Tarabotti: most notably Catherine's rejection, after an early vision of Christ, of her parent's order that she should marry, instead insisting on following her own path. After fasting and jubilantly cutting her own hair in rebellion (whereas for Tarabotti the tonsure ritual was much more complicated, an ambivalent submission[32]), Catherine embraced Christ as her true bridegroom in what she described as a mystical marriage, eventually receiving the stigmata, which she wore internally.[33] In *Paradiso monacale*, Tarabotti—who chronicles her own fervent but unsuccessful aspirations to the spiritual fulfillment of the voluntary nun—begs to be wounded "alla sinistra parte, come Caterina da Siena" ("on the left side, like Catherine of Siena").[34]

Determined to pursue a life of prayer, devotion, and virginity outside convent walls, Catherine lived as a lay member of the Dominican order. She was at once actively involved in political matters—traveling to Avignon to help secure the return of the papacy to Rome in 1377 and negotiating with Pope Gregory XI on behalf of the Republic of Florence, which had been placed under papal interdict in 1376—and marked as Christ's own through the stigmata.[35] The tensions between Catherine's spiritual and public personae presented challenges for her hagiographers, who, as Luongo notes, had to balance her "exceptionally active and public career with the standard expectations of female sanctity."[36] Particularly in the aftermath of Gregory's return to Rome and the subsequent schism that persisted until 1417, Catherine's defenders sought to deflect criticism of the saint as a disruptive presence, similar to her contemporary Birgitta of Sweden, also a critic of power who sought a return of the papacy to Rome and who urged church leaders to address moral corruption within their ranks.[37] In her *Dialogo della Divina Providenza* (*Dialogue on Divine Providence*), Catherine describes the issues that were weakening the Church, including increasing secular power, the corruption of clergy, and the lack of urgently needed reform.[38]

Although Catherine's experience was markedly different from that of Tarabotti—who writes enviously of secular brides and struggled mightily to develop a religious vocation and to accept her own nun's bond to Christ—the saint's rebellion against the expectations of familial and societal norms that prescribed marriage or convent walls, her mystical connection to Christ, and her activism and literary example surely called to Tarabotti. Just as significantly for Tarabotti, Catherine of Siena turned to exemplars of female sanctity to authorize her voice, drawing foremost on the example of Mary. While Marian devotion, as we will see below, emphasized the Virgin's role as an intercessor for all humanity, it traditionally foregrounded her humility and submission. Catherine of Siena instead underscored Mary's active and authoritative role in verbally acceding to the conception of Christ: as Jane Tylus notes, "there was no conception until Mary willed it."[39] Catherine's Mary is driven and determined, a teacher who urges the apostles out into the world to spread the word of Christ. Indeed, Catherine's letters often include a dual salutation in the name of both Christ and the Virgin, a reflection of the equal importance Mary held for her.[40] Catherine observed Marian feasts and customs (such as fasting on Saturdays, dedicated to the Virgin) with special devotion, and, significantly, Mary plays an important role for Catherine as an exemplar of consecrated virginity and the figure to whom she turns to authorize her spiritual marriage with Christ.[41] Catherine's Mary is capable of active intervention, from helping to provide an appropriate spiritual director (in the form of Raimondo of Capua) to bringing about and blessing her union with Christ; in several of her visions, she describes Mary literally handing the newborn Christ child to her and placing him in her arms.[42] As both the epitome of holy virginity and an active and powerful force able to impose authority on earthly matters, Mary thus represented may have helped inspire Tarabotti's own literary and spiritual relationship to the Virgin as the pinnacle of female sanctity.

### Tarabotti and the Virgin Mary: A Literary Exploration of Gender, Authority, and the Church

If Catherine of Siena provides an implicit frame story against which Tarabotti could reconfigure her own experience of enclosure and activism, it is Mary herself, as the highest embodiment of female spiritual authority, whom she positions at the center of her religious vision. Tarabotti's literary exploration of Mary is most extensively evidenced in *Convent Paradise*, in which she embraces the Virgin Mother as a spiritual guide, highlighting her special status both as a model of female virtue and as a divine intercessor for sinners. As was common in early-modern texts, Tarabotti emphasizes the maternal grief at the center of Mary's experience, which the Virgin transforms into understanding and compassion for all human error. Addressing Christ, Tarabotti writes:

> . . . humilissimamente supplico Maria, riffugio de' piu disperati peccatori, ad interponersi intercedente per me, che se la gravezza delle mie colpe non meritera indulgenza, la meritera in soprabondanza uno di quei soli sospiri pieni di dolore ch'ella trasse all'hora che a' piedi dell'infausto Legno della Croce, stava mirando l'orribile spettacolo del vostro lacerato corpo, per opera de' miei delitti la su' confitto.

> . . . I most humbly beg Mary, shelter of the most desperate sinners, to step in, interceding on my behalf. If the gravity of my sins does not merit pardon, surely she will merit it by the mere means of one of those sorrowful sighs she let out when, at the foot of that unhappy wooden cross, she stood gazing at the horrific spectacle of your lacerated body, nailed up there by my sins.[43]

Tarabotti draws comfort from the Virgin, even though she herself, by means of her sins (which represent those of all humankind), caused Christ's death and Mary's unspeakable anguish.

The early-modern period saw a proliferation of Marian art and literature, which emphasized Mary's role as Mother of all Christians, coredemptrix with her son, and mediatrix, though these precepts were not accepted as dogma. As Virginia Cox notes, theologians made it clear that Mary's status could not be considered equal to that of Christ, yet "popular and elite religious tended to elevate her to a role almost of co-protagonist in salvation."[44] This devotion took on a special political importance with the schism between Catholics and Protestants after the Council of Trent: Susan Haskins observes, "[d]evotion to the Virgin, which was particularly encouraged by the Jesuits, was one of the strongest resources cultivated by the Counter-Reformation."[45] Several aspects of Tarabotti's characterization have even deeper historical roots: nuns attributed a particular significance to Mary, who from the earliest centuries of Christianity was recognized as a symbol of female sexual purity and a pillar of the Christian ideal of virginity.[46] The notion of Mary as "the model of virgins" is foundational to the Patristic tradition—a lesson that Tarabotti absorbed deeply, inspired by the authority imbued by Mary's integrity; as Andrew Hopkins writes, "[Mary's] power came through her virginity, which rendered her uncorrupt and gave her strength and purity, and because of which she was assumed body and soul into Heaven and assumed as its Queen."[47] The cult of Mary was promoted by figures such as Ambrose, bishop of Milan (ca. 339–97), who celebrated her role in salvation, and Saint Augustine of Hippo (354–430), who underscored her personal sanctity and her vow of virginity.[48] Saint Bernard of Clairvaux (1090–1153) transformed the cult of Mary in the West into an intense fervor of love and devotion to the Virgin—an aspect we see clearly in Tarabotti's depiction—while the period of the Crusades, when Christ's Passion played an important role, saw a new emphasis on Mary as sorrowful mother, also central to Tarabotti's representation. But other aspects of the traditional representation are sharply at odds with Tarabotti's: by the Middle Ages, Mary was represented as "humble, meek, silent, and passive, the ideal woman molded to the desiderata of the Church's male hierarchy."[49] The Council of Trent ratified Mary's importance within the Church by implicitly giving canonical authority to traditional beliefs (many of which concerned Mary); by exempting Mary from the decree of original sin; and by stressing the efficacy of invoking saints. By 1563, Mary was a central weapon in Counter-Reformation ideology, though, as Haskins notes, her role remained "passively combative."[50]

Tarabotti's emphasis on Mary is rooted in a Counter-Reformation ideology that has Mary as a cornerstone, but she transforms the quietly powerful role officially prescribed to Mary into an explicitly forceful and active one. Tarabotti's foregrounding of the Virgin connected also to Venetian civic mythology, which considered Mary the special protector of the Republic. Legend dated the city's founding in 421 to March 25, or the date of the Annunciation, and the city closely associated itself with the salvation that the event represented. By the middle of the fifteenth century, there were twenty-one churches in the city dedicated to Mary.[51] David Rosand notes that Venice was not unique in adopting Mary as patroness, but "more than, say, Florence or Siena, Venice subtly but aggressively appropriated the image of the Virgin for its own self-representation."[52] The city was also mythologized as a "virgin city," inviolate and unconquered over its millennial history—a long dominion considered both a marker and a result of the special relationship with the Virgin. The devastating plague that killed up to a third of Venice's population in 1629–31 reinvigorated the cult of Mary: already by October 1630, the Senate decided to commission a new church in honor of the Virgin, to be called Santa Maria della Salute, courting "her powers of intercession with Christ her Son to save the city from the plague."[53]

Tarabotti repeatedly situates Mary at the center of the Christian religious experience. Early in the first book of *Convent Paradise*, she writes, for example, "Solo, solo i religiosi veri, spinti da un'auretta soave, e guidati dalla Tramontana Maria, arrivano col lor legno sano, & salvo al Porto della salute" ("Only true men and women religious, pushed by a gentle breeze and guided by Mary—the north wind—arrive at the harbor of salvation with their ship intact and safe").[54] In the third book, she insists even more forcefully on Mary's multivalent power in the Church, calling her "escort, mother, tutor, mistress, liberator, physician, deliverance, and hope of every Catholic."[55] Drawing on the Song of Songs, Tarabotti describes Mary as the "neck" of the Church:

> Lo Spirito Santo, ò Maria, vi disse Colle del mistico corpo della Chiesa, di cui è Capo Dio. *Ipsum constituit caput super omnem Ecclesiam.* Voi sete la più vicina a' lui. *Una est columba mea proxima mea.* Ad ogni moto del Collo si moverà il Capo. Ad ogni vostro cenno Dio perdonerà ogni colpa. Insomma nelle vostre mani, ò Regina Grande, stanno riposte tutte le gratie, onde fu chi di voi disse: *Manus eius distillaverunt miram*
>
> The Holy Spirit, oh Mary, said you were the neck of the mystical body of the Church, whose head is God. *He hath constituted him head over all the Church.* You are the closest to him. *One is my dove, she is near to me.* At every movement of the neck, the head moves. At your every sign, God will forgive every sin. In short, in your hands, oh great queen, all of the graces are held, and thus one said of you, *her hand dripped with myrrh.*[56]

Medieval theologians had developed a corporeal analogy around St. Paul's description of the Church as the body of Christ, with Christ as its head.[57] San Bernardino of Siena explained that Mary represented an important intermediate role, channeling the Holy Spirit to the Church: "For since Christ is our head, from whom every stream of divine grace flows into the mystical body, the Blessed Virgin is the neck, through which this stream passes into the members of the body."[58] Tarabotti reads this analogy in a much more powerful way, understanding the neck not only as an intermediary between the body (the Church) and the head (God) but in fact, a force that influences the movement of God himself.

Alongside this mystical understanding of Mary's instrumental role within the Church, Tarabotti uses Mary to recast the role of women in the history of the Church hierarchy—the religious complement to her defense of women in a secular context. Tarabotti first begins to trace her own and other nuns' spiritual genealogy by including praise for Saint Benedict, founder of her order. But she quickly clarifies that by mentioning him, she does not mean to give men undue credit in the history of Christianity that has led women to the religious "paradise" of the convent. She corrects: "Non vadano però fastosi gli huomini, se trattando io che i Monasteri di Donne siano Paradisi, ragiono di Santi del viril sesso, poiche à me non mancherebbe il modo di formare un perfettissimo Paradiso, col ramentare quante santissime femmine habbiano con l'integrità d'una vita Angelica fatte vedere quà giù in terra le celle trasformate in Cieli, e i Chiostri in Olimpi" ("Men should not strut about proudly, if as I describe women's convents as paradise, I also speak about saints of the male sex. In fact, I would have no trouble forming a most perfect paradise by recalling how many extremely saintly women, through the perfect example of their angelic lives, have transformed their cells here on earth into celestial abodes, and the cloister into an Olympus").[59] These lines echo Tarabotti's polemical works, where she anticipates that antagonistic male readers will try to twist the meaning of her words to fit their own misogynistic understanding of the world. She attempts to short-circuit this process by shifting the focus to the legions of female saints whom women religious can use as models and inspiration. She suggests, in other words, the viability of a self-contained female spiritual system not dependent on male authority and, especially, not subject to destructive male interference. But at the same time, she imagines men—unsettled at her preference for female spiritual models—rattling at the grates, insisting on the centrality of male figures in Christianity. To answer these critics, Tarabotti again makes recourse to the most inviolate of women, claiming for her a unique role at the very heart of the Church.

> Taccia dunque la pretension virile, che se quelli, che diedero i fondamenti, & institutioni alle Regole Monastiche furono huomini, da Maria, e non da

> altri appresero la norma, & esemplare del vivere Religioso. E chi sarà ardito a negarlo? Ella doppo morto il suo figliuolo, fù in un certo modo prima di S. Pietro ad esercitare l'officio di Pontefice nella Chiesa Christiana, poiche da lei, e dalla sua sovr'humana dottrina tutti apprendeuano documenti, & imparauano il modo di viuer conforme alla Diuina volontà, si ch'ella fù il Capo, e la Maestra di tutti i Religiosi.
>
> Let masculine arrogance be silent, since if those who founded and regulated monastic orders were men, they learned from Mary, and no one else, the true precepts and rules for religious life. And who will be so bold as to deny this? After the death of her son, she was in a way the first—before Saint Peter—to exercise the role of pontiff in the Christian Church, because everyone received teachings from her and her superhuman erudition, and learned how to live in accordance with divine will. Therefore, she was the mistress and teacher of all saints.[60]

With this statement, Tarabotti pushes the devoted worship of Mary that was characteristic of the Counter-Reformation past orthodox bounds by naming her, rather than Peter, as the very founder of the Catholic Church.[61] If Saint Catherine's interpretation of Mary's power was subtle—for example, by emphasizing Mary's will in the incarnation of Christ—in Tarabotti it is overt: she positions the Virgin Mother as an exemplar and a proof of female authority at the very origins of Christianity. Not only is she the mystical "neck" of the Church; she is also the very bedrock of its teachings.

In addition to positioning Mary as the foundation of the Church, Tarabotti suggests that its female saints are the mortar that supports it. Indeed, she provocatively writes that female saints exceed—in number and in fervor—their saintly brethren.

> Se Benedetto fu Santo, e riceuè da Dio fauori, che ponno star a fronte á concessi ad Abraamo, la sua Sorella Santa Scolastica il trapassò di molto, com'egli stesso confessa, poiche miracolosamente fè piovere, e fulminar dal Cielo, acciò ch'egli non ripartisse dai di lei colloquij, mentre per non dimorare fuori dal suo Convento, non voleva à modo veruno condescender alle di lei preghiere. Non solo nella qualità della vita Santa, e Religiosa, ma anche nella quantità del numero soprauanzano di gran longa le femmine sante i Religiosi e buoni del viril sesso. Il testimonia à bastanza quell'Orsola, che [si è] fatta Duce d'un intero esercito d'undecimila Vergini.

> If Benedict was a saint, and received favors from God that can be compared to those granted to Abraham, his sister Saint Scholastica greatly surpassed him, as he himself admits. She performed the miracle of making rain and bolts of lightning come down from heaven so that he would not leave in the middle of conversation with her, for he refused to bend to her entreaties to stay, because he did not want to remain outside his monastery. Female saints surpass men of virtue and religion not only qualitatively, in terms of the holiness and religiosity of their life, but also quantitatively, in their number. Sufficient testimony to this comes from Ursula, who led an entire army of eleven thousand virgins.[62]

Tarabotti's insistence on women's spiritual superiority and her desire for autonomy from a male-dominated system echo many of her polemic texts, where she yearns for both a symbolic and a social order that women control and populate. Yet, in *Paradiso monacale*, she seems to fear that this feminist message is at odds with the devotional genre. She seeks to put an end to her argument, saying: "Ma perche non è lecito introdur le contese sospette di qualche livore in Paradiso, voglio di novo replicar ch'Abraamo fù l'idea delle vere Religiose" ("But since it is not proper to make polemics that might seem spiteful in heaven, I would like to repeat again that true nuns take inspiration from Abraham . . .").[63] Backing away from her attempts to create an exclusively female spiritual sphere, Tarabotti acquiesces to a spiritual genealogy for women that foregrounds men. But she indicates that she does so out of a sense of generic propriety—gender polemics are not proper in a religious text (she plays on the meaning of "paradiso" as both "heaven" and as her text, *Paradiso monacale*)—and not because she doubts the validity of her reasoning. In other words, Tarabotti reaches the brink of declaring female spiritual independence, but she steps back because of the limits of devotional literature.

Even here, however, she decides to make one final jab, returning for a moment to the argument at the core of all her works: that forced monachization is a perversion of spirituality. She concludes the comparison between Abraham and nuns by saying: "se il di lui pellegrinaggio finì in beneditioni donateli da Dio, i viaggi di queste, doppo qualche spatio di vita, terminano nel Paradiso d'un Monastero pieno di tutte le felicità che possano pretendersi da un'anima rassegnata in sua Divina Maestà; poscia che le volontarie, e non sforzate Religiose sono maggioni Celesti, e habitationi di Beati in Terra . . ." ("if his pilgrimage ended in the blessings given to him by God, the voyage of these women, after some time in the secular world, will end in the heaven of a convent filled with all of the delights a soul that has given itself over to His Divine Majesty could want. Therefore the cloisters that house perfect nuns—that is willing, not unwilling nuns—are celestial abodes and residences for the blessed on earth").[64] Tarabotti wrote in her *Lettere* that she had "un certo genio che m'invita a pigliar la penna, già che non posso la spada, per diffender il mio sesso" ("a certain disposition that invites me to take up the pen, since I cannot wield the sword, to defend my sex").[65] She gives a true measure of this statement in *Paradiso monacale*, as she engages in gender polemics, even as she tries to back away from them. Always conscious of the numerous wrongs—cultural, social, political, symbolic—that women suffer, Tarabotti cannot stay silent.

## Lucrezia Marinella's Use of Female Saints

To better contextualize Tarabotti's provocative use of female religious figures, and particularly of Mary, within the devotional genre, it is useful to consider the example of her contemporary Lucrezia Marinella, a prolific author who published a number of works devoted to female saints.[66] Marinella's *La Vita di Maria Vergine, imperatrice dell'universo* (1602)—the work that cemented her contemporary fame—both drew on and contributed to the contemporary cult of the Virgin (see Figure 9.2).[67]

The work is consonant with Marinella's sustained interest across her literary career in narrating women's experience and, in particular, charting female spirituality (though it necessarily differs in tone and approach from *La nobiltà et l'eccellenza delle donne co' diffetti e mancamenti de gli huomini* [*The Nobility and Excellence of Women, and the Defects and Vices of Men*, 1600],[68] her secular treatise that forthrightly asserts women's moral and intellectual superiority over men). *La vita di Maria Vergine* is a hagiography whose nuanced approach appears at first glance to be in keeping with prevailing Counter-Reformation ideals for women. As Haskins observes, Marinella centers her attention here on matrimony and the family "in keeping with the Catholic Church's post-Tridentine stress on the sacrament and on family ideology."[69] In fact, the text narrates Mary's miraculous life by focusing on her dutiful and perfect execution of roles within a family structure—as a daughter, as a wife, as a mother. The text also conforms to other notions of female propriety in Counter-Reformation Italy, such as obedience. Retelling the story of the Annunciation, Marinella quotes Mary as saying "'Ecco, ò Padre onnipotente, la bassezza, & l'indignità della tua serva, la quale ubidiente, & humile accetta la lume delle

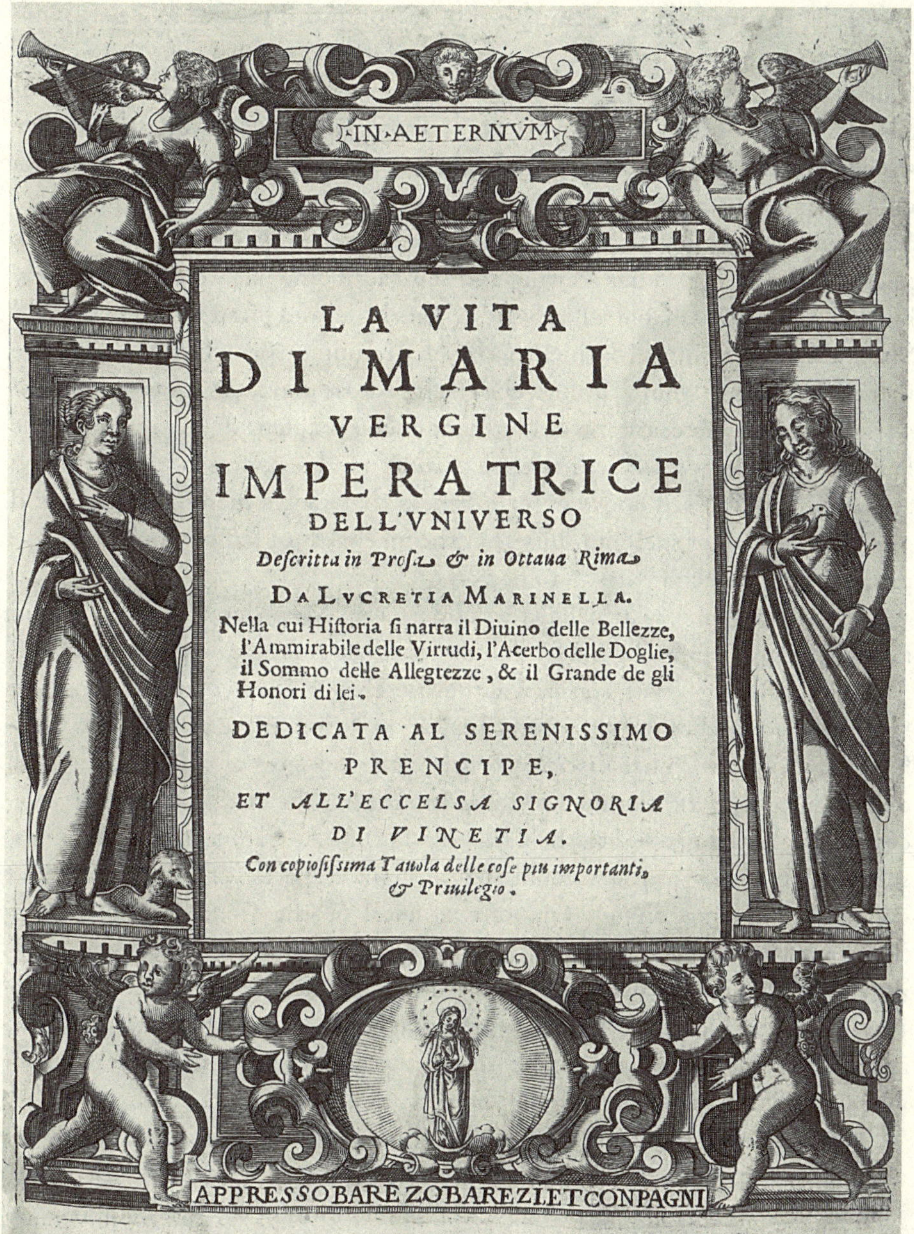


Figure 9.2. Title page of Lucrezia Marinella's *La vita di Maria Vergine, imperatrice dell'universo* (1602). From the Hanna Holborn Gray Special Collections Research Center, The University of Chicago Library.

parole del tuo messaggier sacrato, e ti offre non pur il ventre, & il petto, ma l'anima & il cuore'" ("'behold, O omnipotent father, the loneliness and unworthiness of your maidservant, who obediently and humbly accepts the truth hidden in the light of the words of your holy messenger, and offers you not only her womb and breast, but also her soul and heart'").[70] Marinella puts the emphasis on Mary's acceptance, rather than her will—in contrast, for example, to St. Catherine's reading of the same episode.[71] Marinella also underscores Mary's purity, innocence, and her retiring and self-sacrificing nature: she frequently blushes, lacks "punishable talkativeness," eats little, and often feels unworthy.[72] She is above all humble: Marinella writes, for example, that when Mary has the Christ child in her womb, "avenga che ella si vedesse inalzata sopra ogni altezza che possi dare la pietosa mano di Dio, nondimeno era piena di tanta humiltà che la mansuetudine de gli agnelli sarebbe paruta superbia appresso lei" ("although she saw herself raised above every loftiness that God's merciful hand could give, she was full of such humility that the meekness of lambs would have appeared as pride in comparison to her.")[73]

At the same time, Marinella's text underscores Mary's powerful role within the early Church, imbuing the feminine virtues she embodies—patience, obedience, and suffering—with spiritual authority. Through prayer, meditations, and fasting, Mary teaches the path toward salvation.[74] Even more striking, Marinella's Mary—who with her disciples revisited the key sites of Christ's life—was central in preserving the memory and in shaping the story of her son's life, converting "many people" to the Christian faith.[75] As Eleonora Carinci notes, such an active view of Mary contrasted in many respects with the passive and obedient representation of Mary often typical of the Counter-Reformation. Marinella's depiction drew on Pietro Aretino's *Vita di Maria Vergine* (1539), which instead highlighted Mary's authoritative role, as Carinci demonstrates.[76] Jennifer Haraguchi observes that Marinella's portrayal of Mary presents her as an "active spiritual role model for women," her meditative and contemplative practice serving as a path to lead women to build their own relationship with God.[77]

Marinella's biography of the Virgin emphasized her power in other ways as well. She cast her life of Mary as a prose epic, an unusual choice. Prose narratives were rarely devoted to sacred material, and most epics were composed in verse. By writing Mary's life as a prose epic, Marinella entered into an ongoing literary debate about Aristotelian poetics, as well as the characteristics of Christian epic, and made Mary—a female saint, not a male, secular hero—the center of her focus. Marinella also attributes a political facet to Mary by foregrounding her role in the work's title as "Empress of the Universe"—evoking the same set of civic and political associations with the Virgin that Tarabotti called upon—and she dedicates the work to Venice's doge (not unlike Tarabotti, who dedicates her *Paradiso monacale* to the Patriarch Corner).[78] Carinci adds that by presenting the Virgin as "Empress," Marinella underscores her power and exceptionality instead of simply offering her as an imitable role model for virgins, wives, and mothers. While admitting that the text at times presents Mary more traditionally as modest, chaste, and humble, Carinci sees these elements as of secondary importance, even if they constitute an important thrust of the text.[79]

Marinella's *De' gesti heroici, e della vita meravigliosa della serafica S. Caterina* (*The Heroic Deeds and Marvelous Life of the Seraphic Saint Catherine*)—her longest devotional work, which came out two decades after *La vita di Maria Vergine*—likewise maintains a careful balance between underscoring the authority of female models of sanctity and highlighting idealized feminine virtues. For example, Marinella attributes to Mary a powerful role in blessing Catherine's spiritual marriage by virtue of holy virginity: it is through Mary that Catherine approaches Christ, asking the Holy Mother to pray that her son accept the "integrità del mio corpo verginale" ("integrity of my virginal body"). As in *La vita di Maria Vergine*, Marinella devotes many pages to the traditionally feminine virtues displayed by her protagonist: humility, chastity, virginity. While Marinella's Catherine exhibits a quiet but steely force in her commitment to spiritual perfection and mystical union with Christ, Marinella downplays Catherine's political activism and interactions with popes and leaders—as well as her literary significance—avoiding, Letizia Panizza notes, "any recognition of the awesome authority [Catherine] wielded in contemporary Italian religious and political history."[80] Her presentation of Catherine is deeply interior, domestic, circumscribed, with the first three books dedicated to a close examination of Catherine's girlhood awakening to her vocation and to her subsequent struggle to pursue this spiritual path rather than the worldly one laid out by her parents.

As in *La vita di Maria Vergine*, Marinella again pays close attention to the family. Here, however, Marinella's Catherine exerts agency by rejecting her parents' plans for her, though her defiance is undertaken in the service of God. While Tarabotti was unable to defy her family's decision about her future, and she struggled with her religious calling, she could have read this account of familial conflict with interest, interpreting it as an expression of Catherine's power and autonomy. (Notably, Marinella's intensely psychological portrayal focuses most closely on the power dynamic between Catherine and her mother, rather than her father—almost the obverse to Tarabotti's works, in which fathers are explicitly called to task and mothers are largely absent).[81] Likewise, when Marinella's Catherine cuts off her hair, she does so by her own hand and of her own volition: at once an act of autonomy and a true expression of religious will.[82] Like Marinella's Mary, her Catherine, too, is always deeply humble, and her steadfast commitment to Christ plays out on the body, as she flagellates herself in secret. Even when praising Catherine's authority as a *maestra* and a preacher, Marinella highlights her feminine humility and stresses that her ability to move her audience (whether comprised of nuns, priests, or heads of state) is authorized by an angel and by Christ himself; Marinella notes that Catherine becomes *savia* (wise) following a vision of Christ in papal garments.[83] When Catherine expresses doubts about her suitability, as a woman, to evangelize, Christ himself urges her on, promising "'io ti darò le parole, il senso, il senno, e la forza a persuader, a vincere, e a volgere l'ostinato de' cuori, e il perverso delle altrui volontadi; onde rimarranno vinti, e confusi con loro scorno, e gloria tua'" ("I will give you the words, the meaning, the wisdom, and the strength to persuade, to win over, and turn the stubborn-hearted and those swayed by others' wills, whence they will be vanquished and bewildered, to their shame and your glory").[84] Illiterate until blessed by God, Catherine is a vessel of God's authority, as Marinella underscores, though she also equates her to the likes of the Apostles John or Paul.[85]

Only in Book V does Marinella finally—and glancingly—address some of the public actions of Catherine that would also have interested Tarabotti deeply: her interventions with Gregory XI for the return of the papacy to Rome and her mission on behalf of the Republic of Florence (whose current Medici rulers Marinella's text, dedicated to Maria Maddelena of Austria, is meant to celebrate). However, on a broader level, Marinella embeds Catherine's political significance within the structure of the work. Similar to *La vita di Maria Vergine*, the *Gesti heroici*—literally, Catherine's "heroic acts"—evoke the saint as an epic heroine. And Marinella's lengthy digression on Medici genealogy here is inspired by the women who were effectively cogoverning Tuscany: Christine of Lorraine and Maria Maddalena; as Michael Subialka writes, the encomium thus serves as "a legitimating force behind the regency of two women and also a transformative account of the virtues of the politician."[86] Even so, Marinella is careful to show Catherine's "tanta sapienza" ("abundant wisdom") as existing hand in hand with her "modi pieni di rispetto, e di riverenza; con atti adorni di humiltà e di amore" ("respectful, reverent ways; her actions rich with humility and love").[87] Despite her divinely imparted gift for teaching, Marinella's Catherine always prefers the "solitudine della sua nuda cella"[88]—that is, the "solitary bare cell" of her own making—unlike Tarabotti, who yearns to be in the world. Most interesting, finally, given that Marinella was herself a respected and prolific author, her account does not describe Catherine as a literary figure or a writer of letters, though this was a widely known aspect of Catherine's legacy in seventeenth-century Venice. Only in Marinella's treatise *Della Nobiltà et Eccllenza delle donne*, her work closest to Tarabotti's in terms of its feminist spirit, does Marinella emphasize Catherine's significance as an author of letters and dialogue, which "dimonstrano di quanto sapere dotata fosse" ("show us the wisdom with which she was gifted").[89]

While not as radical as Tarabotti, who in her most important devotional work boldly positions Mary as the first pontiff, Marinella deftly sketches a representation of Mary, and Catherine, that subtly challenges more passive and submissive depictions. Taken together, Tarabotti's and Marinella's texts point to the continuum of approaches to female religious figures that early-modern women writers could take, as they sought to build their case for women's worth within a patriarchal religious order. Tarabotti knew directly of Marinella's *La vita di Maria Vergine*,[90] and it is likely that she also knew *De' gesti heroici*, given her knowledge of contemporary Venetian literature, her interest in female writers and saints, and her literary acquaintance with Marinella. It is therefore instructive to read these texts in parallel, since they share an emphasis on the female religious experience and on female sanctity and locate female spiritual icons within a political context. Tarabotti's female saints, however, take a more outwardly activist—and unequivocally vocal—role, a sign of Tarabotti's more combative approach to advocating for female power in both the secular and religious spheres. Other works in her oeuvre show her using female saints' authority even more directly to speak against men's usurpation of power. In *La tirannia paterna*, for instance, a more overtly political work, Tarabotti unmistakably positions Mary as proof of women's righteousness and men's depravity. She writes that God:

> . . . costante con l'amore verso l'uomo ingrato, si rissolse d'elegger donna che con verità' potesse esser acclamata *mulierem fortem*, a confusione di così gran mostri d'ingratitudine, come sète voi. Questa fu Maria Vergine. . . . In lei sola sul principio confidò la Trinità Santissima il mistero dell'Incarnazione, e per nove mesi fidò sigillato nel scrignetto dell'alvo suo sacratissimo il più prezioso tesoro del cielo, al dispetto di quelle lingue perfide che gracch[iano] con le loro solite bugie.[91]

> . . . remaining true to His love for ungrateful mankind . . . resolved to choose a woman who could be rightly acclaimed "the strong woman"—to the confusion of all ungrateful monsters, I mean, you men. This was the Virgin Mary . . . In her alone did the Holy Trinity entrust within her sealed womb Heaven's most precious treasure—to confound men's treacherous tongues, croaking their usual lies.[92]

Whereas in *Paradiso monacale* Tarabotti ascribes to Mary the role of founder of the Church, in *La tirannia paterna* she depicts Mary as man's superior, highlighting her privileged position over all of humankind and men's necessary submission to her. In *Che le donne siano,* Tarabotti extends Mary's role as intermediary into evidence of women's spiritual superiority, writing that "graces do not come into the world if not dispensed by a woman" and, following from this, that "women are dearer to God, more pleasing to the angels, and their merit will add to the perfection of heaven through the divine will."[93] By recasting Mary's worth as a broad statement of women's value, Tarabotti reveals the hypocrisy of an institution—and a society—that would lift one woman so high but keep all others in submission. Across her texts, Mary's unassailable worth becomes the linchpin in Tarabotti's comprehensive attempt to rebuild the gender hierarchy—in the Church and in the world—to favor women. Tarabotti uses Mary's example to castigate men and to celebrate women, and by amplifying her role, establishes a uniquely forceful model for female power within the Church.

In the note to the reader that precedes *Paradiso monacale,* Tarabotti explicitly states that her decision not to publish her most polemical denunciations of forced monachization, *Inferno monacale* and *La tirannia paterna,* stemmed not from her repudiation of the argument of those works but rather from her certainty that men would condemn them out of political—not religious—motivations: "Se mai capitassero alla luce del Mondo, mi protesto innanzi a Dio, & a' miei Superiori, che ciò riuscirebbe a mia eccessiva mortificatione, non già perch'io conosca in loro detti scandalosi, ò men che pij, ma perche intendo quanto più prema agli huomini l'osservanza delle loro politiche che dei precetti Diuini" ("Were [these manuscripts] ever to see the light of day, I declare before God and my superiors that this would cause me extreme mortification, not because I believe they contain words that are scandalous or anything less than pious, but because I know men care much more about political matters than they do divine precepts").[94] She echoes this sentiment in an extant autograph letter, stating that if the content of *La tirannia paterna* is "thorny" ("materia scabrosa"), it challenges political, rather than religious, life ("contraria al politico vivere, non al cattolico").[95] Tarabotti took care to distinguish activism from orthodoxy, but as is evident in *Paradiso monacale*, the threads cannot be easily disentangled. In addition to this work's spiritual and interior focus, it also includes, as we have seen, many openly polemical moments in which Tarabotti rails against men's arrogance and in particular their appropriation of religious discourse for their own—decidedly self-interested—ends. These sentiments are given particularly free rein at the very opening of Book I, where Tarabotti makes this caustic observation: "Iddio Benedetto ama tutte le Creature, ma particolarmente la Donna, e poi l'huomo, bench'egli non lo meriti, e per ispiegare di che qualità sia l'amor suo verso ingratissimo animale, basta il dire, che l'immortal Creatore l'ama veramente da Dio" ("God loves all creatures, but in particular Woman, and then Man, even if he does not deserve it. And in order to explain the nature of his love for that most ungrateful creature, it suffices to say that the eternal Creator loves him as only God could").[96] By foregrounding gender polemics, from the very start, in her celebration of religious life, Tarabotti makes clear that not even the genre of devotional literature will entirely blunt her sharp pen (already evident in her manuscript works) and that no aspect of the text that follows in any way diminishes her advocacy for women nor her derision of men's treachery. Even as she takes pains to highlight her own religious correctness, she takes an activist stance in her sustained criticism of the ecclesiastical practices and mechanisms that result in the suppression of women's free will—especially forced monachization, which she sees as a practice closely linked to women's broader subjugation. Critics have largely failed to recognize that Tarabotti constructs a coherent feminist critique across her works through her use of female religious figures. As this essay has shown, however, Tarabotti alternately emphasizes their authority and their Catholic virtue to advocate, radically, for women's interests. Immersed in a culture of devotion that permeates every aspect of her life, Tarabotti uses the Catholic Church's own symbolic system to affirm women's central place and fundamental worth in the Church and in society.

Notes

1. Elissa Weaver was instrumental in attracting critical attention to the work of Arcangela Tarabotti, beginning with the international conference on Tarabotti and her context organized at the University of Chicago in 1997. The conference was funded by a faculty-student grant for the study of Tarabotti awarded to Weaver and the authors of the present essay. The resulting collaboration, in which Weaver generously invested her time and knowledge, nurtured what would become a long-standing scholarly focus for us all. The papers from the conference were published as *Arcangela Tarabotti: A Literary Nun in Baroque Venice*, edited by Weaver, the first volume of its kind devoted to Tarabotti and her work (Ravenna: Longo, 2006). The conference fueled scholarly interest in the nun, and now most of her oeuvre is available in modern editions and/or translations.

2. Seventeenth-century Venice was home to more than thirty convents housing nearly three thousand female inhabitants (for figures and discussion of the factors that helped drive monachization, see, for example, Jutta Sperling, *Convents and the Body Politic in Late Renaissance Venice* [Chicago: The University of Chicago Press, 1999], 28, Table 2). In her work *Inferno monacale* (*Convent Hell*), Tarabotti writes of the sacrifice of daughters "a forza incarcerate nell'abisso" ("imprisoned by force in an abyss"), a sacrifice that is "puzzolente alle nari di Dio" ("offends God with its stench") (see L'*Inferno monacale di Arcangela Tarabotti*, ed. Francesca Medioli [Turin: Rosenberg & Sellier, 1990], 92); in her letters she describes the convent as not a prison, but "un Inferno dove non può entrar speranza di uscirne" ("a hell where no hope of leaving can enter") (*Lettere familiari e di complimento*, eds. Meredith Ray and Lynn Westwater [Turin: Rosenberg & Sellier, 2009], 220); *Letters Familiar and Formal*, eds. and trans. Meredith K. Ray and Lynn Lara Westwater (Toronto: Centre for Reformation and Renaissance Studies, 2012), 210.

3. Some scholars have begun to look at Tarabotti's use of biblical examples: see, for example, Joy A. Schroeder, "Envying Jepthah's Daughter: Judges 11 in the Thought of Arcangela Tarabotti (1604–1652)," in *Strangely Familiar: Protofeminist Interpretations of Patriarchal Biblical Texts*, eds. Nancy Calvert-Koyzis and Heather E. Weir (Atlanta: Society of Biblical Literature, 2009), 75–91, and Schroeder, "Tarabotti, Arcangela: 1604–1652," in *Handbook of Women Biblical Interpreters: A Historical and Biographical Guide*, eds. Marion Ann Taylor and Agnes Choi (Grand Rapids, MI: Baker, 2012), 491–493.

4. As Virginia Cox notes, some female-authored Marian texts of this period speak "a more explicit language of protofeminist vindication" by emphasizing Mary's role in redeeming women from the stain of Eve's fall (Cox, *The Prodigious Muse* [Baltimore: Johns Hopkins University Press, 2011], 66).

5. Arcangela Tarabotti, *Paradiso monacale* (Venice: Presso Guglielmo Oddoni, 1643), 49; Arcangela Tarabotti, *Convent Paradise*, eds. and trans. Meredith K. Ray and Lynn Lara Westwater (Toronto: Iter Press/Tempe, AZ: ACMR, 2020), 120. Minimal intervention has been made in the original text where necessary for clarity. All translations are taken from Ray and Westwater's edition.

6. Tarabotti, *Convent Paradise*, 120.

7. Tarabotti, *L''Inferno Monacale'*, 69. Translations are our own throughout, unless otherwise noted.

8. See, for example, her contrast between the garments of secular women and nuns (Tarabotti, *L''Inferno Monacale'*, 40).

9. Arcangela Tarabotti, *La semplicità ingannata*, ed. Simona Bortot (Padua: Il Poligrafo, 2007), 217.

10. See Tarabotti, *Convent Paradise*, 43; for the encomiastic compositions, see *Convent Paradise*, 69–79, 243–248.

11. Chapter 17 of the Decree on Regulars and Nuns, formulated in the last session of the Council of Trent in 1563, required that girls be examined before they took the veil to make sure they did so freely. See Giuseppe Alberigo et al., eds., *Conciliarum oecumenicorum decreta* (Bologna: Edizioni Dehoniane, 1991), 781.

12. For examples of female saints, see Arcangela Tarabotti, *Paternal Tyranny*, ed. Letizia Panizza (Chicago: The University of Chicago Press, 2004), 61, 64, 98, 145; on Adam and Eve, see Tarabotti, *Paternal Tyranny*, 51–54. On this subject, see Elissa Weaver, "Arcangela Tarabotti's Thoughts on Eve and Her Debate with Giovanni Francesco Loredano" (forthcoming in a volume edited by Xenia Von Tippelskirch and Àngela Muñoz).

13. Tarabotti's efforts to see this work published are partially documented in her letter book (see *Letters Familiar and Formal*, 12 n 29). For a detailed discussion, see Lynn Lara Westwater, "A Cloistered Nun Abroad: Arcangela Tarabotti's International Literary Career," *Intersections: Yearbook for Early Modern Studies* 14: *Women Writing Back, Writing Women Back: Transnational Perspectives from the Late Middle Ages to the Dawn of the Modern Era*, eds. Alicia Montoya, Anke Gilleir, Suzan van Dijk (Leiden: Brill, 2010): 283–308; Westwater, "A Rediscovered Friendship in the Republic of Letters: The Unpublished Correspondence of Arcangela Tarabotti and Ismael Boulliau," *Renaissance Quarterly* 65, no. 1 (2012): 67–134.

14. On the work's condemnation, see Natalia Costa-Zalessow, "Tarabotti's 'La semplicità ingannata' and its Twentieth-Century Interpreters, with Unpublished Documents Regarding its Condemnation to the Index," *Italica* 78, no. 3 (2002): 315–325.

15. This work, which likely addressed the situation of women who sought refuge in female institutions after their marriages had ended because of physical, financial, or other conflict, is mentioned in *Letters* (see 49 and 126–27). Although it is not known with certainty the order in which Tarabotti composed the trilogy, it is likely that *Purgatory of Ill-Married Women* was written after both *Convent Hell* and *Convent Paradise* (1643). In the letter to the reader that prefaces her later work, *Antisatira* (1644), Tarabotti indicates that she has planned but not yet composed the work (Arcangela Tarabotti, "Antisatira," in *Satira e Antisatira*, ed. Elissa Weaver, 56–105 (Rome: Salerno, 1998), 59; Arcangela Tarabotti, *Antisatire: In Defense of Women Against Francesco Buoninsegni*, ed. and trans. Elissa Weaver (Toronto: Iter, 2020), 55–93, here 57.

16. The modern edition and translation are by Elissa Weaver. See note 15 above.

17. See Tarabotti, *Antisatire*, 17.

18. Tarabotti, *Antisatira*, 66 (*Antisatire*, 63).

19. See Tarabotti's letter to the reader ("Lettore") that prefaces the *Antisatira*, in which she claims to have been compelled to accede to the "prieghi di chi dovea e potea commandarmi, non ostante che la mia mortificazione fosse grande" (*Antisatira*, 56) ("to satisfy the requests of persons who should and could command me . . . despite my being greatly mortified" [*Antisatire*, 55]).

20. On Tarabotti's letters and her epistolary network, see Ray and Westwater's Introduction to Tarabotti, *Letters Familiar and Formal*, 22–31. See also Meredith K. Ray, "Letters from the Cloister: Defending the Literary Self in Arcangela Tarabotti's *Lettere familiari e di complimento*," *Italica* 81, no. 1 (2004): 24–43.

21. On this phenomenon and early-modern women writers, see Meredith K. Ray, *Writing Gender in Women's Letter Collections of the Italian Renaissance* (Toronto: University of Toronto Press, 2009).

22. On the strategic use of *Le lagrime*, see Meredith K. Ray, "Making the Private Public: Arcangela Tarabotti's *Lettere familiari*," in Elissa B. Weaver, ed., *Arcangela Tarabotti: A Literary Nun in Baroque Venice* (Ravenna: Longo, 2006), 173–189; see also the discussion by Ray and Westwater in *Letters Familiar and Formal* (38–40). An edition and translation of *Le Lagrime* that situates the work with respect to early-modern devotional literature is forthcoming by Ray and Westwater.

23. Tarabotti emphasizes Regina's devotion to Mary, noting that her "consorella" "perfettamente addottrinata in ogni virtù teologale e cristiana [sapeva] che senza sperar nella Vergine Madre, s'inarridiscono le foglie della speme"("[who was] perfectly educated in all the theological and Christian virtues, knew that without placing hope in the Virgin Mary, the leaves of hope dry out"), and had "perciò eletta [Maria] per tramontana fedele in questo tempestoso mare del mondo, ripieno di scogli precipitosi e di vorragini minaccianti l'eterna morte" ("therefore elected [Mary] as a faithful north star in this stormy sea of a world, full of dangerous cliffs and chasms threatening eternal death"), causing those around her to marvel at her "rari eccessi di divozione verso Maria, d'amore verso il suo sposo, e di speranze di paradiso" ("unique excesses of devotion to Mary, of love for her bridegroom, and of hope in paradise"]) (Arcangela Tarabotti, *Le lagrime di Arcangela Tarabotti per la morte dell'illustriss. signora Regina Donati* [Venice: Appresso li Guerigli, 1650], 346).

24. Tarabotti, *Le lagrime*, 357. Notably, Tarabotti also compares Regina to secular female examples, including Amazons, figures examined in this volume by Nathalie Hester.

25. As if to solidify the bridge that connected the two works, Tarabotti fills her *Lagrime*, like her *Lettere*, with erudite, secular references, though in this case largely to classical literature and culture; she quotes Ovid and Homer and features Asclepius and Marcus Tullius alongside religious luminaries.

26. Arcangela Tarabotti [Galerana Barcitotti, pseud.], *Che le donne siano della spetie degli uomini: Difesa delle donne di Galerana Barcitotti contro Horatio Plato . . .* (Nuremberg [Venice]: Cherchenberger, 1651). The work is in a modern edition by Letizia Panizza, *Che le donne siano della spezie degli huomini: Women Are No Less Rational Than Men* (London: Institute of Romance Studies, 1994) and has been translated by Theresa M. Kenney as *Women Are of the Human Species*, in *"Women are Not Human": An Anonymous Treatise and Responses*, ed. and trans. Theresa M. Kenney (New York: The Crossroad Publishing Company, 1998), 89–159.

27. See, for example, Tarabotti's argument against the claim that the Bible has no instances of Christ or the Apostles giving Communion to women and that therefore Christ did not die for them. Tarabotti responds: "The Apostles did give Communion to women. . . . The body of Christ . . . was washed by their tears and buried by them. . . . The more devout sex is baptized, believes, receives Communion, hopes and is saved. And there is no doubt that the one sacrament leads us to argue the other, because Holy Communion will be of little use to those who are not baptized. . . . St. Catherine would not have received the ring from her beloved Spouse Jesus if she had not first gone to the hermit to be baptized by the order of the Virgin herself" (*Women Are of the Human Species*, 144).

28. See Tarabotti, *Letters Familiar and Formal*, 82–83.

29. F. Thomas Luongo, "The Historical Reception of Catherine of Siena," in *A Companion to Catherina of Siena*, eds. Carolyn Muessig, George Ferzoco, and Beverly Mayne Kienzle (Leiden: Brill, 2012), 24.

30. Lucrezia Marinella, *De gesti heroici, e della vita meravigliosa della serafica S. Caterina . . . libri sei* (Venice: Barezzo Barezzi, 1624).

31. Catherine of Siena, *Il Dialogo de la serafica virgine Sancta Catherina da Siena dela divina providentia* (Venice: Matteo Capasca for Luc-Antonio Giunta, 1494); Catherine of Siena, *Epistole devotissime de S. Catharina da Siena (e orazioni)* (Venice: Aldus Manutius, 1500).

32. See Tarabotti, *Convent Paradise*, 49.

33. Catherine requested to bear the stigmata invisibly. In 1478 papal legislation established that only St. Francis of Assisi could be depicted with the stigmata (see Jane Tylus, *Reclaiming Catherine of Siena: Literacy, Literature and the Signs of Others* [Chicago: The University of Chicago Press, 2009], 278). For a consideration of Catherine of Siena in relation to the question of gender and stigmata, see Carolyn Meussig, *The Stigmata in Medieval and Early Modern Europe* (Oxford: Oxford University Press, 2020), 138–189.

34. Tarabotti, *Paradiso monacale*, 31 (*Convent Paradise*, 106).

35. See Unn Falkeid, *The Avignon Papacy Contested: An Intellectual History from Dante to Catherine of Siena* (Cambridge, MA: Harvard University Press, 2017).

36. F. Thomas Luongo, *The Saintly Politics of Catherine of Siena* (Ithaca: Cornell University Press, 2006), 8.

37. See Falkeid, *The Avignon Papacy Contested*.

38. Falkeid, *The Avignon Papacy Contested*, 189–190.

39. Tylus, *Reclaiming Catherine of Siena*, 142.

40. Many of Catherine's writings contain the formula, "In the name of Jesus Christ crucified and gentle Mary" or some variation on this (see Denis Vincent Wiseman, O.P., "Jesus Christ Crucified and Gentle Mary: Salvation and Mary in the Life and Writings of Catherine of Siena," *Marian Library Studies* 27 (2005–2006), 208). On Catherine, Mary, and Mary Magdalene—a figure who is also invoked on occasion by Tarabotti—see Unn Falkeid, "Constructing Female Authority: Birgitta of Sweden, Catherine of Siena, and the Two Marys," in Maria H. Oen and Unn Falkeid, *Sanctity and Female Authorship: Birgitta of Sweden and Catherine of Siena* (New York: Routledge, 2020), 54–73.

41. Wiseman, "Jesus Christ Crucified and Gentle Mary," 206–9.

42. Wiseman, 211–13, 218–19.

43. Tarabotti, *Paradiso monacale*, 5 (*Convent Paradise*, 83).

44. Cox, *Prodigious Muse*, 65.

45. Susan Haskins, "Volume Editor's Introduction," in *Who Is Mary? Three Early Modern Women on the Idea of the Virgin Mary*, ed. and trans. Susan Haskin (Chicago: The University of Chicago Press, 2008), 1. On the importance of Mary in this period, see also Eleonora Carinci, "Una riscrittura di Pietro Aretino: *La Vita di Maria Vergine* di Lucrezia Marinella e le sue fonti," *The Italianist* 33, no. 3 (2013), 362.

46. Haskins, "Introduction," 12. The insistence on Mary's virginity, which can be seen, for instance, in Matthew 1.25 ("And he [Joseph] knew her not till she brought forth her firstborn son: and he called his name JESUS."), came from the mistranslation of the Hebrew word "almah", which meant a nubile, marriageable young woman, into the Greek word "parthenos," which connotes the physical nature of intact virginity (Haskins, "Introduction," 12.)

47. Wiseman, "Jesus Christ Crucified and Gentle Mary," 210; Andrew Hopkins, *Santa Maria della Salute: Architecture and Ceremony in Baroque Venice* (Cambridge: Cambridge University Press, 2000), 6.

48. Here and below, see Haskins, "Introduction," 16–36.

49. Haskins, "Introduction," 30.

50. Haskins, "Introduction," 35–36.

51. Hopkins, *Santa Maria della Salute*, 5.

52. David Rosand, *Myths of Venice: The Figuration of a State* (Chapel Hill & London: The University of North Carolina Press, 2001), 13. See also Edward Muir, *Civic Ritual in Renaissance Venice* (Princeton, NJ: Princeton University Press, 1981), esp. 139–156.

53. See Hopkins, *Santa Maria della Salute*, 3–7. The Republic chose to focus devotion on Mary, as opposed to traditional plague saints like Sebastian or Roch, "because supplication to her was especially attractive in the context of seventeenth-century Venice" (Hopkins, *Santa Maria della Salute*, 5); in the 1620s, Marian devotion intensified through the efforts of Giovanni Tiepolo, patriarch of Venice from 1619 to 1631 (Hopkins, *Santa Maria della Salute*, 6), the immediate predecessor in this role to Federico Corner, *Paradiso monacale*'s dedicatee.

54. Tarabotti, *Paradiso monacale*, 49 (*Convent Paradise*, 120).

55. Tarabotti, *Paradiso monacale*, 206 (*Convent Paradise*, 237).

56. Tarabotti, *Paradiso monacale*, 204 (*Convent Paradise*, 235).

57. See 1 Corinthians 12.12-27. On the development of this analogy, see Donna Spivey Ellington, *From Sacred Body to Angelic Soul: Understanding Mary in Late Medieval and Early Modern Europe* (Washington DC: The Catholic University of America Press, 2001), 129. It was an offshoot of Saint Bernard of Clairvaux's metaphor of the aqueduct to describe Mary's position as mediator, which Ellington summarizes as, "She is herself the conduit through which the waters of grace flow from God to his Church" (128).

58. Quoted in Ellington, *From Sacred Body to Angelic Soul*, 129.

59. Tarabotti, *Paradiso monacale*, 52 (*Convent Paradise*, 122).

60. Tarabotti, *Paradiso monacale*, 52–53 (*Convent Paradise*, 123).

61. Later in the text, Tarabotti pursues a similar argument, saying that Mary transcends in virtues and merits all the saints of paradise (*Convent Paradise*, 199).

62. Tarabotti, *Paradiso monacale*, 53 (*Convent Paradise*, 123). Saint Scholastica (ca. 480–543) was the sister of Benedict of Nursia and the patron saint of Benedictine women's com-

munities. Tarabotti's reference here comes from book 2, chapter XXXIII of *Dialogues*, a work traditionally attributed to Pope Gregory the Great. "Ursula" refers to the fourth-century Saint Ursula, martyred after setting out on a pilgrimage with 11,000 virginal handmaidens.

63. Tarabotti, *Paradiso monacale*, 53 (*Convent Paradise*, 123).

64. Tarabotti, *Paradiso monacale*, 53–54 (*Convent Paradise*, 123).

65. Tarabotti, *Lettere familiari e di complimento*, 78 (*Letters Familiar and Formal*, 79).

66. These include *La Colomba sacra, poema eroico* (Venice: Gio Battista Ciotti Senese, al segno della minerva, 1595); *La vita di Maria Vergine imperatrice dell'universo* (Venice: appresso Barezo Barezi et conpagni, 1602); *Vita di Santa Giustina in ottava rima* (Florence: 1606); *De' gesti eroici e della vita maravigliosa della serafica Santa Caterina da Siena* (Venice: per Barezzo Barezzi, 1624); *Le vittorie di Francesco il serafico. Li passi gloriosi della diva Chiara. Di cui si narrano li fatti eroici, le penitenze acerbe, la vita mortificata e le fatiche insuperabili. . . . Con ragionamenti, ammaestramenti e sensi aristotelici, platonici, e theologici* (Padua: Giulio Crivellari, 1642); *Olocausto d'amore della vergine Santa Giustina in ottava rima* (Venice: Presso Matteo Leni, 1648).

67. First printed in 1602, this work was reprinted in 1604, 1610, and twice in 1617, with increasingly extensive changes; see Carinci, "Una riscrittura," 379–80. Marinella was accused of having plagiarized her *Vita* of Mary (perhaps on the basis of parallels to Aretino; see Carinci, "Una riscrittura," 379). Her publisher Giovan Battista Ciotti defends her against these charges in his presentation to her *Arcadia felice* (Venice: Gio. Battista Ciotti, 1605).

68. Lucrezia Marinella, *La nobiltà ed eccellenza delle donne et i diffetti e mancamenti degli uomini* (Venice: Giovan Battista Ciotti Senese, 1600). The volume was republished in a much expanded form the next year: Lucrezia Marinella, *La nobiltà e l'eccellenza delle donne co' diffetti e mancamenti degli uomini* (Venice: G.B. Ciotti, 1601). It was republished in 1621 and 1622.

69. Haskins, *Who is Mary*, 3.

70. Marinella, *La vita di Maria Vergine*, 26r; Lucrezia Marinella, "Lucrezia Marinella's *Life of the Virgin Mary, Empress of the Universe*," in *Who Is Mary? Three Early Modern Women on the Idea of the Virgin Mary*, ed. and trans. Susan Haskins (Chicago: The University of Chicago Press, 2008), 166.

71. Marinella's Mary is also obedient to political power. Marinella recounts, for example, that in response to Augustus's census order, Mary and Joseph "as upright persons, and full of humility" went to Bethlehem to register and pay taxes (see Marinella, "Lucrezia Marinella's *Life of the Virgin Mary*," 172).

72. Marinella, *La vita di Maria Vergine*, 14v; Marinella, "Lucrezia Marinella's *Life of the Virgin Mary*," 149.

73. Marinella, *La vita di Maria Vergine*, 27r; Marinella, "Lucrezia Marinella's *Life of the Virgin Mary*," 167.

74. See Marinella, *La vita di Maria Vergine*, 59r; Marinella, "Lucrezia Marinella's *Life of the Virgin Mary*," 234; Carinci, "Una riscrittura," 373.

75. Marinella, *La vita di Maria Vergine*, 59r-v; Marinella, "Lucrezia Marinella's *Life of the Virgin Mary*," 234.

76. Carinci, "Una riscrittura," 367–379. In subsequent editions of *La vita di Maria Vergine*, Marinella reduced her reliance of Aretino's text (Carinci, "Una riscrittura," 381).

77. Jennifer Haraguchi, "The Virgin Mary in the Early Modern Italian Writings of Vittoria Colonna, Lucrezia Marinella, and Eleonora Montalvo," *Religions* 9, no. 59 (2018): 5. See also Cox, who notes that Marian texts held a "particular, authorizing function," because they permitted women to model themselves against an "exemplary model of female faith" (Cox, *Prodigious Muse,* 65).

78. As Cox notes, Marinella's prior verse for the Virgin held similar patriotic elements, where she evokes the connection between Mary and Venice via the Annunciation (to which the city tied its foundation) in the sonnet "Di glorie oggi, di gemme, e di splendori. . . ." In her secular epic poem *L'Enrico,* she grants Venice both the "gift of immaculate conception" ("bearing sons, you will yet remain a chaste virgin") and empire (giving Venice the "scepter of Italy, indeed of the world") (Cox, *Prodigious Muse,* 69).

79. Carinci, "Una riscrittura," 378.

80. Marinella, *The Nobility and Excellence of Women and the Defects and Vices of Men,* ed. Anne Dunhill, introduction by Letizia Panizza (Chicago: The University of Chicago Press, 1999), 12.

81. See Cox, *Prodigious Muse,* 155–156, who notes that few early-modern works depict the mother-daughter relationship in such detail.

82. Marinella, *De' gesti heroici,* 74. On the tonsure episode, see note 32 above.

83. Marinella, *De' gesti heroici,* 9, 228, 192.

84. Marinella, *De' gesti heroici,* 156.

85. See Cox, *Prodigious Muse,* 157.

86. Michael Subialka, "Heroic Sainthood: Marinella's Genealogy of the Medici Aristocracy and Saint Catherine's 'Gesti Heroici' as a Rewriting of the Gender of Virtue," in Lucrezia Marinella, *De' gesti heroici e della vita marvigliosa della Serafica S. Caterina da Siena,* ed. Armando Maggi et al. (Ravenna: Longo, 2011), 163–92, esp. 173.

87. Marinella, *De' gesti heroici* (1624), 240.

88. Marinella, *De' gesti heroici* (1624), 157.

89. Lucrezia Marinella, *La nobiltà et l'eccellenza delle donne, co' difetti e mancamenti degli huomini* (Venice: Combi, 1621), 59; Marinella, *The Nobility and Excellence of Women,* 92.

90. Tarabotti, *La semplicità ingannata,* 300–301.

91. Tarabotti, *La semplicità ingannata,* 336–338.

92. Tarabotti, *Paternal Tyranny,* 125–126.

93. Tarabotti, *Women Are of the Human Species,* 147.

94. Tarabotti, *Paradiso monacale,* 39 (*Convent Paradise,* 113).

95. Francesca Medioli, "Alcune lettere autografe di Arcangela Tarabotti: Autocensura e immagine di sé," *Rivista di storia e letteratura religiosa* 32 (1996): 147.

96. Tarabotti, *Paradiso monacale,* 41 (*Convent Paradise,* 115).

# Bibliography


## Primary Sources

Accademia della Crusca. *Compendio del Vocabolario degli Accademici della Crusca formato sulla edizione quarta del medesimo*. Vol. 1. Florence: Appresso Domenico Maria Manni, 1739.

Ademollo, Alessandro. *Una famiglia di comici italiani nel secolo decimottavo*. Florence: C. Ademollo, 1855.

Alberti, Leon Battista. *I libri della famiglia*. Edited by Ruggiero Romano and Alberto Tenenti. Turin: Einaudi, 1969.

Alighieri, Dante. *Purgatorio*. Translated and edited by Robert M. Durling and Ronald J. Martinez. New York: Oxford University Press, 2003.

———. *Vita Nova*. Translated by Andrew Frisardi. Evanston, IL: Northwestern University Press, 2012.

Andreucci, Andrea Girolamo. "*Ragguaglio della vita della serva di Dio, Rosa Venerini, Viterbese Institutrice delle scuole e Maestre Pie (1732).*" In *Le vite delle due Maestre Pie Rosa Venerini e Lucia Filippini*, 1–174. Rome: Stamperia della S. Congr. De Propag. Fide, 1868.

Anghiera, Peter Martyr of. "Sommario dell'istoria dell'Indie occidentali." In Giovanni Battista Ramusio, *Navigazioni e viaggi*, edited by Marica Milanesi, 19–205. Vol. 5. Turin: Einaudi, 1985.

Augustine. *On the Free Choice of the Will, On Grace and Free Choice, and Other Writings*. Edited by Peter King. Cambridge: Cambridge University Press, 2010.

Baldinucci, Filippo. *Notizie de' professori del disegno da Cimabue in qua*. Vol. 1. Florence: Santi Franchi, 1681.

Barbaro, Francesco. "On Wifely Duties." In *The Earthly Republic: Italian Humanists on Government and Society*, translated by Benjamin G. Kohl, edited by Benjamin G. Kohl and Ronald G. Witt, 177–228. Philadelphia: University of Pennsylvania Press, 1978.

———. *The Wealth of Wives: A Fifteenth-Century Marriage Manual*. Translated and edited by Margaret L. King. Toronto, Ontario: Iter Academic Press; Tempe: Arizona Center for Medieval and Renaissance Studies, 2015.

Bartolomei Smeducci, Girolamo. *L'America*. Rome: Lodovico Grignani, 1650.

Beverini, Bartolomeo. *Vita di S. Cecilia vergine e martire descritta dal padre Bartolomeo Beverini della Congreg. della Madre di Dio, con alcune annotationi historiche, e morali*. Lucca: Iacinto Paci, 1663.

Bigolina, Giulia. *Urania: The Story of a Young Woman's Love, & The Novella of Giulia Camposanpiero and Thesibaldo Vitaliani*. Translated and edited by Christopher Nissen. Tempe: Arizona Center for Medieval and Renaissance Studies, 2004.

———. *Urania: A Romance*. Translated and edited by Valeria Finucci. Chicago: The University of Chicago Press, 2005.

Boccaccio, Giovanni. *Delle donne illustre*. Translated by Giuseppe Bertussi. Florence: Giunti, 1606.

———. *Opere. Decameron. Elegia di Madonna Fiammetta. Ninfe Fieoslane*. Edited by Cesare Segre, with notes by Maria Consigli Segre. Milan: Mursia, 1966.

———. *Decameron*. Translated by G. H. McWilliam. New York: Penguin Books, 1984.

———. *Decameron*. Edited by Vittore Branca. Milan: Mondadori, 1976.

———. *Decameron*. Translated and edited by Wayne Rebhorn. New York: W. W. Norton, 2013.

Borgia, Lucrezia. *Lettere di Lucrezia Borgia: 1494–1519*. Edited by Diane Ghirardo. Mantua: Tre Lune, 2020.

Brasavola, Antonio Musa. *Antoni Muse Brasauoli Ferrariensis Examen omnium simplicium medicamentorum, quorum in officinis vsus est, ad Illustriss. & sereniss. Principes Herculem Estensem Ferrarie Ducem et Renatam Gallam*. Rome: Antonii Bladi de Asula, 1536.

———. *Antonii Musae Brasauoli Ferrariensis Examen omnium syruporum, quorum publicus vsus est: ad illustriss. & pudicissimam virginem Elleonoram Estensem*. Venice: per D. Bernardinum Stagninum, 1538.

———. *La vita di Iesu Cristo*. Edited by Adriano and Anna Prosperi. Vol. 3. Turin: Aragno, 2020.

Buoninsegni, Francesco, and Arcangela Tarabotti. *Satira ed Antisatira*. Edited and with an introduction by Elissa Weaver. Rome: Salerno Editrice, 1998.

*Capitolo di Cuccagna dove se intendono le maravigliose cose che sono in quel paese, dove chi piu dorme piu guadagna, & a chi parla di lavorare li sono rotte le braccia* (n.d., n.p.).

Castiglione, Baldassarre. *The Book of the Courtier*. Translated by George Bull. New York: Penguin Books, 1981.

———. *Il libro del Cortegiano*. Edited by Walter Barberis. Turin: Einaudi, 1998.

Catherine of Bologna. See Caterina Vigri, *Libro deuoto de la beata Chaterina bolognese de lordine [sic] dil seraphico San Francesco elqual [sic] essa lascio scripto de sua man propria*. Bologna: Antonio de li Benedicti, May 8, 1500.

Catherine of Siena. *Il Dialogo de la serafica virgine Sancta Catherina da Siena dela divina providentia*. Venice: Matteo Capasca for Luc-Antonio Giunta, 1494.

———. *Epistole devotissime de S. Catharina da Siena (e orazioni)*. Venice: Aldus Manutius, 1500.

Cherubino da Siena, *Regole della Vita Matrimoniale di Frate Cherubino da Siena*. Edited by Francesco Zambrini and Carlo Negroni. Bologna: Romagnoli-dall'Acqua, 1888.

Columbus, Christopher. "Lettera al Santángel." In *Scopritori e viaggiatori del Cinquecento*, edited by Ilaria Luzzana Caraci, 25–41. Vol. 1. Milan: Ricciardi Editore, 1996.

Costa, Margherita. *La chitarra della signora Margherita Costa romana, canzoniere amoroso*. Francfort: Daniel Wastch, 1638.

———. *Lettere amorose della signora Margherita Costa romana*. Venice: s.n., 1639.

———. *La selva dei cipressi: opera lugubre di Margherita Costa romana*. Florence: Massi & Landi, 1640.

———. *Cecilia martire poema sacro di Margherita Costa romana, all'Emin.mo Prencipe Francesco Card. Barberino, Vicecancelliero di Santa Chiesa*. Rome: Mascardi, 1644.

———. *La tromba del parnaso*. Paris: Sebastian Craimoisy, 1647.

———. *The Buffoons, a Ridiculous Comedy: A Bilingual Edition*. Translated and edited by Sara E. Dìaz and Jessica Goethals. Tempe: Arizona Center for Medieval and Renaissance Studies, 2018.

da Bisticci, Vespasiano. "Lamento d'Italia per la presa d'Otranto fatta dai Turchi nel 1480." *Archivio Storico Italiano* 4, no. 1 (1843): 452–463.

De Luca, Giovanni Battista. "*Theatrum veritatis et justitiae, sive Decisivi discursus per materias*, Liber 14, I, *De Regularibus et monialibus* (Venetiis: apud Paulum Balleonium, 1706), in "Il dono di Santa Rosa Venerini a M. Cecilia Baij," by Suor Eliana Massimi, MPV. In *M. Cecilia Baij e le altre donne in ricerca di Dio nel Settecento viterbese*, edited by Nadia Togni and Annamaria Valli, 46. Viterbo: Graffietti, 2018.

del Sera, Beatrice. *Amor di virtù: Commedia in cinque atti (1548)*. Edited by Elissa Weaver. Ravenna: Longhi Editore, 1990.

Dominici, Giovanni. *Regola del governo di cura familiare: compilata dal beato Giovanni Dominici*. Florence: A. Garinei, 1860.

Fonte, Moderata. "Due novelle." Edited by Anicio Bonucci. *L'eccitamento: giornale di filologia, letteratura ed amenità* no. 1 (1858): 742–750.

———. *Due novelle*. Edited by Anicio Bonucci. Bologna: Tipografia delle scienze, 1859.

———. *Il merito delle donne*. Edited by Adriana Chemello. Mirano-Venice: Eidos, 1988.

———. *The Worth of Women: Wherein Is Clearly Revealed Their Nobility and Their Superiority to Men*. Translated and edited by Virginia Cox. Chicago: The University of Chicago Press, 1997.

———. "*Le feste*: Written by Moderata Fonte." Translated and edited by Courtney Quaintance. In *Scenes from Italian Convent Life: An Anthology of Convent Theatrical Texts and Contexts*, edited by Elissa B. Weaver, 193–231. Ravenna, Italy: Longo Editore, 2009.

Gambara, Lorenzo. *De navigatione Christophori Columbi*. Rome: Bartolomeo Bonfadini and Tito Diani, 1581.

Giorgini, Giovanni. *Il mondo nuovo*. Iesi: Pietro Farri, 1596.

Goulas, Nicolas. *Mémoires de Nicolas Goulas: 1643–1648*. Vol. 2. Paris: Librairie Renouard, 1879.

Gualterotti, Raffaello. *L'America*. Florence: Giunti, 1611.

*Historia di Lionbruno con un capitolo di Pamphilo Sasso*. Siena: Francescho di Simeno, 1550.

*Historia di Liombruno il quale fu lasciato dal padre per povertà in preda del diavolo, & scampando fu portato da una donna in forma d'Aquila in una Città, & facendo egli dipoi varij viaggi rubò a certi malandrini un Mantello, & un par di Stivali con li quali andò invisibile, & vinse il vento. Con un capitolo di Panfilo Sasso Nuovamente Ristampato*. Florence: Giovanni Baleni, 1583.

*Le vite delle due Maestre Pie Rosa Venerini e Lucia Filippini*. Rome: Stamperia della S. Congr. De Propag. Fide, 1868.

Machiavelli, Niccolò. *Il Principe e altre opere politiche*. Edited by Stefano Andretta and with an introduction by Delio Cantimori. 14th ed. Milan: Garzanti, 1994.

———. *Machiavelli: Political, Historical and Literary Writings*. Translated by Meredith K. Ray. Edited by Mark Jurdjevic and Meredith K. Ray. Philadelphia: University of Pennsylvania Press, 2019.

Marangoni, Giovanni. *Vita del servo di Dio Cardinal Marcantonio Barbarigo, Vescovo di Montefiascone e Corneto* (1716). Enrici Chierichetti, tunc vicarii generalis Montisfalisci, 1930. In Sacra Rituum Congregatio. *Romana seu Faliscodunen. Beatificationis et canonizationis Ven. Servae Dei Luciae Filippini, fundatricis atque Antistitae Instituti Magistrarum Piarum ab eius cognomine nuncupatarum, Positio super virtutibus*, 150–57. Rome: Typis polyglottis Vaticanis, 1923.

Marinella, Lucrezia. *La colomba sacra, poema eroico*. Venice: Gio. Battista Ciotti Senese, al segno della minerva, 1595.

———. *La nobiltà ed eccellenza delle donne et i diffetti e mancamenti degli uomini*. Venice: Giovan Battista Ciotti Senese, 1600.

———. *La nobiltà e l'eccellenza delle donne co' diffetti e mancamenti degli uomini*. Venice: G. B. Ciotti, 1601.

———. *La vita di Maria Vergine imperatrice dell'universo*. Venice: appresso Barezo Barezi et conpagni, 1602.

———. *Vita di Santa Giustina in ottava rima*. Florence: 1606.

———. *La nobiltà et l'eccellenza delle donne, co' difetti e mancamenti degli huomini*. Venice: Combi, 1621.

———. *De' gesti eroici e della vita maravigliosa della serafica santa Caterina da Siena*. Venice: Barezzo Barezzi, 1624.

———. *Le vittorie di Francesco il serafico. Li passi gloriosi della diva Chiara. Di cui si narrano li fatti eroici, le penitenze acerbe, la vita mortificata e le fatiche insuperabili . . . Con ragionamenti, ammaestramenti e sensi aristotelici, platonici, e theologici*. Padua: Giulio Crivellari, 1642.

———. *Olocausto d'amore della vergine Santa Giustina in ottava rima*. Venice: Matteo Leni, 1648.

———. "Lucrezia Marinella's *Life of the Virgin Mary, Empress of the Universe*." In *Who Is Mary? Three Early Modern Women on the Idea of the Virgin Mary*, translated and edited by Susan Haskins, 119–246. Chicago: The University of Chicago Press, 2008.

Marino, Giambattista. *Lira. Parte Terza*. Venice: Ciotti, 1638.

*Memoriale dei padri di famiglia, 12 dicembre 1711*. In Sacra Rituum Congregatio. *Romana seu Faliscodunen. Beatificationis et canonizationis Ven. Servae Dei Luciae Filippini, fundatricis atque Antistitae Instituti Magistrarum Piarum ab eius cognomine nuncupatarum, Positio super*, 214–16. Rome: Typis polyglottis Vaticanis, 1923.

Nogarola, Isotta. *Complete Writings: Letterbook, Dialogue on Adam and Eve, and Orations*. Edited by Margaret L. King and Diana Robin. Chicago: The University of Chicago Press, 2003.

Ottonelli, Giovanni Domenico. *Della pericolosa conversatione con le donne, o poco modeste, o ritirate, o cantatrici, o accademiche*. Florence: Luca Franceschini & Alessandro Logi, 1646.

Patrignani, Giuseppe Antonio. *Menologio di pie memorie d'alcuni religiosi della Compagnia di Gesù*, vol. 2. Venezia: 1730. In Sacra Rituum Congregatio. *Romana seu Faliscodunen. Beatificationis et canonizationis Ven. Servae Dei Luciae Filippini, fundatricis atque Antistitae Instituti Magistrarum Piarum ab eius cognomine nuncupatarum, Positio super virtutibus*, 95–105. Rome: Typis polyglottis Vaticanis, 1923.

Petrarch, Francesco. "How a Ruler Ought to Govern His State." In *The Earthly Republic: Italian Humanists on Government and Society*. Translated by Benjamin G. Kohl, edited by Benjamin G. Kohl and Ronald J. Witt, 35–80. Philadelphia: University of Pennsylvania Press, 1978.

Picinelli, Filippo. *Mondo simbolico, o sia Uniuersità d'imprese scelte, spiegate, ed'illustrate con sentenze, ed eruditioni sacre, e profane*. Milan: Francesco Mognagha, 1653.

Pigafetta, Filippo. *Relatione del reame di Congo e delle circonvicine contrade*. Rome: Bartolomeo Grassi, 1591.

Plato. *Timaeus*. Translated by Donald J. Zeyl. Indianapolis: Hackett, 2000.

———. *The Collected Dialogues*. Translated by Benjamin Jowett. Edited by Edith Hamilton and Huntington Cairns. Princeton, NJ: Princeton University Press, 1985.

Pulci, Antonia. *Florentine Drama for Convent and Festival: Seven Sacred Plays*. Translated by James Wyatt Cook. Edited by James Wyatt Cook and Barbara Collier Cook. Chicago: The University of Chicago Press, 1996.

———. *Saints' Lives and Bible Stories for the Stage: A Bi-lingual Edition*. Translated by James Wyatt Cook. Edited and with an introduction by Elissa B. Weaver. Toronto: Iter Press/Centre for Reformation and Renaissance Studies, 2010.

Ramusio, Giovanni Battista. *Navigazioni e viaggi*. Edited by Marica Milanesi. Vol. 2. Turin: Einaudi, 1979.

*Regole per le maestre pie dell'Istituto della serva di Dio Rosa Venerini, ricavate dalla vita, dalla relazione e dai manoscritti della medesima*. Rome: 1837.

Sacra Rituum Congregatio. *Romana seu Faliscodunen. Beatificationis et canonizationis Ven. Servae Dei Luciae Filippini, fundatricis atque Antistitae Instituti Magistrarum Piarum ab eius cognomine nuncupatarum, Positio super virtutibus*. Rome: Typis polyglottis Vaticanis, 1923.

———. *Romana seu Viterbien. Beatificationis et canonizationis Servae Dei Rosae Venerini, fundatricis Magistrarum Piarum quae ab eius cognomine nuncupantur († 1728), Positio super virtutibus ex officio compilata*. Rome: Typis polyglottis Vaticanis, 1943.

Santos, João dos. *Ethiopia Orientale. L'Afrique de l'Est et l'océan Indien au XVIe siècle. La Relation de João dos Santos (1609)*. Edited by Florence Pabiou-Duchamp. Paris: Chandeigne, 2011.

Savonarola, Girolamo. *A Guide to Righteous Living and Other Works*. Translated and edited by Konrad Eisenbichler. Toronto: University of Toronto Press, 2003.

———. *Selected Writings of Girolamo Savonarola: Religion and Politics, 1490–1498*. Translated and edited by Donald Beebe, Anne Borelli, and Maria Pastore Passaro. Forward by Giuseppe Mazzotta. New Haven, CT: Yale University Press, 2006.

Stigliani, Tommaso. *Il mondo nuovo*. Rome: Mascardi, 1928.

Tarabotti, Arcangela. *Paradiso monacale*. Venice: Guglielmo Oddoni, 1643.

——— [Galerana Barcitotti, pseud.]. *Che le donne siano della spetie degli uomini: Difesa delle donne di Galerana Barcitotti contro Horatio Plato ....* Nuremberg [Venice]: Cherchenberger, 1651.

———. *L'"Inferno monacale' di Arcangela Tarabotti.* Edited by Francesca Medioli. Turin: Rosenberg & Sellier, 1990.

———. *Che le donne siano della spezie degli huomini: Women Are No Less Rational Than Men.* Translated and edited by Letizia Panizza. London: Institute of Romance Studies, 1994.

———.*Women Are of the Human Species.* In *"Women are Not Human": An Anonymous Treatise and Responses,* Translated and edited by Theresa M. Kenney, 89–159. New York: The Crossroad Publishing Company, 1998.

———. *La Semplicità ingannata.* Edited by Simona Bortot. Padua: Il Poligrafo, 2007.

———. *Lettere familiari e di complimento.* Edited by Meredith K. Ray and Lynn Lara Westwater. Turin: Rosenberg & Sellier, 2009.

———. *Letters Familiar and Formal.* Translated and edited by Meredith K. Ray and Lynn Lara Westwater. Toronto: Centre for Reformation and Renaissance Studies, 2012.

———. *Antisatire: In Defense of Women Against Francesco Buoninsegni.* Translated and edited and with an introduction by Elissa B. Weaver. Toronto: Iter Press/Tempe: ACMRS, 2020.

———. *Convent Paradise.* Translated and edited by Meredith K. Ray and Lynn Lara Westwater. Toronto: Iter Press/Tempe: ACMR, 2020.

*The Story of Lionbruno.* Translated and edited by Beatrice Corrigan. Toronto: Toronto Public Library, 1976.

Tornabuoni, Lucrezia. *Sacred Narratives.* Translated and edited by Jane Tylus. Chicago: The University of Chicago Press, 2001.

———. *Poemetti sacri.* Edited by Fulvio Pezzarossa. Firenze: Olschki, 1978.

Vasari, Giorgio. *Le vite de' più eccellenti pittori, scultori, ed architettori.* 2 vols. Florence: Giunti, 1568.

———. *Lives of the Most Eminent Painters, Sculptors & Architects.* Translated by Gaston du C. du Vere. London: Macmillan & The Medici Society, 1912–1914.

Verdizotti, Giovanni Maria. *Cento favole morali dei più illustri antichi et moderni autori Greci e Latini.* Venice: Francesco Ziletti, 1586.

Vigri, Caterina. ———. *Intus ed Extra. Un formulario epistolare delle Clarisse bolognesi (seconda metà del XV secolo).* Edited by Letizia Pellegrini. Rome: Edizioni di Storia e Letteratura, in press.

———. *Libro deuoto de la beata Chaterina bolognese de lordine [sic] dil seraphico San Francesco elqual [sic] essa lascio scripto de sua man propria.* Bologna: Antonio de li Benedicti, May 8, 1500.

———. *Laudi, trattati e lettere.* Edited by Silvia Serventi. Florence: SISMEL Edizioni del Galluzzo, 2000.

———. *Libro deuoto de la beata Chaterina bolognese de lordine [sic] dil seraphico San Francesco elqual [sic] essa lascio scripto de sua man propria.* Bologna: Antonio de li Benedicti, May 8, 1500.

———. *Pregare con le immagini: il breviario di Caterina Vigri.* Edited by Vera Fortunati and Claudio Leonardi. Florence: SISMEL Edizioni del Galluzzo, Bologna, 2004.

———. *Le sette armi spirituali.* Edited by Antonella Degl'Innocenti. Florence: SISMEL, Edizioni del Galluzzo, 2000.

Virgil. *Eclogues. Georgics. Aeneid Books 1–6.* Translated by H. Rushton Fairclough. Cambridge, MA: Loeb Classical Library, 1999.

———. *L'Enea* . . . . Translated by Lodovico Dolce. Venice: Giovanni Varisco, 1567.

Vives, Juan Luis. *The Education of a Christian Woman.* Translated and edited by Charles Fantazzi. Chicago: The University of Chicago Press, 2000.

Zerbinati, Giovanni Maria. *Croniche di Ferrara: quali comenzano del anno 1500 sino al 1527.* Edited by Maria Giuseppina Muzzarelli. Ferrara: Deputazione provinciale ferrarese di storia patria, 1989.

**Secondary Sources**

*Abiti e lavori delle monache di Bologna: in una serie di disegni del secolo XVIII.* With an introduction by Mario Fanti. Bologna: Tamari, 1972.

Alberigo, Giuseppe, and Hubert Jedin, eds. *Conciliorum oecumenicorum decreta.* Bologna: Edizioni Dehoniane, 1991.

Aloè, Carla. "The New World Mythology in New World Epic Poetry, 1492–1650." PhD diss., University of Birmingham, 2015.

Arlia, Constantino. "Un bandito e una cortigiana letterati." *Il bibliofilo* 2, no. 8–9 (August-September, 1881): 164–166.

Banfi, Luigi, ed. *Teatro del Quattrocento: sacre rappresentazioni.* Turin: UTET, 1963.

Barocchi, Paola, and Giovanna Gaeta Bertelà, eds. *Collezionismo mediceo e storia artistica,* Vol. 3. Il Cardinale Giovan Carlo, Mattias e Leopoldo 1628–1667. Florence: SPES, 2005.

Barolini, Teodolinda. "The Scholar and the Widow: Corrupt Appetite and Moral Failure in Society's Intellectual Elite (VIII.7)." In *The Decameron Eighth Day in Perspective,* 148–89. Toronto: University of Toronto Press, 2020.

Baskins, Cristelle. "Trecento Rome: The Poetics and Politics of Widowhood." In *Widowhood and Visual Culture in Early Modern Europe,* edited by Allison Levy, 197–209. London: Routledge, 2003.

Baxandall, Michael. *Painting and Experience in Fifteenth-Century Italy: A Primer on the Social History of Pictorial Style.* Oxford: Oxford University Press, 1988.

Beckwith, Sarah. "A Very Material Mysticism: The Medieval Mysticism of Margery Kempe." In *Medieval Literature: History, Criticism, and Ideology,* edited by David Aers, 78–111. New York: St. Martin's press, 1986.

Bellesi, Sandro. "I ritratti delle sorelle Costa di Cesare Dandini e Stefano della Bella." In *Con dolce forza: Donne nell'universo musicale del Cinque e Seicento,* edited by Laura Donati, 65–74. Florence: Edizioni Polistampa, 2018.

Belligni, Eleonora. *Renata di Francia (1510–1575): un'eresia di corte.* Turin: UTET, 2011.

Benedetti, Marina. *Io non sono Dio. Guglielma di Milano e i Figli dello Spirito Santo.* Milan: Biblioteca Francescana, 1998.

———. *Milano 1300. I processi inquisitoriali contro le devote e i devoti di Santa Guglielma.* Milan: Libri Scheiwiller, 1999.

———. "Di regine, sante e eretiche. Su Guglielma e sulla recente storiografia." *Reti Medievali Rivista* 19, no. 1(2018): 211–230. doi: 10.6092/1593-2214/5535.

Bergamaschi, Pietro. *Vita del Servo di Dio Card. Marc'Antonio Barbarigo Vescovo di Montefiascone e Corneto*. Vol. 2. Rome: Tipografia Poliglotta Vaticana, 1919.

———. *Vita della serva di Dio Donna Maria Cecilia Baij*. Viterbo: Agnesotti, 1923.

Bhasin, Christine Scippa. "Prostitutes, Nuns, Actresses: Breaking the Convent Wall in Seventeenth-Century Venice." *Theatre Journal* 66, no. 1 (2014): 19–35.

Bilinkoff, Jodi. *Related Lives: Confessors and Their Female Penitents, 1450–1750*. Ithaca, NY: Cornell University Press, 2005.

Biondi, Angelo. *Le maestre pie Filippini nella Maremma sovanese dal '700 al '900: Una istituzione anticipatrice dell'educazione alle donne*. Grosseto: Laurum Editrice, 2003.

Bisaha, Nancy. *Creating East and West: Renaissance Humanists and the Ottoman Turks*. Philadelphia: University of Pennsylvania Press, 2004.

Black, Nancy B. *Medieval Narratives of Accused Queens*. Gainesville: University Press of Florida, 2003.

Blunt, Anthony. *Artistic Theory in Italy 1450–1600*. Oxford: Oxford University Press, 1940.

Bottigheimer, Ruth B. "Cupid and Psyche vs. Beauty and the Beast: The Milesian and the Modern." *Marvels and Tales*, 3, no. 1 (1989): 4–14.

Brege, Brian, "Renaissance Florentines in the Tropics: Brazil, The Grand Duchy of Tuscany, and the Limits of Empire." In *The New World in Early Modern Italy, 1492–1750*, edited by Elizabeth Horodowich and Lia Markey, 206–22. Cambridge: Cambridge University Press, 2017.

Brosius, Amy. "'Il suon, lo sguardo, il canto': The Function of Portraits of Mid-Seventeenth-Century *Virtuose* in Rome." *Italian Studies* 63, no. 1 (2008): 17–40.

———. "'Il suon, lo sguardo, il canto': *Virtuose* of the Roman Conversazioni in the Mid-Seventeenth Century." PhD diss., New York University, 2009.

Brown, Cynthia. "The Reconstruction of an Author in Print: Christine de Pizan in the 15th and 16th Centuries." In *Christine de Pizan and the Categories of Difference*, edited by Marilynn Desmond, 215–35. Minneapolis: University of Minnesota Press, 1998.

Butler, Judith. *Gender Trouble: Feminism and the Subversion of Identity*. 2nd ed. New York: Routledge, 1999.

Bryce, Judith. "Adjusting the Canon for Later Fifteenth-Century Florence: The Case of Antonia Pulci." In *The Renaissance Theatre: Texts, Performance, Design*, edited by Christopher Cairns, 133–45. Aldershot: Ashgate, 1999.

———. "Vernacular Poetry and Mystery Plays." In *A History of Women's Writing in Italy*, edited by Letizia Panizza and Sharon Wood, 31–36. Cambridge: Cambridge University Press, 2000.

———. "'Or altra via mi convìen cercare': Marriage, Salvation and Sanctity in Antonia Tanini Pulci's Rappresentazione di Santa Guglielma." In *Theatre, Opera, and Performance in Italy from the Fifteenth Century to the Present: Essays in Honour of Richard Andrews*, edited by Brian Richardson, Simon Gilson, and Catherine Keen, 23–38. Leeds: The Society for Italian Studies, 2004), 28.

———. "Les Livres des Florentines. Reconsidering Women's Literacy in Quattrocento Florence." In *At the Margins. Minority Groups in Premodern Italy*, edited by Stephen J. Milner, 133–61. Minneapolis: The University of Minnesota Press, 2005.

Byatt, Lucy. "Ippolito d'Este." In *Dizionario biografico degli Italiani* 43 (1993): https://www.treccani.it/enciclopedia/ippolito-d-este_%28Dizionario-Biografico%29/.

Bynum, Caroline W. "Religious Women in the Later Middle Ages." In *Christian Spirituality: High Middle Ages and Reformation*, edited by Jill Raitt, 121–39. New York: Crossroads, 1987.

———. "Women's Stories, Women's Symbols: A Critique of Victor Turner's Theory of Liminality." In *Anthropology and the Study of Religion*, edited by Frank Reynolds and Robert Moore, 105–25. Chicago: Center for the Scientific Study of Religion, 1984.

Caffiero, Marina. *Religione e modernità in Italia, secoli XVII-XIX*. Pisa: Istituti Editoriali e Poligrafici Internazionali, 2000.

Calogero, Elena Laura. "'Sweet alluring harmony': Heavenly and Earthly Sirens in Sixteenth- and Seventeenth-Century Literary and Visual Culture." In *Music of the Sirens*, edited by Lynda Phyllis Austern and Inna Narodistskaya, 140–175. Bloomington: Indiana University Press, 2006.

Capucci, Martino. "Costa, Margherita (Maria Margherita)." In *Dizionario biografico degli italiani*, 233–34. Rome: Istituto della Enciclopedia italiana, 1984.

Carinci, Eleonora. "Una lettera autografa inedita di Moderata Fonte (al granduca di Toscana Francesco I)." *Critica del Testo* 5, no. 3 (2002): 1–11.

———. "Una riscrittura di Pietro Aretino: *La Vita di Maria Vergine* di Lucrezia Marinella e le sue fonti." *The Italianist* 33, no. 3 (2013), 361–389.

Carlsmith, Christopher. *A Renaissance Education: Schooling in Bergamo and the Venetian Republic, 1500–1650*. Toronto: University of Toronto Press, 2010.

———. "The Three Rs: Education in Early Modern Rome." In *A Companion to Early Modern Rome, 1492–1692*, edited by Pamela M. Jones, Barbara Wisch, and Simon Ditchfield, 500–14. Leiden: Brill, 2019.

Carney, Emanuela. "Antonia Pulci's *Rappresentazione di santa Domitilla* and the Defense of Virginity in Quattrocento Florence." In *Scenes from Italian Convent Life: An Anthology of Theatrical Texts and Contexts*, edited by Elissa B. Weaver, 11–36. Ravenna: Longo, 2009.

Carvajal, Gaspar de. *Descubrimento del río de la Amazonas*. Bogotà: Prensas de la Biblioteca Nacional, 1942. http://www.cervantesvirtual.com/obra-visor/descubrimiento-del-rio-de-las-amazonas—0/html/0039c0ae-82b2-11df-acc7-002185ce6064_7.html.

Casciano, Paola. "Il cantare di santa Guglielma." In *Editori ed edizioni a Roma nel Rinascimento*, edited by Paola Farenga, 23–43. Rome: Roma nel Rinascimento, 2005.

Cavallo, Jo Ann. *The World beyond Europe in the Romance Epics of Boiardo and Ariosto*. Toronto: University of Toronto Press, 2013.

Cazelles, Brigitte. *The Lady as Saint. A Collection of French Hagiographic Romances of the Thirteenth Century*. Philadelphia: University of Pennsylvania Press, 1991.

Chemello, Adriana, "La donna, il modello, e l'immaginario: Moderata Fonte e Lucrezia Marinella." In *Nel cerchio della luna: figure di donne in aclune testi del XVI*, edited by Marina Zancan, 95–170. Venice: Marsilio, 1983.

———. "Letteratura di Condotta e vita delle donne nelle opera di Moderata fonte e Lucrezia Marinella." In *Conduct Literature for and about Women in Italy, 1470–1900: Prescribing and Describing Life*, edited by Helena Sanson and Francesco Lucioli, 137–158. Paris: Classiques Garnier, 2016.

Chiappini, Luciano. *Gli Estensi*. 3rd ed. Varese: dall'Oglio editore, 1967.

Ciletti, Elena. "Patriarchal Ideology in the Renaissance Iconography of Judith." In *Refiguring Woman: Perspectives on Gender and the Italian Renaissance*, edited by Marilyn Migiel and Juliana Schiesari, 35–70. Ithaca, NY: Cornell University Press, 1991.

Clark, Elizabeth A. "Dissuading from Marriage: Jerome and the Asceticization of Satire." In *Satiric Advice on Women and Marriage: From Plautus to Chaucer*, edited by Warren S. Smith, 154–81. Ann Arbor: University of Michigan Press, 2005.

Collina, Beatrice. "Moderata Fonte e *Il Merito delle donne*." *Annali d'italianistica* 7 (1989): 142–165.

———. "Thought Pieces for Elissa Weaver." *Modern Philology* 106, no. 4 (May 2009): 704–6.

Colomb de Batines, Paul. *Bibliografia delle antiche rappresentazioni italiane sacre e profane stampate nei secoli XV e XVI*. Florence: Società Tipografica, 1852.

Connolly, Thomas. *Mourning into Joy: Music, Raphael, and Saint Cecilia*. New Haven, CT: Yale University Press, 1994.

Connors, Joseph. "Chi era Ottonelli?" In *Pietro da Cortona: Atti del convegno internazionale, Roma-Firenze 12–15 novembre 1997*, edited by Christoph L. Frommel and Sebastian Schütze, 29–35. Milan: Electa, 1998.

Costa, Patrizia Maria. *Guglielma la Boema. L'"eretica" di Chiaravalle*. Milan: Nuove Edizioni Duomo, 1985.

Costa-Zalessow, Natalia. "Tarabotti's 'La semplicità ingannata' and its Twentieth-Century Interpreters, with Unpublished Documents Regarding its Condemnation to the Index." *Italica* 78 (2002): 315–325.

———. "Margherita Costa." In *Seventeenth-Century Italian Poets and Dramatists. Dictionary of Literary Biography*, 113–18. Farmington Hills: Gale Publishing, 2008.

———, ed. *Voice of a Virtuosa and Courtesan: Selected Poems of Margherita Costa*. New York: Bordighera Press, 2015.

Cox, Virginia. "Moderata Fonte and *The Worth of Women*." *In The Worth of Women Wherein is Clearly Revealed Their Nobility and Superiority to Men*, translated and edited by Virginia Cox, 1–23. Chicago: The University of Chicago Press, 1997.

———. *Women's Writing in Italy 1400–1650*. Baltimore: The Johns Hopkins University Press, 2008.

———. *The Prodigious Muse*. Baltimore: The Johns Hopkins University Press, 2011.

Cremonini, Patrizia. "Il rabarbaro di Lucrezia Borgia e la lettera di frà Nicolò da Tossignano, custode di Terra Santa. Questione d'oriente, spezie, medici e commerci." *Quaderni estensi. Rivista* 2 (2010): 273–305. http://www.archivi.beniculturali.it/QE,2,2010.

Cusick, Suzanne G. "'Thinking from Women's Lives': Francesca Caccini after 1627." *The Musical Quarterly* 77, no. 3 (1993): 484–507.

———. "A Soprano Subjectivity: The Compositional Voice of Francesca Caccini." In *Crossing Boundaries: Attending to Early Modern Women*, edited by Jane Donaworth and Adele Seeff, 80–98. Cranbury, NJ: Associated University Presses, 2000.

———. *Francesca Caccini at the Medici Court: Music and the Circulation of Power*. Chicago: The University of Chicago Press, 2009.

D'Ancona, Alessandro. *Origini del teatro italiano*. 2 vols. Turin: Loescher, 1891.

———, ed. *Sacre rappresentazioni dei secoli XIV, XV e XVI*. 3 vols. Florence: Successori Le Monnier, 1872.

Debby, Nirit Ben-Aryeh. *Renaissance Florence in the Rhetoric of Two Popular Preachers: Giovanni Dominici (1356–1419) and Bernardino da Siena (1380–1444)*. Turnhout: Brepols Publishers, 2001.

De Chirico, Leonardo, and Daniel Walker, eds. *Giovanni Calvino, Renata di Francia, Lealtà in tensione: un carteggio protestante tra Ferrara e l'Europa (1537–1564)*. Caltanissetta: Alfa & Omega, 2009.

De Dominicis, Giulia. "I teatri di Roma nell'età di Pio VI." *Archivio della Società Romana della Storia Patria* 46 (1922): 74–76.

Degl'Innocenti, Antonella. "Spose e madri nell'agiografia medievale." In *Religione domestica: Medioevo, età moderna*, 9–54. Caselle di Sommacampagna: Cierre, 2001.

Delehaye, Hippolyte. *Étude sur le légendier romain: Les saints de Novembre et de Décembre*. Brussels: Société des Bollandistes, 1936.

Diefendorf, Barbara F. "Rethinking the Catholic Reformation: The Role of Women." In *Women, Religion, and the Atlantic World (1600–1800)*, edited by Daniella Kostroun and Lisa Vollendorf, 31–59. Toronto: University of Toronto Press, 2009.

Dionisotti, Carlo. "La letteratura italiana nell'età del concilio di Trento." In *Geografia e storia della letteratura italiana*, 183–204. Turin: Giulio Einaudi Editore, 1967.

Di Simone, Francesco. "Della vita della serva di Dio Lucia Filippini, Superiora delle Scuole Pie (1732)." In *Le vite delle due Maestre Pie Rosa Venerini e Lucia Filippini*, 1–222. Rome: Stamperia della S. Congr. De Propag. Fide, 1868.

Ditchfield, Simon. *Liturgy, Sanctity and History in Tridentine Italy: Pietro Maria Campi and the Preservation of the Particular*. Cambridge: Cambridge University Press, 1995.

Duby, Georges, and Michelle Perrot, eds. *A History of Women*. Cambridge, MA: Harvard University Press, 1992.

Earle, T. F., and K.J.P. Lowe, eds. *Black Africans in Renaissance Europe*. Cambridge: Cambridge University Press, 2005.

Edgar, Swift, and Angela M. Kinney. *The Vulgate Bible: Douay-Rheims Translation*. Cambridge, MA: Harvard University Press, 2010.

Eisenbichler, Konrad. "At Marriage End: Girolamo Savonarola and the Question of Widows in Late Fifteenth-Century Florence." In *The Medieval Marriage Scene: Prudence, Passion, Policy*, edited by Sherry Roush and Cristelle L. Baskins, 23–35. Tempe: ACMRS, 2005.

Ellington, Donna Spivey. *From Sacred Body to Angelic Soul: Understanding Mary in Late Medieval and Early Modern Europe*. Washington DC: The Catholic University of America Press, 2001.

Elliott, Dyan. *Spiritual Marriages: Sexual Abstinence in Medieval Wedlock*. Princeton, NJ: Princeton University Press, 1995.

Fabene, Fabio, and Lydia Saraca Colonnelli, eds. *Il Cardinale Marco Antonio Barbarigo e il suo tempo: catalogo e mostra*. Montefiascone, Chiesa di S. Andrea, Saloni di rappresentanza della Banca Cattolica, 4 agosto 2006–2020 ottobre 2006.

Falkeid, Unn. *The Avignon Papacy Contested: An Intellectual History from Dante to Catherine of Siena*. Cambridge, MA: Harvard University Press, 2017.

———. "Constructing Female Authority: Birgitta of Sweden, Catherine of Siena, and the Two Marys." In *Sanctity and Female Authorship: Birgitta of Sweden and Catherine of Siena*, edited by Maria H. Oen and Unn Falkeid, 54–73. New York: Routledge, 2020.

Falvay, Dávid. "Il mito del re ungherese nella letteratura religiosa del Quattrocento." *Nuova Corvina: rivista di italianistica* 20 (2008): 54–62.

Ferrari, Monica. *"Per non manchare in tuto del debito mio": l'educazione dei bambini Sforza nel Quattrocento*. Milan: Franco Angeli, 2000.

Festa, Lisa. "Representations of Saint Cecilia in Italian Renaissance and Baroque Painting and Sculpture." PhD diss., Rutgers University, 2003.

Findlay, Alison. *Playing Spaces in Early Women's Drama*. Cambridge: Cambridge University Press, 2006.

Finucci, Valeria. *The Lady Vanishes: Subjectivity and Representation in Castiglione and Ariosto*. Stanford, CA: Stanford University Press, 1992.

———. "Moderata Fonte and the Genre of Women's Chivalric Romances." In *Floridoro, A Chivalric Romance by Moderata Fonte*, translated by Julia Kisacky, 1–33. Chicago: The University of Chicago Press, 2006.

Garavaglia, Andrea. *Il mito delle Amazzoni nell'opera barocca italiana*. Milan: LED Edizioni universitarie, 2015.

Garin, Eugenio. *L'umanesimo italiano. Filosofia e vita civile nel Rinascimento*. Bari: Laterza, 1981.

Gigli, Giacinto. *Diario romano (1608–1670)*. Edited by Giuseppe Ricciotti. Rome: Tumminelli, 1958.

Gill, Katherine Jane. "Penitents, Pinzochere and Mantellate: Varieties of Women's Religious Communities in Central Italy, c. 1300–1520." PhD diss., Princeton University, 1994.

Glixon, Beth. "Private Lives of Public Women: Prima Donnas in Mid-Seventeenth-Century Venice." *Music & Letters* 76, no. 4 (1995): 509–531.

———. "La sirena antica dell'Adriatico: Caterina Porri, a Seventeenth-Century Roman Prima Donna on the Stages of Venice, Bologna, and Pavia." In *Musical Voices of Early Modern Women: Many-Headed Melodies*, edited by Thomasin LaMay, 211–238. Aldershot: Ashgate, 2005.

Goethals, Jessica. "The Bizarre Muse: The Literary Persona of Margherita Costa." *Early Modern Women* 12, no. 1 (2017): 48–72.

———. "The Patronage Politics of Equestrian Ballet: Allegory, Allusion, and Satire in the Courts of Seventeenth-Century Italy and France." *Renaissance Quarterly* 70, no. 4 (2017): 1397–1448.

———. "The Singing Saint: The Martyrdom of Saint Cecilia in Seventeenth-Century Literature and Theatre." *Women Language Literature in Italy/ Donne Lingua Letteratura in Italia* 2 (2020): 43–61.

Goodich, Michael. "The Contours of Female Piety in Later Medieval Hagiography." *Church History* 50, no. 1 (March 1981): 20–32.

Gordon, Colby. "Trans Mayhem in *Samson Agonistes*." University of Toronto Early Modern Critical Race Studies Working Group, December 18, 2020. https://play.library.utoronto.ca/play/dd23ce95dd579116d8fad0be16b1cefd.

Gregorio, O. "Falcoia, Tommaso." In *Dizionario degli Istituti di Perfezione*, edited by Guerrino Pelliccia and Giancarlo Rocca, 1386–87. Vol. 3. Rome: Edizioni Paoline, 1975.

Groppi, Angela. *I conservatori della virtù: Donne recluse nella Roma dei Papi*. Rome: Editori Laterza, 1994.

———. "Lavoro e proprietà delle donne in età moderna." In *Il lavoro delle donne*, edited by Angela Groppi, 136–137. Bari: Editori Laterza, 1996.

———, ed. *Il lavoro delle donne*. Bari: Editori Laterza, 1996.

Guerra Medici, Maria Teresa. "Thought Pieces for Elissa Weaver." *Modern Philology* 106, no. 4 (May 2009): 707–709.

Hair, P.E.H., and Jonathan D. Davies. "Sierra Leone and the Grand Duke of Tuscany." *History in Africa* 20 (1993): 61–69.

Hammond, Frederick. *Music and Spectacle in Baroque Rome*. New Haven, CT: Yale University Press, 1994.

———. *The Ruined Bridge: Studies in Barberini Patronage of Music and Spectacle 1631–1679*. Sterling Heights, MI: Harmonie Park Press, 2010.

Haraguchi, Jennifer. "Convent Alternatives for Rich and Poor Girls in Seventeenth-Century Florence: The Lay Conservatories of Eleonora Ramirez di Montalvo (1602–59)." In *Devout Laywomen in the Early Modern World*, edited by Alison Weber, 255–275. London: Routledge, 2016.

———. "The Virgin Mary in the Early Modern Italian Writings of Vittoria Colonna, Lucrezia Marinella, and Eleonora Montalvo," *Religions* 9, no. 59 (2018). DOI:10.3390/rel9020059

Haskin, Susan. "Volume Editor's Introduction." In *Who Is Mary? Three Early Modern Women on the Idea of the Virgin Mary*, translated and edited by Susan Haskin, ix–xxviii. Chicago: The University of Chicago Press, 2008.

Henderson, John. *Florence Under Siege: Surviving Plague in an Early Modern City*. New Haven, CT: Yale University Press, 2019.

Heng, Geraldine. *The Invention of Race in the European Middle Ages*. Cambridge: Cambridge University Press, 2018.

Herlihy, David, and Christiane Klapisch-Zuber. *Tuscans and Their Families: A Study of the Florentine Catasto of 1427*. New Haven, CT: Yale University Press, 1985.

Herzig, Tamar. *Savonarola's Women: Visions and Reform in Renaissance Italy*. Chicago: The University of Chicago Press, 2008.

Hester, Nathalie. "Transnationalism and the Epic Tradition in Baroque Italian Travel Literature." In *Transnational Italian Studies*, edited by Charles Burdett and Loredana Polezzi, 107–124. Liverpool: Liverpool University Press, 2020.

Hollingsworth, Mary. *The Cardinal's Hat: Money, Ambition, and Everyday Life in the Court of a Borgia Prince*. Woodstock, NY: Overlook Press, 2004.

Holmes, Olivia. *Dante's Two Beloveds: Ethics and Erotics in the* Divine Comedy. New Haven, CT: Yale University Press, 2008.

Hopkins, Andrew. *Santa Maria della Salute: Architecture and Ceremony in Baroque Venice*. Cambridge: Cambridge University Press, 2000.

Hopkins, David. *Childish Things*. Edinburgh: Fruitmarket Gallery, 2010.

Hornbeck, Robert. "Harlequin as Theatergram: Transmitting the Timeworn Black Mask, Ancient to Antebellum." In Hornbeck, *Racism and Early Blackface Comic Traditions, From the Old World to the New*, 35–69. New York: Palgrave Macmillan, 2018.

Jolles, André, *Simple Forms: Legend, Saga, Myth, Riddle, Saying, Case, Memorabile, Fairytale, Joke*, translated by Peter J. Schwarz, with a forward by Frederic Jameson. London: Verso, 2017. Kindle edition.

Jordan, Constance. *Pulci's* Morgante: *Poetry and History in Fifteenth-Century Florence*. Washington, DC: The Folger Shakespeare Library, 1986.

Joyce, Lillian. "Roma and the Virtuous Breast." *Memoirs of the American Academy in Rome* 59/60 (2014): 1–49.

Kent, Francis William. *Household and Lineage in Renaissance Florence: The Family Life of the Capponi, Ginori and Rucellai*. Princeton, NJ: Princeton University Press, 1977.

———. "A Proposal by Savonarola for the Self-Reform of Florentine Women (March 1496)." *Memorie domenicane*, n.s., 14 (1983): 335–341.

Kieckhefer, Richard. *Unquiet Souls: Fourteenth-Century Saints and Their Religious Milieu*. Chicago: The University of Chicago Press, 2004.

Kinney, Angela M., ed. *The Vulgate Bible: The New Testament, Douay-Rheims Translation*. Vol. 6. Cambridge, MA: Harvard University Press, 2013.

Klapisch-Zuber, Christiane. "Le chiavi fiorentine di Barbablù: L'apprendimento della lettura a Firenze nel XV secolo." *Quaderni Storici* 57 (1984): 765–792.

———. "The 'Cruel Mother': Maternity, Widowhood, and Dowry in Florence in the Fourteenth and Fifteenth Centuries." In Klapisch-Zuber, *Women, Family, and Ritual in Renaissance Italy*, 117–31. Chicago: The University of Chicago Press, 1985.

———. *Women, Family, and Ritual in Renaissance Italy*. Chicago: The University of Chicago Press, 1985.

Kolsky, Stephen. "Moderata Fonte, Lucrezia Marinella, Giuseppe Passi: An Early Seventeenth-Century Feminist Controversy." *Modern Language Review* 96, no. 4 (October 2001): 973–989.

———. "The *Decameron* and *Il Libro del Cortegiano*: Story of a Conversation." *Heliotropia* 5 (2008): 1–17.

Kovács, Zsuzsa. "La leggenda di santa Guglielma, figlia del re d'Inghilterra e donna del re d'Ungheria." *Rivista di studi ungheresi* 9 (2010): 27–44.

Kühner, Hans. "Ein Unbekannter Brief Von Guillaume Dufay." *Acta Musicologica* 11, no. 3 (1939): 114–115.

Lamothe, Virginia Christy. " The Theater of Piety: Sacred Operas for the Barberini Family (1632–1643)." PhD diss., University of North Carolina at Chapel Hill, 2009.

Lanham, Richard. *The Motives of Eloquence: Literary Rhetoric in the Renaissance*. New Haven, CT: Yale University Press, 1976.

Lawless, Catherine. "Widowhood was the time of her greatest perfection: Ideals of Widowhood and Sanctity in Florentine Art." In *Widowhood and Visual Culture in Early Modern Europe*, edited by Allison Levy, 19–38. London: Routledge, 2003.

Lehtsalu, Liise. "A Welcome Presence: The Custodial Activities of Third Order Women Religious in Seventeenth- and Eighteenth-Century Italy." *Journal of Early Modern History* 22 (2018): 49–66.

Lenzi, Maria Ludovica. *Donne e madonne: L'educazione femminile nel primo Rinascimento italiano*. Turin: Loescher, 1982.

Leonardi, Claudio, ed. *Caterina Vigri: la santa e la città: atti del Convegno, Bologna, 13–15 novembre 2002*. Florence: SISMEL Edizioni del Galluzzo, 2004.

Leoni, Juri. "'A ciò che la regola nostra promessa meglio possiati observare.' Le ordinazioni delle Clarisse del Corpus Domini di Bologna." *Archivum Franciscanum Historicum* 109 (2016): 517–535.

Lesage, G. "Congregazione religiosa." In *Dizionario degli Istituti di Perfezione*, edited by Guerrino Pelliccia and Giancarlo Rocca, 1559–72. Vol. 2. Rome: Edizioni Paoline, 1975.

Liboni, Gionata. "Imitare le sante donne. Medicina e religione in una lettera dedicatoria di Antonio Musa Braşavola a Eleonora d'Este." *Schifanoia* 40–41 (2011): 119–126.

———. "L'experimentum nella medicina pratica di Antonio Musa Brasavola." *Schifanoia* 50–51 (2016): 21–33.

———. "Antonio Musa Brasavola sul digiuno: devozione, medicina e riforma della Chiesa." *I castelli di Yale online* 5, no.1 (2017): 41–87.

Lingo, Estelle. *Mochi's Edge and Bernini's Baroque*. London: Harvey Miller, 2017.

Lirosi, Alessia. "Il corpo di santa Cecilia (Roma, III-XVII secolo)." *Mélanges de l'École française de Rome: Italie et Méditerranée modernes et contemporaines* 122, no.1 (2010): 5–51.

Lombardi, Teodosio. *I francescani a Ferrara*. Vol. 4, *I monasteri delle Clarisse: S. Guglielmo, Corpus Domini, S. Bernardino, S. Chiara*. Bologna: Grafiche Dehoniane, 1975.

———. *Gli estensi ed il Monastero del Corpus Domini di Ferrara*. Ferrara: Industrie grafiche, 1980.

Luongo, F. Thomas. *The Saintly Politics of Catherine of Siena*. Ithaca, NY: Cornell University Press, 2006.

———. "The Historical Reception of Catherine of Siena." In *A Companion to Catherina of Siena*, edited by Carolyn Muessig, George Ferzoco, and Beverly Mayne Kienzle, 23–46. Leiden: Brill, 2012.

Mac Carthy, Ita. *The Grace of the Italian Renaissance*. Princeton, NJ: Princeton University Press, 2020.

Macchietti, Sira Serenella. "Le scuole delle Maestre Pie: esperienze di educazione femminile e popolare nel '600." *Pedagogia e vita* 38 (1977): 633–646.

———. *Rosa Venerini all'origine della scuola popolare femminile: L'azione educativa del suo istituto dal 1685 A.D. oggi*. Brescia: Editrice La Scuola, 1986.

Magnanini, Suzanne. "Una selva luminosa: The Second Day of Moderata Fonte's *Il merito delle donne*." *Modern Philology* 101, no. 2 (2003): 278–296.

———. "Moderata Fonte." In *Oxford Bibliographies: Renaissance and Reformation*. Oxford: Oxford University Press, 2019, https://www-oxfordbibliographies-com.colorado.idm.oclc.org/view/document/obo-9780195399301/obo-9780195399301-0416.xml; doi:10.1093/obo/9780195399301-0416.

Malpezzi-Price, Paola. *Moderata Fonte: Women and Life in Sixteenth-Century Venice*. Madison, NJ: Farleigh Dickinson University Press, 2003.

Marchi, Lucia. "For Whom the Fire Burns: Medieval Images of Saint Cecilia and Music." *Recercare* 27, no.1–2 (2015): 5–22.

Marcocchi, Massimo. "Le origini del Collegio della Beata Vergine di Cremona, Istituzione della Riforma Cattolica (1610)." *Annali della Biblioteca Statale e Libreria Civica di Cremona* 24 (1973): 7–156.

Markey, Lia. *Imagining the Americas in Medici Florence.* University Park, PA: Pennsylvania University Press, 2016.

Martinelli Braglia, Graziella. "Donna Giulia Felice, figlia del Cardinale Alessandro d'Este. Una monaca musicista nel monastero di San Geminiano a Modena." *Atti e memorie della deputazione di storia patria per le antiche province modenesi* 11, no. 42 (2020): 175–207.

———. "Musica claustrale e controriforma. Suor Sulpizia Cesis del monastero di San Geminiano." *Terra e Identità 85, Il Ducato* 46 (2018): 3–17.

Martines, Lauro. *Fire in the City: Savonarola and the Struggle for the Soul of the Renaissance.* Oxford: Oxford University Press, 2006.

Martinez, Ronald J. "Dante between Hope and Despair: The Tradition of Lamentations in the Divine Comedy." *Logos: A Journal of Catholic Thought and Culture* 5, no. 3 (2002): 45–76.

———. "Mourning Beatrice: The Rhetoric of Threnody in the *Vita nuova.*" *MLN* 113, no. 1 (1998): 1–29.

Massimi, Suor Eliana. "Il dono di Santa Rosa Venerini a M. Cecilia Baij." In *M. Cecilia Baij e le altre donne in ricerca di Dio nel Settecento viterbese,* edited by Nadia Togni and Annamaria Valli, 43–50. Viterbo: Graffietti, 2018.

Mazzeo, Joseph Anthony. *Renaissance and Revolution: The Remaking of European Thought.* New York: Pantheon Books, 1965.

Mazzinelli, Alessandro. *Istruzione per regolamento delle scuole della Dottrina Cristiana delle Maestre Pie Filippini* (1717). Viterbo: Tipografia AEMME Grafica, 1994.

McAra, Catriona, and David Calvin. "Introduction." In *Anti-Tales: The Uses of Disenchantement,* edited by Catriona McAra and David Calvin, 1–15. Cambridge: Cambridge Scholars Publishing, 2011.

McKenna, Katherine. "Women in the Garden: *The Decameron* Reimagined in Moderata Fonte's *Il Merito Delle Donne.*" *Early Modern Women: An Interdisciplinary Journal* 13, no. 2 (2019): 58–80. doi:10.1353/emw.2019.0003.

Medioli, Francesca. "Alcune lettere autografe di Arcangela Tarabotti: Autocensura e immagine di sé." *Rivista di storia e letteratura religiosa* 32 (1996): 133–155.

Merlo, Grado Giovanni. "Guglielma la Boema: Tra santità ed eresia al femminile." In *Eresie ed eretici medievali,* 113–18. Bologna: Il Mulino, 1989.

Meserve, Margaret. *Empires of Islam in Renaissance Historical Thought.* Cambridge, MA: Harvard University Press, 2008.

Messa, Pietro, and Filippo Sedda, eds. *Dalla corte al chiostro: santa Caterina Vigri e i suoi scritti: atti della VI giornata di studio sull'Osservanza francescana al femminile: 5 novembre 2011.* Assisi: Porziuncola, 2013.

Meussig, Carolyn. *The Stigmata in Medieval and Early Modern Europe.* Oxford: Oxford University Press, 2020.

Miglio, Luisa. "'Un mondo a parte': libri da donne, libri di donne." In *Religione domestica: medioevo, età moderna,* 219–48. Caselle di Sommacampagna: Cierri Edizione, 2001.

Milligan, Gerry. *Moral Combat. Women, Gender, and War in Italian Renaissance Literature*. Toronto: University of Toronto Press, 2018.

Molinari, Cesare. *Spettacoli fiorentini del Quattrocento: contributi allo studio delle sacre rappresentazioni*. Venice: Neri Pozza, 1961.

Molini, Giuseppe. *Operette bibliografiche*. Florence: Cellini, 1858.

Monson, Craig A. "Ancora uno sguardo sulle suore musiciste di Bologna." In *I monasteri femminili come centri di cultura fra Rinascimento e barocco: atti del Convegno storico internazionale: Bologna, 8–10 dicembre 2000*, edited by Gianna Pomata and Gabriella Zarri, 3–26. Rome: Edizioni di storia e letteratura, 2005.

Mossakowski, Stanisław. "Raphael's 'St. Cecilia': An Iconographical Study." *Zeitschrift für Kunstegeschichte* 31, no. 1 (1968): 1–26.

Motta, Uberto. *Castiglione e il mito di Urbino. Studi sulla elaborazione del "Cortegiano."* Milan: Vita e Pensiero, 2003.

Moudarres, Andrea. *The Enemy in Italian Renaissance Epic: Images of Hostility from Dante to Tasso*. Newark, DE: University of Delaware Press, 2019.

Mudimbé, V. Y. *The Idea of Africa*. Bloomington, Indiana: University of Indiana Press, 1994.

Muir, Edward. *Civic Ritual in Renaissance Venice*. Princeton, NJ: Princeton University Press, 1981.

Mullett, Michael. *Popular Culture and Popular Protest in Late Medieval and Early Modern Europe*. London: Croom Helm, 1987.

Murano, Giovanna, ed. *Donne, sante e madonne: (da Matilde di Canossa ad Artemisia Gentileschi)*. Imola: La mandragora, 2018.

Muraro, Luisa. *Guglielma e Maifreda Storia di un'eresia femminista*. Milan: La Tartaruga Edizioni, 1985.

Murata, Margaret. *Operas for the Papal Court (1631–1668)*. Ann Arbor, MI: UMI Research Press, 1981.

———. "Why the First Opera Given in Paris Wasn't Roman." *Cambridge Opera Journal* 7, no. 2 (July 1995): 87–105.

"Mwene Matapa." https://www.britannica.com/topic/Mwene-Matapa. Article published July 20, 1999. Last modified February 27, 2009.

Najemy, John M. "Giannozzo and His Elders: Alberti's Critique of Renaissance Patriarchy." In *Society and Individual in Renaissance Florence*, edited by William J. Connell, 51–78. Berkeley: University of California Press, 2002.

Neveu, Marc, "The Space of the Mask: From Stage to Ridotto." In *Architectural Space in Eighteenth-Century Europe: Constructing Identities and Interiors*, edited by Denise Amy Baxter and Meredith Martin, 149–68. London and New York: Routledge, 2010.

Newbigin, Nerida. "Antonia Pulci and the First Anthology of Sacre Rappresentazioni (1483?)." *La Bibliofilía* 118, no. 3 (2016): 337–362.

Newbigin, Nerida. *Feste D'Oltrarno: Plays in Churches in Fifteenth-century Florence*. 2 vols. Florence: Leo Olschki, 1996.

———. *Making a Play for God: The* Sacre Rappresentazioni *of Renaissance Florence*. Toronto: University of Toronto Press, 2021.

Newman, Barbara. "WomanSpirit, Woman Pope." In *From Virile Woman to WomanChrist: Studies in Medieval Religion and Literature*, 182–223. Philadelphia: University of Pennsylvania Press, 1995.

———. "The Heretic Saint: Guglielma of Bohemia, Milan, and Brunate." *Church History* 74, no. 1 (2005): 1–38.

Niccoli, Ottavia. "Creanza e disciplina: Buone maniere per i fanciulli nell'Italia della Controriforma." In *Disciplina dell'anima, disciplina del corpo e disciplina della società tra medieovo ed età moderna*, edited by Paolo Prodi, 929–63. Bologna: Il Mulino, 1994.

Noè, Virgilio. *I santi fondatori nella Basilica Vaticana*. Modena: Panini, 1996.

Noreen, Kirstin. "Sant'Urbano alla Caffarella, Rome: The Reconstruction of an Ancient Memorial." *Memoirs of the American Academy in Rome* 47 (2002): 57–82. https://doi.org/10.2307/4238792.

Ori, Anna Maria, ed. *Le Clarisse in Carpi. Cinque secoli di storia XVI-XX*. Vol. 2, *Testi*. Reggio Emilia: Fondazione Cassa di Risparmio di Carpi, 2003.

Paolocci, Claudio, ed. *Congregazioni laicali femminili e promozione della donna in Italia nei secoli XVI e XVII*, Atti della giornata di studio in occasione del quarto centenario delle Medee, Genova, 3 giugno 1994. Genoa: Associazione Amici della Biblioteca Franzoniana, 1995.

Papi, Anna Benvenuti. "Mendicant Friars and Female Pinzochere in Tuscany: From Social Marginality to Models of Sanctity." In *Women and Religion in Medieval and Renaissance Italy*, edited by Daniel Borstein and Roberto Rusconi, 85–106. Chicago: The University of Chicago Press, 1996.

Park, Katherine. *Secrets of Women: Gender, Generation, and the Origins of Human Dissection*. New York: Zone, 2006.

Passano, Giambattista. *I novellieri italiani in prosa*. Milan: Libreria Antica e Moderna di G. Schiepatti, 1864.

———. *I novellieri in verso indicati e descritti da Giambattista Passano*. Bologna: Gaetano Romagnoli, 1868.

Pelliccia, Guerrino. "Nuove note sulla educazione femminile popolare a Roma nei secoli XVI-XVII." *Quaderni* 1 (1980): 293–346.

———. "Scuole di catechismo e scuole rionali per fanciulle nella Roma del Seicento." *Ricerche per la storia religiosa di Roma*, 4 (1980): 237–268.

———. *La scuola primaria a Roma dal secolo XVI al XIX: L'istruzione popolare e la catechesi ai fanciulli, nell'ambito della parocchia e dello "Studium Urbis," da Leone X a Leone XII (1513–1829)*. Rome: Edizioni dell'Ateneo, 1985.

Pelliccia, Guerrino,and Giancarlo Rocca, eds. *Dizionario degli Istituti di Perfezione*, vols. 1–10. Rome: Edizioni Paoline, 1974–2003.

Perocco, Daria. "Thought Pieces for Elissa Weaver." *Modern Philology* 106, no. 4 (2009): 711–713.

Peverada, Enrico. "Documenti per la storia organaria dei monasteri femminili ferraresi (secc. XVI-XVII)." *L'Organo. Rivista di storia organaria e organistica* 30 (1996): 119–193.

Piantoni, Luca. "*Le lettere amorose* (1639) di Margherita Costa tra sperimentalismo e 'divertissement'." *Studi secenteschi* 59 (2018): 33–51.

Polizzotto, Lorenzo. "When Saints Fall Out: Women and the Savonarolan Reform in Early Sixteenth-Century Florence." *Renaissance Quarterly* 46, no. 3 (1993): 486–490.

———. "Savonarola, Savonaroliani e la riforma della donna." In *Studi savonaroliani*, edited by Gian Carlo Garfagnini, 229–232. Florence: Edizioni del Galluzzo, 1996.

Pomata, Gianna "Medicina delle monache. Pratiche terapeutiche nei monasteri femminili di Bologna in età moderna." In *I monasteri femminili come centri di cultura fra Rinascimento e barocco: atti del Convegno storico internazionale: Bologna, 8–10 dicembre 2000*, edited by Gianna Pomata and Gabriella Zarri, 331–363. Rome: Edizioni di storia e letteratura, 2005.

Ponte, Giovanni, ed. *Sacre rappresentazioni fiorentine del Quattrocento*. Milan: Marzorati, 1994.

Presciuttini, Mario. "Santa Lucia Filippini, catechista." *Rivista lasalliana: trimestrale dei fratelli delle scuole cristiane* 4, no. 46 (1979): 299–322.

Propp, Vladimir. *Morphology of the Folktale*. Translated by Laurence Scott. Edited by Louis Wagner, with an introduction by Alan Dundes. 13th ed. Austin: University of Texas Press, 1996.

Pullia, Anna, and Dávid Falvay. "La Sacra Rappresentazione Fiorentina di Santa Guglielma, Regina d'Ungheria." In *Sul filo di ragno della memoria. Studi in onore di Ilona Fried*, edited by Franciska d'Elhoungne Hervai and Dávid Falvay, 235–48. Budapest: ELTE, 2012.

Quint, David. "Courtier, Prince, Lady: The Design of the *Book of the Courtier*." *Italian Quarterly* 37 (2000): 185–195.

Quondam, Amedeo. *"Questo povero Cortegiano." Castiglione, il Libro, la Storia*. Rome: Bulzoni Editore, 2000.

Ray, Meredith K. *Daughters of Alchemy: Women and Scientific Culture in Early Modern Italy*. Cambridge, MA: Harvard University Press, 2015.

———. "Letters From the Cloister: Defending the Literary Self in Arcangela Tarabotti's *Lettere familiari e di complimento*." *Italica* 81.1 (2004): 24–43.

———. "Making the Private Public: Arcangela Tarabotti's *Lettere familiari*." In *Arcangela Tarabotti: A Literary Nun in Baroque Venice*, edited by Elissa Weaver, 173–189. Ravenna: Longo, 2006.

———. "Scientific Culture and the Renaissance *Querelle des Femmes*: Moderata Fonte and Lucrezia Marinella." In Ray, *Daughters of Alchemy: Women and Scientific Culture in Early Modern Italy*, 73–110. Cambridge, MA: Harvard University Press, 2015.

———. *Writing Gender in Women's Letter Collections of the Italian Renaissance*. Toronto: University of Toronto Press, 2009.

Robertson, Duncan. *The Medieval Saints' Lives: Spiritual Renewal and Old French Literature*. Lexington, KY: French Forum, 1995.

Rocca, Mafaldina. *Una luce nella chiesa: Santa Lucia Filippini (1627–1732), Fondatrice delle Maestre Pie Filippini*. Rome: Brossura, 1969.

Romanello, Marina. "Duglioli, Elena." In *Dizionario Biografico degli Italiani*. Treccani: 1992.

Rosand, David. *Myths of Venice: The Figuration of a State*. Chapel Hill: The University of North Carolina Press, 2001.

Rosenmeyer, Patricia A. *The Language of Ruins: Greek and Latin Inscriptions on the Memnon Colossus*. Oxford: Oxford University Press, 2018.

Ross, Sarah Gwyneth. *The Birth of Feminism: Woman as Intellect in Renaissance Italy and England*. Cambridge, MA: Harvard University Press, 2009.

Rowe, Erin. *Black Saints in Early Modern Global Catholicism*. Cambridge: Cambridge University Press, 2019.

Rowland, Ingrid D. *The Ecstatic Journey: Athanasius Kircher in Baroque Rome*. Chicago: The University of Chicago Press, 2000.

Rubini, Luisa. "Fiabe in ottava rima: Il cantare fiabesco a stampa (1475–1530)." In *Il cantare italiano fra folklore e letteratura*, edited by Michelangelo Piccone and Luisa Rubini Messerli, 414–440. Florence: Olschki, 2007.

Saccone, Eduardo. "*Grazia, Sprezzatura, Affettazione* in the *Courtier*." In *Castiglione: The Ideal and the Real in Renaissance Culture*, edited by Robert W. Hanning and David Rosand, 45–67. New Haven, CT: Yale University Press, 1983.

Salotti, Carlo. *La Beata Lucia Filippini: Fondatrice e Superiora dell'Istituto delle Maestre Pie Filippini*. Rome: Casa Generalizia delle Maestre Pie Filippini, 1926.

Sambin De Norcen, Maria Teresa. "Romei, Giovanni." In *Dizionario Biografico degli italiani* 88 (2017): https://www.treccani.it/enciclopedia/giovanni-romei_(Dizionario-Biografico)/.

Sanson, Helena. "Conduct for the *Real* Widow: Giulio Cesare Cabei's *Ornamenti della gentildonna vedova* (1574)." In *Conduct Literature for and about Women in Italy 1470–1900: Prescribing and Describing Life*, edited by Helena Sanson and Francesco Lucioli, 41–61. Paris: Classiques Garnier, 2016.

Sardo, Andrea, ed. *Ferrara. Il Museo di Casa Romei guida alla visita*. Cinisello Balsamo: Silvana Editoriale, 2019.

Schroeder, Joy A. "Envying Jepthah's Daughter: Judges 11 in the Thought of Arcangela Tarabotti (1604–1652)." In *Strangely Familiar: Protofeminist Interpretations of Patriarchal Biblical Texts*, edited by Nancy Calvert-Koyzis and Heather E. Weir, 75–91. Atlanta, GA: Society of Biblical Literature, 2009.

———. "Tarabotti, Arcangela: 1604–1652." In *Handbook of Women Biblical Interpreters: A Historical and Biographical Guide*, edited by Marion Ann Taylor and Agnes Choi, 491–93. Grand Rapids, MI: Baker, 2012.

Schulenberg, Jane Tibbets. "Female Sanctity: Public and Private Roles, ca. 500–1100." In *Women and Power in the Middle Ages*, edited by Mary Carpenter Erler and Maryanne Kowaleski, 102–125. Athens, GA: University of Georgia Press, 1988.

Scott, Joan W. "Gender: A Useful Category of Historical Analysis." *American Historical Review* 91, no. 5 (1986): 1053–1075.

Segarizzi, Arnoldo. *Bibliografia delle stampe popolari italiane: Stampe Popolari delle Biblioteca Marciana*. Bergamo: Istituto D'Arti Grafiche, 1913.

Smarr, Janet Levarie. *Joining the Conversation: Dialogues by Renaissance Women*. University of Michigan Press, 2005.

Smith, Ian. *Race and Rhetoric in the Renaissance: Barbarian Errors*. New York: Palgrave Macmillan, 2010.

Solum, Stefanie. *Women, Patronage, and Salvation in Renaissance Florence: Lucrezia Tornabuoni and the Chapel of the Medici Palace*. Burlington, VT: Ashgate Publishing, 2015.

Sperling, Jutta. *Convents and the Body Politic in Late Renaissance Venice*. Chicago: The University of Chicago Press, 1999.

Staiti, Nico. "'L'estasi di Santa Cecilia e quattro santi' di Raffaello: Riflessioni su pittura e musica." *Il Saggiatore musicale* 8, no. 2 (2001): 177–192.

Stefaniak, Regina. "Raphael's *Santa Cecilia*: A Fine and Private Vision of Virginity." *Art History* 14, no. 3 (1991): 345–371.

Stolzenberg, Daniel. *Egyptian Oedipus: Athanasius Kircher and the Secrets of Antiquity*. Chicago: The University of Chicago Press, 2013.

Stoppato, Lisa Goldenberg. "Arcangela Paladini and the Medici." In *Women Artists in Early Modern Italy: Careers, Fame, and Collectors*, edited by Sheila Barker, 81–95. Turnhout: Brepols, 2016.

Stoppino, Eleonora. *Genealogies of Fiction: Women Warriors and the Dynastic Imagination in the* Orlando Furioso. New York: Fordham University Press, 2012.

Stras, Laurie. *Women and Music in Sixteenth-Century Ferrara*. Cambridge: Cambridge University Press, 2018.

Strocchia, Sharon T. *Death and Ritual in Renaissance Florence*. Baltimore: Johns Hopkins University Press, 1992.

———. *Forgotten Healers: Women and the Pursuit of Health in Late Renaissance Italy*. Cambridge, MA: Harvard University Press, 2019.

———. "Learning the Virtues: Convent Schools and Female Culture in Renaissance Florence." In *Women's Education in Early Modern Europe: A History-1500–1800*, edited by Barbara J. Whitehead, 3–46. New York: Garland, 1999.

———. "The Nun Apothecaries of Renaissance Florence: Marketing Medicines in the Convent." *Renaissance Studies* 25, no. 5 (2011): 627–647.

Subialka, Michael. "Heroic Sainthood: Marinella's Genealogy of the Medici Aristocracy and Saint Catherine's 'Gesti Heroici' as a Rewriting of the Gender of Virtue." In Lucrezia Marinella, *De' gesti heroici e della vita marvigliosa della Serafica S. Caterina da Siena*, ed. Armando Maggi, 163–192. Ravenna: Longo, 2011.

Swain, Melissa. "Spousal Sovereignty: The Ruling Couple and Its Representations in Quattrocento Italy." PhD diss., New York University, 2016.

Terpstra, Nicholas. *Abandoned Children of the Italian Renaissance: Orphan Care in Florence and Bologna*. Baltimore: The Johns Hopkins University Press, 2005.

———. *Lost Girls: Sex and Death in Renaissance Florence*. Baltimore: The Johns Hopkins University Press, 2010.

———. *Cultures of Charity: Women, Politics, and the Reform of Poor Relief in Renaissance Italy*. Cambridge, MA: Harvard University Press, 2013.

Testore, Celestino. "Baldinucci, Antonio, beato." In *Enciclopedia Cattolica*, vol. II. Città del Vaticano: Ente per l'Enciclopedia Cattolica e per il Libro Cattolico, 1949, 735.

Tinagli, Paola. "Womanly Virtues in Quattrocento Florentine Marriage Furnishings." In *Women in Italian Renaissance Culture and Society*, edited by Letizia Panizza, 265–284. Oxford: Humanities Research Centre, University of Oxford, 2000.

Trexler, Richard. "A Widow's Asylum of the Renaissance: The Orbatello of Florence." In *The Women of Renaissance Florence. Power and Dependence in Renaissance Florence*, vol. 2, 66–98. Binghamton, NY: Medieval and Renaissance Texts and Studies, 1993.

Tylus, Jane. Introduction to "The Story of Judith, Hebrew Widow." In Lucrezia Tornabuoni de' Medici, *Sacred Narratives*. Translated and edited by Jane Tylus, 118–122. Chicago: The University of Chicago Press. 2001.

———. *Reclaiming Catherine of Siena: Literacy, Literature, and the Signs of Others*. Chicago: The University of Chicago Press, 2009.

Ulysse, George. "Un Couple d'écrivains: les sacre rappresentazioni de Bernardo et Antonia Pulci." In *Les femmes écrivains en Italie au Moyen ge et à la Renaissance*, edited by George Ulysse, 177–96. Aix-en-Provence: Publications de l'Université de Provençe, 1994.

Vauchez, André. *The Laity in the Middle Ages: Religious Beliefs and Devotional Practices*. Translated by Margery J. Schneider. Notre Dame, IN: Notre Dame University Press, 1993.

Vecchio, Silvana. "The Good Wife." In *Silences of the Middle Ages*, edited by Christiane Klapisch-Zuber, 105–135. Vol. 2. Cambridge, MA: Harvard University Press, 1992.

Ventrone, Paola. "Per una morfologia della sacra rappresentazione fiorentina." In *Teatro e culture della rappresentazione: lo spettacolo in Italia nel Quattrocento*, edited by Raimondo Guarino, 195–225. Bologna: Il Mulino, 1988.

———. *Gli araldi della commedia: teatro a Firenze nel Rinascimento*. Ospedaletto [Pisa]: Pacini Editore, 1993.

———. "Acting and Reading Drama: Notes on Florentine *sacre rappresentazioni* in Print." *Journal of Early Modern Studies* 8 (2019): 69–132.

Verrier, Frédérique. *Le miroir des Amazones. Amazones, viragos et guerrières dans la littérature italienne des XVe et XVIe siècles*. Paris: L'Harmattan, 2003.

Vickers, Nancy J. "Widowed Words: Dante, Petrarch, and the Metaphors of Mourning." In *Discourses of Authority in Medieval and Renaissance Literature*, edited by Kevin Brownlee and Walter Stephens, 97–108. Hanover, NH: University Press of New England, 1989.

"Vita e morte di Tiberio Squilletti, detto comunemente Fra Paolo (1677)." In *Le prigioni più rinomate d'Italia*, 604–614. Florence: Jacopo Grazzini, 1854.

Wainwright, Anna. "A Simple Virgin Speaks: Authorial Identity and Persuasion in Isabella Cervoni's Oration to Pope Clement VIII." *The Italianist* 37, no. 1 (2017): 1–19.

———. "Teaching Widowed Women, Community, and Devotion in Quattrocento Florence with Lucrezia Tornabuoni and Antonia Tanini Pulci." *Religions* 9 (3), no.76 (2018): 1–13.

Walker, Jonathan. "Gambling and Venetian Noblemen c.1500–1700." *Past & Present*, 162, no. 1 (1999): 28–69.

Walter, Katherine Clark. *The Profession of Widowhood: Widows, Pastoral Care, and Medieval Models of Holiness*. Washington, DC: Catholic University Press, 2018.

Warner, Marina. *From the Beast to the Blonde: On Fairy Tales and Their Tellers*. New York: Farrar, Staus, Giroux, 1994.

———. *Once Upon a Time: A Short History of Fairy Tale*. London: Oxford University Press, 2014.

Weaver, Elissa. "Antonia Pulci e la sacra rappresentazione al femminile." In *La maschera e il volto. Il teatro in Italia*, edited by Francesco Bruni, 3–19. Venice: Fondazione Giorgio Cini: Saggi Marsilio, 2002.

———. "Antonia Tanini (1452–1501), Playwright, and Wife of Bernardo Pulci (1438–88)." In *Essays in honor of Marga Cottino-Jones*, edited by Laura White, Andrea Fedi, and Kristin Phillips, 23–37. Fiesole: Edizioni Cadmo, 2003.

———, ed. *Arcangela Tarabotti: A Literary Nun in Baroque Venice*. With an introduction by Elissa B. Weaver. Ravenna: Longo Editore, 2006.

———. "Convent Comedy and the World: The Farces of Suor Annalena Odaldi (1572–1638)." *Annali d'italianistica* 7, Women's Voices in Italian Literature (1989): 182–192.

———. "The Convent Muses: The Secular Writing of Italian Nuns, 1450–1650." In *Women and Faith: Catholic Religious Life in Italy from Late Antiquity to the Present*, edited by Lucetta Scaraffia and Gabriella Zarri, 129–143. Cambridge, MA: Harvard University Press, 1999.

———. *Convent Theatre in Early Modern Italy: Spiritual Fun and Learning for Women*. Cambridge: Cambridge University Press, 2002.

———, ed. *The Decameron First Day in Perspective*. With an introduction and bibliography by Elissa B. Weaver. Toronto: University of Toronto Press, 2004.

———. "Editor's Introduction." In Antonia Pulci, *Saints' Lives and Bible Stories for the Stage: A Bilingual Edition*, translated by James W. Cook, edited by Elissa B. Weaver, 1–65. Toronto: Iter Press/Centre for Reformation and Renaissance Studies, 2010.

———. "Le muse in convento. La scrittura profana delle monache italiane (1450–1650)." In *Donne e fede. Santità e vita religiosa in Italia*, edited by Lucetta Scaraffia e Gabriella Zarri, 253–276. Rome-Bari: Laterza, 1994.

———. Review of *The Fortunes of the Warrior Heroine in Italian Literature*, by Margaret Tomalin. *Renaissance Quarterly* 36, no. 3 (Autumn 1983): 456–459.

———, ed. *Scenes from Italian Convent Life: An Anthology of Theatrical Texts and Contexts*. Ravenna: Longo Editore, 2010.

Weber, Alison. "Introduction, Devout Laywomen in the Early Modern World: The Historiographic Challenge." In *Devout Laywomen in the Early Modern World*, edited by Alison Weber, 1–28. London: Routledge, 2016.

Weinstein, Donald. *Savonarola and Florence: Prophecy and Patriotism in the Renaissance*. Princeton, NJ: Princeton University Press, 1970.

Weinstein, Donald, and Rudolph M. Bell. *Saints and Society: The Two Worlds of Western Christendom, 1000–1700*. Chicago: The University of Chicago Press, 1986.

Westwater, Lynn Lara, "A Cloistered Nun Abroad: Arcangela Tarabotti's International Literary Career." In *Intersections: Yearbook for Early Modern Studies*. Vol.14 of *Women Writing Back, Writing Women Back: Transnational Perspectives from the Late Middle Ages to the Dawn of the Modern Era*, edited by Alicia Montoya, Anke Gilleir, and Suzan van Dijk, 283–308. Leiden: Brill, 2010.

———. "A Rediscovered Friendship in the Republic of Letters: The Unpublished Correspondence of Arcangela Tarabotti and Ismael Boulliau." *Renaissance Quarterly* 65.1 (2012): 67–134.

Wiesner-Hanks, Merry. "Review of *Devout Laywomen in the Early Modern World*, edited by Alison Weber." *The Sixteenth Century Journal* 48, no. 1 (Spring 2017): 259–261.

Wiseman, Denis Vincent O.P. "Jesus Christ Crucified and Gentle Mary: Salvation and Mary in the Life and Writings of Catherine of Siena." *Marian Library Studies* 27 (2005–2006): 200–19.

Zarri, Gabriella. "Le istituzioni dell'educazione femminile." In *Le sedi della cultura nell'Emilia-Romagna. I secoli moderni. Le istituzioni e il pensiero*, edited by Adriano Prosperi and Cinisello Balsamo, 84–109. Milan: A. Pizzi, 1987.

———. *Le sante vive. Profezie di corte e devozione femminile tra '400 e '500*. Torino: Rosenberg & Sellier, 1990.

———. "Disciplina regolare e pratica di coscienza: le virtù e i comportamenti sociali in comunità femminili (secc. XVI–XVIII)." In *Disciplina dell'anima, disciplina del corpo e disciplina della società tra medieovo ed età moderna*, edited by Paolo Prodi, 257–278. Bologna: Il Mulino, 1994.

———. "Christian good manners: spiritual and monastic rules in the Quattro- and Cinquecento." In *Women in Italian Renaissance Culture and Society*, edited by Letizia Panizza, 76-91. Cambridge: Legenda, 2000.

———. *Recinti. Donne, clausura e matrimonio nella prima età moderna*. Bologna: Il Mulino, 2000.

———. "The Third Status." In *Time, Space and Women's Lives in Early Modern Europe*, edited by Anne Jacobson Schutte, Thomas Kuehn, and Silvana Seidel Menchi, 181–199. Kirksville, MO: Truman State University Press, 2001.

———. *La religione di Lucrezia Borgia. Le lettere inedite del confessore*. Rome: Roma nel Rinascimento, 2006.

———. "Culture nel chiostro. Tra arte e vita." In *Artiste nel chiostro. Produzione artistica nei monasteri femminili in età moderna*, ed. Sheila Barker and Luciano Cinelli. *Memorie domenicane*, n. s., 46 (2015): 19–29.

———. "Why Become a Poor Clare? Presenting the Observant Franciscan Life to Fifteenth-Century Women." In *Select Proceedings from the First International Conference on Franciscan Studies, The World of St. Francis of Assisi, Siena, Italy, July 16–20, 2015*, 217–223. Siena: Betti Editrice, 2017.

———, ed. *Donna, disciplina, creanza cristiana dal XV al XVII secolo: studi e testi a stampa*. Rome: Edizioni di Storia e Letteratura, 1996.

———, ed. *Le Clarisse in Carpi. Cinque secoli di storia XVI–XX*. Vol. 1, *Saggi*. Reggio Emilia: Fondazione Cassa di Risparmio di Carpi, 2003.

# Contributors

**Emanuela Zanotti Carney** earned a PhD in Italian Literature from the University of Chicago and is a senior lecturer and an assistant Director of the Italian Language Program at the University of Illinois at Chicago. Her recent publications include articles, coauthored with Chiara Fabbian, on topics such as women's education in postunification Italy, and curricular development, critical pedagogy, and social justice in Second Language Education. She is currently working on a book about the nineteenth-century writer Tommasina Guidi.

**Jennifer Haraguchi** is associate professor of Italian at Brigham Young University. Her research focuses on women's social and religious history in early-modern Italy, women writers, and women's education. She has published articles in *The Sixteenth Century Journal*, *Early Modern Women: An Interdisciplinary Journal*, and *I Tatti Studies in the Italian Renaissance*.

**Nathalie Hester** is associate professor of French and Italian and the director of European Studies at the University of Oregon. She is the author of *Literature and Identity in Italian Baroque Travel Writing* and the editor and translator of Marie-Gigault de Bellefonds, *Letters from Spain: A Seventeenth-Century Noblewoman at the Spanish Royal Court*.

**Suzanne Magnanini** is associate professor and president's teaching scholar in the Department of French and Italian at the University of Colorado, Boulder, where she teaches courses on early-modern Italian fairy tales, Dante, and Boccaccio. Her research focuses on early-modern fairy tales and issues of alterity. She is the author of *Fairy-Tale Science: Monstrous Generation in the Tales of Straparola and Basile*, and the editor and translator of Giovan Francesco

Straparola's *The Pleasant Nights*. Most recently, she has edited the volume *A Cultural History of the Fairy Tale in the Age of the Marvelous*.

**Courtney Quaintance** is an independent scholar and freelance translator based in Rome, Italy. She is the author of *Textual Masculinity and the Exchange of Women in Renaissance Italy* and articles on Moderata Fonte and Veronica Franco. She is currently completing a book on women singers in seventeenth-century Italy.

**Meredith K. Ray** is Elias Ahuja Professor of Italian at the University of Delaware. She is the author of *Margherita Sarrocchi's Letters to Galileo: Astronomy, Astrology, and Poetics in Seventeenth-Century Italy*, *Daughters of Alchemy: Women and Scientific Culture in Early Modern Italy*, and *Writing Gender in Women's Letter Collections of the Italian Renaissance*. Her translations include *Machiavelli: Political, Historical, and Literary Writings*, coedited with Mark Jurdjevic; and with Lynn Lara Westwater, Arcangela Tarabotti's *Letters Familiar and Formal* and *Convent Paradise*.

**Michael Sherberg** is professor of Italian at Washington University in St. Louis. He has written on authors ranging from Dante to Collodi. He is the author of *The Governance of Friendship: Law and Gender in the* Decameron, and he coedited *Boccaccio: A Critical Guide to the Complete Works*. More recently, he edited *The* Decameron *Fourth Day in Perspective*. He is completing a translation of Jacopo Passavanti's *Specchio della vera penitenzia*.

**Anna Wainwright** is assistant professor of Italian Studies at the University of New Hampshire. Her research considers gender, race, and emotion in early modern Italy. She is a coeditor of three volumes: *Innovation in the Italian Counter-Reformation* (University of Delaware Press); *Race in the European Renaissance: A Classroom Guide* (ACMRS); and *The Legacy of Birgitta of Sweden: Women, Politics, and Reform in Renaissance Italy* (Brill, forthcoming). She is currently completing her first monograph, *Widow City: Gender, Politics and Community in the Italian Renaissance*, which is forthcoming from the University of Delaware Press.

**Lynn Lara Westwater** is professor of Italian at George Washington University. Her books include *Sarra Copia Sulam: A Salonnière and the Press in Counter-*

*Reformation Venice*; with Meredith K. Ray, critical editions of Arcangela Tarabotti's *Letters Familiar and Formal* and *Convent Paradise*; and with Diana Robin, a critical edition of Ippolita Sforza's works, *Duchess and Hostage in Renaissance Naples: Letters and Orations.*

**Gabriella Zarri** served as professor of History in the faculty of Lettere e Filosofie at the University of Florence, and has held positions at the University of Bologna and the University of Udine. Her research examines ecclesiastical institutions and religious life between 1400 and 1600, with particular attention to religious orders for men and women, women's condition, and sanctity. Her numerous publications include *Le sante vive. Cultura e religiosità femminile nella prima età moderna*; *Recinti. Donne, clausura e matrimonio nella prima età moderna*; *La religione di Lucrezia Borgia. Le lettere inedite del confessore*; and *La chiesa dei principi e delle città tra medioevo e prima età moderna.*

# Index

Page numbers in italics indicate figures. Page numbers followed by n denote notes.